The Struggle over Law in Europe

This book examines the role of law in Europe at a time when economic policies have become dominant not only on this continent but globally. Can law be seen as a mere infrastructure? Or does it contribute to defining the social and legal order through its own inherent rules? If the second hypothesis is true, what might these rules be, and how may they be identified? Lastly, to what extent can agreeing a definition of the role of law affect the future of Europe? With the Next Generation European Union, the EU has introduced an unprecedented investment plan for economic recovery and resilience. In doing so, it has become the most important financial intermediary on the continent. But is this simply the prelude to a European economic and financial revival, or does it also aim to strengthen the European legal order in social, political, and constitutional terms? This book argues that the role of law in Europe should be to achieve a balanced relationship between freedom and solidarity; encouraging economic competition, but also social cohesion. Analyzing the role of law in the project of European integration, it maintains that law should be more than an infrastructure for finance and economics, showing how it can act as a guide and a binding force to achieve a more balanced relationship between economics, politics, and law. This book will be of interest to scholars in the fields of public law, European law, law and economics, the philosophy of law, legal history, political theory, and political science, as well as others concerned with the future of European integration.

Aldo Sandulli is Professor of Administrative Law at the LUISS Guido Carli of Rome, Italy.

Law and Politics: continental perspectives

for information about the series and details of previous and forthcoming titles, see https://www.routledge.com/law/series/LPCP

The Struggle over Law in Europe

Aldo Sandulli

Routledge
Taylor & Francis Group
a GlassHouse book

First published 2024
by Routledge
4 Park Square, Milton Park, Abingdon, Oxon OX14 4RN

and by Routledge
605 Third Avenue, New York, NY 10158

a GlassHouse book

Routledge is an imprint of the Taylor & Francis Group, an informa business

British Library Cataloguing-in-Publication Data
A catalogue record for this book is available from the British Library

Library of Congress Cataloging-in-Publication Data
Names: Sandulli, Aldo, 1966- author.
Title: The struggle over law in Europe / Aldo Sandulli.
Description: Abingdon, Oxon [UK] ; New York, NY : Routledge, 2024. | Series: Law and politics: continental perspectives | Includes bibliographical references and index. | Summary: -- Provided by publisher.
Identifiers: LCCN 2023055544 (print) | LCCN 2023055545 (ebook) | ISBN 9781032295459 (hardback) | ISBN 9781032295473 (paperback) | ISBN 9781003302094 (ebook)
Subjects: LCSH: Administrative law--European Union countries. | Law--European Union countries.
Classification: LCC KJE5602 .S267 2024 (print) | LCC KJE5602 (ebook) | DDC 342.4--dc23/eng/20231214
LC record available at https://lccn.loc.gov/2023055544
LC ebook record available at https://lccn.loc.gov/2023055545

ISBN: 978-1-032-29545-9 (hbk)
ISBN: 978-1-032-29547-3 (pbk)
ISBN: 978-1-003-30209-4 (ebk)

DOI: 10.4324/9781003302094

Typeset in Sabon
by Taylor & Francis Books

Contents

	Prologue	1
I	The Prismatic Construction of the European Legal Order	13
II	The Relationship between European Law, Economics, and Finance	41
III	Technical Expertise and Democratic Legitimacy in European Law over the Last Quarter Century	85
IV	The Ability of Administrative Law to Adapt and Expand as the European Legal Order Takes Shape	104
V	The Science of Administrative Law and the Role of the Jurist in the Construction of the European Legal System	124
VI	The Law in the New European Legal Order	158
	Epilogue	168
	Bibliography	181
	Index	207

Prologue

1. The European legal system is currently facing a fresh wave of challenges due to the COVID-19 pandemic and the Ukrainian crises, marking a new phase in its relatively brief yet remarkable history of just under three-quarters of a century. During this time, the construction of this legal edifice has assured the peoples of Western Europe an extended era of peace, prosperity, and affluence, perhaps as never before in human history,[1] rivalled only by some decades of the Roman Empire. The European institutions have adeptly turned this time of constant crisis[2] into an opportunity, addressing the integration process with even greater determination[3] in what can be likened to a period of growing pains during which young bodies mature and strengthen. And, of course, the European legal system stands as an ever-evolving legal fiction – a model that, from a legal perspective, can be perceived as an ongoing construction. Indeed, in this context, it resonates with the well-known adage about the traveller for whom the journey holds greater significance than the destination. Numerous criticisms can be levelled at the European Union; however, it is undeniable that it has not remained passive in the face of the recurrent crises of the 2000s.

1 From this perspective, the history of united Europe has been a success story. We may recall the reductionist thesis outlined in A.S. Milward, *The Reconstruction of Western Europe 1945–1951*, first published in 1984 (Abingdon: Routledge, 2013); idem, *The European Rescue of the Nation State*, 2nd ed. (London; New York: Routledge, 2000). According to this view, European unity was not the result of political idealism; rather it sprang from the need for the founding countries to pursue objectives of internal security, economic prosperity (through an organizational model broader than that of individual states), and peace (in response to German resurgence and the spectre of communism in Eastern Europe).

2 On the concept of crisis in modern terms, see R. Koselleck, *Crisi. Per un lessico della modernità*, first published in 1982 (Verona: Ombre corte, 2012).

3 For an interesting analysis of the crises that have befallen Europe, see S. Cassese, 'L'Europa vive di crisi' (2016) *Rivista trimestrale di diritto pubblico* 779 ff. For an interpretation of the economic and financial crisis at the close of the first decade and the early years of the second decade of the new millennium, refer to: E. Nanopoulos and F. Vergis (eds), *The Crisis Behind the Eurocrisis: The Eurocrisis as a Multidimensional Systemic Crisis of the EU* (Cambridge, United Kingdom; New York, USA: Cambridge University Press, 2019).

DOI: 10.4324/9781003315490-1

Despite admirably attaining internal peace among the European member states, the functional agreement they share has shown signs of evident strain in recent times. Suffice it to recall Brexit with its far-reaching consequences,[4] the situation in Catalonia, the risk of secession in certain member states, or the unsettling cracks in the young 'democracies' in Eastern Europe, which are increasingly veering away from the rule of law they committed to uphold when they joined the Treaties. These difficulties stem, in part, from failed attempts to establish a continental constitutional pact and the Union's perhaps over-hasty expansion (but without enlargement, what geopolitical balance could Europe maintain in the light of the Ukrainian conflict?). Dark clouds, reminiscent of past nightmares, are gathering in the skies of Europe.[5] The current situation appears to transcend mere temporary crisis; it denotes a precarious state of health demanding a serious and stringent cure that will have to supersede self-interested and opportunistic national policies (one thinks of European immigration policies and migrant rights or the resistant stance of countries like the Czech Republic, Poland, Slovakia, and Hungary).

In this regard, the current crisis looks different from those that preceded it. It is the longest lasting, beginning with the failure to reach a consensus on a European constitution, and has persisted amid economic and financial turmoil, the COVID-19 emergency, and the present energy and border security emergencies. It is highly complex from the perspective of international relations, as the motives that led the United States to champion the European anti-Soviet axis over many decades have largely disappeared since the fall of the Berlin Wall.

What is more, the tide of economic and financial globalization that has marked the last few decades has receded, giving way to a shift towards new polarization between the USA and China, with the EU called upon to align with the Western front. It is also the most far-reaching of the crises, as, unlike historical precedents, the contemporary European system has had to make a series of substantial political

4 The economic, political, and social effects of Brexit on the United Kingdom may offer crucial insights into the future configuration of the European Union. It will allow a tangible assessment of the costs and benefits of being (or not being) a member of the Union, an assessment that could well translate into a form of *a contrario* legitimation output. Concerning Brexit, see esp., P. Craig, 'Brexit: A Drama in Six Acts' (2016) 41 *European Law Review* 447 ff.; F. Fabbrini (ed.), *The Law and Politics of Brexit* (Oxford: Oxford University Press, 2017).

5 It is no coincidence that the connection between these two crises, which dominated the early 20th century – ultimately culminating in World War II – has been the subject of extensive investigation. The first was the Great Depression, the global economic crisis, triggered by the Wall Street crash in October 1929, and the second was the crisis of democratic-liberal constitutionalism following the collapse of the Weimar Republic and the ascent of Nazism in Germany in 1933. For an exploration of the parallels between the economic crisis of 1929 and the current situation, we may refer, among a number of sources, to N. Roubini and S. Mihm, *La crisi non è finita* (Milan: Feltrinelli, 2010); for a comprehensive treatment of the decline of the Weimar Republic, see, among the many, C. Amirante and S. Gambino (eds), *Weimar e la crisi europea. Economia Costituzione Politica* (Cosenza: Periferia, 2013).

choices on the economic (but also the social) front in order to revitalize the community model and strive to shape a new legal order capable of nurturing the emergence of a European democratic society. Such an endeavour involves engagement with intergovernmental dynamics on the one hand and countering the surge of populist and neo-nationalistic trends on the other. Certainly, the nation-states, whose democratic frameworks have been in crisis for decades, have raised their heads once more. Within these states, political manoeuvring often tilts towards short-term goals, placing more emphasis on opinion polls and electoral cycles than on building a cohesive social fabric and implementing medium-to-long-term public policies. This is particularly evident in relation to immigration policies.

Prevailing currents of national self-interest have had a marked influence on the EU institutions' attempts to find shared solutions. Consequently, the old continent's achievements are currently hanging in the balance: prosperity and social safeguards, and perhaps the very prospect of enduring peace.

Thus, what we see is a crisis of both law and rights. The milestones of civilisation achieved during the latter half of the twentieth century, especially in the area of social welfare, had created the illusion that the evolutionary trajectory of rights and freedoms could only move in one direction, at least in the democracies of Western Europe. It has been a rude awakening.[6] It has become evident that economic and financial considerations have become paramount, with politics and law exhibiting unmistakable signs of financialization. In this evolving landscape, the achievements of the past must be nurtured and defended on a daily basis, both on the cultural front and through the elaboration of shared public policies; this should also be the case at the supranational level.[7] Clearly, the global ascendency of the economy and the market on the part of a handful of corporations stands in stark contrast to the intrinsic imperative of individual freedom and equality, as well as to social formations. These foundational principles of civilisation have been present throughout Europe's history, spanning millennia to become the hallmarks that set apart the concept of the European project.[8] Equally apparent is the imperative to subject private powers to the same constraints that were historically imposed upon public authorities. While economics-based analyses of the cyclic crises have shed light

6 The phenomenon of democratic backsliding is, of course, more widespread outside the European context. As L. Diamond observes in *The Spirit of Democracy: The Struggle to Build Free Society Throughout the World* (New York: Times Books/Henry Holt & Company, 2008) but especially in 'Facing Up to the Democratic Recession' (2015) 26 *Journal of Democracy* 141 ff., democracies worldwide have been in recession since 2006, after more than three decades of continuous expansion, starting in 1975.

7 A strand of scholarly inquiry focusing on cosmopolitan constitutionalism has focussed on this area. See, among others, M. Kumm, 'The Cosmopolitan Turn in Constitutionalism. An Integrated Conception of Public Law' (2013) 20 *Indiana Journal of Global Legal Studies* 605 ff.

8 The cultural reference in this regard remains F. Chabod, *Storia dell'idea di Europa* (Bari: Laterza, 1961).

on certain aspects of the underlying challenges, they often fall short in terms of grasping broader political and social dynamics. This 'illiteracy' in political and social perception results in diagnoses and remedies unable to fully address the ailment, which also encompasses political, social, and legal dimensions.[9] A new long-term European social and legal model can be grounded only upon a balance between the construction of a supranational political sphere and the performance of a 'neutral' function grounded in technical expertise: a European democratic legitimization distinct from the modern state's conventional approaches, which have proven ineffective in tackling the challenges of economic globalization and technological progress. Such a model, built around the principles of art. 2 TEU,[10] aspires to establish a new supranational legal order and infuse new life into the integration process at the constitutional level.[11]

2. From this perspective, it is imperative to determine the prospective role of law: discerning whether, within a scenario where politics and law are ensnared by the pre-eminence of the economy, as Luhmann claims, the advent of a new technocratic and plutocratic millennium has been an obstacle to the development of a truly European society and the unity of the European peoples, or, as we contend, it is still plausible to contemplate a new European legal order[12] grounded in and prompted not only by Vivien Schmidt's 'pragmatic' narrative (which, for the United Kingdom, Scandinavia, and Eastern European, would merely signify a borderless space safeguarding the market and security) but also extending to embrace a culturally and legally 'prescriptive' dimension (a prospect championed by the Western founding nations).[13] In this trajectory we observe growing recognition of the need to return to law or a new process of gradually re-introducing now-waning legal values into society.[14]

In an endeavour to offer some rudimentary answers to this question – regarding the role of law in Europe, it may be instructive to cast a retrospective eye (particularly in chapters I, IV, and V) over the numerous obstacles that have

9 U. Beck, *Europa tedesca. La nuova geografia del potere* (Rome: Laterza, 2012) 11.

10 See A. von Bogdandy, *Strukturwandel des öffentlichen Rechts. Entstehung und Demokratisierung der europäischen Gesellschaft* (Berlin: Suhrkamp, 2022).

11 In this regard, alongside the perspectives that we will discuss later, some radical and utopian solutions have also been put forward. See, for example, J. Zielonka's *Disintegration: How to Save the European Union* (Rome-Bari: Laterza, 2015), suggesting the notion that European integration should continue, but should primarily be built up from the grassroots level. In our view, however, the integration process cannot be deemed viable unless it operates bidirectionally.

12 There has been much discussion on the roles of law and the legal scholar in recent years. Among the many recent analyses, see J. Commaille, *À quoi nous sert le droit?* (Paris: Gallimard, 2015); F. Ost, *À quoi sert le droit? Usages, functions, finalité* (Bruxelles: Bruylant, 2016); V. Di Cataldo, *A che cosa serve il diritto* (Bologna: il Mulino, 2017).

13 V.A. Schmidt, *The Futures of European Capitalism* (Oxford: OUP, 2002); id, *Democracy in Europe* (Oxford: OUP, 2006).

14 See, among the others, P. Grossi, *Ritorno al diritto* (Rome: Laterza, 2015); idem, *L'invenzione del diritto* (Rome: Laterza, 2017).

already been surmounted, focusing on the role of individual legal traditions in comparison with similar studies in other social sciences within the context of the European integration process. Our aim is to undertake a comprehensive assessment of the almost seven decades in which the tapestry of the European legal order has been woven.[15]

We will focus in particular on the ever-increasing importance of European administrative law (both through its impact on national[16] administrative law in the member states and its ties with global[17] administrative law). This area of European law has assumed some unique characteristics, giving rise to the paradox of a shared law that is also situated, i.e., a law that has evolved from a combination of civil law and common law traditions and can adapt to the distinct features of the national legal systems in which it is applied. Our analysis will also explore the ambivalent relationship between administrative and constitutional law (particularly in chapter IV). On the one hand, it is necessary to acknowledge the constitutional fragility and the substantial challenges facing the parallel trajectory of constitutional law in Europe, especially following the failed attempt to adopt a European constitution and the weak hold of European identity – a paradox, as the absence of a shared spirit in post-modern Europe is juxtaposed with the perceived hollowness of a reversion to individual nation-states.[18]

15 There are numerous works on the history of European integration. Among the many, we may refer to B. Olivi, *L'Europa difficile. Storia politica dell'integrazione europea 1948–2000*, 2nd ed. (Bologna: il Mulino, 2000 (1st ed., 1993)); M. Gilbert, *Storia politica dell'integrazione europea* (Rome-Bari: Laterza, 2005); G. Giraudi, *Ripensare l'Europa. Storia, processi e sfide dell'integrazione europea* (Soveria Mannelli: Rubbettino, 2008); A. Varsori, *La Cenerentola d'Europa? L'Italia e l'integrazione europea dal 1947 a oggi* (Soveria Mannelli: Rubbettino, 2010); U. Morelli, *Storia dell'integrazione europea* (Milan: Guerini, 2011); G. D'Ottavio, *L'Europa dei tedeschi. La Repubblica Federale di Germania e l'integrazione europea, 1949–1966* (Bologna: il Mulino, 2012); E. Calandri, M.E. Guasconi, R. Ranieri, *Storia politica e economica dell'integrazione europea. Dal 1945 ad oggi* (Naples: EdiSES, 2015); B. Olivi, R. Santaniello, *Storia dell'integrazione europea. Dalla guerra fredda ai giorni nostri*, 3rd ed. (Bologna: il Mulino, 2015 (1st ed., 2005)); L. Rapone, *Storia dell'integrazione europea*, 2nd ed. (Rome: Carocci, 2015 (1st ed., 2002)); F. Fauri, *L'Unione europea. Una storia economica* (Bologna: il Mulino, 2017); E.R. Papa, *Storia dell'unificazione europea. Le origini e la crisi di un progetto rivoluzionario*, new edition (Florence-Milan: Giunti-Bompiani, 2017 (1st ed., Milan: Bompiani, 2006)).

16 See esp. G. Vesperini, *Il vincolo europeo sui diritti amministrativi nazionali* (Milan, Giuffrè, 2011).

17 See esp. E. Chiti and B.G. Mattarella (eds), *Global Administrative Law and EU Administrative Law. Relationships, Legal Issues and Comparison* (Berlin-Heidelberg: Springer, 2011).

18 These aspects are explored by J.H.H. Weiler, in his article 'To Be a European Citizen-Eros and Civilization', published in the *Journal of European Public Policy*, 1997, 495 ff. As early as the 1930s and 1940s, English economist Lionel Robbins remarked that the divided politics of European nation-states was the result of anti-economic unity: just as gunpowder had rendered the feudal system obsolete, in the same way, the aeroplane has made independent European sovereignties look outdated. The digital technological

On the other hand, the trajectory followed by administrative law can only pave the way for a new and different process of constitutionalization through a European lens, one tending towards an aggregating constitutional moment as opposed to the disaggregation that stems from the impulses of individual social forces.[19] This has been aptly described as a 'metabolic Constitution'.[20] Some argue that administration and administrative law are part of the problem, especially in their more extreme forms of bureaucratism and technicism. Others contend that they could be part of the solution, especially if the approach to challenging situations, as history has shown, entails an even higher level of integration (for example, in areas such as politics, economics, finance, fiscal policies, security, and social welfare).

Therefore, if we wish to reflect on the future prospects for the idea of Europe, it might – after examining some of the issues concerning the relatively young European legal order (chapters II and III) – prove worthwhile to investigate whether administrative law can offer a valuable contribution to revitalizing the European integration process, exploring the possible directions it may take and how it might come about.

This is because, in such a context, if there is one area of law that has played a central role in recent decades, it is – undoubtedly – administrative law, perhaps because it is the legal domain most suited to comparison with other sciences, or conceivably because it is more dynamic and less insular than was commonly believed during the latter half of the nineteenth century and much of the twentieth. It is a story of resurgence and emancipation: administrative law, once thought useful only in the context of the state, has proven more versatile than the other branches of law and has played a part in meeting demands for closer integration, fostering the construction of a gradual path towards unity, while nevertheless preserving diversity.[21]

revolution has created an even wider gap, and sovereignist battles for a return to national sovereignty have every appearance of rearguard actions.

19 Concerning the 'constitutional moment' (and the need to impose limitations on partial systems), we must principally refer to G. Teubner's work, *Nuovi conflitti costituzionali. Norme fondamentali dei regimi transnazionali* (Milan: Bruno Mondadori, 2012).

20 P. Lindseth, 'The metabolic constitution and the limits of EU legal pluralism', in G. Davies and M. Avbelj (eds), *Research Handbook on Legal Pluralism and EU Law* (Northampton, MA: Elgar, 2018) 223–242; C. Fasone, P. Lindseth, "Europe's Fractured Metabolic Constitution: From the Eurozone Crisis to Coronavirus Response", Working Papers Series, SOG-WP61/2020, Luiss School of Government, October 2020.

21 See, in particular, L. Torchia, *Il governo delle differenze. Il principio di equivalenza nell'ordinamento europeo* (Bologna: il Mulino, 2006). More recently, M. D'Alberti, 'Comparazione giuridica, diritto europeo e diritto globale', and G. della Cananea, 'Uniformità e varietà del diritto nello "spazio giuridico europeo"', both in G. della Cananea and C. Franchini (eds), *Il diritto che cambia, Liber amicorum Mario Pilade Chiti* (Naples: Editoriale Scientifica, 2016) 179 ff and 233 ff respectively.

In essence, if – as we will attempt to demonstrate (while aiming to introduce some original elements contrasting with the common view) – the legal history of the European order serves as an *ancilla* and not as a *domina*, unlike the legal history of the nation-state system, which has always had a symbiotic relationship with politics (see chapter I), then the history of administrative law in the construction of Europe emerges as a narrative of emancipation. Like a freed slave, European administrative law has diligently disseminated its paradigms, particularly in recent decades, continuing, however, to reside within the household of the *patronus* and maintaining duties of respect and economic obligations towards the master.

We will direct particular attention to administrative law (chapter V) since, in the journey towards integration through law, the focus has rightly lain almost exclusively on the case law of the European Court of Justice. The parallel and significant role of officials within the major institutions (such as the Commission, the Council, agencies, committees, etc.) in practical implementation and soft law has been acknowledged only to a very limited extent. Furthermore, very little research has been conducted into the role of legal scholarship, and still less on studies in administrative law. This, as we will see, has succeeded, despite its late start and having long been overshadowed by the decisions of the European Court of Justice, in carving out a significant role in shaping administrative law in Europe, contributing significantly to the evolution of the European legal order over the last 25 years. The story of administrative law scholarship has been one of construction 'on the road' through the belated pursuit of transformation driven by the imperatives of economic, political, and institutional integration; it has been accomplished by means of structural and procedural factors.

This trajectory has led administrative law scholars, especially from the 1980s, to make a substantial contribution to constructing the juridical coordinates of the European legal order. The path it has followed is more mature and advanced than the methodologies adopted in international and even European law. It has been more innovative and productive than private law scholarship, and more timely and flexible than that of constitutional law, despite its importance. It may even be considered more effective in achieving the goals of the European legal order itself. Indeed, administrative law scholarship has seamlessly integrated itself into the trajectory that we will attempt to outline here, acting as a driving force not only within the European context but also at the national level. It has driven institutional and administrative reform, prompted in turn by the transformations that have taken place in the supranational legal order.

The final part of the book (chapter VI) will focus once again on the role of law, and especially on how it serves as a balance between various social forces. This role is 'militant' rather than 'neutral', being driven by the pursuit of goals inherent to democratic constitutionalism.

As Karl Polanyi remarked at the close of World War II, when a "partial system" of social sciences[22] (such as economics, law, politics, sociology, etc.) isolates itself from the others and gains prominence, the results are often harmful.[23] The book will examine the consequences of such imbalances within the realm of law and its interactions with other disciplines.

The various partial systems must be unified, balanced, and integrated into a cohesive and complex whole, a task which falls primarily to law. This also applies to legal culture which, together with the entire intellectual sphere, must leave behind what has been termed "the era of the great silence".[24]

3. Before embarking on our inquiry, we should perhaps clarify what the book 'is not' (leaving it to the reader to decide what it actually is).

First and foremost, addressing the vexed question of methodological pluralism, one that has sparked extensive debate across the spectrum of the humanities and among legal scholars (historically defenders of methodological purism and separatism), we must make quite clear that we embrace the call to "beware of single methodologies (after all, a century dominated by the 'pure legal method' ought to have taught us something); in the hope that the economic analysis of law will become more widespread (not as a study of the American economic analysis of law, but as the application of the method to Italian cases) and that alongside it, the historical method for understanding the law, legal philology, political science's analytical approach to law, the sociological method, and (why not?) the legal method – provided this remains as impure as possible – will continue to be used".[25]

This book will examine some of the relationships between law, economics, and politics, but a disclaimer is called for. There can be no question that the boundaries between the social sciences mentioned here are somewhat blurred, especially those separating economics and politics, as their respective domains are closely intertwined. Similarly, the legal sphere often engages closely with the

22 On the constitutional interaction of a plurality of autonomous partial systems evolving on a global scale, see the collection of writings by G. Teubner, *La cultura del diritto nell'epoca della globalizzazione. L'emergere delle costituzioni civili* (Rome: Armando Editore, 2005).

23 In *The Great Transformation. The Political and Economic Origins of Our Time*, 1944 (Boston: Beacon Press, 2001) 71 ff. and 210 ff, K. Polanyi discusses how the distancing of economics from society during the late 19th and early 20th centuries, based on the assumption of the autonomy and completeness of the scientific discipline (an assumption shared by legal scholarship at that time), led to the commodification of labour, land, and money. This process ultimately contributed to the tragedy of World War I and, a few decades later, to the catastrophe of World War II (in the latter case this was due in part to the primacy of politics).

24 On the civil and cultural catastrophe brought about by the 'great silence' of the intellectuals, See A. Asor Rosa, *Il grande silenzio. Intervista sugli intellettuali* (Rome-Bari: Laterza, 2009).

25 S. Cassese, 'Giuristi ed economisti: metodo e metodi nello studio del diritto' (2002) 3 *Giornale di Diritto Amministrativo* 342.

fields of political science and economics (we might recall certain currents within legal realism). These considerations must thus be taken into account when discussing the relationships between the social sciences at issue. But the aims, objectives, and methods of these social sciences can profoundly influence the evolution of legal frameworks in a multitude of ways. It is precisely towards this dynamic development that our attention is directed.

As we shall argue in a subsequent section (chapter IV), we seek to avoid undertaking a path of legal conceptualism and dogmatism (as is sometimes advocated), as doing so would only further exacerbate the already pronounced marginalization of the legal scholar. Our approach does not dismiss as useless or injurious the contributions of the major social sciences, especially economics. On the contrary, the input from economics, politics, and sociology studies is extremely valuable, and jurists must welcome and carefully consider it and integrate it into their work. However, they are also called upon to make an innovative and 'militant' contribution to constructing the new European order.

3.1 This book is not an attack on economics, nor does it emphasize conflicts between disciplinary areas. Rather, it critiques a certain *way* of understanding economics (for instance, an excessive emphasis on neoliberalism and dogmatic reliance on analytical theory) and the dangerous cocktail that has emerged from neoliberalism, new public management, and stringent public finance policies. When taken singly, the measures resulting from these approaches may yield positive effects, but their amalgamation has been a significant factor in the crisis. Later (especially in chapter II), we will briefly address some aspects of the reforms introduced in recent decades, including the corporatization of public administrations, the introduction of managerial principles and engineering methods, the proliferation of deregulation, liberalization, and outsourcing, as well as the imposition of excessive financial constraints linked to the use of algorithms, and the establishment of a relationship of trust between leadership and personnel management. The stability of public finances merits particular attention, and some states have demonstrated a reckless disregard for the state of public finances, burdening future generations and inflating public debt for decades.[26] Similarly, we must not forget the positive effects of competition and the role played by economic regulation and antitrust authorities. Moreover, the emphasis on accountability has intensified due to the widespread implementation of managerial standards, rectifying a historical lack of answerability. Still, concerning the managerial approach, persistent mismanagement leading to the subsequent squandering of public resources cannot be overlooked. However, this observation does not negate the predominant emphasis on economic productivity, with the consequent disruption of the equilibrium

26 For a discussion of intergenerational responsibility, see R. Bifulco, *Diritto e generazioni future. Problemi giuridici della responsabilità intergenerazionale* (Milan: Franco Angeli, 2008).

among the diverse forces that ought to work in concert to foster societal development, an imbalance that has led to a flood of economic methods and objectives. The inundation effect can be harmful, not only when economic aspects prevail over legal ones but equally when the reverse occurs, and law overflows into economics: "The law disrupts the harmony of economic results and does what it should not do, creating disharmonious institutions that can be understood only if one is aware that the law is being used against economics".[27] The objective must therefore be to avoid bidirectional short circuits and find a neutral balance. Doing so will serve not only to assess the resilience of the European legal order but also to gauge its ability to regain a state of dynamic equilibrium after prolonged disruption caused by the dominance of economics and finance.

3.2 This book is not antagonistic to private law; instead, it argues that, fuelled by the process of European integration, a shared legal framework has been evolving, expanding the boundaries between the public and private spheres.[28] Consequently, the priority is to find the right balance to pursue the general interest on a case-by-case basis. The use of private law tools and models has been largely positive, both in terms of the shift from authority to consensus and the increased flexibility of the tools themselves. It would therefore be an oversimplification to overlap the various reasons that have caused the current global 'disorder' and the use of consensus-based tools.[29]

On the other hand, it is firmly established that there is no "biunivocal relationship between public interest and the public law framework".[30] In reality, the challenges that arise possess different characteristics and exhibit a certain duality. On the one hand, we can speak of mutation: when the traditional concept of private law is transplanted into a different context, there is the risk

27 F. Merusi, *Diritto contro economia. Resistenze istituzionali all'innovazione economica* (Turin: Giappichelli, 2006) 2), goes on to clarify that "the lawmaker's main tool is 'dissimulation'; it pretends to innovate but inserts a wedge into the mechanism to make it work without losing complete control over it". Fabio Merusi is a legal scholar who has dedicated the last few decades to an extensive study of the relationship between law and economics. His *oeuvre* includes: *Democrazia e autorità indipendenti. Un romanzo "quasi" giallo* (Bologna: il Mulino, 2000); idem, *Sentieri interrotti della legalità. La decostruzione del diritto amministrativo* (Bologna: il Mulino, 2007); idem, *La legalità amministrativa. Altri sentieri interrotti* (Bologna: il Mulino, 2012); idem, *La legalità amministrativa fra passato e futuro. Vicende italiane* (Naples: Editoriale Scientifica, 2016).

28 See G. Napolitano, *Pubblico e privato nel diritto amministrativo* (Milan: Giuffrè, 2003).

29 Among others, see M.R. Ferrarese, *Diritto sconfinato. Inventiva giuridica e spazi nel mondo globale* (Rome-Bari: Laterza, 2006) 28 ff.

30 A. Moliterni, *Amministrazione consensuale e diritto privato* (Milan: Giuffrè, 2016) 477. For further discussion on this topic, also refer, out of the many, to V. Cerulli Irelli, *Amministrazione pubblica e diritto privato* (Turin: Giappichelli, 2011) 239 ff.; M. D'Alberti, 'Diritto amministrativo e diritto privato: nuove emersioni di una questione antica' (2012) *Rivista trimestrale di diritto pubblico* 1019 f.

that some of its original[31] characteristics may be lost, spawning hybrid forms that can occasionally lead to practical problems of application.[32] On the other hand, private law is not always necessarily and universally the most suitable means of fulfilling a given objective, and the most appropriate approach must be tailored to each circumstance.

One last question revolves around the potential abuse of private law and, therefore, the use of private law principles to circumvent constitutional constraints. These issues are particularly pertinent in the United States, having emerged during the Obama presidency and spilled over into the early stages of the Trump presidency.[33] However, these are entirely separate issues from those under consideration here and will not be explored further in this forum.[34]

3.3 Similarly, this book is not opposed to institutional and administrative reforms. A series of reforms and adaptations within the member states are essential and desirable, provided they align with their democratic constitutional framework. Building a new European order will require substantial interventions in governance and the organization and functioning of administration. Consider, for instance, the urgent need (even though the European Parliament may well not share the same point of view) for a European law on administrative procedures to introduce procedural safeguards for both specific procedures and law-making processes.[35] Still on the subject of reforms, the challenge lies in maintaining a balance with regard to content. For instance, irrespective of the specific outcomes it will yield in practical terms, the reform of the inter-agency consultation process within the framework of the Madia reforms[36] pursues a dual purpose through Legislative Decree No. 127 of July 30, 2016. On the one hand, it aims to foster simplification and efficiency; on the other, it favours coordination and the adoption of a well-balanced decision that will take into account the interests that need to be balanced.

3.4 Lastly, this book does not look back with nostalgia to a time of protectionism and state monopolies, territorial boundaries, or closed legal systems. Nor does it yearn for the dominance of political parties on the national stage (to use the term in a broader, non-technical sense, in the light of the drift towards

31 Suffice it to mention on this subject A. Watson's classic study, *Il trapianto di norme giuridiche. Un "approccio" di diritto comparato*, 1974 (Naples: ESI, 1984).

32 The reference is mainly to the studies of M. Dugato, *Atipicità e funzionalizzazione nell'attività amministrativa per contratti* (Milan: Giuffrè, 1996); idem, *Le società per la gestione dei servizi pubblici locali* (Milan: Ipsoa, 2001).

33 See Davidoff Solomon and D. Zaring's recent 'The Dealmaking State: Executive Power in the Trump Administration' (2018) 106 *Georgetown Law Journal* 1097.

34 See the comprehensive and in-depth monograph by A. Moliterni, *Amministrazione consensuale e diritto privato*, op. cit. fn 29.

35 Referencing this, see esp. G. della Cananea and D.U. Galetta (eds), *Codice ReNEUAL del procedimento amministrativo dell'Unione europea* (Naples: Editoriale Scientifica, 2016).

36 B.G. Mattarella, *Burocrazia e riforme. L'innovazione nella pubblica amministrazione* (Bologna: il Mulino 2017).

charismatic leadership on the one hand and movement-oriented approaches on the other). The Europe we hope for is a Europe of peoples: the goal is to improve the European legal framework in order to bring it to fruition.

4. Thus, the role of law becomes the tipping point in the post-modern era, where paradoxically, the sphere of juridicity is widening, but, at the same time, its centrality is being brought into question. There is great need for a new and different role, grounded in what has been described here. It will serve as a sorting mechanism, a crossroads, and a compass within the social sciences. Above all, it will mean re-establishing connections with these disciplines, modernizing the tools and investigative methods that the institutions adopt. Otherwise, if room is made for other driving forces, the heritage that has matured over 15 centuries of European civilisation, fundamentally shaped by the shared "circulating mentality" of legal principles may be prematurely lost.[37]

However, this cardinal point will be revisited in the concluding chapter. For the present, in the chapters that follow, we must shift our focus towards a more in-depth exploration of the evolution of European administrative law. This branch of law, often likened to a 'fire alarm', as mentioned in this prologue, permits a conscious analysis of its evolutionary path and makes it possible to identify the coordinates for defining the role of law and jurists within the renewed and problematic European landscape.

5. This book is the product of a team effort and is the outcome of the sacrifices to which I have subjected my family. I extend my gratitude to Maria Stella and our daughters (Maria Beatrice, Aurora, and Luna) for their enduring patience (which by now has perhaps begun to resemble resignation).

I started working on this volume back in the latter half of 2014, and the time I spent as a visiting professor in Heidelberg in 2015 played an important role in shaping its progress. I would like to express my heartfelt thanks to Armin von Bogdandy and Anne Peters for their kind hospitality at the *Max Planck-Institut für Ausländisches Öffentliches Recht und Völkerrecht*, which provided an ideal environment for in-depth study of Europe-related topics.

I had the privilege of working on this book during my time at Suor Orsola Benincasa University in Naples and later at the Luiss Guido Carli University in Rome, both of which are bastions of open and unfettered knowledge. I thank all my colleagues for the opportunity they gave me to exchange ideas and work on projects together.

I would like to thank Adrian Bedford for his skilful translation work, and Paola Monaco, for her valuable help in editing.

The book was originally published in Italian in 2018. However, significant changes have unfolded over the past five years due to the COVID-19 pandemic and the Ukrainian crisis. As a result, the current version of the text has undergone substantial modifications and updates with respect to its previous iteration, although the essential framework of the original has been maintained.

37 P. Grossi, *L'Europa del diritto* (Rome-Bari: Laterza, 2009) 141.

Chapter 1

The Prismatic Construction of the European Legal Order

1 Law as a 'formant' of European history
2 The modern state 'speaks' law, the European legal system is a polyglot
3 Models of European integration

1. Law as a 'formant' of European history

According to a well-known theory[1], a legal formant is the basis upon which the legal order of a society develops. There are three legal formants: statutes, case law, and scholarship.

By extrapolating this concept from the field of law and applying it to the history of Europe in a broader and less technical manner, we can attempt to ascertain which of the main human sciences (law, economics, or politics) has had the greatest impact on the evolution of Europe throughout its history. The answer is clear and unambiguous: law (along with philosophy and theology) is the discipline that has contributed most to giving European history its form. However, a second question, namely 'is this still the case? Is law still the scientific-social formant?', underpins this entire volume. The answer, as we shall see in the next chapter, is no. But the outcome of the concluding chapters of the book is that the role of the law must be recovered for a balanced and democratic development of European society. However, we must proceed slowly, step by step.

In his famous historical[2] essay, Paolo Grossi showed how the evolution of democracy, the conquest of freedoms, and the advancement of culture and wealth in Western Europe came about under the aegis of the law (hand in hand with the ideal guide of philosophy) and the achievements of legal science. At

1 R. Sacco, 'Legal Formants: A Dynamic Approach to Comparative Law' (Installment I of II) (1991) 39(1) *The American Journal of Comparative Law* 1 ff.; idem, 'Legal Formants: A Dynamic Approach to Comparative Law (Installment II of II)' (1991) 39(2) *The American Journal of Comparative Law* 343 ff.

2 P. Grossi, *A History of European Law* (Hoboken: Wiley-Blackwell, 2010); Italian edition, *L'Europa del diritto* (Rome: Laterza, 2009).

DOI: 10.4324/9781003302094-2

around the same time, another study[3] of the same name traced the emergence of European identity on the philosophical plane, taking Carl Schmitt's essay on European legal science, written at the end of World War II, as a starting point. It explored the past, present, and future of European integration, the product of a melting pot of legal systems and traditions. Lastly, performing a diachronic analysis, another fundamental work[4] emphasized the substantial unity of continental legal thinking along its multi-millennial history.

These three studies constitute only the most recent step in a centuries-long intellectual journey that has been examined in numerous works, including, in particular, the writings of two icons of twentieth-century socio-political thought, both of whom well versed in legal studies. On the one hand, Max Weber[5] for whom rational religion is a guide to salvation and, via legal and theological systematisation, constitutes one of the foundations of the legitimising power of political authority and the social order of the privileged classes. On the other, Carl Schmitt,[6] for whom today's secularized legal order is the product of theological dogmatics, since, for him, the main concepts of the doctrine of statehood are all secularized theological concepts. For both, religion (from the Protestant and Catholic standpoints respectively) and their theological constructs, among other things, form the basis of the spirit of Western capitalism, thriving in the liberal legal order.[7]

Before briefly piecing together the stages of this journey – an essential premise for analyzing the European legal system – three points require clarification. First of all, it must be observed that today's clear dividing[8] lines between the

3 M. Barberis, *Europa del diritto. Sull'identità giuridica europea* (Bologna: il Mulino, 2008).

4 A.M. Hespanha, *La culture juridique Européenne. Synthèse d'un millenaire* (Aix-en-provence: Le poisson volant, 2015); Italian edition. *La cultura giuridica europea* (Bologna: il Mulino, 2012).

5 See, in particular, M. Weber, *The Protestant Ethic and the Spirit of Capitalism*, 1920 (Oxford: OUP, 2010; *Die Protestantische Ethik und der Geist des Kapitalismus*, 1904–1905).

6 See, in particular, C. Schmitt, *Political Theology: Four Chapters on the Concept of Sovereignty* (Chicago, University of Chicago Press, 2006; *Politische Theologie. Vier Kapitel zur Lehre von der Souveränität*, 1922)

7 Calvinism especially – as masterfully set out in M. Weber, *The Protestant Ethic and the Spirit of Capitalism*, op. cit., according to which, falling into debt is a punishable offence, and economic success is a heavenly reward for austere and ethical living – underlies the capitalist logic of Northern European countries. Weber's text is still a fundamental key to understanding the mental processes behind the decisions of European institutions during the euro crisis.

8 To see the effects of 'Taylorisation' on the system of scientific knowledge, suffice it to examine the taxonomy of academic disciplines in some Western European countries concerning university appointments, especially in France, Italy, and Spain. However, with the fourth (technological and digital) industrial revolution, interdisciplinarity – and especially the ability to work in research teams comprising experts from different fields – have been substantially reappraised. European research is pushing hard to overcome scientific and academic compartmentalisation.

various fields of study[9] were unknown in previous centuries, so our remarks concerning the relationships between disciplines must be read with this in mind. Second, our observations concerning historical development are mostly applicable to advances in continental civil law countries up to the early twentieth century. The common law countries took a different path (which, particularly in the last quarter of the twentieth century, had a strong impact on the formation and legal development of the European legal system[10]), both with regard to the relationship between *ius* and *lex* (especially in the light of the differing role of the judge in these systems) and the relationships between legal knowledge and other social sciences, which were, especially during the nineteenth and twentieth centuries, more fluid and dynamic than on the continent. Third, our account is, of course, an oversimplification because, as has been remarked in reference to European identity, it "presupposes a continuity in European history that has never existed", since European society has morphed and set itself apart over the centuries.[11] Lastly, we will take a look at the scientific and methodological guidance that law and philosophy (two social sciences that have been structured in some way since antiquity) can give, but we are careful to keep in mind that civilisations have also been built on other premises, the most powerful of which, as we have mentioned, is religion, which conditioned societal models for centuries. However, with the exception of theology, these forces did not take their structure from the scientific method.

Law and philosophy were the drivers of the economic, political, and social development of continental Europe, especially in the wake of the principal societal model in the second half of the last millennium, namely the modern state, with its decidedly law-based DNA, due in particular to its science and its relationship with factuality. It was law (hand in hand with philosophy) that, apparently acting instrumentally, slowly wrought the decline of the absolute monarchies typical of the early states.

Rooted in the Roman tradition, the law was fundamental to the workings of society.[12] The culture of knowledge was manifest, in fact, through the two most advanced human sciences: philosophy and law. In the absence of any structured

9 History supplies many examples of intellectuals who are difficult to identify with a specific social science. Just to cite a few examples from Italy, in the 16th century we have Francesco Guicciardini and Niccolò Machiavelli; in the 17th and 18th centuries, Giambattista Vico; in the 18th, Pietro Verri and Cesare Beccaria, and, straddling the 18th and 19th centuries, Gian Domenico Romagnosi and Vincenzo Cuoco.

10 Discussed in chapter IV of this volume.

11 P. Rossi, *L'identità dell'Europa* (Bologna: il Mulino, 2007) 13. See also P. Rossi (ed.), *The Boundaries of Europe, From the Fall of the Ancient World to the Age of Decolonisation* (Berlin: De Gruyter Akademie Forschung, 2015).

12 Naturally, this was also true much earlier, dating back to Ancient Rome. See the authoritative A. Schiavone, *Ius. L'invention de droit en Occident* (Paris: Belin Editeur, 2011); Italian edition, *Ius. L'invenzione del diritto in Occidente* (Turin: Einaudi, 2010).

science of politics or economics, it fell to law (with its authoritative and respected store of knowledge) to bring order to the emerging societal realities, especially in the economic and political spheres. The law interpreted and transformed this material reality into precepts, also thanks to academic speculation in the *universitas*, engendering a shared, multistranded, and universal law to bring order[13] to society. It was understood as a true science by the scholars of the day. In the Middle Ages, religion, the spiritual sphere, guided the development of Western legal systems (which, in a sense, accompanied and nurtured religious momentum, bringing earthly order to the divine), sanctioning the juridical unity of the Church and its independence from the secular institutions that sometimes held power. We might say that it endowed the law with order and structure (which branched out into various fields: feudal law, mercantile law, and the laws of cities and kingdoms). One may recall, for instance, the substantial impact on legal traditions of the Protestant Reformation in the sixteenth century and the English Revolution in the seventeenth.[14]

During the Middle Ages, however, it was law that channelled economic and socio-political factors on the methodological level: an anthropocentric vision gradually emerged, mainly thanks to the enfranchisement of the small and medium merchant classes. At the same time, the political realities that would give rise to the modern states in the centuries to follow began to take shape.

Of course, humanism and the discovery of the Americas constituted an epoch-making caesura thanks to the cultural revolution wrought by faith in the mathematical and natural sciences. In fact, beginning in the sixteenth and, especially, the seventeenth, centuries, a true osmosis developed between the emerging language of science and the construction of legal systems. Suffice it to recall the geometric method of Baruch Spinoza's *Ethica*, Thomas Hobbes's *De Cive* and *Leviathan*, and Hugo Grotius's *Etsi Deus non daretur*. All this

13 Obviously, the mediaeval concept of 'bringing order' was unlike what is usually meant by the expression in the modern state, being structurally distinct from typical modern orders. In the Middle Ages, the major point of reference was the Thomist theory of law, defined as an 'ordering of reason', a mere reflection of the order of reality; it was thus limited to reproducing the (hierarchical) order of reality, interpreting and regulating it with no claim to changing it. This too indicates an active role of law, which chooses to interpret reality precisely in order to preserve and perpetuate the way it is organized; but the theoretical justification for this conception grants the law an ancillary role: it modifies what God and nature have ordained. The new proposition in the Modern Age, with the advent of modern natural law (which gave rise to the theory of sovereignty and the state for this very purpose), was that law not only interprets but moulds and transforms reality. Thus, the Modern Age conception of law was freed from the sway of religion as cultural driver of the social order: it would fall to the law of the state to bring order to society.

14 On the importance of religion in the development of the European legal tradition, see, in particular, the two volumes of H.J. Berman, *Law and Revolution*, vol. I, *The Origin of the Western Legal Tradition* (Cambridge, MA: Belknap Press, 1998); idem, *Law and Revolution*, vol. II, *The Impact of the Protestant Reformation on the Western Legal Tradition* (London; Cambridge, MA: Belknap Press, 2003).

sustained the ideal of boundless scientific knowledge devoid of inter-disciplinary barriers, while the birth of *homo oeconomicus* pointed the way to the accumulation of capital and the option of pursuing earthly wealth rather than eternal salvation.

The stirrings of a move towards economic policy can be found in fourteenth-century English mercantilism. And as early as the sixteenth century, embryonic attempts were made to organize the foundations of political science and economics scientifically. In this, the role of Niccolò Machiavelli[15] was central, but Francesco Guicciardini, at least, is also worth a mention. Yet, a true scientific basis for economics (and, from another perspective, the foundation of political science) was still far off.

In the seventeenth and eighteenth centuries, reflecting the influence of natural law, the law took on a constructive role in terms of political sovereignty and returned to its age-old centrality (albeit with different interpretations from those of the mediaeval era) through the elaboration of objective and abstract universal rules with the goal of constructing a new social order founded on the right to property and the protection of individual freedoms: a new social order that would lead to the affirmation of the bourgeoisie through law. Proposals for political reform emerged during the Age of Enlightenment (with Montesquieu playing a fundamental role), aiming to enhance the role of the sovereign legislator and find a remedy for the disorder and uncertainty caused by referring to custom and the technicalities of the judiciary and scholarship. It should, of course, be borne in mind that the eighteenth century was still a time of passport-free travel, with no customs formalities, and there was still a strong and cohesive cultural fabric, a common European spirit.[16]

As we mentioned earlier, there were no disciplinary fences artificially separating the various branches of science: the example of Machiavelli and Guicciardini in the sixteenth century has already been cited. But we might also consider the influence of philosopher and legal scholar Jeremy Bentham, the chief exponent of English utilitarianism in the eighteenth and nineteenth centuries on subsequent developments in the economic sphere. We might also recall the versatility of the exponents of the Milanese Enlightenment: Cesare

15 The literature on Machiavelli and political science is vast and cannot be summarized here, but see, among many others, L. Strauss, *Thoughts on Machiavelli* (Glencoe, Ill.: The Free Press, 1958); C.H. Zuckert, *Machiavelli's Politics* (Chicago: University of Chicago Press, 2017); C. Holman, *Machiavelli and the Politics of Democratic Innovation* (Toronto: University of Toronto Press, 2018); R.J. Schmidt Jr., *Reading Politics with Machiavelli* (Oxford: OUP, 2018). On Machiavelli and economics see in particular, P. Harris, A. Lock, P. Rees (eds), *Machiavelli, Marketing and Management* (London: Routledge, 2000); P. Ciocca, 'Machiavelli e l'economia' (2013) *Rivista di storia economica* 249 ff. On Machiavelli and law see, among others, G. Labriola and F. Romeo (eds), *Niccolò Machiavelli e la tradizione giuridica europea* (Naples: Editoriale Scientifica, 2016).

16 See, among others, J.A. Armstrong, *Nations before Nationalism*, 1982 (Chapel Hill: UNC Press Enduring Editions, 2009), according to whom, before the 17th century there had been no nations, let alone any form of nationalism.

Beccaria (philosopher, jurist, economist, and man of letters) and Pietro Verri (philosopher, economist, historian, and man of letters).

It was in this period, especially with the emergence of physiocracy,[17] that economic analysis first developed, seeking to attribute the true value of the excess production of agricultural goods at the moment of exchange. This analysis was determined by mercantilism and highlighted the relationship between political-social factuality and the decisions of princes to the benefit of collective utility through a sort of enlightened despotism. This was an important driver for Adam Smith in founding the science of economics in the late eighteenth century, subsequently followed by Ricardo, Malthus, Say, and Stuart Mill, among others. Economics therefore began to take its first mature steps during the nineteenth century. Similarly, the foundations of the modern state were laid in the philosophical and political writings of Jean Bodin, and, with the Peace of Westphalia in 1648, political balances were drawn: the primacy of politics on which the state model would develop for three-and-a-half centuries was established. But political science, as is well known, only matured in the second half of the nineteenth century, with Gaetano Mosca and Vilfredo Pareto.

Not that economics and politics had been unimportant until then: we might even say that they had been fundamental from the very beginning. They were, however, merely social trends and impulses, lacking a scientific substratum and construction. Economics and politics had certainly held centre stage in previous millennia, but they lacked the necessary science to theorise their paradigms and were, therefore, devoid of economic and political[18] method.

In the legal sphere, the sovereign became the holder of absolute power as the modern state became a reality, and legislation ousted natural law; in contrast, there emerged a sense of the individual with a claim to civil and political rights and freedoms. Then, with the French Revolution, the state became sovereign, and the laws adopted by the parliamentary assembly gained primacy; the individual acquired constitutional rights and freedoms through the constitutional assertion of the principles of the rule of law. The supremacy of *lex* over *ius*, in fact, completed a gradual and slow rethinking of the pre-eminence of legal cetuality that supported the oligarchy of the privileged classes: the law thus became both instrument and expression of the principle of equality. But this primacy of the individual translated into a growing plurality of contradictions. For example, in the liberal single-class state, it gave rise to the oxymoron of 'progressive conservatism' due to the

17 On this theme see, among others, E. Fox-Genovese, *The Origins of Physiocracy, Economic Revolution and Social Order in Eighteenth Century France* (Ithaca, NY: Cornell University Press, 1976); G.M. Labriola, *La fisiocrazia come scienza nuova. Economia e diritto tra antico e moderno* (Naples: Editoriale Scientifica, 2004).

18 For the consequences of these aspects, see chapter II.

presence of both drivers of social factors, as in the well-known Böckenförde[19] dilemma.

In the modern state, the law guaranteed that the social order remained closed and thus ensured full sovereignty.

Following the unity of political power, the state came to hold the monopoly in the use of force, and its operative arm was the law (*instrumentum regni*, to preserve the established power and the status quo), understood also in a unitary sense and as a dogmatic expression of the general theory of law. In the dialectical relationship between the individualistic and idealistic Kantian perspective, which made it possible to supersede metaphysical dogmatism, and the statist Hegelian perspective, the latter came to the fore during the second half of the nineteenth century, leading, thanks to German public law especially, to the personalisation of the state as sovereign.

All this took place under the aegis of law[20] and legal science, albeit with divergent conceptions of the role of the jurist, depending on either the structuralist[21] or

19 According to this scholar, close to Carl Schmitt and strongly influenced by his views, the liberal state protects the freedom of its citizens endogenously through the moral strength of individuals and social cohesion; but if it uses legal coercion to guarantee freedom, it fails in its liberal intentions: E.-W. Böckenförde, *Staat, Gesellschaft, Freiheit. Studien zur Staatstheorie und zum Verfassungsrecht* (Berlin: Suhrkamp, 1976) 60 ff. On Schmitt's influence on Böckenförde, see, in particular, M. Künkler and T. Stein, 'Carl Schmitt in Ernst-Wolfgang Böckenförde's work: 'Carrying Weimar constitutional theory into the Bonn Republic' (2018) *Constellations* 225 ff.

20 The term 'legal science' has already been used, and will be used, extensively in this volume. We must first understand the non-technical meaning attributed to the term. 'Science' refers here to the social science known as 'law', and the term 'legal science' will be used to refer to the *scholarship* on the social science of 'law'. These terms are not used prescriptively nor with the desire to add to the vast discussion surrounding the centuries-old debate on the nature of law and the dilemma between science and legal technique. There is no doubt that in the age of natural law, law itself was considered a science, since the universalist mindset rendered it an area of study based on rational criteria, capable of leading to immutable and absolute solutions. Friedrich von Savigny and his pupil Rudolf von Jhering offer commendable theoretical reflections on law as a science. They approach the subject from different angles but arrive at the same conclusions. The positivist approach was somewhat different. Its proponents emphasized the exegetical aspect, highlighting the limits resulting from the wording of statutes, often characterized by arbitrariness and contingency, thus bringing the idea of law as a science into question.

21 We have approached this theme again through Kelsen's structuralist approach, in which law is structure and form and, therefore, seeks its own forms of expression, which are essentially coercive and consequently linked to the exercise of power: it is not the aims that the legal system sets itself that count, but the legal system in and of itself, its structure and the set of rules that emanate from it. A legal order that, as a structure, is autonomous and self-sufficient and constitutes a true legal system: in this sense, only some norms within the system can be valid, while others remain outside it. In Kelsen's construction, law becomes a fully self-sufficient system (this, of course, is a simplification, as some openness can already be found in Kelsen's

functionalist[22] leanings of scholars. For a few decades, legal scientists once again became the overlords of the state and many of them also assumed leading political

work). In this sense, law really *is* a science, responding to its own internal principles and criteria, remaining uncontaminated and impermeable to the outside world and therefore separate from the other social sciences. A different view of the scientific nature of law shows through in Carl Schmitt's 1950 essay, *Die Lage der europäischen Rechtswissenschaft*, which starts from the divergence between *ius* and *lex* to carve out a scientific role for the jurist. As the law gained primacy, scholarly writing lost its scientific characteristics and value in the course of the nineteenth century: "Positive law transforms the jurist into a worm in rotten wood", says Schmitt, quoting Julius von Kirchmann's famous phrase pronounced at the 1847 Berlin conference. The situation worsened even more at the turn of the short century, with the concept of 'motorized law' making it impossible for legal science to keep up with sudden normative changes, so that technicians and practitioners, with their commentaries, substituted academics. The advent of European constitutionalism, however, saw a return to public lawyers interpreting general public law, and this would lead to much experimentation in the resistance of European legal science to *lex*: "Beyond the various national borders a common vision has been achieved that allows every scientifically educated jurist in one European state to navigate the legal universe of another."

22 From a functionalist perspective, it is imperative to open up to the outside world and, in particular, to political influences, which indicate the benchmarks of legitimation, and society, determining the goals to be pursued. Openness to the outside world weakens the system's internal tightness, but it is a necessary choice because, to fully understand the legal needs of a community – a social reality – clues from other sciences (history, philosophy, political science, sociology, etc.) with very different goals must be used. For example, sociologists of law are interested in the effects of law on the social fabric and how society is subject to change under its influence. Nevertheless, even from the functionalist perspective, law can be understood as a science, since those who study law essentially seek to understand its nature, i.e., what it is rather than what it ought to be. It has become increasingly difficult to consider law as a science, especially assuming that science, as in the case of the empirical sciences, concerns the discovery of predictable features of law through concepts, rules, and methods able to qualify it as such (among others, N. Irti, *Il diritto incalcolabile* (Milan: Giuffrè, 2016)). In sum, it is no easy task to affirm that law is rational and definitive, since it is necessarily bound to a specific society and a precise setting. Furthermore, at a time when the prescriptive power of law-making (European, national, and regional) is waning, and the interpretative role of the courts, sometimes in dialogue/conflict with each other, is on the rise, the technical aspect inevitably prevails over the scientific one. Moreover, in the course of the 20th century, especially during the second half, law not only increasingly encroached on and intermingled with other human sciences but also gradually ceded ground to them, in as much as it was no longer perceived as central to the development of society, increasingly taking a back seat to the political, sociological, anthropological, and even economic sciences. This is also because it became evident that underlying the prescriptive effect of a norm there must be a balance between understanding and interpreting the interests that stem from social reality, resolved upstream of the legal development of the precept, pertaining, if anything, to the politics of law or, at best, to the theory of justice. Among the main problems concerning the role of the jurist and legal science in the contemporary age is precisely that of having abandoned (intentionally or through weakness) the importance of

roles between the second half of the nineteenth and first half of the twentieth centuries. Demarcation into closed, autopoietic legal orders did not, as we well know, produce positive results: indeed, it gave rise to two world wars. The propensity of law to play an ancillary function in relation to politics (and the parliamentary majority within a cetual system) rather than guiding evolution in the interests of justice, showed the weakness of a law-based system as power exercised by the strongest. This called for a new humanism for the modern age, built on the correlation between legal systems and social sciences and a new pluralistic pact between the citizens of Europe, based on the rights and freedoms enshrined in strict[23] constitutional charters. This resulted in the largest area of freedom in the world, in terms of the quantity and quality of the recognition of these freedoms. From the discussion so far, it is clear that law was now becoming a less isolated area of the human sciences and was being increasingly encircled by other disciplines. It was no longer the soloist, but just a rank-and-file musician playing in the orchestra. In fact, the problem was now reversed: as law became just one player, it lost its role as guide and provider of order at the risk of engendering social dysfunction and malaise in a scenario not so different from that of our own day.

And it can also be inferred that in other areas of the human sciences, including economics, scientific growth was slower and would come later. It may

selecting interests, leaving it to legal practitioners (and judges in particular) or, worse still, to sciences outside the legal sphere (economics especially).

23 The thorny question of the social openness of law and, therefore, of the (political and social) purpose of legal analysis had already been foreshadowed at the dawn of the 20th century, both in Italy, by Santi Romano (subsequently by Massimo Severo Giannini and Feliciano Benvenuti), and more forcefully in France and Germany. Beyond the Alps, in the shadow of Émile Durkheim's studies, Léon Duguit formulated in his *service public* theory a conception of law that would show the shortfalls of the idea of the state as a person and the need to recognize legal sociologism. On the other hand, François Gény, one of the greatest exponents of jusliberalism, dealt a fierce blow to the theory of the closed and self-sufficient legal order, revealing the shortcomings of the exegetical method and arguing for a re-established hermeneutics rooted in the rediscovery of natural law on the one hand and the practical requirements of life in society on the other. In Germany, where the eclectic studies of Rudolf von Jhering and Hugo Preuss, among others, had previously met with great success, having studied the history of mediaeval law, Hermann Kantorowicz, the leading German exponent of the free-law doctrine, posited the need to return to the equitable decision of the judge in place of positive law. From another angle, Gustav Radbruch, adopting a neo-Kantian position, had evidenced the split between the concept of law and jus-positivism, he too undermining the idea of the primacy of state law where it conflicted with the principles of equality and substantive justice. We must not overlook the fundamental contribution of Max Weber, critiquing dogmatic and formalistic conceptions of law from the sociological perspective. The functional goal-based conception of law, rather than the merely structural impetus of legal development (as described by Norberto Bobbio, among others), became widespread in late twentieth-century Europe.

be deduced that studies in the field of economics were still unripe and difficult to classify within the panorama of the European social sciences. We may cite the example of Benedetto Croce's studies around the time of the First World War, in which he emphasized the late conceptualization of the economic principle and the economic (but also legal) 'premorality' of the practical spirit of the modern age.[24] Croce was interested in resolving the thorny question of the distinction between the useful and the moral, between theory and practice, which had also been addressed by Giovanni Gentile. For Croce, law and economics are synonymous: law can only flourish on economic terrain as both serve a utilitarian and practical purpose. In seeking to discern whether law is an economic or a moral phenomenon, he leans towards the idea that the practice of law and economics are one and the same. This contributed to the consolidation of historicist legalism, the relativization of the principles of justice, and the creative importance of the practical interpretative dimension of the courts. For Croce, law does not engender concepts, but only pseudo-concepts, de facto present in reality (deriving from positive law). Gentile, on the other hand, held that law is not a mere fact, but constitutes the reality of the spirit in a dialectical process. Therefore, law and, in particular, the philosophy of law, have a gnoseological vocation, helping to form a critical awareness of reality: thus, law and economics inhabit different planes, and law and morality enter a shared dialogue. Somewhat later, in the 1930s, Croce came to see economics simply as a means of distinguishing in the sphere of the moral life, confirming the superiority of the paradigms of moral philosophy over the practical one of economics.[25] However, Croce's taxonomy began to show traces of disquiet regarding such a "position of the 'economic', faced with the realisation of how problematic its very 'instrumentality' was, being capable of fostering moral life and civil progress and leading to a long historical eclipse of freedom".[26]

2. The modern state 'speaks' law, the European legal system is a polyglot

This brief preliminary summary shows how the law, for millennia, has been the instrumental and functional foundation upon which social models have been built, especially in Europe. The phenomenon was further accentuated by the birth of the modern state (the state of the rule of law) under the aegis of law and its science. It is a path dating back a couple of millennia that seems, however, to have reached a caesura with the European legal experience, which, as we shall see, has taken the continent in a new and distinct direction.

24 B. Croce, *Riduzione della filosofia del diritto alla filosofia dell'economia*, 1907 (Milan: Giuffrè, 2016).

25 B. Croce, *Storia d'Europa nel secolo decimonono* (Bari: Laterza, 1932) 364.

26 P. Bonetti, *Introduzione a Croce* (Rome-Bari: Laterza, 2005) 86.

Indeed, the growing role of law (and its science) in the construction of the European legal system opens the door to a whole new[27] avenue of exploration. This is not (only) so much by virtue of the special nature of the European legal system, which has already been addressed from various angles by scholars studying the European[28] institutions, but in terms of the balance between law and the other social sciences (and their respective scientific methods and aims) underpinning the foundations of this system.

The brief excursus offered in the preceding section affirms that when the foundations of the modern state[29] were being laid between the seventeenth and eighteenth centuries, law was an ancient and established science (albeit in the guise of the law of private individuals), whereas economics was little more than a rudimentary discipline (classical political economics developed between the second half of the eighteenth and the first half of the nineteenth century), and sociology was yet to emerge (taking its first steps in the nineteenth century). There are two circumstances to consider. The first is that the distinctions between the sciences, and especially the social sciences, were extremely tenuous, with a general tendency for robust hybridization. Second, even at that time, decisions were still taken by rulers in the light of political and economic considerations. These, however, were merely factual in nature: there was no method and no solid framework for economics, sociology, or political science, so decisions were goal-related; whereas law was already a solid given, both in terms of methodology and with regard to tradition and practice, so its purposes were pursued according to a scheme, following a scientific method.

In eighteenth- and nineteenth-century Western societies (especially in continental Europe civil law systems), the relationship between the state and law proved to be decisive in the evolution of the institutions. Law was the basis for

27 The monograph by G. Itzcovich, *Teorie e ideologie del diritto comunitario* (Theories and ideologies of community law) (Turin: Giappichelli, 2006), is fundamental here. Adopting a neo-constitutionalist approach and offering an analysis of the incisive role of the European courts in constructing the European legal system and addressing the relationship between the courts and scholarship, Itzcovich highlights how even a pluralist theory of the legal system is no longer adequate for interpreting the institutional order.

28 There are two contrasting visions. On the one hand, the conviction that the European legal system is composite, and that everything should be done to promote integration: in support of this position we find S. Cassese, *La crisi dello Stato* (Rome-Bari: Laterza, 2001); idem, *Lo spazio giuridico globale* (Rome-Bari: Laterza, 2003); G. della Cananea, *L'Unione europea. Un ordinamento composito* (Rome-Bari: Laterza, 2003). Others hold that the European order has been incomplete and flawed from the outset and that its governance is potentially harmful to its member states. For this opinion, see in particular, E. Jones, R.D. Kelemen, S. Meunier, 'Failing Foward? The Euro Crisis and the Incomplete Nature of European Integration' (2016) 49(7) *Comparative Political Studies* 1010–1034.

29 A construction linked, like all social constructions, to a well-defined space and time. In this sense, see B. Badie, P. Birnbaum, *Sociologie de l'Etat* (Paris: Grasset, 1979).

organising political power through which its exercise was planned, in a sort of consubstantiation between state and law and between law and state. Law was understood as functional to the state, and the state existed as a function of law; all this through a process of the 'legalization' of politics and/or politicisation of law. The interaction between politics and law intensified above all during the nineteenth century with the affirmation of the primacy of law and positive law, namely legislation created by the state as a manifestation of the sovereign power of command over its subjects; but it also expanded in the form of individual guarantees recognized by the rule of law. The state 'speaks the law' in almost every aspect of its actions.[30] The idea of sovereignty, a 'closed' conception of the state, the direct relationship between state and citizen that excludes the intermediation of other bodies,[31] rests on the neutral and absolutizing construction of the law. This process of 'legalization' of the state reached its peak during the nineteenth century, assuming the form of Weberian rational-legal dominance: the state possesses an administrative and legal order that can be changed by legislation and to which the organized activities of the administration, it too controlled by legislation,[32] tend.

It follows that, with the rapid developments in public law, legal science[33], with its paradigms and modes of interpretation, has played a leading role in the

30 G. Poggi, *The State: Its Nature, Development and Prospects* (Milton, Australia: Polity, 2013); Italian edition, *Lo Stato* (Bologna: Il Mulino, 1992) 42–48. See also idem, *Forms of Power* (Milton, Australia: Polity, 2013).

31 This is, of course, a simplification: the presence of intermediate bodies was remarked by Montesquieu and Tocqueville, while aggregated social groups were recognized by Althusius, Pufendorf, and Gierke.

32 M. Weber, 'Economy and Society', vol. I, part III, 'Forms of Power'; vol. IV, part IX, 'Sociology of Power', Section II, 1922 (Berkeley, Los Angeles, London: University of California Press, 1978).

33 The thorny question of law as science and technique is discussed above. Even today there are numerous attempts to theorise the substantially scientific nature of law, such as the neo-pandectist and neo-constructivist theories of both private and public law. For the former, see the German neo-pandectist theories of the last quarter-century. The greatest exponent of this approach is Reinhard Zimmermann, professor at the Max Planck Institute in Hamburg and author, among other works, of *The Law of Obligations: Roman Foundations of the Civilian Tradition* (Oxford: Oxford University Press, 1996), now in its third edition. It focuses, on the one hand, on the underestimation of the eighteenth- and nineteenth-century process of codification and the return to *ius commune*, and above all to the Roman tradition (not for their historical value but due to their influence on positive law today) and, on the other, legal purism and dogmatism, thus creating a distance from the social context in which the law operates. For the neo-pandectists, codification amounted to a sort of deviation to be resisted so as to bring it back to the abandoned Romanist binaries; codes are nothing more than porous and flexible repositories of Romanist wisdom; these are, as Zimmermann claims, pandectism coagulated into law. This line of thought sees law as an autonomous product, originating in, and driven by, its own dynamics, untouched by the social context, economic factors, and political conditioning. All this is built upon a vague and amorphous concept of

construction of the state. The 'language' of the institution that is the 'state' was purely legal, and the jurist, particularly between the second half of the nineteenth century and the First World War, was the *dominus* in this organizational model. All this came about mainly through the extraordinary expansion of state bureaucracy and administrative apparatus, starting from the late nineteenth century and throughout much of the twentieth.

The events of the European supranational order in the aftermath of World War II and during the second half of the twentieth century were diverse. Alongside law, other sciences, such as economics, sociology, political science, and statistics diverged to become sciences in their own right. We should consider, for example, Luhmann's observation that the primacy of economics in contemporary society manifests itself in the political sphere through the extent to which political success or failure is judged on the basis of economic success or failure.[34] The so-called crisis of the law, which we have been debating for over a century, was in fact a crisis of a certain neutral and autonomous non-secularized idea of law; together with the secularization of European society, the law has become one of the causes, and a part of, a more complex model,

the unity of law. For a severe critique of the neo-pandectist standpoint see, among others, P. Caroni, *La solitudine dello storico del diritto. Appunti sull'inerenza di una disciplina altra* (Milan: Giuffrè, 2009), stating that the disparaging interpretation of codification constitutes the *wreck of historicity* since legal purism domesticates the code and leads to making the past appear to be a prefiguration of the present. He, on the contrary, assumes that codification did not actually change the game itself, but directly altered its rules, refocusing everything. And it did so in the light of the changing social context, a factor that purists entirely ignore. For this author, neo-pandectism is an illusion, a historical investigation essentially seeking "in the past some message that confirms the goodness of the law in force and legitimises it. Their incursion into the mainland behind us is reminiscent of police searches: they break into the wanted man's home, seize the materials they find; they unscrupulously but not haphazardly sort through them, and come running back with the loot they need" (p. 201). Essentially, Zimmermann and the neo-pandectists have succeeded in restoring the history of Roman law to law faculties as a core subject: but at the price of prioritising mythology and pure legal conceptualism. In the realm of public law, see, among others, the neo-constructivist views of A. von Bogdandy in 'The Past and Promise of Doctrinal Constructivism: A Strategy for Responding to the Challenges Facing Constitutional Scholarship in Europe' (2009) *I-Con* 364 ff.; idem, 'Le sfide della scienza giuridica nello spazio giuridico europeo' (2012) Il diritto dell'Unione europea 225 ff. These authors do not shy away from the issues outlined above; see the exhaustive M. Brutti, 'Per la scienza giuridica europea (riflessioni su un dibattito in corso)' (2012) *Rivista trimestrale di diritto pubblico* 905 ff., and S. Civitarese Matteucci, 'L'identità delle scienze giuridiche nel mondo giuridico "plurale" – "Questa è l'acqua"', in V. Barsotti (ed.), *L'identità delle scienze giuridiche in ordinamenti multilivello* (Rimini: Maggioli, 2014) 29 ff. For a more formalistic approach see P. Forte, 'Oggetti giuridici. Note e primi appunti sulla loro esistenza' (2015) *Costituzionalismo* 45 ff., to which we also refer for the extensive bibliography on the subject.

34 N. Luhmann, 'Selbst-thematisierungen des Gesellschaftssystems', in *Soziologische Aufklärung*, vol. II (Köln: Westdeutscher, 1975) 72 ff. and, in particular, 90–95.

intermingled with political, social, and economic[35] elements. Hence the absolute need for an interdisciplinary approach (born, of course, as far as jurists are concerned, from a legal interest and pursuing a legal goal) to the study of legal systems and, in particular, that of Europe. It must be interdisciplinary both in terms of the relationship between law and the other human sciences and also with regard to the relationships between the various branches of legal[36] science.

This is because the DNA of the European legal system is, for the reasons shown above, profoundly different from that of state legal systems and the result of contamination among the different sciences. Moreover, how this system has been constructed, and the instruments used to achieve it, have followed different trajectories: suffice it to recall the circumstance that the integration process has been instrumentally affected by trends in political and economic theory, no longer constrained by the fundamental objectives and goals pursued. As we shall see in the next section, when discussing the main theories underpinning the European order (neo-functionalism, liberal intergovernmentalism, transgovernmentalism, neo-institutionalism, etc.), scholars mostly debate the validity of theories developed by political scientists and economists in order to identify their weaknesses and assess their degree of compatibility with democratic[37] constitutionalism.

Nevertheless, the task of the law, although only partially differing from its historical role, has been no less significant: to stem and channel the powerful influence of economics and politics (somewhat like the globalization process) and to give

35 On these questions, see, among others, S. Cassese, 'Le rivoluzioni politiche del ventesimo secolo e la secolarizzazione della scienza giuridica', in Aa.Vv., *Nuovi moti per la formazione del diritto*, Atti del Convegno Internazionale, Rome, C.N.R., 2–3 June 1987 (Padua: Cedam, 1988) 379–386. But see also, from a historical perspective, the fine essay by E. Böckenförde, 'The Rise of the State as a Process of Secularization', 1967, idem, *Religion, Law and Democracy: Selected Writings*, section II, *Law and Secularity* (Oxford: OUP, 2020) 152 ff.

36 From this point of view, German legal science has proved to be precursory. Of interest in this regard are the studies produced by the Arbeitskreis Europäische Integration (AEI) of the Institut für Europaische Politik. It is the oldest and largest independent association dedicated to the interdisciplinary study of European integration. As the association's website states, the "AEI has about 400 members, consisting of professors, lecturers and researchers in the fields of law, economics, political science and EU history, and of people working in various institutions and organisations connected to European politics and policies. AEI was founded in 1969. Among the founders were the first President of the European Commission, Professor Dr. Walter Hallstein, and State Secretary Professor Dr. Alfred Müller-Armack. AEI is a founding member of the European Community Studies Association World, the global umbrella organisation of all national European studies associations". The AEI has been operating since 1969 and has so far produced eighty-five volumes of research, in addition to the publications contained in its journal, Integration.

37 For a summary, see P. Craig, 'The Nature of the Community: Integration, Democracy, and Legitimacy', in P. Craig, G. de Búrca (eds), *The Evolution of EU Law*, 2nd ed. (Oxford: OUP, 2011) 13 ff.

concrete constitutional force to the integration process at moments of *impasse*.[38] Hence the initial effort of the founders, but also that of the judges of the European Court of Justice ('Der EuGH als "Motor der Europäisierung" in historischer Darstellung'[39]), who performed an essentially political role ("Der EuGH als pragmatischer 'political player'"[40]), especially in the first quarter-century of the Treaties[41] (so-called Integration through Law,[42] whereby law is both object and instrument of integration[43]). Thanks to its long-standing tradition, law was for many years the vehicular 'language' of integration, the instrument of cultural communication between national systems: this was especially true of administrative law, in part due to the predominantly legal training of national bureaucrats.

On the other hand, the 'causal nexus' linking democracies and supranational[44] law was different. The aim of the former was primarily (as is clear from Article 1 of the Italian Constitution) to institutionalize the social conflict between capital and labour and to govern it through the instruments of representative democracy. Conversely, the second was principally intended to regulate conflicts arising from the economic interdependence of member states and the circulation of goods in order to promote efficient market arrangements. As we shall see, it is only natural

38 A very effective and convincing treatment of the historical reconstruction seen from the legal perspective is offered in A.K. Mangold, *Gemeinschaftsrecht und deutsches Recht* (Tübingen: Mohr Siebeck, 2011) 31 ff. This work highlights the asymmetries and sometimes even the conflicts underlying the political and legal construction of Europe. For a historical reconstruction from the political angle, still emphasizing the founding role of the European Court of Justice in constructing the Community edifice, see, among many others, C. Zorgbibe, *Histoire de la construction européenne* (Paris: Puf, 1993); B. Olivi, *L'Europa difficile. Storia politica dell'integrazione europea 1948–2000*, op. cit., Prologue; P. Gerbet, *La construction de l'Europe*, 4th ed. (1st ed., 1983), (Paris: Armand Colin, 2007); G. Courty, G. Devin, *La construction européenne*, 3rd ed. (1st ed., 2001), (Paris: La Découverte, 2010).

39 This is the meaningful title of chapter 5 in the book by A.K. Mangold, *Gemeinschaftsrecht und deutsches Recht*, op. cit., 86 ff.

40 This is the title of the subsequent chapter in A.K. Mangold, *Gemeinschaftsrecht und deutsches Recht*, op. cit., 138 ff. (chapter 6).

41 See the canonical studies by E. Stein, 'Lawyers, Judges and the Making of a Transnational Constitution' (1981) 75 *American Journal of International Law* 1 ff.; H. Rasmussen, *On Law and Policy in the European Court of Justice: A Comparative Study in Judicial Policy-Making* (Dordrecht: Nijohoff, 1986); J.H.H. Weiler, 'The Transformation of Europe' (1991) 100 *Yale Law Journal* 2403 ff.; A. Stone Sweet, *The Juridical Construction of Europe* (Oxford: OUP, 2000).

42 See the seminal essays by Joseph Weiler, including, in addition to the one mentioned in the previous footnote, J.H.H. Weiler, 'The Community System: The Dual Character of Supranationalism' (1981) *Yearbook of European Law* 267 ff.

43 On the topics of negative integration (the removal of barriers to integration) and positive integration (the creation of EU legal frameworks to replace national ones), see the definitive A. Stone Sweet, *The Juridical Construction of Europe*, op. cit.; idem, 'La Corte di Giustizia europea', in S. Fabbrini (ed.), *L'Unione europea. Le istituzioni e gli attori di un sistema sovranazionale* (Rome-Bari: Laterza, 2002) 73 ff.

44 See, in particular, M. Dani, *Il diritto pubblico europeo nella prospettiva dei conflitti* (Padua: Cedam, 2013), with particular reference to the first part.

that the different constitutional logics must entail European institutions and member states taking divergent positions, resulting in conflicts and the consequent need to reconcile opposing interests. These conflicts, after an initial period in which a virtuous equilibrium was established, have come to a head in recent decades.

The diversified genome of the European order has produced a many-voiced framework within which the means for reaching objectives and goals are to be reached, displaying a gradual and consistent shift of the centre of gravity towards the theoretical *instrumentarium* of the economy in particular. Indeed, some of the most influential contemporary scholars have variously questioned the possibility of the survival of a liberal-democratic order, with its extraordinary cultural and scientific past, due to the pre-eminent thrust of economics.[45] But this shifting axis has consequently given the law a more diversified role in the construction of the European legal system compared with the dominant role it plays in the construction of a state (as well as a return to this methodological approach which, following the Europeanisation of national law, has affected state systems too). In essence, in the first phase of the construction of Europe, economics was also allowed to play a part in exploring and guiding the direction that integration would take. Law was above all central to the institutional construction of the first phase and then, at a later stage, the judicial level. It was subsequently left waiting for a legal and political Godot in the expectation of a second, constitutional, phase. Admittedly, the supranational order grew from legal sources (the result of lengthy collaboration also at the technical and legal levels) and underwent a change of pace thanks to the creative function of the European Court of Justice (and, therefore, due to a sort of judicial seigniory over the European institutions) and a substantial output of *soft law*.[46] But the original paradigms and interpretative techniques expanded from a scientific melting pot rather than the predominantly legal (and symbiotically political) experience of the modern state.

Essentially, we hypothesize that the European order was born with a primarily legal and economic genetic makeup (while the political one was consciously limited to the supranational level, leaving it largely in the hands of the states), aiming for integration through the market, also through legal means. This balance was maintained in the early stages, with the legal aspect prevailing at certain times (suffice it to recall the fundamental jurisprudence of the Court of Justice in the

45 See, among others, albeit with different sensitivities and perspectives, and with varying degrees of criticism of the architecture of the European Union, R. Dahrendorf, *Reflections on the Revolution in Europe* (London: Routledge, 2017); J. Habermas, *Time of Transitions* (Cambridge, UK; Malden, MA: Polity, 2006); idem, *The Crisis of the European Union. A Response* (Cambridge, UK; Malden, MA: Polity, 2012); idem, *Europe. The Faltering Project* (Cambridge, UK; Malden, MA: Polity, 2014); idem, *The Lure of Technocracy* (Cambridge, UK; Malden, MA: Polity, 2015). For a particularly insightful interpretation, see M. Goldmann, 'The Great Recurrence. Karl Polanyi and the Crises of the European Union' (2017) 23 *European Law Journal* 272–289.

46 For an outline, stocktaking, and critical analysis of soft law production in the European legal system, see L. Senden, *Soft Law in European Community Law* (Oxford, UK; Portland, Oregon: Hart, 2004).

1960s). However, this balance began to shift towards the economic side of the scales from the late 1980s. Precisely because of the mixed genetic heritage mentioned above, economic considerations came to prevail over the others. In the light of the crisis of the previous years, it became imperative to effect a reorganization.

The history of European law is therefore quite different from that of the law of states, and the role played by legal science differs from that of the previous three centuries. In particular, it is interesting to ask why, in a cultural context different from that leading to the birth of the modern state, the construction of the European legal system nevertheless took place through law-based mechanisms, and why the role of law changed over time. Why was law so central in the decades following the Second World War, still characterized by nationalistic closure and deep-rooted normative positivism.

What we have discussed so far also leads to a reflection on two further points.

First of all, on the empirical side, some reflection is due not only in relation to how 'legalization' has contributed to the European integration process but also on the environmental conditions and broader scientific context (institutional, economic, geopolitical and socio-political conflicts, technological innovation, etc.) that have affected, conditioned, and crossed its pathway. This is particularly true in periods of profound transformation,[47] characterized, as today, by a change in the geopolitical order in the direction of a scission of economic and military power relations into new Eastern and Western blocs and the emerging power of private bodies (particularly Big Tech and Big Pharma) capable of confronting national and supranational public powers. At the regional level, on the other hand, we see a marked post-Covid paradigm shift within the European legal system (from pro-competitive economic regulation to functionalised economic programming), albeit continuing to prioritize financial interests in socio-economic policy-making choices.

Second, on the theoretical side, it is striking that the framework of the European integration process is unsuited to the intricacy of the intertwining disciplines: they remain parallel and, for the most part, autonomous. Depending on the angle from which scholars consider the historical path that led to the Union, individual scholars are convinced that it was either law, economics, or political science that provided the direction for the evolution of the European order. This, of course, leads to only a partial vision of the phenomenon.

3. Models of European integration

That the evolution of the European legal system has, from its very beginnings, represented a discourse in its own right with respect to that of modern states can be demonstrated by an examination of the theories underlying the European integration[48] process.

47 Discussed in greater detail in chapter II.
48 From the legal perspective, see the overview by P. Craig, 'The Nature of the Community: Integration, Democracy, and Legitimacy', in P. Craig, G. de Búrca (eds),

The earliest theories were drawn up by political scientists and, in particular, by scholars of international relations, embracing some elements from the economic sciences. This would seem reasonable, given that the European Community was formally constructed upon international relationships between states governed through treaties. Indeed, until the late 1960s it was scrutinized by scholars of international law from a variety of backgrounds, who, it must be said, did not fully grasp the originality of the new structure.

Of the various early theories, two became particularly widespread.

The neo-functionalist hypothesis, inspired by theories from international relations policy and economics,[49] was grounded in the economic concept of spill-over (a theory based on the idea of communicating vessels), i.e., the circumstance that as European integration grew in certain market sectors, it would gradually expand into other areas as a result of pressures from various directions, especially from interest groups from below and European bureaucracies from above, also leading to political spill-over, which would gradually result in increased economic interdependence and political pressure for greater integration. The theory originated with David Mitrany's[50] functionalism, which he developed in the 1930s and 1940s. It was later adopted in the political sphere by Robert Schuman and Jean Monnet.[51] This rational and technocratic approach

The Evolution of EU Law, op. cit., 13 ff. On the theories of integration, see also E. Chiti, C. Franchini, *L'integrazione amministrativa europea* (Bologna: il Mulino, 2003) esp. 120 ff. Also interesting from the constitutional point of view is F. Palermo's, *La forma di Stato dell'Unione europea. Per una teoria costituzionale dell'integrazione sovranazionale* (Padua: Cedam, 2005). From the political science perspective, an accurate overview is provided in S. Saurugger, *Theoretical Approaches to European Integration* (New York: Palgrave MacMillan, 2014); but also see L. Raffini, *La democrazia in mutamento. Dallo Stato-Nazione all'Europa* (Florence: FUP, 2010). For an economic approach to European integration, see, among others, R. Baldwin and C. Wymplosz, *The Economics of European Integration*, 5th ed. (Maidenhead: MacGraw-Hill Education, 2015).

49 The ultimate reference is, of course, E.B. Haas's monograph *The Uniting of Europe. Political, Social, and Economic Forces 1950–57* (Stanford: Stanford University Press, 1958). See also L.N. Lindberg, *The Political Dynamics of European Economic Integration* (Stanford: Stanford University Press, 1963); S.A. Scheingold, *The Law in Political Integration: The Evolution and Integrative Implications of Regional Legal Processes in the European Community* (Harvard: Harvard University Center for International Affairs, 1971).

50 D. Mitrany, *A Working Peace System. An Argument for the Functional Development of International Organization*, 1943 (Chicago: Quadranglite Books, 1966).

51 In fact, as has been claimed in P. Gouzy, *Les pioniers de l'Europe communautaire* (Losanne: Centre des Recherches Européennes, 1968) 143, "Jean Monnet a toujours été l'homme d'une seule idée, et d'une idée simple: il préconisa une percée européenne sur un point limité: 'Il faut, disait-il, instaurer une coopération supranationale européenne dans le domaine de l'utilisation de l'énergie atomique à des fins pacifiques'. Sans le proclamer, Jean Monnet jugeait hasardeux, parce-que mettant en cause trop d'interêts disparates, les projects de marché commun qui avaient plutôt la faveur de M. Spaak." A different version claimed that both Monnet and Spaak

would necessarily bring about, among other things, a gradual shift in citizens' loyalty towards the new institutions and guarantee a long period of peace, reducing the likelihood of armed[52] conflict. With the hiatus brought about by French president General de Gaulle's 'empty chair' policy in 1965[53] (de Gaulle envisaged Europe as a confederation, unlike others, including Hallstein, who were pushing for a federal model[54]), and the subsequent Luxembourg compromise, it became clear that the gradualist thesis could not be endorsed in full as it relied too much on economic and technical factors and too little on ideology and social cohesion. The theory centred, in fact, on politicians and technocrats, with particular reference to national and supranational elites, but it underestimated the problem of transferring loyalty from the state to the supranational level. This difficulty had actually been grasped as far back as the 1950s, causing a rift between those who supported the need for functionaries independent of the states to which they belonged and those who, on the other hand, considered it helpful to maintain a link with national administrations.[55]

had doubts about the common market, whereas it was Dutch foreign minister Jacques Beyen who pushed in that direction. Monnet's uncertain stance is confirmed in both versions.

52 E. Böckenförde's criticism in 'The Constituent Power of the People: A Liminal Concept of Constitutional Law', 1982, in *Constitutional and Political Theory. Selected Writings*, section II, *Constitutional Theory* (Oxford: OUP, 2017) is well known. For Böckenförde, the functionalist project of European unification starting from economic integration was doomed to failure from the outset, as it was thought that the paradigms of the modern state could be slavishly applied to the European supranational order. Such paradigms, however, cannot be transferred to another historical and social context as they are: they require radical reworking.

53 See, in particular, N. Piers Ludlow, 'Challenging French Leadership in Europe: Germany, Italy, the Netherlands and the Outbreak of the Empty Chair Crisis of 1965–1966' (1999) 8 *Contemporary European History* 231–248; P. Caraffini, 'De Gaulle, the 'Empty Chair Crisis' and the European Movement' (2015) 7 *Perspectives on Federalism* 163–189.

54 The strong disagreement between de Gaulle and Hallstein is well known. See, among others, E.R. Papa, *Storia dell'unificazione europea. Le origini e la crisi di un progetto rivoluzionario*, new edition (Florence-Milan: Giunti-Bompiani, 2017 (1st ed., Milan: Bompiani, 2006)) 159-160, according to which De Gaulle considered Hallstein "a sort of monarch of the 'European super-State': a super-State, he wrote in his memoirs, that the polemical and turbulent German, 'ardently espoused' from Brussels, where he reigned as in 'his own capital, robed in the apparel of sovereignty, intent on directing his colleagues among whom he 'distributed tasks, armed with several thousand officials (...) receiving letters of credentials from ambassadors, and demanding special honours on his official visits'. He was, the General wrote, 'a German ambitious for his homeland', anxious for a Europe where Germany could regain its 'respectability', a leadership role: everything that 'Hitler's defeat had caused it to lose'."

55 See, in this sense, the analysis in A. Grilli, *Le origini del diritto dell'Unione europea* (Bologna: il Mulino, 2009) ch. VII.

Conversely, intergovernmental liberalism (or perhaps liberal intergovernmentalis,[56] also emanating from international relations), with the grafting of economic institutes and notions linked to collective and public choice, was based on states making rational choices by means of cost-benefit balancing, liberal national preferences, and intergovernmental analysis of inter-state negotiation. Thus, political choices came from below due to pressure from domestic interest groups and were then translated, if appropriate, into supranational integration models via inter-state negotiation, through a sort of economic interdependence between member states in the direction of greater integration. In this approach, rational and efficient choice prevailed, so that the existence of the supranational system satisfied the need to reduce transaction costs and allowed a positive cost-benefit balance. The pivotal role of the Court of Justice was also appreciated in terms of economic rationality; it served to prevent the prisoner's dilemma and avert the problem of free riders. This theory, favouring inter-statism and individualism, essentially reinforced state sovereignty and was incompatible with the goal of constructing a supranational democratic order.

These early theories were succeeded by others from the political sciences, more aligned with communitarianism.

The multi-level governance theory[57] emphasized the Community's three-level government structure (sub-national, national, and supranational), where all the nation-states play an equal part, thus breaking the inter-state monopoly of national governments, since supranational institutions also contribute substantially to decision-making. In an interconnected and networked political scenario, on the one hand, member states lose influence and control over the EU institutions due to their multiple and divergent positions, information asymmetries, and the unexpected consequences of institutional transformations. On the other hand, a significant role is played not only by governments but also by various levels of bureaucracy and interest groups in general. Straddling multi-governance theory and intergovernmental theory is a variant of this outlook: historical institutionalism.[58]

56 For an extensive treatment of this theory, see A. Moravcsik, *The Choice for Europe: Social Purpose and State Power (from Messina to Maastricht)* (Ithaca: Cornell University Press, 1998), stating that "the essential lines of European integration since 1955 reflect three main factors: economic advantage, the relative bargaining power of important governments, and incentives to enhance the credibility of commitments between States. Of these, the most prominent is undoubtedly commercial interest. European integration is the result of a series of rational choices by the leaders of various countries, who were constantly pursuing economic interests – firstly the trade interests of domestic lobbies, and secondly the macroeconomic preferences of national coalitions of governments – that gradually became a response to the structural incentives of the global economy" (p. 3).

57 For a detailed analysis of this theory, see L. Hooghe, G. Marks, *Multi-Level Governance and European Integration* (Lanham: Rowman & Littlefield, 2001); idem, 'European Integration and Democratic Competition' (2004) *Europäische Politik* 1 ff.

58 See, among others, P. Pierson, 'The Path to European Integration: A Historical Institutionalist Analysis' (1996) 29(2) *Comparative Political Studies* 123 ff.

The neo-institutionalists sought to prioritize the independence of political institutions, particularly Community institutions, as structures tasked with defining and defending values, norms, interests, and identities originating from below, from society. The prioritization of supranational organization meant that transnational society established the basis for interaction and dictated the rules defining political life. Neo-institutionalist theory guaranteed supranational structures greater autonomy and the ability of transnational actors to choose whether to influence politics at the national or Community levels, with greater awareness. This necessarily entailed a gradual shift of competences to the supranational level.[59]

In the 1990s, the 'rational choice institutionalism' and 'social constructionism' models emerged: the former was more inspired by economic theories whereas the latter more strictly derived from political science. In the former, the stakeholders' choice of institutional structure is dictated by the fact that it brings greater benefits than alternative institutional architectures; in practice, the chosen institutional structure is the one that best pursues the benefits of cooperation. For the latter, the role of institutions is understood in a broader sense as they also contribute, through soft law, to enabling the social development of preferences and identities. Here, the focus shifts from the rationality of strategic choices towards ideal and identity-based sociological aspects and the legal strategies espoused in the various conceptions of regulation.

The situation has become even more complex in the new millennium, with several, sometimes mixed, coexisting models, leading in some cases to even more advanced forms of integration by stealth, unbeknownst to the public. As has been observed by Luisa Torchia, the mere opposition between the Community method and the intergovernmental method has long since ceased to reflect the complex reality of the Union, in which different models of federalism, centralized and decentralized administrative systems, institutions and powers with very different regulatory bases, wider and narrower circles of rules and apparatuses, and intersections between different models and systems of governance coexist. The chief example of this *mélange* is currently the new architecture of the European financial institutions, where the decentralized model coexists with the centralized pattern. Here, different combinations, in variously wider and narrower circles, are found from time to time, so an argument has been made for variable-geometry integration according to the different segments[60] of financial supervision.[61] In particular, the European System of Financial

59 L. Torchia, 'In crisi per sempre? L'Europa tra ideali e realtà' (2016) *Rivista trimestrale di diritto pubblico* 619.

60 L. Torchia, 'In crisi per sempre? L'Europa tra ideali e realtà', op. cit., 620. See also L. Torchia, *Il governo delle differenze. Il principio di equivalenza nell'ordinamento europeo* (Bologna, il Mulino, 2006).

61 See, in particular, M. De Bellis, 'European Financial Supervision after the Crisis: Multi-Speed Models within a Two-Track Framework', in E. Chiti and G. Vesperini (eds), *The Administrative Architecture of Financial Integration: Institutional Design, Legal Issues, Perspectives* (Bologna: il Mulino, 2015) 61 ff.

Supervision interacts in several ways with the European Banking Union. For example, ESMA, the European Securities and Markets Authority, is part of the ESFS, but it also has increasing competences within the EBU.[62]

It has been demonstrated, however, that none of the scientific theories referred to so far, which seek to outline the structure and role of the European legal system for the purposes of integration, have come from legal science: they originated with political science and economics, and jurists used them for instrumental purposes. And this came about despite the institutional theory famously developed by jurists (Hauriou and Romano), working on the borderline between sociology and political science.

The instrumental role of law as an economic and financial driver has been confirmed during the crises of the last twenty years, which produced a twofold and decisive paradigm shift. First, with the austerity policies in place between 2008 and 2019, the relationships between the European institutions and the member states (and between the states themselves) radically changed[63]: the intergovernmental method[64] and the technical role of the European Central Bank (which has become, with the Council, the leading institution in the European order) were strengthened, introducing a complex series of mostly financial conditions, which have broadened the gap between the creditor countries of Northern Europe and the debtor countries of the South.[65] Then, thanks to economic recovery policies, the Community method gained the upper hand once more, with the Commission regaining its central position and the creation of a model based on economic planning led by the European institutions, in addition to the imposition of a further series of conditions. Finance was still pre-eminent (with the EU budget and the protection of Euro-unitary financial interests assuming greater importance[66]), but by now some value-based conditions and public policies with a broad constitutional scope were developing.

62 The gradual shift of competences to the supranational level raised the issue, and not only in the area of financial markets, of the attribution and legitimation of authority with respect to the exercise of powers: on this topic, among others, see P. Lindseth, *Power and Legitimacy: Reconciling Europe and the Nation-State* (New York; Oxford: OUP, 2010); J. Mendes and I. Venzke (eds), *Allocating Authority: Who Should Do What in European and International Law?* (Oxford, UK; Portland, Oregon: Hart Publishing / Bloomsbury, 2020).

63 Among many, see F. Fabbrini, *Economic Governance in Europe: Comparative Paradoxes and Constitutional Challenges* (Oxford: OUP, 2016).

64 On intergovernmental methodology, see, among others, S. Fabbrini, 'Intergovernmentalism and Its Limits: Assessing the European Union's Answer to the Euro Crisis' (2013) 46 *Comparative Political Studies* 1003–1029.

65 C. Pinelli, 'Conditionality and Economic Constitutionalism in the Eurozone' (2019) 11 *Italian Journal of Public Law* 22 ff.

66 Among others, C. Fasone and N. Lupo, 'The Union Budget and the Budgetary Procedure', in R. Schütze and T. Tridimas (eds), *Oxford Principles of European Union Law*, vol. I, *The European Union Legal Order* (Oxford: OUP, 2018) 809–843; L. Zamparini and U. Villani-Lubelli (eds), *Features and Challenges of the EU Budget* (Cheltenham: Edward Elgar, 2019). This has led, among other things, to an

As we shall see in the next chapter, despite progressive financialization – with the tip of the iceberg discernible in the massive reinforcement of safeguards protecting the European Union's financial interests – the most significant legal integration model of the last half-century, known, thanks to the term coined by Joseph Weiler, as integration through law, has once more gained ground.

In the past, this phenomenon, which will be discussed later on, mostly involved the role of the European courts in disseminating legal principles and institutions. Today, as we shall see, it also provides the European institutions with technical-political content, and this is especially true of the European Commission.

Apart from the 'integration through law' model, the only ones of even partially juridical origin are federalist (stemming, from a European standpoint, from the Ventotene Manifesto). We may recall in particular the comparative federalism model, which looks at the European legal system through the lens of the major federal states (especially the USA, Canada, and Germany) and comparing it with the confederal model.

There is still a strain of thought, which has gained ground over the last twenty years and whose main exponents are mostly jurists and political scientists, that sees the construction of a European federal state, the United States of Europe, as the only option to guarantee the establishment of a European order devoid of its current democratic deficiencies.[67] This vision – which, of course,

ever-increasing overlap between the Euro-EU budget and that of the member states (see, among others, C. Fasone, 'Towards a Strengthened Coordination between the EU and National Budgets: A Complementary Role and a Joint Control for Parliaments?' (2018) 40 *Journal of European Integration* 265–279) and the increasing prominence of independent financial institutions within the member states' legal systems, which play a significant role in the European Semester (on this, see C. Fasone, 'The Constitutional Role of Independent Fiscal Institutions in the Eurozone' (2019) 23 *German Law Journal* 257–279).

67 For a description of federal mechanisms and suggestions for possible adaptation to the European order, see the monograph by R. Schütze, *From Dual to Cooperative Federalism: The Changing Structure of European Law* (Oxford: OUP, 2009), studying models of dual and cooperative federalism through the lens of the United States. The bibliography on the European shift towards federalism and alternative models (confederation, a Europe of the regions, differentiated integration, etc.) is vast. We cite but a few studies here: M. Burgess, *Federalism and European Union: Political Ideas, Influences, and Strategies in the European Community 1972–1986* (London; New York: Routledge, 1989); M. Burgess, *Federalism and the European Union: The Building of Europe, 1950–2000* (London; New York: Routledge, 2000); D. McKay, *Federalism and European Union: A Political Economy Perspective* (Oxford: OUP, 2000); A. Heinemann-Grüder (ed.), *Federalism Doomed? European Federalism Between Integration and Separation* (New York: Berghahn Books, 2002); S. Fabbrini (ed.), *Democracy and Federalism in the European Union and the United States: Exploring Post-National Governance* (London; New York: Routledge, 2004); F. Laursen (ed.), *The EU and Federalism: Polities and Policies Compared* (London; New York: Routledge, 2010); E. Cloots, G. De Baere, S. Sottiaux (eds), *Federalism in the European Union* (Oxford, UK; Portland, Oregon: Hart Publishing, 2012); I. C. Saliba, *The Influence of Federalism on the Process of European Integration*

dates back to the nineteenth century and invited the reflections of Gian Domenico Romagnosi and, above all, his best pupil, Carlo Cattaneo, taken up again in the early twentieth century by some exponents of *Giustizia e Libertà*, including Carlo Rosselli, Silvio Trentin and Andrea Caffi – was theorized by a group of anti-Fascist politicians (the Ventotene Manifesto of 1941 was drafted by Altiero Spinelli, with the help of Ernesto Rossi and Eugenio Colorni) in the wake of the tragedy of World War II and was essentially inspired by the liberal-socialist values of freedom, equality and justice.[68] For Spinelli, the new order was "a society in which a strong sense of solidarity takes precedence over individual interest without stifling it" and "in which all citizens are assured the same opportunities to develop their abilities".[69] It is no coincidence that the only model to also have a juridical substratum (discernible above all in Umberto Campagnolo's intricate European federalist project of 1943[70]) is the one most clearly inspired by social-democratic constitutions, affirming universal principles of justice.

Apart from the case just mentioned, legal science has otherwise been mostly on the defensive, reflecting the extent to which the various theories coincide with the democratic principle and its corollaries. These developments have sought above all to emphasize the democratic deficit arising from the European institutions' lack of legitimacy.[71] Weaknesses include the circumstance that those exercising power are not answerable to the electorate, the predominance of the executive due to the limited importance of the European Parliament, the preponderance of bureaucratic concerns and interest groups in decision-making processes, the greater distance between the *locus* of decision-making and citizens, and the complexity and lack of

(Saarbrücken: Lambert Academic Publishing, 2014); F. Requejo and K.-J. Nagel (eds), *Federalism beyond Federations: Asymmetry and Processes of Resymmetrisation in Europe* (London; New York: Routledge, 2016); D. Bataveljic, *European Federalism* (Saarbrücken: Lambert Academic Publishing, 2018); B. Kovačević, *Europe's Hidden Federalism: Federal Experiences of European Integration* (London; New York: Routledge, 2019).

68 See in particular P. Costa, *Civitas. Storia della cittadinanza in Europa*, IV, *L'età dei totalitarismi e della democrazia* (Rome-Bari, Laterza, 2001) 439 ff.

69 A. Spinelli, *Il piano economico della democrazia italiana*, 1944, in A. Spinelli, *La rivoluzione federalista. Scritti 1944–1947*, edited by P. Graglia (Bologna: Il Mulino, 1996) 119. See also J. Pinder, *Altiero Spinelli and the British Federalists: Writings by Beveridge, Robins and Spinelli* (London: Federal Trust for Education, 2005); A. Glencross and A.H. Trechsel (eds), *EU Federalism and Constitutionalism: The Legacy of Altiero Spinelli* (Lanham, MD: Lexington, 2010).

70 U. Campagnolo, *Verso una Costituzione federale per l'Europa. Una proposta inedita del 1943* (Milan: Giuffrè, 2003); idem, *Repubblica Federale Europea. Unificazione giuridica dell'Europa*, 1945 (Soveria Mannelli: Rubbettino, 2004).

71 For a multi-faceted summary of the issues related to the so-called democratic deficit of the European Union, see, among others, M. Böhme, *Why We Need to Renew Democracy in Europe: A Brief Excursus on the Democratic Deficit of the European Union* (GRIN, 2013); A. Vauchez, *Democratizing Europe: The Centrality and Salience of Europe's Independent Branch* (New York: Palgrave, 2015); A. Psygkas, *From the 'Democratic Deficit' to a 'Democratic Surplus' in Europe* (New York: OUP, 2017).

transparency of procedures. On these issues, the principles that underpin legal discourse, such as legality[72] and legal certainty have collided and been forced to reckon with principles such as efficiency and quality, which originate in other areas of the social sciences. As for the democratic deficit,[73] it has been observed that it serves little purpose to consider it a mere accident in the construction of the European Union since, in the functionalist model (not fully embracing the ordoliberal system), separation from the political aspect was part of the original programme: "It is the idea that the social order – which is effectively the economic order – should be kept separate, as far as possible, from the political order. This is certainly not a new idea: it has animated liberal thought since the Restoration."[74]

This is, of course, the heart of the ethical-political deficit, explored in depth, by the German *Staatslehre*, concerning the modern state, and which Ernst Forsthoff deemed to be closely connected to technical and scientific progress, with the result that technical achievement affects the social environment and forms of political domination, fundamentally transforming the aims of the legal system, whose primary concern is no longer to protect freedoms and the *Daseinvorsorge*.[75]

While it must be agreed that the problem of the technocracy of the European institutions lies partly in the nature of things, namely the very genesis of the Union, as a reflection of the functional changes described by Forsthoff, this does not imply that certain flaws in its inception and development cannot be identified in order to suggest some corrective measures. These include at least the following: the failure of the European institutions to see the profound social conflicts taking place at state level, the opacity of the decision-making processes at supranational level, at odds with the transparency imposed on the member states, and the circumstance that the Court of Justice now operates as a protector of fundamental rights but operates as a constraint on the member states, essentially upholding the four freedoms favouring competition and the market, often to the detriment of social[76]

72 As we will attempt to demonstrate in the closing chapter, the law cannot constitute the translation into norms of the will of those who exercise power; it expresses and realizes an endogenous form of justice. It is assumed, therefore, that there is an 'ethical' sphere of law, beyond anything the sovereign may dispose. This is precisely one of the characteristics of the constitutional rule of law, on which the German Staatslehre has dwelt so much. See, in this regard, at least E.-W. Böckenforde, *Staat, Verfassung, Demokratie. Studien zur Verfassungstheorie und zum Verfassungsrecht* (Berlin: Suhrkamp, 1991), where account must be taken of Staatsrecht and the fundamental rights of the individual. The democratic principle must also be respected.

73 See chapter III below.

74 R. Bin, P. Caretti, G. Pitruzzella, *Profili costituzionali dell'Unione europea. Processo costituente e* governance *economica*, 2nd ed. (Bologna: Il Mulino, 2015) 351.

75 E. Forsthoff, *Der Staat der Industriegesellschaft. Dargestellt am Beispiel der Bundesrepublik Deutschland* (Berlin: Beck, 1984).

76 M. D'Alberti also remarks on the problem of the inadequate protection of social rights in Europe in 'L'Unione europea e i diritti' (2016) *Rivista trimestrale di diritto pubblico* esp. 772 ff, according to which, despite the principles of social market economy and solidarity enshrined in the Treaties, "beyond the proclamations, the

rights in the European balancing act (historically contributing to building citizenship, whereas today the idea has taken hold that "the only possible form of social integration into citizenship is that guaranteed by the market"[77]). Another problem area is unsatisfactory neutrality in the concrete choices of the European institutions, lurking behind the mask of neutrality and technicality and favouring certain interests over others, most likely as a consequence of the genetic imprint of the European order (one example is ESMA's measures regarding the arbitrary downgrading of sovereign ratings by rating agencies[78]). Yet another issue is the adoption of economic and financial measures to tackle the crisis, which leads to further accentuating already substantial inequalities, with serious repercussions on social cohesion.[79]

It is important in all this not to lose sight of the original objectives of integration: first and foremost, to build peace among the peoples of Europe and to ensure that the economy and the Common Market constitute a means and not an end, as can be deduced from Walter Hallstein's well-known view on the relationship between economics and politics: "We are not integrating economies, we are integrating politics."[80] In this respect, it will be important to see

Union's legal system has to a large extent left the protection of social rights to the legislation and administration of the Member States: eloquent testimony to this is precisely the Nice Charter, which, regarding the recognition and the manner of exercising social rights refers to 'national legislation and practice'." The literature on social rights in Europe is vast. Among the key studies, we single out: G. de Búrca, B. de Witte (eds), *Social Rights in Europe* (Oxford: OUP, 2005); M. Mazziotti di Celso, 'Diritti sociali', in *Enciclopedia del diritto*, vol. XII (Milan: Giuffrè, 1964) 806 ff.; G. Corso, 'I diritti sociali nella Costituzione italiana' (1981) *Rivista trimestrale di diritto pubblico* 755 ff.; M. Luciani, 'Nuovi diritti fondamentali e nuovi rapporti fra cittadini e pubblica amministrazione' (1985) *Rivista critica del diritto privato* 71 ff.; idem, 'Sui diritti sociali', in *Studi in onore di Manlio Mazziotti di Celso*, vol. II (Padua: Cedam, 1995) 101 ff.; A. Baldassarre, 'Diritti sociali', in *Enciclopedia giuridica*, vol. XI (Roma: Istituto della Enciclopedia italiana,1989) 1 ff. On the jurisprudence of the Constitutional Court on social rights, see the recent M. Luciani, 'Diritti sociali e livelli essenziali delle prestazioni pubbliche nei sessant'anni della Corte costituzionale' (2016) 3 *Rivista* AIC 1 ff.

It has been posited that downsizing the welfare state could be instrumental, from a liberal perspective, in the realisation of a new age of rights, a sort of return to the rule of law: D. Zolo, 'Teoria e critica dello Stato di diritto', in P. Costa and D. Zolo, Milan (eds), *Lo Stato di diritto. Storia, teoria, critica* (Milano: Feltrinelli, 2002) 17 ff.

77 G. Preterossi, *Ciò che resta della democrazia* (Rome-Bari: Laterza, 2015) 27.

78 For example, Standard and Poor's unjustified downgrading of France deserved heavier sanctions from the ESMA; however, for reasons of expediency, driven by political and economic interests, the consequence was no more than a public warning. Regarding these events see, among others, M. De Bellis, 'Unificazione, differenziazione e tecnificazione nella regolazione europea dei mercati finanziari' (2015) *Rivista italiana di diritto pubblico comunitario* 1553 ff., in particular 1556–57.

79 On all these aspects, see the closing chapter of R. Bin, P. Caretti, G. Pitruzzella, *Profili costituzionali dell'Unione europea*, op. cit., 339 ff.

80 Hallstein's well-known phrase dates back to 1958, to the speech he gave before the European Parliament in which he also noted that "Our Community is itself a

whether the European Union, unlike what seems to have happened in this early period, will be able to play a significant role in fostering peace and closer integration following the events of the Ukrainian war. And yet, although the current Euro-Union governance does not favour implementing joint foreign policy and common defence solutions, the conclusions of the European Council of 25 March 2022[81] showed a unified reaction to Ukrainian aggression, taking a small step towards political community and, in particular, shared defence.

The result is a series of short-circuits in relations between the European institutions and the member states, largely due to the excessive politicization of national decisions and those of European bodies that have espoused the intergovernmental method, as well as the marked absence of political consensus in the decisions of European bodies adhering to the community method. We may recall, for example, the failure of the Open Method of Coordination, which, at the beginning of the millennium, and in the context of the Lisbon Strategy, was meant to advance the integration process in certain sectors (education and vocational training, social policies, and employment) through instruments of cooperation based on soft law, peer review, benchmarking, and risk management. Another example is the European Commission's 2001 white paper, which

political body, a zoon politicon" (BdS, *Allocuzione del Prof. Walter Hallstein, Presidente della Commissione, dinanzi all'Assemblea parlamentare a Strasburgo, 20 marzo 1958*, Luxembourg, 1958, 7).

Much earlier, during the preparatory work for the Schuman Plan Conference, Hallstein had clearly stated what would be ideological fabric from which integration was to be woven: "The German government confirms that the Schuman Plan is primarily of political importance. From such a perspective, economic problems, however important, take second place: for them some solution will always be found. The German delegation therefore puts an urgent request to all the participants at this conference to put economic interests before the greater political goal" (on this, see, E.R. Papa, *Storia dell'unificazione europea*, op. cit., 160). But see also the Commission's 1962 memorandum taking stock of the situation five years after the Treaty of Rome (BdS, Commission of the European Economic Community, *Memorandum of the Commission on the Action Programme of the Community in the Second Stage*, Brussels, 1962). Hallstein called for a fully integrated Europe, not just a sectoral one. He believed that the economy was political and should not be considered separately, as they follow a single trajectory: "European 'economic' integration is, in its essence, a political phenomenon. The European Economic Community constitutes, with the European Coal and Steel Community and the European Atomic Energy Community, a political union in the economic and social field. (...) The European Economic Community is therefore not a purely economic enterprise that should now be accompanied by a political enterprise. On the contrary, it can be said that the Community is the starting point for political integration in a very broad area, while other areas – cultural policy, other fields of foreign policy, defence policy – are still the responsibility of the member States."

On these aspects see, in particular, A. Grilli, *Le origini del diritto dell'Unione europea* (Bologna: il Mulino, 2009) 58 ff.

81 https://data.consilium.europa.eu/doc/document/ST-1-2022-INIT/en/pdf.

outlined the need for new governance in place of the representative democracy of the modern[82] state.

We will return to some of these aspects later in the light of recent changes to the landscape. In the wake of the pandemic and the Ukrainian crisis, alongside the massive impact on society and the protection of rights[83], the European institutions have shown a marked change in their attitude to financial austerity adopted in the fifteen years preceding the pandemic.[84] What is immediately striking is that the main reflections on these issues have focused on the unique nature of the European legal system and have attempted to show that transposing principles, institutions, interpretations, and state law into the European legal system is a far from ideal solution. On the one hand, the European order has a nature, structure, and functions of its own, hence, for example, our reflections on institutional balancing in the European[85] legal system and our focus on its composite make up.[86] Consequently, the policies adopted by the government of a member state now require not only consensus from within, approved by the political majority, but also exogenous assent, as the member states are part of a strengthening supranational network. On the other hand, this legal order not only concerns the nation-states but has constructed a dense network of legal and, especially, administrative ties with bodies operating on a global scale.[87] This is a development that will certainly also impinge on its internal organization.

82 C. Pinelli, 'Il doppio cappello dei governi tra Stati e Unione europea' (2016) *Rivista trimestrale di diritto pubblico* 642–643.

83 Among many, see, M. Maduro and P. Kahn (eds), *Democracy in Times of Pandemic* (Cambridge, UK; New York: CUP, 2020).

84 On the push for greater European integration following the pandemic crisis, see, among others, N. Brack, S. Gürkan (eds), *Theorizing the crises of the European Union* (London: Routledge, 2020); V.A. Schmidt, 'Theorizing Institutional Change and Governance in European Responses to the COVID-19 Pandemic' (2020) 42(8) *Journal of European Integration* 1177–1193.

85 See the incisive chapter in P. Craig, *Institutions, Power, and Institutional Balance*, in P. Craig and G. de Bùrca (eds), *The Evolution of EU Law*, op. cit., 41 ff.

86 The bibliography on this subject is vast. See, among others, S. Cassese, *La crisi dello Stato* (Roma-Bari: Laterza, 2001); idem, *Lo spazio giuridico globale* (Rome-Bari: Laterza, 2003); G. della Cananea, *L'Unione europea. Un ordinamento composito* (Rome-Bari: Laterza, 2003); E. Schmidt-Aßmann, 'Introduction: European Composite Administration and the Role of European Administrative Law', in O. Jansen and B. Schöndorf-Haubold (eds), *The European Composite Administration* (Mortsel: Intersentia, 2011) 2 ff.

87 See, in this regard, the insightful volume E. Chiti and B.G. Mattarella (eds), *Global Administrative Law and EU Administrative Law. Relationships, Legal Issues and Comparison* (Berlin-Heidelberg: Springer, 2011).

Chapter II

The Relationship between European Law, Economics, and Finance

1 Methodological pluralism and a new 'hybrid' rule of law in Europe
2 European law shifting towards economics and finance
3 The financialization of the rule of law in Europe
4 The logic of economics in public law
5 From formal legality to administrative efficiency
6 The instrumental use of law as infrastructure and functional imbalance in favour of economics and finance

1. Methodological pluralism and a new 'hybrid' rule of law in Europe

An important characteristic of the models described – and the European legal system itself – is that they presuppose a new European rule of law or rather the end of mere state-level rule of law as it was understood in the late nineteenth century and throughout the twentieth. A new European rule of law which, as we have seen, "was hybrid from birth: its legitimacy derives not only from *auctoritas* (formally valid 'legislative' law) but also, and above all, from the *ratio* (the substantive and procedural rights and principles of justice)".[1] The

1 The bibliography on the development of the principle of the rule of law and contemporary approaches to it is vast. Essential texts include P. Costa and D. Zolo (eds), *The Rule of Law: History, Theory and Criticism* (Dordrecht: Springer, 2007); J. Waldron, 'Legislation and the Rule of Law' (2007) *Legisprudence* 91 ff.; M. Vogliotti, *Les nouveaux chemins de la légalité. Au-delà de la modernité juridique* (Bruxelles: Presses de l'Université Saint-Louis, 2020); G. Pino, V. Villa (eds), *Rule of Law. L'ideale della legalità* (Bologna: il Mulino, 2016), to which we also refer for references to the extensive bibliography itself. The words quoted here are taken from M. Vogliotti, 'Legalità', in *Enciclopedia del diritto*, Annali, vol. VI (Milano: Giuffrè, 2013) 371 ff., in particular, 410 ff.

For an updated reconstruction of the rule of law in the European legal order, see, among others, L. Pech, 'The Rule of Law in the EU: The Evolution of the Treaty Framework and the Rule of Law Toolbox', *Reconnect Project*, WP 7, March 2020, 11 ff.

DOI: 10.4324/9781003302094-3

transformation brought about by the legal fiction of shared[2] sovereignty is a move away from the rule of law to the community of law, stemming from the rule of law itself and identified by the Court of Justice as a way of indicating the blend that derives from the European treaties and the general principles of the legal system recognized by the Court[3]: thus, the courts, which ensure the correct application of principles through judicial review, have become the new lords of the European legal system. The "'pillar' of the law, as the *auctoritas* at the summit of the pyramid of sources and supporting the validity of the entire legal system", is replaced by "a 'fabric' of intimately related *auctoritates* and *rationes*; if the former are to be valid, they must conform to the *rationes* of law (*ex parte societatis*); and to be valid, the latter must be transformed into *auctoritates*, assuming suitable forms and following correct procedural models".[4] This has led, among other things, to the gradual dilution of political-administrative direction within a hybrid technical-bureaucratic form of institutionalism.

But, as described above, this rule of law was born hybrid, due, in part, to its varied genetic heritage: it stems from a functionalist European model, which develops in, and for, the market, adopting methods that are at the same time economic, sociological, and political.[5] It is no coincidence that we find in it a number of general principles underlying the European order, such as subsidiarity, highlighting its plural nature and potentially indistinct legal framework, proportionality, a notoriously polymorphic principle expressed in more than one social science, carrying the gene of the cost/benefit balance from the field of economics,

2 On the prismatic concept of shared sovereignty, the first point of reference is surely J.H.H. Weiler, 'The Transformation of Europe' (1991) *Yale Law Journal* 2403 ff., the functional subtlety of the European project between the mid-1980s and the early 1990s. For more recent contributions, see, among others, F. Capogrosso, *Shared Sovereignty and Denationalisation of Statehood in the European Union: Has Governance Eclipsed Government?* (GRIN, 2009); T. van den Brink, M. Luchtman, M. Scholten (eds), *Sovereignty in the Shared Legal Order of the Eu: Core Values of Regulation and Enforcement* (Cambridge, UK: Intersentia Uitgevers, 2015). For an interesting reconstruction of the historical precedents of shared sovereignty, see C. W. Close, *State Formation and Shared Sovereignty: The Holy Roman Empire and the Dutch Republic, 1488–1696* (Cambridge: CUP, 2021). For an evolutionary reconstruction of the concept of sovereignty, see, among others, Deliverable 4.3 of the Reconnect Project, R. Bifulco and A. Nato (eds), *The Concept of Sovereignty in the EU: Past, Present and the Future*, in https://reconnect-europe.eu/wp-content/uploads/2020/05/D4.3.pdf, 2020.

3 Concerning the European fundamental principles see, among many, A. von Bogdandy and J. Bast, *Principles of European Constitutional Law* (London: Hart-Beck-Nomos, 2011). On the spread of general principles of law beyond the state, see, among others, S. Cassese, *Advanced Introduction to Global Administrative Law* (London: Elgar, 2021).

4 M. Vogliotti, 'Legalità', op. cit., 420.

5 Concerning this evolutionary and conceptual framework see, in particular, E.-W. Böckenförde, *Staat-Nation-Europa: Studien zur Staatslehre, Verfassungstheorie und Rechtsphilosophie* (Frankfurt am Main: Suhrkamp Verlag 1999).

and the 'useful' effect, which emphasises the need to balance and weigh interests for the sake of effectiveness and obtaining the most favourable result.

Thus, rather than the formal expression of power, what is important in the European legal system is how power is exercised and the concrete substantive effect through which it is pursued. These are aspects – the convergence of interests, procedure, effectiveness, and the relationship between politics and technology – on which administrative law, especially in continental Europe, has been able to reflect, and which it has been able to metabolise at greater length than other branches of law.

Another consequence of the hybridization process is the methodological variety of the work and laws produced in the European legal system, guiding the development of the European integration process.

The most exemplary case is that of the economic sciences. There have essentially been three main developments along the European journey: the Customs Union, from 1958 to 1968, with the abolition of duties and quotas in European domestic trade; the Single Market, which eliminated many non-tariff barriers and liberalized capital flows within the system; while Economic and Monetary Union led to a single currency for the member states. Choosing the functionalist path to European integration – namely, piloting the development of attempted political and social union in Europe, taking its cue from the constitution of a single market and the construction of an ever-closer connection between the economic and financial systems of European countries – has almost spontaneously led to the development of mechanisms for constructing the European model typically found in economic analysis.[6] As has been noted, "European integration has always been driven by political factors (...). Yet, while the goals were always political, the means were always economic."[7]

This has meant that the creation of rules has also been understood by operators as a set of incentives and a cost-benefit system guiding their behaviour in terms of economic benefits and losses and the relationship between ends and means. The focus is therefore on 'useful effect' or 'effectiveness' on the one hand and proportionality on the other, on the general principles defined by the Community institutions and especially the Court of Justice as the cornerstones of the European order. There can be no doubt, in this case, that an empirical methodology dominates, putting the study of public and private

6 It is common knowledge that the attempts to form a strictly political union over the past three-quarters of a century have all foundered. Suffice it to think of the European Defence Community (EDC) in the early 1950s, which would have led to political union, encroaching on the core of national sovereignty, or, at the same time, the European Political Community (EPC). In the 1960s, the 'empty chair' crisis was provoked by the French reaction to the trend within the European institutions seeking greater political union. Lastly, we saw the idea of a European Constitution flounder in the early 2000s.

7 R. Baldwin and C. Wyplosz, *The Economics of European Integration*, 5th ed. (Maidenhead, UK: MacGraw-Hill Education, 2015) 31.

behaviour before the formulation of the rule and reasoning not so much in terms of legality, inequality, and solidarity as on the basis of objectives/results and social wellbeing. At the European level, therefore, it may be argued that the concept of the rule of law is also a composite one, as is the nature of the supranational legal system. To be more precise, it consists of a traditional hard core, a legal matrix, which coincides with the requirements defined by the Venice Commission but is also subject to a series of substantial variables that characterize the evolution of the European legal system and connote the external and changing layer of the European rule of law. Among these endogenous features of the European rule of law, we encounter – first and foremost – a process of financialization within the legal environment, examined in greater detail in the next section, whereby the common core deriving from legal science is perforated and permeated by the exogenous incidence of the economic and financial sciences.

Here, we may momentarily conclude that, as this encounter between the "ideal-having-to-be valid" of law and the "real occurrence" of economics, as Max Weber puts it,[8] constitutes an important but hazardous experiment and was considered scarcely practicable until the mid-twentieth century precisely because of the tendency of economics to value fact and effect. Instead, it is thanks to the development and mediation of sociological analysis that the legal system has bridged the gap with reality through 'empirical validity' and the subsequent rationalization of the stakeholders' behaviour within the systems.

2. European law shifting towards economics and finance

The functionalist decision to direct European law towards the construction of a single market meant that, almost naturally, the focus shifted to the economy, albeit with some later adjustments.

In the first phase, the European integration process "featured a healthy mix of market liberalism and governmental regulation that would control social inequalities arising from the market and entice solidarity".[9] At this juncture, the reins of the market were in the tight grip of both political and societal forces. Furthermore, it should be borne in mind that, between the 1950s and 1960s, Western European countries enjoyed the benefits of the massive Marshall Plan[10] (the European Recovery Program – the ERP – which led to the establishment of the OECE and then, from 1961, of the OECD), drawing on funds largely

8 On Weber's concept of legal science, see, in particular, M. Weber, 'R. Stammlers "Überwindung" der materialistischen Geschichtsauffassung', in *Gesammelte Aufsätze zur Wissenschaftslehre* edited by von J. Winckelmann (Tübingen: Mohr, 1988) (1st ed., 1922), 291 ff. and especially 329.

9 M. Goldmann, 'The Great Recurrence: Karl Polanyi and the Crises of the European Union' (2017) 23 European Law Journal 272–289.

10 For a historical reconstruction of the Marshall Plan, see, among many others, B. Steil, *The Marshall Plan. Dawn of the Cold War* (New York: Simon & Schuster, 2018).

allocated for social protection policies. Then, after the 'empty chair' crisis of 1965/6, a process was set in motion which would gradually free the market from politics and society, especially in the wake of the economic crisis of the 1970s. It is well known that a turning point which would revolutionize the international financial system constructed after World War II at the Bretton Woods[11] conference (with the establishment of the International Monetary Fund and the World Bank and the institution of gold as the basis of the currency system and the dollar as the sole reserve currency) occurred on 15 August 1971 thanks to the so-called Nixon shock. This refers to the day when, in order to reduce the strong deficit in the US balance of payments (also due to the costs the Vietnam War), President Nixon put an end to fixed exchange rates between currencies, built on the rule of the convertibility of the dollar into gold for the central banks of the national states (the so-called Gold Standard) and allowed the United States to print money again without having to prove that it possessed a corresponding amount of gold in the Federal Reserve's coffers. This announcement was followed in December by the agreements reached at the Smithsonian Institute in Washington (which determined the new exchange rates and an initial devaluation of the price of gold). The results were fluctuating exchange rates, soaring inflation, deregulation, and economic-financial globalization (with consequent international financial speculation), soon to be followed by the energy crisis caused by the Yom Kippur War in October 1973, with a surge in OPEC oil prices that would have very serious economic and social repercussions, especially in Europe.[12]

It has been observed that in the mid-1970s the market paradigm also began to make itself felt in case law, starting from the *Dassonville* and *Cassis de Dijon* cases: integration through law rather than through politics favoured a market-oriented drift.[13] Since then, the Court of Justice has often appeared to be more sensitive to defending the market and competition (which constitute the hard core of Euro-EU competences) than to solidarity, cohesion, and the protection of fundamental rights. It must be acknowledged, however, that at certain times in its history, the Court of Justice has helped build a platform of legal protection for European social solidarity. This was the case, for example, in the early years of the new millennium, when it promoted access to non-contributory benefits.[14] However, the *Laval quartet* case saw a dramatic and consistent

11 On the International Monetary System that grew from the Bretton Woods agreements, see, among others, F. Cesarano, *Monetary Theory and Bretton Woods. The Construction of an International Monetary Order* (New York: CUP, 2006); E. Helleiner, *Forgotten Foundations of Bretton Woods: International Development and the Making of the Postwar Order* (Ithaca, New York: Cornell University Press, 2014).

12 For a reconstruction of the 1970s oil crisis, F. Venn, *The Oil Crisis* (Routledge, 2002).

13 M. Goldmann, 'The Great Recurrence: Karl Polanyi and the Crises of the European Union', op. cit..

14 See in this regard *Martinez Sala* (C-85/96, decided in 1998), *Grzelczyk* (C-184/99, decided in 2001), *Baumbast* (C-413/99, decided in 2002).

tightening of the protection of social rights at the European level.[15] After this, a move towards the de-Europeanization of social rights began to take shape.[16] Lastly, there seem to be some more recent signs of a reversal of this trend, especially thanks to a push from national constitutional courts.[17]

The subsequent liberalization of markets in the late 1970s and especially the early 1980s thanks to Reagan and Thatcher's Anglo-American deregulation policies accelerated the market expansion process, especially the financial markets. Furthermore, with the fall of the Berlin Wall and the end of the Cold War, interest in peace, which now seemed to be consolidated (returning to the forefront in the light of the Ukrainian crisis), became less urgent, so the direction was now firmly one of economic and financial globalization, and the main European interest was to build the single market, consolidated in the Maastricht Treaty, seeking to increase the Union's economic competitiveness. Maastricht and the advent of the euro brought a 'commodification of public finance, which tortuously led to Article 125 TFEU, subjecting the budgets of the member states to market regulation. At the same time,

> The European constitution also comprised a number of provisions intended to limit government powers but without the corresponding freedom. Rather, they entrench the regulating power of the markets over politics. These provisions include the Maastricht parameters, a set of rather contingent benchmarks for joining the Eurozone, in addition to provisions on budgetary regulation detailed in Art. 126 TFUE, including sanctions for violations, and the requirement of independent central banks in Art. 130 TFUE. None of these provisions guarantee individual liberty, understood in the negative sense as a space from which government is excluded. But they all create zones free from democratic policies, where the state is subject to private market power or the power of an independent central bank whose monetary policy operations rely on the market. One could go so far as to

15 *Laval* (C-341/05, decided in 2007), *Rüffert* (C-346/06, decided in 2008), *Commission vs. Luxembourg* (C-319/06, decided in 2008) and *Viking* (C-438/05, decided in 2007). The causes of the restrictive approach lie in the early stages of the financial and economic crisis.

16 *Brey* (C-140/12, decided in 2013) *Dano* (C-333/13, decided in 2014), *Alimanovic* (C-67/14, decided in 2015), Garcia-Nieto (C-299/14, decided in 2016), *Commission vs. the UK* (C-308/14, decided in 2016).

17 The so-called dialogue between the Courts has somehow helped ensure the protection of social rights at the European and national level after the serious recent crises. As already mentioned, the Court of Justice has implemented (with the 'Laval quartet') self-restraint on welfare following the economic and financial crisis that marked the first two decades of the new millennium. Recent case law has led to a new approach – in particular under the influence of the judgments of the National Constitutional Courts (see, in particular, Italian Constitutional Court, n. 275/2016 and nos. 120 and 194/2018). The global health emergency caused by the pandemic crisis has further accentuated this drive for change.

> say that while nineteenth-century constitutions ensured the right of elected politicians to govern, the European constitution handed parts of that right to the market.[18]

A further decisive step towards freeing the financial markets occurred in 1998 with the setting aside of the 1933 Glass Steagall Act at the end of the Clinton presidency. This law established the separation of banking into commercial and investment banks, prohibiting the former from using citizens' deposits and savings in speculative and high-risk financial transactions.

This summary of Europe's economic development shows, on the one hand, that the economic and market approach has been present from the outset and that, although it was initially harnessed by a balance of forces, it contributed from the theoretical and methodological points of view to the genesis and first steps of the supranational order. On the other hand, it shows that an ever-increasing imbalance and separation between economics/finance and other social forces emerged, particularly in the 1980s. This led, also through the juridification of economic and financial paradigms, to these mechanisms and methods dominating those of the other sciences, a process, on the other hand, with both European and global dimensions, as Ernst Böckenförde also observed in relation to the evolution of the relationship between state and society. For him, the state is a mere helper in the economic-industrial process.[19]

This dominance was also noticeable thanks to increased methodological contamination, through the development of the hybrid disciplines of the social sciences, which sought to combine the economic method with others. These mixed disciplines have the undoubted merit of bringing together scientific areas that had always been totally separate, representing fertile terrain for experimentation in the virgin soil of the European legal system.[20]

The best-known example is the so-called Law & Economics (L&A) discipline. As is well known, this subject was introduced in the United States in 1960 thanks to the pioneering studies of Ronald Coase[21] – who had already developed a neo-institutionalist vision of the theory of the firm[22] before the Second World War – on the problem of social cost and the theory of transaction costs, which plays a primary role in establishing the terms of the

18 M. Goldmann, 'The Great Recurrence: Karl Polanyi and the Crises of the European Union'.

19 See E.-W. Böckenförde, 'The Rise of the State as a Process of Secularization', 1967, in Religion, Law and Democracy: Selected Writings, section II, 'Law and Secularity' (Oxford: Oxford University Press, 2020) 152–167.

20 These disciplines have much to offer and can make a useful and concrete contribution to scientific advancement. They are not problematic in themselves: hybridizations between the social sciences can be mutually beneficial, but balance among them may be lost. Indeed, in recent years, economics has come to predominate over the others to a remarkable degree.

21 R.H. Coase, 'The Problem of Social Cost' (1960) 3 *Journal of Law & Economics* 1–44.

22 R.H. Coase, 'The Nature of the Firm' (1937) 4 *Economica* 386–405.

relationship between law and the market, and Guido Calabresi[23] on the application of economic thinking to the regulation of civil liability. The European Economic Community and L&E are practically coetaneous, and the Chicago School developed and expanded (suffice it to recall Richard Posner's seminal handbook on the *Economic Analysis of Law*, in the early 1970s[24]) at the same time as the Court of Justice, establishing general principles, allowed the European legal system to free itself of the political stranglehold of sovereign states. The issue of the law's loss of autonomy from other social sciences and, above all, economics became a topic of debate in the United States at the very time Europe was heading towards the Maastricht Treaty.[25]

We should also recall that public choice theories were formulated at around that time (following Duncan Black's pioneering studies,[26] the work of James Buchanan and Gordon Tullock in 1962[27] is recognized as being of fundamental importance). These theories attempted to explore the true role of politics in developing decision-making processes, which tend to link political science to economics, with repercussions on public law.

The following decades – with the European legal system functioning as a testing ground – were a period of construction and contamination, seeking to strike a balance between the economic criterion of allocative efficiency and the legal and social criteria of pursuing equity and justice.[28]

This development curve spanned the entire course of the twentieth century and gradually shifted the content and methodological barycentre away from the political philosophy/law binomial (with law holding centre stage as the immediate consequence of the ideal philosophical construction). This shift led to the birth of the libertarian and egalitarian constitutions of the modern states (ending, it should not be forgotten, in two bloody world wars) and the pairing of economics with the political sciences, while law still made its presence felt, albeit in an instrumental and incidental role.

23 G. Calabresi, 'Some Thoughts on Risk Distribution and the Law of Torts' (1961) 70 *Yale Law Journal* 499–553.

24 R.A. Posner, *Economic Analysis of Law* (Boston: Little Brown & Co., 1973).

25 R.A. Posner, 'The Decline of Law as an Autonomous Discipline' (1987) 100 *Harvard Law Review* 761–780.

26 D. Black, 'On the Rationale of Group Decision-making' (1948) 56 *Journal of Political Economy* 23–34; idem, *The Theory of Committees and Elections* (Cambridge: CUP, 1958).

27 J.M. Buchanan & G. Tullock, *The Calculus of Consent. Logical Foundations of Constitutional Democracies* (Ann Arbor: University of Michigan Press, 1962).

28 An example, among others, is the Constitutional Political Economy of the 1980s and 1990s and especially, in the 1990s, that of the New Political Economy, which studies the macroeconomic impact of institutional arrangements. On all the theoretical and cultural movements mentioned in these pages, see the definitive and accurate reconstruction by G. Napolitano and M. Abrescia, *Analisi economica del diritto pubblico* (Bologna: il Mulino, 2009) 15 ff.

Over time, the ordoliberal theory of the Freiburg School (heavily influencing the drafting of the *Grundgesetz*) came to the fore. It sprang up in Germany in the late 1930s and was strongly influenced by opposition to state totalitarianism (the Nazi experience was considered the unwholesome culmination of Hobbesian and Hegelian approaches) and therefore to the centralization of public power in the state, as well as market liberalism, which also brought negative consequence.[29] The original exponents of the Freiburg School were Walter Eucken (professor of political economics in Freiburg and founder of the journal *Ordo* in 1936, hence the term ordoliberalism), Franz Böhm, Hans Grossmann-Dörth, Constantin von Dietz, Adolf Lampe, and scholars from outside who referred to it from the cultural perspective, including Alfred Müller-Armack, Alexander Rüstow, and especially Wilhelm Röpke. They hypothesized a 'third way', a middle way between economic planning and economic/financial deregulation[30]: the social market economy. In their view, society was divided into a plurality of distinct circles of equal rank (law, politics, economy), closely interconnected and restored to unity through subsidiarity. The outcome of this vision of society is a transition from the interventionist to the regulatory state in terms of the economy[31]: the state cannot leave the market to itself, but neither can it intervene as a monopoly-holder in economic affairs. The powers of the state must produce the *ordo*, that is, a legal locus of rules which places the market within a justice-centred framework. This gives the law a fundamental role, not just as a mere superstructure, but in giving form and content to the economy, which is nothing more than the social and legal orders working together. The smooth functioning of markets and, in particular, the principle of free competition relies on the coexistence of economics, politics, and law. The latter determines economic growth and therefore social progress. This is an

29 There is an ample literature on ordoliberalism, but the most important studies are fairly recent. See, among others, P. Koslowski (ed.), *The Theory of Capitalism in the German Economic Tradition. Historism, Ordo-liberalism, Critical Theory, Solidarism* (Berlin, Heidelberg: Springer, 2000); D.A. Crane, 'Ordoliberalism and the Freiburg School', in D.A. Crane and H. Hovenkamp (eds), *The Making of Competition Policy. Legal and Economic Sources* (New York: OUP, 2013) 252–281. At the legal level, of particular note is J. Hien and C. Joerges (eds), *Ordoliberalism, Law and the Rule of Economics* (Oxford, UK; Portland, OR: Hart, 2017), taking a historical-reconstructive approach, aimed at isolating the original ordoliberal theories from subsequent contamination by various economic ones and highlighting their influence on the process of European integration. In this vein, see also K. Dyson, *Conservative Liberalism, Ordo-liberalism, and the State: Disciplining Democracy and the Market* (Oxford: OUP, 2021).

30 On the ordoliberal idea of *laissez-faire* as an empty formula, see, in particular, D. M. Woodruff, 'Ordoliberalism, Polanyi, and the Theodicy of Markets', in J. Hien and C. Joerges (eds), *Ordoliberalism, Law and the Rule of Economics.*

31 On the Regulatory State in Europe, see G. Majone, 'The Rise of Regulatory State in Europe' (1994) 17 *West European Politics* 77–101. See also the later R. Baldwin, M. Cave, M. Lodge (eds), *Understanding Regulation: Theory, Strategy, and Practice* (Oxford, New York: OUP, 2012).

institutional conception of economics in which the legal system is geared towards the fundamental goal of protecting competition in the market, which becomes the primary public interest to be safeguarded. In this context, public institutions play an active role, protecting the economic order and a holistic conception of the economy and the market. Hence the constant interaction between economics and law, both on a procedural level and in relation to how the system's operating rules are constructed.

As Böckenförde[32] observes, there was an apparent paradox in the first phase of development, whereby notwithstanding the welfare state and the recognition of social rights (factors that had ensured the redistribution of wealth and the implementation of the principle of substantial equality in European democracies) which developed in the member states at the same time thanks to an *embedded liberalism* model,[33] an economic rationale and the protection of competition took root in the Community order, which kept the economic level – geared towards integration – separate from the social level, which was left to the states and was underpinned by differentiation.[34]

During the second half of the twentieth century, the difficulty of bearing the financial cost of social rights became apparent and, at the same time, responsibility for the common good was divided between the European and national systems.[35] This led to a rapprochement of member states' regulations through the reduction of welfare benefits, limiting them to what was socially useful and economically justifiable, with financial constraint becoming the *deus ex machina* of public policies. A twofold asymmetry was created, favouring non-political actors at the European level, which led to negative rather than positive integration.[36] Following the ordoliberal diktat, filtering the European principles of subsidiarity and proportionality of state decisions was one of the factors that determined the move away from the welfare state to the regulatory state, with the consequent reversal of the relationship between the state and the market. Abandoning the idea that the state, rather than the market, is tasked with the provision of welfare services and the political correction of the market when this interferes with the fulfilment of citizens' primary needs and those of going beyond the level of the single individual, the principles introduced by the European treaties mark a transition to the idea that, in reality, the market tends to

32 E.-W. Böckenförde, *Staat-Nation-Europa: Studien zur Staatslehre, Verfassungstheorie und Rechtsphilosophie*, op. cit., fn. 5.
33 J.G. Ruggie, 'International Regimes, Transactions, and Change: Embedded Liberalism in the Postwar Economic Order' (1982) *International Organization* 379 ff.
34 See, among others, R. Ursi, *Le stagioni dell'efficienza. I paradigmi giuridici della buona amministrazione* (Rimini: Maggioli, 2016) 201 ff.
35 This profile has been highlighted by E. Böckenförde, *Diritto e secolarizzazione. Dallo Stato moderno all'Europa unita* (Rome-Bari: Laterza, 2007) 182–183.
36 F.W. Scharpf, 'The Asimmetry of European Integration or Why the EU Cannot Be a "Social Market Economy"' (2010) 8 *Socio-Economic Review* 211–250.

respond to the demands of social welfare only if it is allowed to develop free competition to the full. For this to happen, "the state must only intervene when it has to remove an obstacle to real competition, which must not only be free but above all private".[37] Such interventions have necessarily shifted the centre of gravity in the direction of guaranteeing economic freedoms to the detriment of 'social citizenship'.[38] This is demonstrated by the fact that social cohesion, which has become a full part of European concerns, "is not seen as a constraint on the market as a counterweight: a financial instrument rather than an inspiring principle underpinning public policy" in order to avoid social dumping.[39] All in all, even with the NGEU, which was meant to constitute a sort of new Marshall Plan[40] and a clear paradigm shift by the Euro-unitary institutions, recourse to territorial and social cohesion policies was instrumental to the economic recovery of the member states, which had jeopardized the economic-financial resilience of the supranational order.

A radical twofold transformation of the socio-economic context took place in the 1990s, favouring deregulation and, at the same time, the corporatization of public administrations along the lines of the reforms introduced in the English-speaking countries, especially in the United States and Great Britain. It has been observed that "the market emerges forcefully from its 'ancillary' role – as a docile instrument producing resources to be redistributed for purposes of general emancipation and social equalisation – which had been carved out for it, placing itself (again) at the top of the rank of ends".[41]

There was an initial departure from the social market economy theorized by the Freiburg School, which, as we have just seen, was based on the close links between economics, politics, and law in a shift towards the neo-liberalism of the Chicago School, theorized principally by Milton Friedman and George

37 R. Ursi, *Le stagioni dell'efficienza*, op. cit, 215.

38 As observed in N. Irti, *Nichilismo giuridico* (Rome-Bari: Laterza, 2004) 114 f., the market produces a depersonalizing and limiting effect on individual freedom and identity, reducing the individual to a category. Individuals are in fact reduced "to functions of the market: no longer this or that individual, but abstract categories of 'consumers', 'professionals', 'sellers', etc. Upon entering the market (and thus into a 'department store', as it were), individuals lose their own identity, becoming, together with millions and millions of like-minded people, anonymous and repetitive."

39 R. Ursi, *Le stagioni dell'efficienza*, op. cit., 216. For some significant examples of the reduction of institutions working to develop social citizenship, see A. Nato, *La cittadinanza sociale al tempo della crisi economica* (Rome: Cacucci, 2020).

40 In this regard, a debate has developed as to whether the NGEU constituted a Hamilton moment: S. Kapoor, 'This isn't Europe's "Hamilton' moment", on politico.eu, 22 May 2020; M. Copelovitch, 'No, this isn't Europe's "Hamiltonian moment"', on washingtonpost.com, 27 May 2020; J. Weeks, 'A "Hamiltonian moment" for Europe', on socialeurope.eu, 14 July 2020; O. Issing, 'The COVID-19 Crisis: A Hamilton Moment for the European Union?' (2020) *International Finance* 340 ff.

41 S. Giubboni, *Social Rights and Market Freedoms in the European Constitution: A Labour Law Perspective* (Cambridge: CUP, 2009).

Stigler in a move inspired by privatization and liberalization policies, together with an inveterate faith in mechanisms (e.g., tendering, liabilities, etc.) that allowed the deconstruction of public structures.[42] The most interesting aspect of all this from a methodological point of view is that this change, excellently described in Friedman's famous 1953 essay,[43] also took place thanks to a decisive turn in the direction of the analytical approach and econometrics (and thus through the development of mathematically valid algorithms), leading to distancing from a realist vision and separation from the other social sciences on the assumption of the systematic completeness of economics and its scientific nature, separating itself from the other social sciences under the illusion of being related to the exact sciences. *Mutatis mutandis*, these were the same sins of suprematism, abstractionism and dogmatism that had beset legal science in the late nineteenth and early twentieth centuries.

Second, Thatcher's *New Public Management* transplanted organization and corporate management methods (*management by objectives*, managerial responsibility, internal controls and performance appraisal, prudent resource allocation, staff self-discipline, and transparency) into the public system, spawning the 'corporatization' system, dubbed 'results administration'. In this transformation, the role of business economics, the constructions of public choice, the economic analysis of law, conveyed and facilitated by the process of European integration, were of the utmost importance. Therefore, an instrumental, productivist, contractualistic, and teleocratic vision of the legal order prevailed, setting aside the nomocratic vision typical of political philosophy that had developed over centuries in European legal and political culture.[44]

But what were the concrete consequences of the shifting centre of gravity of theoretical development and methodology? The effects showed through more markedly during the financial crisis of the second decade of the new millennium, the so-called euro crisis, which brought profound changes not only to relations between the European institutions and the member states thanks to a tendency to favour the intergovernmental method, but also between the member states themselves (especially between Northern Europe and the states in the Mediterranean area).[45]

It may be appropriate at this juncture to consider a few concrete examples to clarify the concept.

42 On the stark differences between the Freiburg and Chicago Schools, see, most recently, B. Young, 'What is Neoliberal in Germany's and Europe's Crisis Politics?', in Hien and C. Joerges (eds), *Ordoliberalism, Law and the Rule of Economics*.

43 M. Friedman, 'The Methodology of Positive Economics', in idem, *Essays in Positive Economics* (Chicago: University of Chicago Press, 1953) 3 ff. and 30 ff.

44 The reference is to M. Oakeshott, *Rationalism in Politics and Other Essays*, New expanded ed. (Indianapolis: Liberty Fund, 1991) (1st ed., 1962).

45 Among others, see F. Fabbrini, *Economic Governance in Europe: Comparative Paradoxes and Constitutional Changes* (Oxford: OUP, 2016).

As of 2014, the European Statistical Office began to include some illegal activities in its Gross Domestic Product (GDP) calculations, namely prostitution, drug trafficking, and cigarette smuggling. Eurostat's intention was to include "all income-generating activities, regardless of their legal status", but also to harmonize GDP calculation estimates among member countries, considering that even before 2014, Germany, Hungary, and Greece had included prostitution, and the Netherlands had included drug trafficking.[46] Today, the asymmetry between the calculation of wealth and that of legality is evident since the wealth parameter disregards both the legality or illegality of the activity and the consequences for society in question in terms of values.[47] This sharp divide would not be a problem were it not for the fact that the solution has been legally codified, since it is contained in the EU Regulation (549/2013) published on 26 June 2013, which regulates the European System of Accounts, i. e., the European System of National and Regional Accounts (ESA), namely the macroeconomic accounting scheme that quantitatively describes national economic activity in monetary terms, in the form of a coherent set of accounts. This is an extreme example, but it gives an idea of the repercussions of the change in perspective. Law becomes a mere infrastructure[48] and is used to achieve an economic result.

There are other examples illustrating, *mutatis mutandis*, the characteristics of the phenomenon. One that comes to mind is the 'Double Irish, Dutch sandwich', i.e., the substantial tax avoidance regulations adopted in Ireland and the Netherlands to attract companies and, in particular, multinationals. Others are the regulations on derivatives (or, rather, their absence or inadequacy): the choice not to regulate derivatives, before the crisis, was heavily influenced by lobbies and driven by the fact that they appealed to investors with greater expertise.[49] After the crisis, the option of banning some derivatives altogether,[50] suggested by several parties, was not followed, while transparency obligations were introduced, as was the idea of trading on a sort of derivatives exchange, the CCPs, on which the risk of failure is shifted. The competences relating to CCPs, moreover, were not centralized under the European Supervisory

46 I. Sales and S. Melorio, 'Le mafie nel PIL', in E. Ciconte, F. Forgione, I. Sales (eds), *Atlante delle mafie. Storia, economia, società, cultura*, vol. IV (Soveria Mannelli: Rubbettino, 2016) 15 ff.

47 In this respect, the debate on the role that a legal order should play vis-à-vis gambling is vast: there may be an enormous range of answers, depending on whether the problem is addressed from a legal, economic, sociological, or ethical perspective.

48 Regarding the use of law as a tool see, among others, N. Irti and E. Severino, *Dialogo su Diritto e tecnica* (Rome-Bari: Laterza, 2001).

49 See, among others, M. De Bellis, *La regolazione dei mercati finanziari* (Milan: Giuffrè, 2012) 191–192; idem, 'Public Law and Private Regulators in the Global Legal Space' (2011) *International Journal of Constitutional Law* 425 ff.

50 Among others, F. Merusi, 'Per un divieto di cartolarizzazione del rischio di credito' (2009) *Banca borsa e titoli di credito* 253 ff.

Authority (ESMA) because, even if this were possible, the risk of having to bail out the CCP at the European level would have been high, while the costs continue to be sustained at national level for now.[51]

Hence, due to the different methodological framework produced by virtue of the new European legal and social model, the meaning of the principle of the rule of law has been profoundly reconceptualized and is now anchored to different parameters concerning the economic as well as (or instead of) legal rationale. As for its repercussions on administrative law, it has been observed that "the model of the legal rationale behind administrative action up to now, considered to be the only one that conforms to the requirements of social life, is destined to fade into the background as soon as this binomial seems to become effective": if, in fact, legal action is no longer synonymous with efficient action, it is disastrous that it is the latter which inspires the legal reconstruction of administrative action, such that

> if the social interest is directed towards economically efficient administration as a whole, it will no longer be possible to assess, in terms of mere legal conformity, even the single instances through which this activity is authoritatively expressed, because attaining this goal will also become relevant (and soon predominant, as will their ability to fulfil, even in single cases, the interests at stake).[52]

It has also been remarked that the legal codification of such conceptions inspired by, and borrowed from, economics and its methodology, while endowing these principles and institutions with a new and different scope and dimension, also "seem barely compatible with a managerial rationale" as "management is essentially a pragmatic activity: pursuing a decidedly utilitarian and clearly functional purpose; it starts from concrete practice, the problems that organizations have to face, and seeks to define the rules that will enable them to achieve their objectives with the greatest efficiency".[53]

The quarter of a century between the end of the last millennium and the first two decades of the new one saw a process of expansion – not so much in terms of economics as a very specific economic methodology, which has also

51 See, in particular, M. De Bellis, 'Unificazione, differenziazione e tecnificazione' (2015) *Rivista italiana di diritto pubblico comunitario* 1565–1566. This example highlights at least two further points. Despite gradual adjustments to foster greater transparency, the post-crisis regulatory model is barely different from that of the twenty years before the crisis. Second, in the event of bail-out risks for the public, it becomes a matter for the individual states, and the process of European integration grinds to a halt.

52 A. Romano Tassone, 'Sulla formula "amministrazione per risultati"', in *Scritti in onore di Elio Casetta*, vol. II (Naples: Jovene, 2001) 813 ff, in particular 823.

53 J. Chevallier, 'Management public and droit' (2008) *Politiques et management public* 93 ff.

overlapped alternative and different methods within the economy itself. Recently, however, other areas and sensitivities have emerged in the economic sciences, such as behavioural science, circular science, innovation and sustainability, and so on, which have drawn strength from the crises of the last few years and allowed them to have a place once more in the decision-making processes that use instruments from economics, which, especially in Europe, ended up flanking – and then marginalizing – other sciences and methods: law, sociology and political science. It has, indeed, been said that "law has an on-off relationship with economics: from the sovereignty of the State over the economy we swing to the sovereignty of the economy over the state".[54] Economic globalization and the financial and pandemic crises have highlighted this process,[55] so that decisions have long been taken on the basis of an economic-financial perspective.[56] This has introduced the risk of a return to the methodological hegemony[57] and dominion (this time) of economists over other social scientists. We have already seen that this cannot work with regard to the legal system as this method of decision-making creates more problems than it solves.

However, the series of crises in the most recent phase of Europe's history has shown the European legal system's ability to find in these events a stimulus to relaunch the process of European integration using finance either recessively or expansively.

Let us look, first of all, at the global financial crisis between the first and second decades of the new millennium. It caused the social re-feudalization[58] or desocialization of contemporary society.[59] This, in turn, has had serious social and political consequences, particularly in the European Mediterranean area, with notable repercussions on the disconnection of citizens from the European institutions, but it has also led to an awareness of the weaknesses of the economic sciences, which indeed proved incapable of holding their own alongside

54 S. Cassese, *L'educazione del giurista*, Lecture given at Bocconi University in Milan on 17 May 2011, 23 of typescript.

55 Moreover, see M. Buti, *The Man Inside: A European Journey Through Two Crises* (Milan: BUP, 2021), which reconstructs the two crises from within the European institutions. From the same author see also *Jean Monnet aveva ragione? Costruire l'Europa in tempi di crisi* (Milan, BUP, 2023).

56 On the global dimension of the financial crisis see, in particular, G. Di Gaspare, *Teoria e critica della globalizzazione finanziaria. Dinamiche del potere finanziario e crisi sistemiche* (Padua: Cedam, 2011).

57 On the distinction between balance and hegemony see, among others, G. Dorso, 'Equilibrio ed egemonia' (1944) *Aretusa* 93–94. See, on the concept of hegemony, the masterly work by H. Triepel, *Die Hegemonie. Ein Buch von führenden Staaten* (Stuttgart-Berlin: Kolhammer, 1938), now a classic.

58 The "critical weight of re-feudalisation" is amply discussed in M. De Carolis, *Il rovescio della libertà. Tramonto del neoliberalismo e disagio della civiltà* (Macerata: Quodlibet, 2017).

59 An analysis of Habermas's theory is proposed, among others, in R. Esposito, *A Philospby for Europe. From the Outside* (Cambridge, UK; Medford, MA, USA: Polity Press, 2018).

the so-called exact sciences. The crisis triggered a significant transformation in economic theory, having highlighted the fundamental limits of the most promising avenues of research and thus leading to the abandonment of economic research pursuing holistic goals. Moreover, this was not, unlike past research, overcome by changes in theoretical direction but by the pragmatism of the European Central Bank's monetary and financial policies and the use of legal resources as an infrastructure to convey these solutions, thus weakening the connection between theory and concrete economic-policy decisions.[60] This, in addition to highlighting the fact that experimentation has come to prevail over theory, and realism over dogma, is a clear symptom of the absence of a shared perspective regarding the origins and deep-seated reasons underlying the crisis and, perhaps, also the incidental nature of overcoming it, barring an axiological return to at least the original social market economy.[61] By strengthening the intergovernmental model, the constraints arising from compliance with financial standards became even stronger, so the recipe for solving the crisis was financial austerity and the centrality of the European Central Bank's technical decisions.

Turning, however, to the pandemic crisis, we observe a radical change in both the model and the role of the European institutions, founded on the technical partnership between economic policy and administrative law.[62]

First, we note a distinct revival of the Community model, with the European Commission regaining, and exceeding, its central role in managing economic and financial policies, while the ECB has maintained its role of protecting monetary stability, now also acting to promote social cohesion.

Second, the response to the pandemic crisis has not been marked by austerity and restrictive economic and financial policies but by an openness to expansion, with new tools for economic planning, focusing on investments in infrastructure and increased public spending, firmly constrained by European regulatory policy. Financial mechanisms have taken centre stage, but the form they assume changes according to circumstances.

Third, these economic and financial mechanisms have been put in place thanks to the legal infrastructure through a stronger process of financialization

60 See the slides accompanying the lecture given at Luiss University on 14 March 2018, by M. Messori, 'Processo all'economia. Demografia, democrazia, mercati, felicità' (2018) *Astrid-online.it*.

61 C. Joerges, 'The Overburdening of Law by Ordoliberalism and the Integration Project', in J. Hien and C. Joerges (eds), *Ordoliberalism, Law and the Rule of Economics*, op cit., 179 ff., shows how the original ordoliberal theories gradually shifted towards Anglo-Saxon forms of neo-liberalism, irreconcilable with the rule of law and democratic principles.

62 M. Dani, E. Chiti, J. Mendes, A.J. Menéndez, H. Schepel and M. Wilkinson, '"It's the political economy…!" A moment of truth for the Eurozone and the EU' (2021) 19 *International Journal of Constitutional Law* 309–327, section 6; M. Dani, J. Mendes, A.J. Menendez, M. Wilkinson, H. Schepel, E. Chiti, 'At the End of the Law: A Moment of Truth for the Eurozone and the EU', *VerfBlog*, 15 May 2020.

of the European rule of law,[63] one that focuses on strengthening the protection of the EU's financial interests.

Moreover, all this has always taken place within the framework of economic and financial rules: the RRF is still linked to the mechanisms of the European Semester (which has been only temporarily suspended); the logic of NGEU reporting reflects the 'efficiency' performance/output-based model, but this may end up 'reining in investment', especially regarding the countries most in debt distress; the pursuit of some of the main policy objectives of the NGEU, e.g., that of ecological transition, has been seriously jeopardized by the Ukrainian war and the energy crisis (which the European institutions believe they can remedy through the RePowerEU, by standardizing the anti-crisis function of economic/financial planning in a federalist and expansive key).

At this point, we would do well to reflect in greater detail on the juridical financialization process, starting with the NGEU itself.

3. The financialization of the rule of law in Europe

The NGEU has had a profound effect on the paradigm of European economic governance,[64] which, through the Community method, has constituted a great boost to European integration.[65] All this is due to placing the protection of the financial interests of the European Union at the heart of the European legal order, which must be the key to ensuring that the integration process starts again.[66]

Before EU Regulation n. 883/2013, safeguarding the financial interests of the European Union was an important, but not central, issue not least because the European budget was much smaller than those of the member states themselves. In 2020, the EU had a turnover of 172 billion euro, while Amazon's turnover was around twice as much (386 billion), and that of Germany was almost twenty times more (roughly 3,300 billion euros). In recent years, however, it has

63 For an overview of the European rule of law before the pandemic crisis, see, among others, T. Kostantinides, *The Rule of Law in the European Union. The Internal Dimension* (Oxford, UK; Portland, OR: Hart, 2017).

64 For a description of the radical paradigm shift in European economic governance, see F. Fabbrini, *Next Generation EU. Il futuro di Europa e Italia dopo la pandemia* (Bologna: il Mulino, 2022). F. Fabbrini, 'The Legal Architecture of the Economic Responses to COVID-19: EMU beyond the Pandemic' (2021) 60 *Journal of Common Market Studies* 186–203. On the problems of the previous structure of European economic governance, see esp., F. Fabbrini (ed.), *Economic Governance in Europe*, op. cit., fn. 45.

65 B. De Witte, 'The European Union's COVID-19 Recovery Plan: The Legal Engineering of an Economic Policy Shift' (2021) 58 *Common Market Law Review* 635–682.

66 On the debate during the NGEU approval stage, see, among others, J. Núñez Ferrer, 'Reading between the lines of Council agreement on the MFF and Next Generation EU', CEPS Policy Insights No. 2020–18, July 2020. J. Echebarria Fernández, 'A Critical Analysis on the European Union's Measures to Overcome the Economic Impact of the COVID-19 Pandemic', in *European Papers*, no. 5, 2020.

become increasingly important to defend the EU's financial interests, even becoming, as it were, an ontological component of the European legal system.

In the rule-of-law model, financial and budgetary profiles have long been considered instrumental, serving the pursuit of the functions set out in the constitutional pact, namely the welfare of citizens, the creation of infrastructures, the will to power, and so on. More recently, with the structuring of the supranational legal space, the protection of financial interests has become one of the main goals of the legal system itself, modifying the essence of the legal order.

Financial interests have become a shaping partner of the European rule of law, and one of the criteria for establishing whether a member state can remain in the Union is the financial risk it poses to the Union through its failure to respect the founding values of the treaties.

We can thus deduce four consequences.

A) First of all, financial interests are no longer instrumental but have become an end in themselves and shifted from marginal to central. Thanks to economic-financial globalization, the resilience of a legal system has become an essential element for its survival, also by virtue of the full hybridization of the financial and economic markets. The findings of rating agencies are decisive in guiding purchase choices by institutional players, so a particularly negative rating can lead to default and distancing from the markets. Hence the importance of a shift in the role of finance from instrumental to central, so that the primary guide to governments' political choices becomes public expenditure. Let us consider the following example: in the early years of the twenty-first century, the European institutions held that fighting corruption, especially white-collar corruption, could have a considerable impact on the economic-financial framework and foster competition between economic operators, particularly in public procurement. Twenty years later, this function, albeit still cultivated at the European level, seems to have become less central and plays a more marginal role in the strategic landscape of European objectives.

On the contrary, with the NGEU, digital and, above all, the ecological transition, together with the New Green Deal,[67] constitute the new strategic centre of Euro-EU policies.[68] This is an epoch-making change, as we shall see, because the RRF places the European Commission in a position from which it can influence the policies of the member states in terms of the results achieved in relation to a specific function predefined at the European level: ecological and

67 See, among others, J. Rifkin, *The Green New Deal: Why the Fossil Fuel Civilization Will Collapse by 2028, and the Bold Economic Plan to Save Life on Earth* (New York: St. Martin's Press, 2019).

68 On this topic, see, above all, E. Chiti, 'Managing the Ecological Transition of the EU: The European Green Deal as a Regulatory Process' (2022) 59(1) *Common Market Law Review* 19–48, for which the *New Green Deal* redefines the purpose of the European legal system, effecting a renewal of the *acquis communautaire*; the author also points out, however, the weakness of this project, which is partly due to its ambivalent approach to international and global regulation.

digital transition. But, going deeper, in addition to pursuing a social goal, namely sustainable development and the protection of future generations, the New Green Deal also has a decisive economic-financial goal: the strategy of concentrating efforts on sustainability is thought to produce beneficial effects on the economies of the member states in the medium-to-long term, making the continent globally more competitive. We may deduce, therefore, that the financial target can no longer be considered instrumental as previously ("finance will follow") but has taken centre stage.

B) The European rule of law is now financialized, insofar as the financial element is a shaping partner of it. In this, Regulation 2020/2092, on the general regime of conditions to safeguard the EU budget, is emblematic. As is well known, this Regulation, closely linked to the package of measures included in the MFF 2021–2027 and Next Generation EU, establishes a new legal instrument to protect the financial interests of the EU from violations of the rule of law. This resulted from the search for an instrumental solution to the democratic emergency produced by rule of law back-sliding: the European institutions, following the ineffectiveness of the mechanisms of Art. 7 TEU and the consequent rulings of the Court of Justice, felt they had to adopt measures that would guarantee punitive effectiveness, and the most useful instrument turned out to be financial sanctions. However, linking respect for the essential features of the rule of law to the protection of the financial interests of the European Union has had important repercussions, also with regard to the very substance of the rule of law.[69]

Let us consider, in this respect, the well-known cases of Hungary and Poland, which are still ongoing and give rise to a perennial tug-of-war between the European institutions and the two member states led by populist governments. Poland and Hungary are among the net beneficiaries of the European budget, and their illiberal governments have gained consensus also thanks to massive European resources. With the help of European funding, the Hungarian and Polish governments first consolidated their legislative and executive power before taking control of the judiciary, the security services, and the media, thus reducing room for opposition. Lastly, they changed the electoral laws, effectively sabotaging electoral competition; essentially, they introduced illiberal regimes that leave no room for civil society, either in terms of individual freedom of expression or organized opposition. This amounts to a true regression of the rule of law. It is a process by which elected public authorities deliberately take measures to systematically weaken, annihilate, or acquire, internal control over the power to pull apart the liberal democratic state and strengthen long-term government hegemony.[70]

69 M. Blauberger, V. van Hüllen, 'Conditionality of EU Funds: An Instrument to Enforce EU Fundamental Values?' (2021) 43(1) *Journal of European Integration* 1–16.

70 L. Pech, K. Scheppele, 'Illiberalism Within: Rule of Law Backsliding in the EU' (2017) 19 *Cambridge Yearbook of European Legal Studies* 3–47; G. de Búrca, 'Poland and Hungary's EU Membership: On Not Confronting Authoritarian Governments' (2022) 20 *International Journal of Constitutional Law* 13–34.

In 2018, seeking to remedy the changes to the rule of law, unacceptable in the European legal system by virtue of the fundamental principles laid down in the TEU, the European Commission drew up a proposal to deem rule of law as a prerequisite, aiming to bind respect for the rule of law to the protection of the EU's financial interests.[71] This proposal sought to punish broader shortcomings in the protection of the rule of law at national level harmful to the financial interests of the Union. The final version of the regulation, unfortunately, came out weaker than the original, following negotiations between the member states for the approval of the NGEU.[72] In particular, the procedure for adopting

71 P. Lindseth, C. Fasone, 'Rule-of-Law Conditionality and Resource Mobilization: The Foundations of a Genuinely "Constitutional" EU?', 12 *Verfassungsblog* (11 December 2020), https://verfassungsblog.de/rule-of-law-conditionality-and-resource-mobilization-the-foundations-of-a-genuinely-constitutional-eu/; A. Baraggia and M. Bonelli, 'Linking Money to Values: The New Rule of Law Conditionality Regulation and its Constitutional Challenges' (2022) 23 *German Law Journal* 131–156; J. Beqiraj and L. Moxham, 'Reconciling the Theory and the Practice of the Rule of Law in the European Union Measuring the Rule of Law' (2022) 14 *Hague Journal on the Rule of Law* 1–26.

72 J. Grogan, J. Beqiraj, 'The Rule of Law as the Perimeter of Legitimacy for COVID-19 Responses', in J. Grogan, A. Donald (eds), *Routledge Handbook of Law and the COVID-19 Pandemic* (Abingdon, Oxon; New York: Routledge 2022). See also Deliverable n. 2 of the Betkosol Project (https://betkosol.luiss.it): "The legal basis of the regulation is Art. 322 (1)(a) TFEU and provides for the adoption of appropriate measures where breaches of the rule of law seriously affect or threaten to affect the principles of sound financial management or the protection of the financial interests of the EU. Indeed, the rule of law is a fundamental element in compliance with the principle of sound financial management (Art. 317 TFEU). Proper management of funds can only be ensured if national authorities act under the law, effectively prosecute fraud, conflict of interest, and fight corruption, and illegal actions are subject to review by an independent judiciary (Tridimas, 2020, XII; Beqirai, 2020). Moreover, the regulation establishes the conditions under which measures can be taken, as well as their content, and the procedure for their adoption and withdrawal. According to Art. 4 of Regulation EU 2020/2092, measures against the member states can be taken when two conditions are met. First, there must be some violation of the principles of the rule of law. Second, any such breach must undermine or seriously risk affecting the sound financial management of the Union budget or the protection of the Union's financial interests in a sufficiently direct way and cannot be effectively tackled otherwise (Tridimas, 2020, XI; Benqiraj, 2020). The measures can be activated after a series of violations of the rule of law have been detected. Art. 3 of regulation 2020/2092 provides for some specific violations of the rule of law that trigger the sanction mechanism, namely endangering the independence of the judiciary, failing to prevent, correct, or sanction arbitrary or unlawful public authority decisions, and limiting the availability and effectiveness of legal remedies. These breaches may be committed by any branch of government or any authority exercising public power and can be the result of either law or practice (Tridimas, 2020, XIII). Furthermore, the regulation provides for a closed list of areas that a breach of the rule of law must concern. According to Art. 4(2) of Regulation 2020/2092, these are as follows: the proper functioning of the authorities implementing the EU budget, including loans and other instruments guaranteed by

measures extends a central role to the Commission but lays the final decision with the Council," which decides by a qualified majority vote.[73]

Despite these weaknesses, the condition that links the violation of the rule of law to the protection of the Union's financial interests is still the most effective instrument among those available to the European institutions: it is the best available response of the European institutions to regimes that use European funds but fail to comply with the fundamental principles of the identity of the European order. The introduction of negative conditionality is an important

the EU budget – especially in the framework of public procurement or grant procedures, the proper functioning of authorities carrying out financial control, monitoring and audit, the proper functioning of the investigation and prosecution of fraud, and effective judicial review by independent courts. Quite different are the prevention and sanctioning of fraud and corruption or the protection of EU financial interests, the recovery of unduly paid funds, co-operation with Olaf and the EPPO, and any conduct by authorities of relevance to the sound financial management of the EU budget or protection of the financial interests of the EU. This is a closed list. Art. 4(1) provides a second prerequisite for establishing measures whereby violations of the principles of the rule of law must seriously affect or risk undermining the sound financial management of the EU budget or the protection of the EU's financial interests in a sufficiently direct way. The definition of "sufficiently directly link" should be understood in the light of the objectives of Regulation 2020/2092. In general, there is a strong link between respect for the rule of law, mutual trust, and financial solidarity among the member states. The condition is therefore fulfilled when infringement of the rule is liable to directly affect that mutual trust (Tridimas, 2020, XVI). It should be noted that the fact that a violation may impact other areas not concerned with the European Union budget does not mean that the financial interests of the EU are not directly affected (Tridimas, 2020, XVI). Furthermore, systemic violation is the most significant for triggering the mechanism. For example, violation of the principle of judicial independence could well fulfil the circumstance of the branch of the rule of law. Art. 5 of Regulation 2020/2092 establishes the measures that the European institutions can take when the conditions of Art. 4 are satisfied. These measures involve the suspension or interruption of payments, the reduction of economic benefits in the context of EU financial instruments, and the prohibition of entering into new agreements. These measures must respect the principle of proportionality, considering elements such as the nature, duration, gravity, and extent of any violations of the rule of law (Beqiraj, 2020; Fasone, 2021b)."

73 "Under Art. 6, the first step in the procedure is for the Commission to notify the Member State in writing, setting out the facts and the specific reasons that justify its conclusions. The Member State must respond within three months. At the same time, the Commission must also inform the European Parliament and the Council. The Commission's assessment must be carried out within one month of receiving any information or observations from the Member State concerned. Within this period, it must decide whether to submit a proposal to the Council for an implementing decision on appropriate measures. At this stage, the Member State concerned could intervene by commenting on the proportionality of the measures proposed by the Commission. The Council should therefore take this decision within one month – exceptionally extendable by two months – and may amend the Commission proposal, adopting the amended text acting by qualified majority (Julinda, 2020; Tridimas, 2020, XIX)."

break with the past. This link, however, implies a series of consequences: there is no doubt that the relationship between the juridical and the financial spheres has been overturned, since the constitutional foundations of the rule of law are subject to protection only if the lack of safeguards results in harm to financial interests. In essence, it is understood that financial aspects take priority over constitutional and juridical ones.

> In other words, if it is true that the instrument of conditionality operates only in the presence of direct prejudice to the rule of law, this is not sanctioned as such but only to the extent that it is detrimental to the EU budget and there are no alternative and more effective instruments in European law to counter it, such as the political procedure that can be activated through Art. 7 TEU (Fasone, 2021b).[74]

In addition, this link means that the economic-financial element also becomes an essential part of the European rule of law, changing its genetic formula as the assessment of compliance with the rule of law will, from now on, imply a prior analysis of effects on the Union's financial interests.[75]

74 See deliverable 2, Betkosol Project (https://betkosol.luiss.it).

75 "However, it must be acknowledged that the Regulation is part of a more general model of EU response to the crisis of the rule of law. This model seeks to strengthen the institutional and regulatory framework to limit breaches by imposing procedural guarantees, recognising new roles for institutions, shaping institutional structure, and providing for substantial measures to counter violations (Tridimas, 2020, XXI). Furthermore, it is important to underline that the 2020/2092 Regulation breaks with the accession logic of reinforcement for reward and tries to introduce negative conditionality (Blauberger, Van Hullen, 2021, 4). This type of conditionality could generate social pressure and persuade Member States to continue violating the rule of law. Moreover, even if the simultaneous threat of sanctions may not be persuasive, the EU could still seek to maintain or create a form of contact that would create a depoliticised context and a highly deliberative quality of interaction with the target government (Blauberger, Van Hullen, 2021, 14; Sedelmeier 2017, 345). The success of regulatory procedures will depend on the determination of other member States. And the pursuit of violations of the rule of law will depend on the willingness of member States to deliver on their commitments. In this regard, the EU institutions must demonstrate institutional personality and resilience. Unfortunately, the premises are not comforting. On 11 March 2021, Hungary and Poland filed a complaint before the European Court of Justice (EJC) against the regulation that links the disbursement of block funds to the situation of the rule of law in the EU Member States (see Court of Justice, 11 March 2021, C-157/21, *Poland vs European Parliament and Council and Court of Justice*, 11 March 2021, C-156/21, *Hungary vs European Parliament and Council*). On March 17, 2021, the European Parliament adopted a resolution (European Parliament resolution on the application of Regulation (EU, Euratom) 2020/2092, the rule-of-law conditionality mechanism (2021/2582(RSP), asking the Commission to promptly implement the Regulation 2020/2092 mechanism against breaching member States (Tridimas, 2020, XX; Piana, Nato, 2020, 57)" (https://betkosol.luiss.it).

The judgments of 2022 (see Court of Justice, 16 February 2022, C-156/21, and 16 February 2022, C-157/21) rejected the appeals of Poland and Hungary and highlighted

C) The protection of financial interests plays an influential role in the process of European integration. In particular, the contents of EU Directive no. 2017/1371, the so-called PIF Directive, have sketched a detailed protection mechanism, both from the point of view of criminal and administrative law. First of all, Article 2 of the Directive introduced the idea of protecting the financial interests of the European Union under criminal law, whereby the focus is on the European budget and the related financial interests. Second, the Directive defines the mechanisms for combating fraud at the European level (through collaboration between OLAF and the EPPO) and, above all, the ways the member states must work to prevent and combat fraud against the Union's financial interests. It follows, then, that the European integration process is considerably strengthened by the organizational structures and administrative and penal procedures that closely link the European and national institutions, both in terms of public administrations and, even more so, as regards judicial systems.

D) The financial interests of the Union are pervasive and can no longer be bound by the single euro budget which, as we have seen, is still very light.

The last of these consequences shows that the EU's financial interests now extend far beyond the European budget, since, as Recital no. 1 of the aforementioned Directive no. 2017/1371 states: "The protection of the Union's financial interests concerns not only the management of budget appropriations but extends to all measures which negatively affect or which threaten to negatively impact its assets and those of the Member States, to the extent that those measures are of relevance to Union policies."

This way of understanding the financial interests of the Union has potentially incisive effects on the economic-financial policies of the member states, particularly when these have access to European funding. Once again, the NGEU provides a striking example, because, after an initial phase in which the Council led the process, the mechanisms established in the RRF devolve significant economic-financial steering powers to the European Commission[76] (with the worrying exclusion of the European Parliament).

the Union's identity dimension and the need to defend the values of the European legal system. In the direction of the promotion and defence of a set of Union values covered by the TEU, see, among others, G. de Búrca, 'Poland and Hungary's EU membership: On Not Confronting Authoritarian Governments' (2022) 20(1) *International Journal of Constitutional Law* 14 ff. For a reconstruction of the effects of the Regulation EU 2020/2092 and the resulting guidelines of Courts rulings, see, *inter alia*, A. Guazzarotti, *Neoliberismo e difesa dello Stato di diritto in Europa. Riflessioni critiche sulla costituzione materiale dell'UE* (Milano: FrancoAngeli, 2023).

76 In this sense, compared with the financial crisis of the previous decade, there has been a shift of leadership role from the Council to the Commission. On the Council's former role, see M. Dawson, F. de Witte, 'Constitutional Balance in the EU after the Euro-crisis' (2013) 73(4) *Modern Law Review* 817–844 (in particular, 830 ff.); E. Bressanelli, N. Chelotti, 'The Shadow of the European Council: Understanding Legislation on Economic Governance' (2016) 38(3) *Journal of European Integration* 509 ff.

Of course, the NGEU is part of a framework of interventions that follow on from previous actions, so there are also strong elements of continuity with respect to older financial and budgetary policies. Suffice it to recall, for example, the conditionality mechanism, which, as a prerequisite and limiting parameter for the allocation of loans, characterized the financial assistance mechanisms set up in the context of the sovereign debt crisis and, in recent times, was set up for the administration of the structural funds themselves.

Moreover, the innovative elements introduced by the NGEU are fundamental because they represent a clear paradigm shift and outline a new form of European economic governance, in which the Commission once again plays an absolutely central role: the decision to issue common debt could constitute a first step towards greater fiscal integration; second, the size of the financing plan and its allocation to states not only in the form of loans but also as grants, means that the European institutions are called upon to act not only as financial intermediaries but also as public helpers; third, the establishment of this instrument within the framework of EU law rather than by means of external intergovernmental instruments (unlike the majority of financial assistance mechanisms adopted in response to the debt crisis), implies a decisive revival of the Community model.

The fact that it is the Commission that identifies the fundamental far-reaching goals and objectives in the pursuit of which the member states are called upon to spend the funds (ecological and digital transition and six other objectives, including social and territorial cohesion, health and resilience, and policies for generational solidarity) means that the conditionality mechanism has profoundly changed and that the Commission directs and plans *ex ante* the overall direction of the funding and reforms (ultimately the development plans) of the individual states. It prefigures a sort of return to economic planning, only it is directed by the European institutions, and especially the Commission. In essence, thanks to the transformation of European economic governance, the economic and financial planning of the member states is no longer carried out within the national legal systems but is elevated to the supranational level, especially by the European Commission. It is clear that, in this context, the process of European integration has been strongly reinforced by the pandemic crisis, not least in terms of greater fiscal integration.[77]

But the European Commission also plays another decisive role in the NGEU, stemming from the connection between the NGEU and the European Semester. National recovery and resilience plans, in fact, must be consistent with the specific priorities identified in the country-by-county recommendations, and it falls to the Commission to perform the monitoring. Thus, the new model of financial assistance launched during the pandemic crisis merges with the

77 P. Dermine, 'The EU's Response to the COVID-19 Crisis and the Trajectory of Fiscal Integration in Europe: Between Continuity and Rupture' (2020) 47(4) *Legal Issues of Economic Integration* 337–358.

national financial monitoring mechanisms introduced in response to the sovereign debt crisis. It follows that the Commission's role of monitoring how recommendations are implemented is strongly reinforced by the authority to sanction non-compliance through the suspension of payments or even the recovery of funds.[78]

In conclusion, while the Council still plays a significant role in the approval phase and has the authority to block NRPs (by a qualified majority), when it comes to control over implementation, the institution that holds almost exclusive power (if we exclude the advisory contribution of the Economic and Financial Committee), is the Commission.[79]

The innovative nature of the steering and monitoring role that the Commission plays within the NGEU may, however, also be influenced and modified by the functioning of mechanisms internal to the mechanism itself that relate to the link between the mechanism, on the one hand, and the European Semester, on the other, to respect the rule of law.[80] However, the fact that the RRF and the

78 The implementation phase starts with the Council's approval of the decision to implement the NRP in response to a proposal by the Commission. The Commission plays a capillary role in assessing the state of implementation of the PNRR twice a year in concomitance with payment requests from the states. If a positive preliminary assessment confirms that states have reached their targets and objectives, the Commission passes its conclusions on to the Economic and Financial Committee, whose opinion will be taken into account. If all is well, the Commission authorises the grant. Should the verdict be negative, possible consequences range from the suspension of payment to termination of the agreement and recovery of the amounts already paid out if the state fails to remedy its failure to reach the targets and objectives.

79 First of all, the Commission's steering power is extended through the *ex-ante* indication of the objectives against which states' investment and reform projects must be directed. The breadth of the six pillars signals the connection with the Commission's broader plans, namely ecological and digital transition, and indeed the functionalization of the financing mechanism approved in the emergency context of the pandemic crisis. These pillars achieve an unprecedented synthesis of public interest objectives in terms of the financial assistance programmes launched in response to the sovereign debt crisis. The Commission's monitoring of the implementation of the NRPs is continuous and thorough, using stringent indicators and quantitative indices. At this early stage, no critical issues have emerged in connection with meeting targets and objectives. However, no forecasts can be made. First of all, the implementation process is currently limited to a small sample of countries. Moreover, the targets and objectives whose implementation is scheduled for later stages are more complex to achieve.

80 Respect for the rule of law and its weaknesses has already been mentioned above, but at least two other limitations should be noted. The first limit to the innovative feature of the conditionality mechanism of the NGEU relates to its temporary and exceptional character, one of the key elements in the political compromise that led to its approval. It could, however, be subject to review, in the sense desired by various parties, thus allowing this model to have a greater impact on long-term dynamics. A second limitation could be the link between the NGEU and the European Semester: in particular, whether the mechanisms typical of the latter can also

European Semester are still linked may be an indication that the economy and finance (and the Northern European creditor countries) have simply taken a strategic step backwards in the wake of the crisis. But are they ready to take two steps forward if the situation changes, stifling the spirit of expansive economic policy of the NGEU? The answer to this question can only be found empirically.

The four points raised here confirm the tendency to financialize the European integration process and the increasing centrality of the protection of the Union's financial interests and budget in the process. But what are the repercussions of this encroachment by a logic of economics onto law-making on the legal environment and the rule of law?

4. The logic of economics in public law

Should the constitution be considered from the perspective of the political and legal content of the social pact made by the people, or should it be evaluated in terms of its compliance with criteria of economic efficiency?

There is no harm in considering it, as some have done,[81] from this last angle because, as mentioned earlier, scientific pluralism and contamination between fields of study can be fruitful in itself. A problem arises if this becomes the *only* perspective or the clearly favoured one, seeking to depoliticize constitutional content (in an attempt to separate body and soul, as it were). If this is the objective, then applying this method becomes dangerous as it is inspired not by a logic of coexistence and exchange between kinds of knowledge but by hegemonic aims.

Nevertheless, it is worth reiterating the caveat already hinted at in the previous chapter: the problem is not the economic method per se nor the juridicization of institutes from the sphere of economics. Many play (or can play) a positive role. Similarly, contaminations in the legal sphere by elements from economics are useful in themselves. What, on the other hand, may constitute a risk is the danger of upsetting the balance between economics, politics, and law, as we shall attempt to show here. It must be borne in mind, in this regard, that there are many different economic methods and approaches (e.g., behavioural, circular, sustainability, and innovation economics) and that our criticism

affect the objectives of the former. The question is whether the ultimate goals, i.e., the wide-ranging requirements to foster ecological and digital transition and to reconcile this with social cohesion have priority, or whether concerns regarding sound public finance management will prevail. This will largely depend on the decisions that will be taken regarding the stability pact. The pact has been suspended due to the coronavirus crisis; discussions on its reform are being hotly debated among states, and the outcome can only have major consequences on how the NGEU develops.

81 J.M. Buchanan, 'Constitutional Economics', in J. Eatwell, M. Milgate, P. Newman (eds), *The Invisible Hand* (London: Macmillan, 1989) 79 ff.

centres on the efficiency approach, with its mainly analytical connotation, stemming from the neo-liberal conception of recent decades. Thus, we repeat, we are not critiquing economics per se but the specific way it has been interpreted in the late twentieth and early twenty-first century mainstream.

As Max Weber points out: capitalist economics also developed, especially since the second half of the nineteenth century, thanks to an infrastructural use of law and, in particular, exploiting its formal and calculable legal framework. In essence, in the modern state, economics uses the legal framework (inherited from ancient Rome) to constitute a suitable social model for constructing the markets. Weber, however, recalls that "the justice of all theocracies and absolute powers is oriented towards the material" and is, therefore, incalculable: "With a law of this kind, capitalism cannot organize the economy; what is required is a law that can be calculated in a machine-like manner; ritual-religious and magical perspectives cannot play any role."[82] As is well known, economic policy originated in England with fourteenth-century mercantilism and substantially developed in parallel with the modern state, precisely by using law as a means, as an infrastructure;[83] it is no coincidence that modern capitalism is rooted in Protestant ethics (with ramifications filtering down even today: in a certain sense, the Calvinist view underlines the logic of austerity with which the Mediterranean countries have been 'punished' for the sin of accumulating debt[84]). Law has helped to "demagicise the world", says Weber, and thus to lift the veil of asceticism that has characterized the long period in history when religion played a fundamental part in shaping social patterns.[85] The period in which the compact between economics and law was at its strongest was the half-century covering the last quarter of the nineteenth and the first quarter of the twentieth centuries: it is no coincidence that this was a time when the legal method held sway, and the period when the theoretical coordinates of political economics and business economics were defined; organizational and bureaucratic models were refined, and technical business efficiency increased.

The combination of economics and law, with the latter at the helm, led to World War I, as Polanyi explains; the unresolved (and indeed aggravated) economic problems and the supremacy of politics, with the latter predominating, produced World War II.

82 M. Weber, *Historia económica general*, 1923, Fondo de cultura económica USA, 2011 (Italian ed., *Storia economica. Linee di una storia universale dell'economia e della società*, 1923 (Rome: Donzelli, 1997) 239).

83 See, among others, F. Galgano, *Lex mercatoria. Storia del diritto commerciale* (Bologna: il Mulino, 1993). But see also K. Pistor, *The Code of Capital. How to Creates Wealth and Inequality* (Princeton, NJ: Princeton University Press, 2019). On Pistor's volume, see A. Sandulli, 'Il diritto quale infrastruttura per i poteri privati? A proposito di un libro di Katharina Pistor' (2021) 27 *Diritto pubblico* 999 ff.

84 K. Dyson, *States, Debt and Power: 'Saints' and 'Sinners' in European History and Integration* (Oxford: OUP 2014).

85 M. Weber, *The Protestant Ethic and the Spirit of Capitalism*, 1920 (New York: OUP, 2010).

The relationship between law and economics as instruments of domination to preserve the status quo began to show their first divergences during the twentieth century and, in particular, after World War II, when, with the proliferation of democratic Constitutions containing a catalogue of values and principles of constitutional rank, law came to be endowed with constitutional substance, becoming also and primarily the goal and index of the development of a democratic social model, aimed at combining freedom and equality, social cohesion and, above all, lasting peace in the European continent (at least in the geopolitical sphere of the United States, in opposition to the Soviet bloc) and ideal conditions for generating wealth from the support for start-ups constituted by the Marshall Plan (in a classic twist of history, the risk of war, opposition between geopolitical blocs, and the economic-financial planning of investments for recovery have returned to the centre of European political agendas, with the pandemic and Ukrainian crises, three-quarters of a century later).

However, as we have seen, in the early days of the European Economic Community, a number of factors, including the social market economy model introduced by the Freiburg School in post-war Germany and transplanted to Europe, managed to hold together the various social sciences and, in particular, their relationship with law by virtue of the realist tendency in ordoliberal thinking to emphasize the close connection between the economy and other forces driving society.

Only later, with the advent of globalization, did economics and finance (no longer an economics of production but one linked to financial markets) cross the barriers between states, especially through the remarkable expansion of the major corporations. The growth (both quantitative and qualitative) of supranational and international legal systems triggered a crisis in the traditional legal-formal order and the 'closed' way of seeing law[86]; confusion regarding the ways law is produced, with the courts taking the leading role, made this incalculable.[87] The phenomenon should have been regulated from both the economic and juridical standpoints: instead, it has developed and expanded in the economic-financial direction alone. Rather, law itself has self-seekingly pushed in that direction. As Joseph Weiler points out, through the diffusion of barely established customary norms and, above all, the multiplication of mostly economic multilateral treaties, the typical dynamics of democracy have become irreconcilable with the law of international bodies, which operate through governance without government.[88] What is striking about the phenomenon is

86 In the contemporary context, state orders are reduced, according to A. Supiot in *Homo Juridicus: On the Anthropoligical Function of the Law* (London, New York: Verso, New ed., 2017), to the sociological significance of mere "forms of local solidarity, permissible only insofar as they do not hinder the free movement of goods and capital".

87 On these aspects, see N. Irti, *Un diritto incalcolabile* (Turin: Giappichelli, 2016).

88 J.H.H. Weiler, 'The Geology of International Law: Governance, Democracy and Legitimacy' (2004) *Heidelberg Journal of International Law* 547 ff.

that it proceeds in waves, i.e., it expands and retracts on the basis of the geopolitical situation: this can be seen at this time, following the growing tensions between the US and the Sino-Russian spheres of influence. The Euro-Union and national regulations establishing controls and limits on foreign direct investment are the most obvious manifestation of this phenomenon.[89]

As we have seen above, the neo-liberal theories of the Chicago School, like the Anglo-American experience of the early 1980s (the first implementation of neo-liberal theories had actually taken place a few years earlier, in Pinochet's Chile) aimed, first and foremost, at radical deregulation on the assumption that the market was capable of regulating itself, and second, at affirming privatization, liberalization, and outsourcing models in order to give private individuals greater scope to act within the economic sphere; and third, transplanting corporate logic into public administrations on the assumption that the organization and operation of private enterprise were more efficient than those of public entities. Thus, economics veered towards an analytical and mathematical approach, towards abstractionism and the theoretical model to be validated sitting at a desk, distancing itself – according to a hegemonic and, moreover, supremacist logic – from comparison with the other social sciences.

Incidentally, the deregulation policies of the 1980s must be put into historical context if their 'philosophy' is to be understood. In the US, these drastic measures were adopted in response to the American industries' loss of international competitiveness in the 1970s. The relaxation of regulatory controls made mergers and acquisitions easier and thus allowed US companies to grow and become competitive across borders again. It is clear that the economic policies applied in the context of another model and another economic, legal, and cultural system cannot be suited to pursuing the same results.[90]

The fact remains, as far as we are concerned, that the crucial point is precisely the one mentioned above: an oppositional dialectic has arisen between the 'substance' of law and that of economics, resulting in a break with democratic constitutionalism.[91] The economic method, in the global disorder, has worked to free itself of the constitutionally oriented legal aims of the traditional models of twentieth-century Western democracies, attempting instead to reproduce an

89 On foreign direct investment see, among others, G. Napolitano (ed.), *Foreign Direct Investment Screening. Il controllo sugli investimenti esteri diretti* (Bologna: il Mulino, 2020).

90 Of interest in this respect are, on the one hand, anthropological research on competition law, on which, in particular, W. Fikentscher, *Culture, Law and Economics* (Berne, Durham: Staempfli and Carolina Academic Press, 2004); on the other hand, studies on the adaptation of competition law and policies to the contexts of developing countries, on which, in particular, M.S. Gal, M. Bakhoum, J. Drexl, E.M. Fox, D.J. Gerber (eds), *The Economic Characteristics of Developing Jurisdictions: Their Implications for Competition Law* (Cheltenham, Northampton: Elgar, 2015).

91 On different ways of understanding constitutionalism in these difficult years of economic and financial crisis, see, in particular, M. Luciani, 'Costituzionalismo irenico e costituzionalismo polemico' (2006) *Giurisprudenza costituzionale* 1643 ff.

instrumental and infrastructural use of juridicality through the judicialization of rules and mechanisms proper to economics.[92]

It is not for us here to assess how this process has developed at the European level and what consequences it brings for the system as a whole, or for the individual states that make it up.

We have seen that the European legal system was came into being with mature and advanced legal, political, and economic methods; however, it has expanded over the last thirty years mainly in the direction of the prevailing economic cultural influence.

To claim that this methodological imprint has overflowed into the field of law, and especially administrative law, is not a value judgement. It does not mean, as mentioned above, that this phenomenon need be interpreted negatively. The hybridization of the social sciences is, in itself, from the perspective of methodological pluralism, a positive element. Hence, mutual influences should generally be viewed with confidence.

Problems can arise, on the other hand, if the balance between the various social sciences breaks down under the weight of different economic and social influences, usually dictated by the tendency of one or more powers and interests to prevail over the others. In the second quarter of the twentieth century, the supremacy of politics was dictated by the nationalist, imperialist, and totalitarian turn of the state. At present, the prevalence of a certain economic imprint seems to take its inspiration from the coordinated disposition of the process of financial globalization, changes in the geopolitical order, relations between superpowers, and private powers transcending state borders to make instrumental use of public powers on the one hand and a certain conception of the role of public administrations and the algorithmic constraints of public finance, on the other.

As Giuliano Amato points out, "Those who think we need more democracy in Europe and learn from the estimates of the output gap and potential GDP that our future hangs on an algorithm can only think 'what have we done to deserve this?'"[93] And, again, "cohabitation is governed by rules, and this flow

92 In recent years, numerous books written by Italian constitutionalists have questioned whether the structures and achievements of 20th-century democratic constitutionalism can hold. See, among others, M. Benvenuti, *Libertà senza liberazione. Per una critica della ragione costituzionale dell'Unione europea* (Naples: Editoriale Scientifica, 2016); O. Chessa, *La Costituzione della moneta. Concorrenza, indipendenza della banca centrale, pareggio di bilancio* (Naples: Jovene, 2016); A. Guazzarotti, *Crisi dell'euro e conflitto sociale. L'illusione della giustizia attraverso il mercato* (Milan: Franco Angeli, 2016); F. Saitto, *Economia e Stato costituzionale. Contributo allo studio della 'Costituzione economica' in Germania* (Milan: Giuffrè, 2016); A. Somma, *Europa a due velocità. Postpolitica dell'Unione europea* (Reggio Emilia: Imprimatur, 2017).

93 G. Amato, 'Conclusioni', in G. Montedoro and E. Reviglio (eds), *La legge di bilancio e di stabilità: le politiche economiche possibili fra diritto costituzionale e diritto europeo. Dibattito fra economisti e giuristi* (Rome: Dike, 2017) 127, which continues as follows: "How is it possible to address our issues, which have all the volatility, the necessity to

of numbers and formulas has opened up, leading – like Google webpages – to the decisive use of an algorithm. Our future lies in an algorithm."[94]

Therefore, we must observe the shifting of balance with concern as it is from disharmonies such as these that the heinous events of the last few centuries have sprung.

As mentioned above, the peculiarity of the evolution that has taken place in the European legal system is that the economic method has 'perforated' the legal space, and the law has been used as an 'infrastructure' to disseminate it within the legal system instrumentally. This phenomenon has been termed 'judicialization' and has affected both politics[95] and, above all, economics,[96] although it has operated very differently in the two cases. For the most part, it has involved the area of law coinciding with administrative law (but it has also affected constitutional law: the balanced budget rule comes to mind), so that it has brought this branch of legal studies to the centre of worldwide attention. But it has now come to involve the constitutional order too, as in the case of some European countries following the addition of the balanced budget rule to the Constitution (Articles 81 and 97 of the Constitution[97] were amended in the Italian system).

be followed with an ability to adopt policies promptly as the situation changes. The one thing all economists are sure of is that an intervention that is appropriately counter-cyclical in September can become procyclical if made in November. Economists reproach institutions with always working to a timetable that ignores the reasons they do things, and they thus spiral into permanent contradiction. So discretion is essential, but we use it only, often improperly, for timing, and for the rest, no less improperly, we get caught up in the rules" (p. 128).

94 G. Amato, 'Conclusioni', op. cit., 129: "Fortunately, this also makes economists unhappy, convinced of what only the best of us jurists have convinced themselves of, namely that there are no certainties in the application of our instruments. They know that they have an enormous responsibility when they claim that what they tell us contains a truth that applies perfectly to every situation. This cannot be so. Yet, in 1992 at Maastricht we got ourselves into this chain of constraints for the opposite purpose of saving national autonomies and prerogatives. This is why our governments decided not to give the European institutions powers that would have curtailed them."

95 See, among others, R. Hirschl, 'The Judicialization of Politics', in G.A. Caldeira, R. D. Kelemen, K.E. Whittington (eds), *The Oxford Handbook of Law and Politics* (Oxford: Oxford University Press, 2008).

96 On the more general trend towards 'juridification', see, in particular, G. Teubner, 'Juridification. Concepts, Aspects, Limits, Solutions', in G. Teubner (ed.), *Juridification of Social Spheres: A Comparative Analysis in the Areas of Labor, Corporate, Antitrust and Social Welfare Law* (Berlin-Boston: De Gruyter, 2012) 3 ff.

97 See, for example, F. Bilancia, 'Spending review *e pareggio di bilancio. Cosa rimane dell'autonomia locale?*' (2014) *Diritto pubblico* 47, according to whom, "Analysis of these issues shows categorical interference between law and economics even in areas where this was never the case. As will become evident when we are forced to react to what the normative texts adopted require, for example, with the revision of Article 81 of the Italian Constitution and the consequent legislative implementation of the prescriptions deriving from it. To cite just a few examples – anticipating the meaning of the 'legal' issues that we will address in the remainder of this reflection – suffice it to consider the meaning of concepts and formulas such as 'economic

Reconstructions of the forms and ways in which the economic method has overflowed into legal methodology have already been carried out: a recent in-depth[98] study describes the temporal phases, analyzing the reasons and different means of putting this process into practice as well as how the criteria of economy and efficiency have spread into the various areas of administrative law.

An interesting aspect is that, despite manifesting itself to its fullest extent over the last three decades, this process traces its roots back to the original genetic heritage of the formation of the European legal system, confirming what has been said in the previous chapters. The European institutions have, in fact, followed a different route from the member states in the thirty years between the Treaty of Rome and the Single European Act, during which, in a Habermasian spirit, while the constitutional states developed redistributive policies underpinned by a mentality of substantial equality, the European institutions, by gradually constitutionalizing the treaties, shaped the face of the European order in terms of the primacy of competition and the protection of economic freedoms, largely deconstructing the protections provided by national social systems.

The neo-liberal dynamics of the last thirty years, which have affected the organization and functioning of the law, especially administrative law, pushing for free-market (or loosely regulated) policies, and, sometimes with nothing to hold them back,[99] would then be grafted onto this initial,

cycle', or 'structural budget balance', or the formulas emerging from the disarticulation of the items that make up the economic and financial 'constraints' deriving from the EU provisions governing public finance. In effect, these are all provisions that impose an *a priori* legal assessment (but not only) of the macroeconomic effects of the financial consolidation measures – or at any rate those affecting public finance budgets – adopted as necessary, the outcomes of which represent the structure of the so-called 'medium-term objectives' a category that *legally* sets out in detail the constitutional notion of *budget balancing*, as now made explicit by Articles 1, para 1(d); 3, paras 2, 3, and 5 of the aforementioned Law no. 243/2012". On this topic see also C. Bergonzini, 'The Italian Constitutional Court and Balancing the Budget: Judgment of 9 February 2015, no. 10; Judgment of 10 March 2015, no. 70' (2016) 12(1) *European Constitutional Law Review* 177–191.

98 R. Ursi, *Le stagioni dell'efficienza*, op. cit., fn. 34, in particular, for the next section, 201 ff.

99 A significant example is the functioning of the energy market in Europe, which, in the light of the Ukraine war and international financial speculation, is generating gigantic profits for financial and economic operators but also economic and social costs for the peoples of Europe and many nation-states. With some of these, however, such as the Netherlands, gaining from this situation because of the Title Transfer Facility - TTF, i.e., the hub, based in Amsterdam, for the exchange of natural gas, which has been chosen by the European Union to set the purchase price of gas: During these first two-thirds of 2022, the Netherlands has doubled its trade surplus, precisely thanks to financial speculation on gas prices, and it is strenuously opposed to any possibility of price capping, while the other major economies in continental Europe have seen their traditionally high surpluses substantially reduced to zero. The lesson to be learned from this is twofold. On the one hand, competition is not a valid recipe for all occasions: it is necessary to distinguish between sectors and manage flexibly and quickly, knowing how to adapt to the

ordoliberal[100] structure, which remained moderate insofar as it implied a strong connection with the institutions operating in the member states in the direction of the public function and public regulation, in both the economic and social fields.

The supranational order was thus born with the imprinting of the economic rationale and in application of the economic method (albeit, in the ordoliberal view, strictly connected to legal and social profiles), leaving instead the management of functions of a more strictly political nature, including those of welfare, to the states (but, in relation to this last point, it is necessary to take into account, in the pandemic era, mitigation through the measures introduced by the NGEU for the sake of social cohesion).

Since the reference parameter – also at regulatory and jurisprudential levels – has become the cost-effectiveness of management, with the necessary ability to cover costs, it is no surprise that the financial constraint represents – now also at constitutional level – the pivotal element in the system, with the inverse consequence that the administration now precedes rather than follows, suddenly finding itself on the front line of public policy choices.

5. From formal legality to administrative efficiency

During the latter part of the nineteenth century and the first half of the twentieth, the legal system was oriented towards compliance with the precepts of formal legality. In Italy, the Republican Constitution signified an important caesura as it enabled a beneficial shift from formal to substantive legality.[101]

Within the European legal system, legality, as mentioned at the beginning of the chapter, has entered a new phase of transformation, resting on foundations dictated mostly by jurisprudential principles: a European body of hard and soft law as interpreted by judges and technical standards.[102] This, at the European level, has led to the eclipse of the traditional political summit in favour of technico-bureaucratic institutionalism. This process of development seems to

contingent situation (in certain circumstances, in the energy sector, long-term contracts, which states have traditionally stipulated with large international companies and which today could be signed directly by the European Commission, can provide greater guarantees). On the other hand, Europe should take the difficult situation onboard, resolutely solving the problem: instead, from this point of view it is currently silent or late to act, although the REPowerEU plan has been announced (and is pending).

100 On the relationship between ordoliberalism and the reforms of the 1980s, see for example M. Everson, 'The Fault of (European) Law in (Political and Social) Economic Crisis' (2013) *Law Critique* 107 ff.

101 This distinction between formal and substantive legality does not apply to Italy alone: see, in this regard, among others, P. Craig, 'Formal and Substantive Conceptions of the Rule of Law: An Analytical Framework' (1997) *Public Law* 467 ff.

102 On soft law in the European legal order, see the recent M. Eliantonio, E. Korkea-Aho, O. Stefan (eds), *EU Soft Law in the Member States: Theoretical Findings and Empirical Evidence* (London: Hart, 2021).

have produced a short circuit (particularly in the economic and financial sectors, and especially at certain times, such as the second decade of the millennium), thereby linking formal legality directly to efficiency, bringing negative consequences due to the depletion of the legal substance of the measures introduced. But in recent years, especially following the European institutions' response to the pandemic, these dysfunctions seem to have been somewhat tempered.

The Maastricht Treaty represented a turning point not only in European integration, as the financial constraint imposed by the prohibition of excessive deficits significantly changed (to some extent to the good) the relationship between public resources and the approach to how public sector expansion is perceived.[103] This brought a reversal of the relationship between the state and the market, with the latter being able to respond to the demands of social wellbeing through the development of free competition: the European Community and the member states became regulators and, as mentioned earlier, social cohesion was now a mere counterbalance to the market, not a limitation.[104]

Alongside these changes, and in line with the original ordoliberal theories, radical transformations of the administrative apparatus came about also thanks to the principle of good administration: a process of intense privatization, liberalization, and outsourcing was accompanied by New Public Management policies, a movement that began in the Anglo-American sphere, viewed as a kind of orthodoxy for approximately twenty years. This model favoured forms of management imported from the private sector and focused on production: "government and administrative action is conceived as a network of transactions and agreements involving the assumption of mutual responsibility between political decision-makers and administrative officials".[105] Efficiency is thus equated, from a business perspective, to the maximization of administrative productivity.

Thanks to these neo-liberal models, reform processes based on privatization, liberalization and outsourcing, the deregulation of markets, especially financial markets[106], performance evaluation mechanisms, and the managerialization of civil servants have all spread across the globe. Methods of producing legal sources have multiplied, with particular reference to so-called soft law, whereby indicators, mechanisms, measurements, ratings, evaluation, benchmarking, protocols, risk analysis (HACCP), statistical data, etc., from the world of economics, languages, and methodologies, aiming at targets dictated by corporate

103 G. Guarino, *Verso l'Europa. Ovvero la fine della politica* (Milan: Mondadori, 1997).

104 Among the first, G. Amato, 'Il mercato nella Costituzione' (1992) 1 *Quaderni costituzionali* 7 ff.

105 R. Ursi, *Le stagioni dell'efficienza*, op. cit., 238.

106 The literature on the fundamental role of law in the regulation of markets is vast. We merely mention the recent *FairEconomy. Crises, Culture, Competition and the Role of Law* edited by W. Fikentscher, P. Hacker, R. Podszun, (Berlin, Heidelberg: Springer, 2013).

logic, have been vested with legal status. Examples of this kind of judicialization can be observed in the introduction into European legislation[107] of uniform accounting standards developed by the International Accounting Standards Board (IASB) or recourse to ratings (to determine the capital requirements of banks) in legislation.

As has been observed, precepts from management have been translated into legal principles, but, in the process, they have mutated in terms of legal rationale thanks to an economics-based mindset, consisting in the reformulation of the paradigms of legality by juridifying efficiency.[108] The result is a split between efficiency and legality, with the rules of social living shifting in the direction of the former. This 'juridified'[109] efficiency has led to an abnormal transformation of the necessarily dynamic character of an economic process, that of achieving a result, into a prescriptive and formal datum, paralyzing and mutating it into legalism, with the consequence of determining a logical and systemic short circuit from which it is difficult to escape.

The global sovereign debt crisis and the restrictive stability and fiscal measures adopted at European level (especially between 2011 and 2013) have further accentuated the tendency[110] to embrace intransigent liberalism (but the crisis has also contributed to bringing out the weaknesses of neo-liberalism): the rules of public finance, starting with the balanced budget rule (constitutionalized in Article 81 of the Italian Constitution),[111] have become absolute priorities (thus reversing the

107 On this see, for example, M. De Bellis, 'EU and Global Private Regulatory Regimes: the Accounting and Auditing Sectors', in E. Chiti and B.G. Mattarella (eds), *Global Administrative Law and EU Administrative Law. Relationships, Legal Issues and Comparison* (Berlin: Springer, 2011) 269 ff.

108 On these aspects, see the apposite reflections of G.M. Salerno, *L'efficienza dei poteri pubblici nei principi dell'ordinamento costituzionale* (Turin: Giappichelli, 1999).

109 Natalino Irti calls the relationship between law as a legal power and other powers 'techno-law'. On the relationship between techno-law and techno-economy, see v. N. Irti, *Il diritto nell'età della tecnica* (Naples: Editoriale Scientifica, 2016) 13 ff.

110 A. Guazzarotti, *Crisi dell'Euro e conflitto sociale. L'illusione della giustizia attraverso il mercato*, op. cit., 21, highlights the distortion of the constitutional foundations of the EMU countries resulting from the fact that the ECB, "on the one hand, is forbidden to create money in favour of the states but, on the other, is allowed to do so in favour of the private banking system, thereby triggering or amplifying speculation on public debt securities and forcing states to hold back funds for social spending to allocate them to debt servicing in favour of in support of financial speculation". On the ability of 'external constraints' to reshape the constitutional regulation of public finance, see, especially, G. della Cananea, *Indirizzo e controllo della finanza pubblica. Un tema al centro del dibattito istituzionale:la finanza pubblica nazionale e l'Unione economica e monetaria* (Bologna: il Mulino, 1996). On the 'constitutional rupture' brought about by the EMU, see, among others, A. Cantaro, *Costituzione e ordine economico* (Acireale: Bonanno, 1994); F. Bilancia, *La crisi dell'ordinamento giuridico dello Stato rappresentativo* (Padua: Cedam, 2000).

111 But we should consider, before that, the revision of the German Grundgesetz of 29 July 2009, which eliminated the golden rule, i.e., the rule that allowed the Federation and the Länder to resort to debt to finance capital expenditure. On these

inveterate habit of some countries, including Italy, of disregarding public accounts for several decades), financial interest has become the priority, and, thanks to bureaucratic primacy, the new economic governance aimed at overseeing European member states in crisis or financial difficulties has given rise to what has been called a (derogating and exceptional) "commissarial dictatorship",[112] where the Commission (in matters of public finance) and the ECB (in matters of banking supervision with the intervention also of the IMF for states benefiting from financial assistance, the so-called Troika) enjoy substantially unlimited powers, being the most powerful administrations, with the lowest degree of democratic control[113]). Thus, the fate of states is linked to a technical assessment of their mathematical compliance with regulatory automatisms possessing firmly regimented economic and budgetary policies. Among other things, as we have seen, although it has been acknowledged in official acts that mistakes were made in the first ten years of economic and monetary union (Recital 8 of EU Reg. 1175/2011), it has long persisted, in the context of strengthened intergovernmental economic governance (ESM, Six Pack, Fiscal Compact),[114] in the inconsistent pursuit of the same economic doctrine deemed unfit for purpose[115] and had to wait for the pandemic

aspects, see M. Matthijs, 'Powerful Rules Governing the Euro: The Perverse Logic of German Ideas' (2015) *Journal of European Public Policy* 375 ff., for whom ideas "as independent variables are at their most powerful when they inform policy decisions that go directly against the material interests of the strongest player, and at the same time lead to perverse 'reality effects' where the ideational discourse actively leads to contrary outcomes. Since 1999, the macroeconomic consensus governing the euro has changed twice, fluctuating between rules and discretion. The Stability and Growth Pact was reformed in 2005, while a series of policy innovations was introduced in response to the euro crisis after 2010. Both developments have been largely driven by the Eurozone's most powerful state, Germany. However, if one thinks of the changing consensus merely as the result of Berlin's shifting interests, then while the first episode can be coded as such, the second cannot. While it regained its budgetary powers in 2005, Germany agreed to give away fiscal and financial powers without recouping any discretion over monetary policy after 2010. Furthermore, adherence to German ideas and ordoliberal "rules" actually turned a Greek fiscal problem into a full-blown systemic crisis, which only receded once those ideas were partially abandoned."

112 See, to this effect, L. De Lucia, '"Pastorato" e "disciplinamento" nella governance economica europea' (2015) *Diritto pubblico* 867 ff. The contribution is interesting due to the application of Michel Foucault's ideas to the mechanisms of new European economic governance.

113 M. Goldmann, 'The Great Recurrence: Karl Polanyi and the Crises of the European Union' (2017) 23 *European Law Journal* 17.

114 B. de Witte, 'Treaty Games: Law as Instrument and as Constraint in the Euro-Ccrisis Policy', in F. Allen, E. Carletti, S. Simonelli (eds), *Governance for the Eurozone: Integration or Disintegration?* (Philadelphia: FIC Press, 2012) 139–160, in particular at 152 et f.; A. Hyvärinen, 'Opening Statements', in A. Kocharov (ed.), *Another Legal Monster? An EUI Debate on the Fiscal Compact Treaty*, EUI Working Paper LAW 2012/09 (Fiesole: European University Institute, 2012) 8.

115 C. Pinelli, 'Il doppio cappello dei governi tra Stati e Unione europea' (2016) *Rivista trimestrale di diritto pubblico* 647.

crisis for an opportune change of course, along the line long since traced by those who believed that a decisive change in economic and financial policies in the direction of less austerity was necessary in order to stimulate investment and greater sensitivity in terms of solidarity.[116] Having ascertained the inadequacy of neo-liberal theories and verified the positive effects of the economic planning of expansive investments, it must be recorded that ordoliberal theories are not suitable in all cases and that, in the presence of serious economic-financial crises, it may be useful and necessary to re-evaluate the hypothesis of recourse to Keynesian-type economic policies.

Under the motto 'Finance will follow!', gains in efficiency have led to the subordination of other public functions: those relating to social and welfare policies but also those concerning infrastructural investments and even those attributable to the hard core of the nation-state, to the need to cut expenditure and reduce public debt, for which the state, through budget squeezing, is constantly under EU scrutiny.

This has led, in particular, to social rights being downgraded and marginalized at the European level,[117] despite statements on the principle of solidarity and the related ancillary nature of general social services with respect to services of general economic interest due to a lack of balance in terms of economic competences. Thus, for example, the main European point of reference in this sense is not the broader container, that of services of general interest (SGI), but what it contains, relating to services of general economic interest (SGEI). On this basis (substantially by subtraction), the social services of general interest (SSGI), which, moreover, cannot but be conditioned by the notion from which they derive, are adjusted.

The European Court of Justice itself, which, from the point of view of the protection of rights, has historically performed a function of institutional rebalancing, has adopted, starting from the first decade of the new millennium (see, in particular, the well-known *Viking, Laval*, and *Rüffert*[118] cases), decisions that highlighted the now more secondary nature of social rights and the

116 M. Goldmann, 'The Great Recurrence: Karl Polanyi and the Crises of the European Union', op. cit., 16.

117 On the fundamental topic of social rights in Europe, see, among others, G. de Búrca (ed.), *EU Law and the Welfare State. In Search of Solidarity* (Oxford: OUP, 2005). Most recently, S. Civitarese Matteucci, S. Halliday (eds), *Social Rights in Europe in an Age of Austerity* (London: Routledge, 2017). How the welfare state has been affected by European financial constraints has been examined by, among others, F. Losurdo, *Lo Stato sociale condizionato. Stabilità e crescita nell'ordinamento costituzionale* (Turin: Giappichelli, 2016).

118 CJEU, Grand Chamber, 11 December 2007, C-438/05, *International Transport Workers' Federation* and *Finnish Seamen's Union v. Viking Line ABP* and *OÜ Viking Line Eesti*; CJEU, Grand Chamber, 18 September 2007, C-341/05, *Laval un Partneri Ltd v. Svenska Byggnadsarbetareförbundet, Svenska Byggnadsarbetareförbundets avdelning 1, Byggettan e* and *Svenska Elektrikerförbundet*; CJEU, Second Chamber, 3 April 2008, C-346/06, *Dirk Rüffert v. Land Niedersachsen.*

protection of employment with respect to the needs of the markets. This trend soon spread to the supreme courts of the main national legal systems.

This tendency eventually made a strong impact on the constitutional order of the member states, producing a series of political and legal consequences.[119] The erosion of the principle of solidarity was highly divisive, prioritizing economic-financial goals over other interests lying outside the economic sphere.

By the close of the first decade of the twenty-first decade, the 'econocratic project' began to show signs of weakness, with the European architecture being jeopardized by the powerful thrust of economic recession in the absence of dual social and political adjustment in terms of responsibility and solidarity.[120] The European institution that assumed the role of breakwater in fighting recession, and which proved most authoritative in regulating the economic and financial fortunes of the member states (with very serious consequences for Greece and the salvation of Italy), was the European Central Bank and, therefore, a technical entity, wholly independent of the traditional democratic circuit. The 'politically' active role of the Central Bank has, of course, sparked – and continues to spark – constitutional debate regarding encroachment on national sovereignty, the threat to constitutional identity, and the theory of counter-limits, leading to dialogue between the courts during which the Second Senate of the German Constitutional Court has been fiercely critical, particularly in its ruling on the PSPP.[121]

In reality, the pandemic crisis and then the energy crisis following the war in Ukraine have triggered a change of direction, a clear change in economic governance, as we saw last year with the NGEU, and now the announced RePowerEU.

119 B. De Witte, 'Euro crisis responses and the EU legal order: Increased institutional variation or constitutional mutation?' (2015) 11 EuConst 434–457; Ka. Tuori, Kl. Tuori, *The Eurozone Crisis: A Constitutional Analysis* (New York: Cambridge University Press, 2014); P. Craig, 'Economic Governance and the Euro Crisis: Constitutional Architecture and Constitutional Implications', in M. Adams, F. Fabbrini, P. Larouche (eds), *The Constitutionalization of European Budgetary Constraints* (Oxford, UK; Portland, OR: Hart, 2014) 19–40; M. Dawson and F. De Witte, 'Constitutional Balance in the EU after the Euro-crisis', op. cit. 6; E. Chiti, P.G. Teixeira, 'The Constitutional Implications of the European Responses to the Financial and Public Debt Crisis' (2013) 50 *Common Market Law Review* 683–708; J.H.H. Weiler, 'Europe in Crisis: On "Political Messianism", "Legitimacy" and the "Rule of Law"' (2012) *Singapore Journal of Legal Studies* 248–268.

120 M. Ferrera, 'Breaking the "Caging" Mentality: Ordoliberalism, Responsibility and Solidarity in the EU', in J. Hien and C. Joerges (eds), *Ordoliberalism, Law and the Rule of Economics*, op. cit., 115 ff.

121 See, in particular, the I•CON symposium on the *PSPP* ruling and, in particular, J. Basedow, J. Dietze, S. Griller, M. Kellerbauer, M. Klamert, L. Malferrari, T. Scharf, D. Schnichels, D. Thym, J. Tomkin, 'European integration: *Quo vadis?* A critical commentary on the PSPP judgment of the German Federal Constitutional Court of May 5, 2020' (2021) 19 *I-CON* 188–207; Editorial Comments: 'Not Mastering the Treaties: The German Federal Constitutional Court's PSPP Judgment' (2020) 57 *Common Market Law Review* 965–978. V. See also, A. Sandulli, 'Il *bazooka* giurisdizionale tedesco e la politica monetaria della Banca Centrale Europea' (2020) *Rivista italiana di diritto pubblico comunitario* 363 ff.

In addition to introducing the new economic governance criteria mentioned above, the NGEU has greatly reinforced the solidarity principle, significantly relaunching policies of social cohesion through the SURE and the RRF. All this is giving the third pillar political solidity, although there is still a long way to go. A final point to note concerns the impact of the new economic governance of which the NGEU is the first indicator on administrative law and, in particular, on the administrative procedures of the member states.

We have already mentioned that, in the end, the European institutions and, in particular, the European Commission, direct and plan national economic development since national plans have to be approved by the Commission first and then by the Council. They then see that the various targets and milestones set in the national plans are met, on which the concrete disbursement of the funding tranches depends. This means, therefore, that if the targets are not met in the established manner and within the envisaged timeframe, a member state does not receive the corresponding tranche of funds.

This has repercussions on the way the member states' National NRRPs are implemented insofar as the different projects that make up each Plan must be implemented in the manner and within the timeframe agreed with the European Commission, which then verifies the correct implementation of the planned activities.

This implies, on the one hand, extraordinary planning ability, farsightedness, and the know-how to devise projects and investments that will be competitive in a few years' time. This capacity for planning in the economic field, if it existed in the past, has been 'mothballed' in many member states for decades, sacrificed on the altar of previous European economic governance (suffice it to note the different names given to economics subjects: from 'economic policy' to 'macroeconomics', precisely to highlight the non-interference of the public sphere in matters of economics), which tended to leave basic development choices to the regulated markets and economic operators.

On the other hand, there is also a substantial impact on the methods of execution, as the public administrations do not simply have to realize the investments envisaged by the Plan through standard tenders and procedures: they must, with special attention to timing, meticulously plan and implement the multiple stages and numerous steps between one tranche of European funding and the next. Essentially, failure to conclude a procedure or one of its phases within the timeframe 'scheduled' in the agreements between the European Commission and the member state implies a breach of supranational obligations, with consequences that, at least in terms of formal strictness, could be extremely damaging to a country's economy.

It follows, therefore, that there is a constraint linked to results tied to the timing of the procedure, which has become more central and decisive than before. We might even say that it has become more important than the actual result arising from the real impact of the investment or reform. The consequences are twofold: on the one hand, the NGEU, as an instrument of economic policy, should enjoy greater freedom as investments might otherwise be discouraged if they are bridled in a tight-meshed legal net; on the other hand, it ends up 'bureaucratizing' performance, which is measured in terms of processes and deadlines rather than on the basis of assessing the outcome.

The fact is that management techniques, corporate project management, and business engineering, which had already worked their way into public administrations, have become absolutely fundamental in this emergency phase of recovery and resilience.

Project management techniques and especially models that have led to the transition from process-based to project-based organization, have now found their way into public administrations at this time of transformation.

It follows that the legal, and therefore highly structured and rigid rules and stages of a procedure involving the set-up, a person responsible, a deadline, fact-finding, decision, and so on, have gone hand in hand with contemporary mechanisms of project-based organization centred on flexibility and speed, flexible personnel management, the ability to adapt to different needs, and a constant and regular reporting system. However, these mechanisms can also have drawbacks, including considerable stress due to the rigid and frequent deadlines that punctuate the entire project; focus on the individual project with the risk of losing sight of the big picture, which must be recuperated within organizations themselves (through the general manager or office manager); numerous projects that may find themselves in mutual competition (e.g., using the same personnel); a relationship with personnel working to complete the project becoming a sort of project manager with all the benefits and costs that this may entail.

This process of integration and change has already taken place in public administrations as far as implementing the NRP is concerned, as we can see for ourselves and are experiencing it right now.

We can assume, however, that this transformation in the way administrations work, this new organization and procedures, can only bring gradual changes to their genetic heritage, resulting in structurally modified administrative procedures adapting to new project management models and techniques.

6. The instrumental use of law as infrastructure and functional imbalance in favour of economics and finance

In an attempt to draw the bottom line regarding the trend over the last quarter century, we can argue that, despite the recent counter-tendencies in the wake of Covid, Europe has seen a shift in the direction of the efficiency of states and organs of state.[122] This process has brought about a constitutional

122 On so-called results-based administration – and, therefore, the three "Es" (efficiency, effectiveness, economy) expressed by the constitutional principle of good performance and the European principle of good administration envisaged in the Nice Charter – see, for example, J. Wakefield, *The Right to Good Administration* (Alphen aan den Rijn: Kluwer, 2007); S. Cassese, 'Il diritto alla buona amministrazione' (2009) *European Review of Public Law* 1037 ff.; B.C. Mihaeschu Evans,

misalignment, at the European level, between impartiality and good performance (an inverse process, therefore, to the trend in some Western European national systems between the 1950s and 1970s). It has come about through the introduction of formally (and procedurally) juridical measures that are also substantial in economic and financial terms. The pursuit of good administration is in itself laudable: the problem is finding the right balance between assurance and efficiency.[123]

The most interesting aspect of the phenomenon is that the effect of substantive de-juridicization of the measures introduced came about through the juridicization of the mechanisms. The economicization of decision-making processes is the result of the infrastructural use of law. As has been noted, there has been a 'juridicization' of such vague concepts as the member states' 'good economic health' or its variants such as 'competitiveness', etc. Previously, this objective was essentially left to the national political/democratic process under the coordination of the Council. This juridicization has resulted in a 'hybrid' system in which different instruments (hard and soft) operate simultaneously and sometimes in contradiction. As has been observed, "on the one hand, legal regulation is presented as a solid web enveloping the macro-economic and fiscal conduct of states; on the other, primary, and especially secondary, legislation give rise to 'creeping de-juridicisation', because they actually 'open up vast spaces of discretionary political assessment to post-democratic technocratic apparatuses'".[124] Consider, for example, the rule-making powers of the financial agencies, which establish technical standards to adopt as Commission regulations, and, at the same time, can also adopt guidelines, which then become soft law (although the Commission retains the power to amend and refer technical standards back to the agencies).

In the light of these considerations, it has been observed that "while legal regulation based on public law occurs essentially in terms of the binomial consisting of the conformity/non-conformity (of conducts and acts) with respect to the norm – that is, it is based on an assessment of lawfulness or/unlawfulness, which then allows for judicial review – the new governance revolves to a large

The right to good administration at the crossroads of the various sources of fundamental rights in the EU integrated administrative system (Baden-Baden: Nomos, 2015); U. Stelkens, A. Andrijauskaitė, *Good Administration and the Council of Europe. Law, Principles and Effectiveness* (Oxford: OUP, 2020).

123 In this regard, the intimate link between the principle of good administration and procedural guarantees has been appositely noted in J. Ponce, 'Good Administrations and Administrative Procedures' (2005) *Indiana Journal of Global Legal Studies* 551 ff.; D.U. Galetta, 'Il diritto a una buona amministrazione europea come fonte di essenziali garanzie procedimentali nei confronti della pubblica amministrazione' (2005) *Rivista italiana di diritto pubblico comunitario* 819 ff.

124 L. De Lucia, '"Pastorato" e "disciplinamento"', nella governance economica europea' (2015) Diritto pubbico, 889, recalling the essay by C. Joerges and S. Giubboni, 'Diritto, politica ed economia nella crisi europea' (2014) *Rivista critica del diritto privato* 343 ff.

extent around assessments, that is, around the different conceptual binomial of success or failure of a state's economic performance and its planned or implemented policies".[125] For confirmation, one need only read, for example, the Commission's documents referring to individual states regarding the alert mechanism.

Thus, a "neo-liberal view that government is not merely the enforcement of a general will but takes on a substance of its own, precisely by adopting the economics paradigm,"[126] has taken root. From this perspective, as Armin von Bogdandy puts it, law is a social infrastructure for the functioning of European integration,[127] since it is conceived as a political project subordinated to economic processes mediated by law.

The result is a formal (and procedural) legality rich in economics-based content, directly reflecting the goal of making states and their public apparatuses more efficient, bypassing substantive legality and thereby endowing European officials with practically unlimited powers. And, under certain circumstances, these technical powers have become substantially immune (or almost immune[128]) even to judicial review of the application of technical

125 L. De Lucia, '"Pastorato" e "disciplinamento"', op. cit., 890.

126 R. Ursi, *Le stagioni dell'efficiena*, op. cit., 378.

127 A. von Bogdandy, 'Founding Principles', in A. von Bogdandy, J. Bast (eds), *Principles of European Constitutional Law* (Oxford; Munich, Hart-Beck, 2010) 17.

128 Consider, for example, the unclear wording of Article 85(3) of Directive 2014/59/EU on the resolution of credit institutions, which provides that "national courts use the complex economic assessments of the facts carried out by the resolution authority as a basis for their own assessment". This provision requires the national court to base its assessment on the technical ones made by the technical body. It is true that the 89th Recital of the Directive does not rule out judicial review: "therefore, it is important to ensure that the complex economic assessments made by national resolution authorities in this context are used as a basis for national courts when reviewing the crisis management measures concerned. However, the complex nature of those assessments should not prevent national courts from examining whether the evidence relied on by the resolution authority is factually accurate, reliable and consistent, whether that evidence contains all relevant information which should be taken into account in order to assess a complex situation and whether it is capable of substantiating the conclusions drawn therefrom." The provision could be merely interpreted as preventing a court from substituting its own assessment for that made by the technical body.

Moreover, precisely on the basis of the ambiguous wording of Article 85 of the Directive, the legislative decree implementing the Directive at the national level and, in particular, Article 95(4), of Legislative Decree no. 95 of 2015, provided that "[i]n judgments against crisis management measures [...] Articles 19 and 63(4), of the Code of Administrative Procedure [...] do not apply", on the subject of checks and technical consultations. When it was submitted to the Chambers for their opinions, the Explanatory Memorandum accompanying the draft decree also clarified that the purpose of the provision was to "limit the technical assessments underlying the decision to those carried out by the resolution authority".

This limitation imposed by national legislation not only looks manifestly unconstitutional but also hardly consistent with European law and seems to exceed the limits imposed by the Directive. The national legislative provision, in fact,

discretion (often accompanied by a deferential attitude of self-restraint in the case law of the Court of Justice and even domestic courts). Thus, the Commission and the ECB effectively hold absolute power: it is necessary to go back to the *ancien regime* to find similar forms of power in Europe, apart from a brief period in the second quarter of the twentieth century.

This power did not diminish in the wake of the pandemic and Ukrainian crises: indeed, if anything, it increased. We have already referred to the new-found central role of the Commission in the light of the NGEU. But the European Central Bank (ECB) has also adopted some significant and 'creative' unconventional monetary policies. We refer in particular to the ECB purchasing bonds placed on the market through the so-called Pandemic Emergency Purchase Programme (PEPP). The introduction of this programme has fuelled a new interpretation of the ECB's institutional mission, opening up new systemic perspectives on the role of European institutions in the economy.

The European Commission and the ECB's clear change of course in relation to the recent past is certainly worthy of note. In this respect, their post-pandemic contribution to greater European integration is extremely significant, with the two European institutions taking the lead in the solid revival of the Community method and the integration process. There is also another element: the Commission has been working on economic policy to safeguard and recoup the economies of the member states, as has the ECB to safeguard monetary stability. But both have also performed the fundamental task of promoting social cohesion, which is particularly striking if we consider the work of the ECB in the decade from 2008 to 2018.

Even leaving aside the overt and covert aims – whether austerity or expansion, competitiveness or cohesion – of the European institutions, the complex path that we have attempted to summarize here raises a number of questions about the European rule of law. These issues regard its theory and application throughout much of the twentieth century[129] and the transformations it has undergone with the emergence of globalization and global[130] law, further

compromises the effectiveness of judicial redress against bank decisions, making it difficult to verify the correctness of the parameters and accounting criteria used for the write-down of so-called non-performing loans or, even further upstream, the very existence of the conditions for declaring a bank insolvent. This happens despite the fact that the subject matter concerns full subjective rights (the credit rights of shareholders and bondholders; the status of a legal entity, whether it is *in bonis* or in liquidation due to insolvency), regarding which, therefore, if the normal insolvency procedures entrusted to the cognizance of the ordinary courts were to be applied, the judge could exercise full control over the conditions of the proceedings.

129 See, most recently G. Pino, V. Villa (eds), *Rule of law. L'ideale della legalità*, op. cit.

130 On the developments and limitations of the global rule of law see, among others, S. Cassese, *Advanced Introduction to Global Administrative Law* (London: Elgar, 2021), 80 et f. On the legal entanglements between systems arising from globalization, see, most recently, N. Krisch (ed.), *Entangled Legalities beyond the State* (Cambridge: CUP, 2022). A characteristic phenomenon from this point of view is

amplified by the crises of recent years. This theme leads on to the crucial and related one of the role of law at this sensitive time.[131]

Before addressing (from the European law standpoint) this important topic, we must first shift our attention to the possible institutional 'opacities' still found in the European legal system, starting from the thorny question of whether there is really an imbalance between the technical and the political, and whether the system itself suffers from a democratic deficit.

inter-legality, on which see J. Klabbers and G. Palombella (eds), *The Challenge of Inter-Legality* (Cambridge, UK; New York: CUP, 2019). Concerning the interaction between legal systems on the global level, see, for example, P.S. Berman, *Global Legal Pluralism: A Jurisprudence of Law beyond the Borders* (New York: CUP, 2012).

131 On this point see, esp. G. Palombella and N. Walker (eds), *Relocating the Rule of Law* (Oxford, UK; Portland, OR: Hart, 2008); L. Morlino and G. Palombella (eds), *Rule of Law and Democracy. Inquiries into Internal and External Issues* (Leiden; Boston: Brill Academic Publishing, 2010); G. Palombella, *È possibile una legalità globale? Il rule of law e la governance del mondo* (Bologna: il Mulino, 2012); S. Cassese, *A World Government?* (Sevilla: Global Law Press/Editorial Derecho Global, 2018).

Chapter III

Technical Expertise and Democratic Legitimacy in European Law over the Last Quarter Century

1 The development of European technical bureaucracy while politics lies quiet
2 The dilemmas of democratic legitimacy
3 Constitutionalizing and democratizing the European order

1. The development of European technical bureaucracy while politics lies quiet

The European spillover has been functionally grounded in technical[1] performance: the primacy of technocracy while politics lies quiet, in a kind of 'output legitimacy',[2] as technocratic legitimacy has been called, which draws its inspiration from the Community's wish to pursue results in favour of general welfare – results that the individual states cannot achieve working alone. The supranational order has consciously developed in an apolitical[3] sense, in an institutional context where political leadership is fragmentary but faith in the virtues of the technical expertise of epistemic communities abounds.[4] It was, on the other hand, an understandable reaction to the political excesses of the second quarter of the twentieth century, which led to the outbreak of World War II. This situation naturally favoured the emergence of administrative law, able to evolve and adapt in an appropriate environment.

1 On the move from social to technocratic performance, see E. Forsthoff, *Lo stato della società industriale* (Milan: Giuffrè, 2011) 29 ff. Forsthoff recalls that Saint Simon, ahead of his time, had already argued that political affairs should be entrusted to industrialists, scientists, and exponents of the positive sciences.
2 G. Majone, 'Europe's 'Democratic Deficit': The Question of Standards' (1998) 4 *European Law Journal* 18 ff.; F.W. Scharpf, *Governing in Europe: Effective and Democratic?* (Oxford: OUP, 1999) 10 ff.
3 Or, rather, the pursuit of policies without politics or the routine translation of the political into the technocratic.
4 P.M. Haas, 'Epistemic Communities and International Policy Coordination' (1992) *International Organization* 1 ff.

DOI: 10.4324/9781003302094-4

In this chapter we will examine the democratic shortcomings brought about by technocracy without politics.[5] This is not to say that technocracy and independent technical regulation are negative in themselves: indeed, they produce beneficial effects[6] and are often also a protection against the growing lack of competence of the political class in almost all democratic states, but they risk causing what may sometimes constitute distortions when they operate in systems not balanced by democratic legitimation mechanisms.[7]

In this respect we must bear in mind that, over the last few decades, we have witnessed in almost all the Western European democracies a sort of marginalization of parliaments and political parties alongside a growth in the weight of executive and political leadership, as well as a corresponding growth in the prominence of technocracy and technical decision-making fora. Does all this indicate a shift from a democratic to a non-democratic system? Not necessarily. A healthy representative political circuit is also a very important sign of the resilience of democracies: however, one must at least bear in mind that the constitutional provisions of liberal democracies have more than one seat for the preservation of democracy. Constitutional systems are built on checks and balances based on a plurality of powers that confront, limit, and control each other. Suffice it to recall the important role in the defence of democracy of the president of the Republic and the Constitutional Court in the Italian legal system. Although they have interpreted their institutional role in different ways, the last three presidents (Ciampi, Napolitano, and Mattarella) have guaranteed the continuity of the democratic life of the country in this difficult quarter century marked by extraordinary executive instability. In the same way, the Constitutional Court has performed the essential task of overseeing the correct application of the Constitution itself, all the while adopting a prudential

5 On the democratic legitimation of bodies with technical expertise, see the recent empirical research by E. Krick and C. Holst (eds), *Experts and Democratic Legitimacy: Tracing the Social Ties of Expert Bodies in Europe* (Abingdon, UK; New York: Routledge, 2021).

6 An indicator of an essentially positive outcome is the fact that those who, at various junctures in European history, have taken a stand against bureaucracy in Brussels have been the very standard-bearers of deregulation policies. See, in this sense, the commendable reflections in G. Napolitano, 'La crisi di legittimazione e di capacità amministrativa dell'Europa' (2016) *Rivista trimestrale di diritto pubblico* 719.

7 This is the well-known objection in A. Spinelli, 'Europeismo', in *Enciclopedia del Novecento* (Rome: Istituto della enciclopedia italiana, 1977), according to which "The weakness of functionalism was that found in all technocratic theories. It substituted the creativity of political power for the executive efficiency of administrative power. An administration is always necessary to realise a political plan, but it tends by its very nature to rigidify and view it as something complete and thus incapable of generating new plans. No European agency could have been a driving force for the other European economies and society without new political stimuli coming from outside the agency itself. But Monnet was convinced that governments would be forced by circumstance to create such new stimuli."

attitude, avoiding judicial activism but intervening, sometimes even assertively, only when no other path was open to it.[8]

And it should also be borne in mind that a lack of legitimacy from the perspective of political representation can be partially balanced by other forms of democratization of the decision-making process, namely procedural[9] legitimization and forms of democratization from below, involving civil society.[10]

1.1. In the beginning are the functions,[11] one might say, since they assert their influence on the construction of the administrative machine, both in terms of organization and personnel. Since the functions assigned to the European institutions were initially directed specifically towards the economic and financial area, and since the institutions themselves are constantly in contact, for the most part, with international bodies (WTO, IMF, World Bank) and member state bodies (independent authorities) also responsible for these areas, it follows that both the facilities and, above all, the training and selection criteria for European administrative officials have been predominantly geared towards economics, business, and finance, with mostly technical responsibilities. Since the 1950s, "the ideal type of European civil servant had to master a panoply of complex, theoretical and practical disciplines (from law to economics to multiple languages in the aftermath of WWII, as French lost ground to English)".[12] The characteristics of the European administration are thus different from the typical state bureaucracies of the continental area.[13] Whereas a generalist type of bureaucracy with a predominantly legal and political basis prevails in the latter (suffice it to think, for example, of parliamentary and government officials, as well as prefectural and diplomatic careers, not to mention manager training in public administrations in Germany, France and Italy, which has only

8 On these points see, among others, S. Cassese, *La democrazia e i suoi limiti* (Milan: Mondadori, 2017).
9 Among others, see J. Mendes, *Participation in EU Rule-Making: A Rights-based Approach* (Oxford; New York: OUP, 2011); G. della Cananea, *Due Process of Law beyond the State: Requirements of Administrative Procedure* (Oxford: OUP, 2016).
10 U. Liebert, A. Gattig, T. Evas (eds), *Democratising the EU from below? Citizenship, Civil Society and the Public Sphere* (London: Routledge, 2018).
11 M.S. Giannini, 'In principio sono le funzioni', 1959, idem, *Scritti*, vol. IV (Milan: Giuffrè, 2004) 719 ff. The terms 'public or administrative functions' refer here to the aims and purposes that public authorities are called upon to pursue by the Constitution and the law in order to satisfy the needs of the community (e.g., the function of public order and safety, education, health, environmental protection, and so on).
12 A. Grilli, *Le origini del diritto dell'Unione europea* (Bologna: il Mulino, 2009) 195.
13 For a detailed reconstruction from the comparative perspective (analyzing the French, British, German, and Russian administrations statistically), of the European administrative elite, see the still essential socio-political study by J.A. Armstrong, *The European Administrative Elite*, 1973 (Princeton: Princeton Legacy Library, 2015). He examines, in particular, the family background, educational achievements, university education, recruitment, and work experience of civil servants, also in order to assess their impact on development and economic growth.

changed in recent years), in the European institutions, the bureaucratic class is predominantly technical, insofar as officials are trained in economics and finance, which, in the member states, is mainly found in authorities independent of the political influence of national governments[14]).

If we add to this the fact that, as we will see in more detail in the next chapter, from the mid-1980s onwards the European legal system has been heavily influenced by the US corporatist model, we can realize how radical the transformation of the European bureaucratic apparatus has been, with subsequent spillover into the legal systems of the member states. The corporatist model typical of private enterprise, based on audit culture and evaluation, spread first to the European institutions and then to the member states. It has been suggested that, through enabling legislation, regulatory powers have been transferred to supranational technical agencies, "to lift the management of the market to a more effective systemic level",[15] not only in order to boost integration without further strengthening the Commission[16] but above all to entrust highly technical subjects to bodies with staff specially trained to fulfil these functions.[17] Alongside the technicization of the content of the supranational bureaucratic apparatus, there has also been a change in the way bureaucratic work is carried out, for example through the flanking (and, in part, replacement) of the traditional bureaucratic model, based on procedural sequences, with a model built around project management and management engineering skills.[18]

It is, therefore, a very different type of bureaucracy from the one described by Weber[19] and criticized by von Mises[20]: a bureaucracy that originated with private enterprise and the process dynamics of the exercise of private authority, which then overflowed into public institutions. As public bureaucracy techniques had inspired Tayloristic industrial models in early-twentieth-century United States, the late twentieth-century engineered corporate model made its way back into the public sphere.

In a famous press conference on 9 September 1965,[21] Charles de Gaulle defined European bureaucracy as an "aréopage technocratique, apatride et

14 Whether this is true independence has been debated for decades. Seminal writings on the subject include C. Sunstein, 'Paradoxes of the Regulatory State' (1990) 57 *University of Chicago Law Review* 407–441.
15 W. Sauter, 'The Economic Constitution of the European Union' (1998) *Columbia Journal of European Law* 66.
16 On this point, M. Shapiro, 'The Problems of Independent Agencies in the United States and the European Union' (1997) *Journal of European Public Policy* 276 ff.
17 G. Majone, 'Delegation of Regulatory Powers in a Mixed Polity' (2002) *European Law Journal* 319 ff.
18 On these points, see paragraph 5, chapter II above.
19 M. Weber, 'Economy and Society', vol. I, part III, 'Forms of Power'; vol. IV, part IX, 'Sociology of Power', Section II, 1922 (Berkeley, Los Angeles, London: University of California Press, 1978), in particular 217 ff. and 956 ff.
20 R. von Mises, *Bureaucracy* (Grove City, PA, Libertarian Press, 1983).
21 V. Conférence de presse de Charles de Gaulle (9 septembre 1965), in *cvce.eu.*

irresponsable". But the most sensitive issue today is no longer these characteristics but rather lack of transparency in the processes of "democracy in transit"[22] – or "throughput", as Vivien Schmidt puts it.[23] For these reasons, too, it would appear essential to return to procedural democracy, more traditionally linked to legally balanced ways of reaching decisions, and this calls for a general law on European administrative procedure.[24]

Having highlighted the critical aspects of technical bodies in the absence of politics, we must reiterate that technical expertise can also bring positive results: suffice it to think of the results achieved at the European and national levels in terms of competition between economic operators and services of general economic interest.[25]

1.2. Alongside this, changes have been affecting the balances arising from the prior establishment of the boundaries between and/or the separation of the two areas between political direction and administrative management. This process has undoubtedly been influenced by, on the one hand, the weakening and inadequacy of the dominant organization model – the nation-state (due to inadequate planning and strategic ability, and its negative effects on a number of fronts, such as healthcare, by too close a link between political leadership and administrative management), and, on the other, the still immature state of the supranational system.

22 G. Pasquino, *L'Europa in trenta lezioni* (Turin: UTET, 2017) 123.

23 See, in particular, V.A. Schmidt, 'Democracy and Legitimacy in the European Union Revisited: Input, Output and "Throughput"' (2013) 61(1) *Political Studies* 2 ff., according to whom "Scholars of the European Union have analysed the EU's legitimacy mainly in terms of two normative criteria: output effectiveness for the people and input participation by the people. This article argues that missing from this theorisation is what goes on in the 'black box' of governance between input and output, or 'throughput'. Throughput consists of governance processes with the people, analysed in terms of their efficacy, accountability, transparency, inclusiveness and openness to interest consultation. This article defines and discusses this third normative criterion as well as the interaction effects of all three normative criteria. It does so by considering EU scholars' institutional and constructivist analyses of EU legitimacy as well as empirical cases of, and proposed, solutions to the EU's democracy problems. The article also suggests that unlike input and output, which affect public perceptions of legitimacy both when they increase or decrease, throughput tends to be most salient when negative, because oppressive, incompetent, corrupt or biased practices throw not just throughput but also input and output into question." There is no shortage of studies on the decision-making processes of European institutions. Among many, see M. Savino, *I comitati dell'Unione europea. La collegialità amministrativa negli ordinamenti compositi* (Milan: Giuffrè, 2005).

24 Proposing a possible Euro-Union regulatory discipline on administrative procedure, see P. Craig (ed.), *ReNEUAL Model Rules on EU Administrative Procedure* (Oxford: OUP, 2017).

25 On SGEI see, most recently, D. Gallo, *Public Services and EU Competition Law: The Social Market Economy in Action* (Abingdon, UK; New York: Routledge-Giappichelli, 2021).

The European states have seen the decline of politics, which was a dominant force during the first three-quarters of the twentieth century,[26] partly due to the crisis of the broad political parties and other ways of aggregating interests in civil society,[27] and also because major decisions are often taken at the international and supranational level or are manoeuvred by judicial decisions.

Looking at Italy in particular, we realize that the technical bodies, a source of pride for the national authorities (e.g., the Genio Civile) between the late nineteenth and early twentieth centuries, have now almost disappeared. There are several reasons for this.

On the one hand, there was a well-known historical factor behind the development of our administration, with the ousting of technical bodies by the traditional administrative bureaucracy, based on standardized and generalist, mostly legal, knowledge.[28] This ostracism was particularly vigorous in the Giolitti era due to special legislation. The technicians were marginalized in three stages: work was conferred outside the state system (in the railways, land reclamation, etc.); special technical bodies were set up in addition to the Genio Civile, leading to its fragmentation and division; express provision was made in 1904 for the director general of the Genio Civile to be only an administrative official (thus excluding engineers at the head of the apparatus). All this was brought about through special laws aiming to re-establish the dominance of the jurist and generalist bureaucrat. This led, within the administration too, to the affirmation, first in academia and then in society, of the idea of the fundamental importance of legal education. The victory of administrative law over the science of administration provided the key to imposing legal formalism, so in the technical careers too, an in-depth knowledge of the legal disciplines became a priority at the expense of overall know-how.

On the other hand, this also depended on the consistent reduction of the public sphere,[29] further exacerbated by the sovereign debt crisis and which, as has been suggested, exposed some countries to the risk of bureaucratic default.[30] This also meant that in-house technical skills became increasingly

26 See, for example, the historical perspective in, A. Tarquini (ed.), *Il primato della politica nell'Italia del Novecento* (Rome-Bari: Laterza, 2016).

27 See, among others, P. Mair, *Governare il vuoto. La fine della democrazia dei partiti* (Soveria Mannelli: Rubbettino, 2016).

28 This phenomenon is reconstructed very well by G. Melis, 'Introduzione', in A. Varni and G. Melis (eds), *Burocrazie non burocratiche. Il lavo ro dei tecnici nelle amministrazioni tra Otto e Novecento* (Turin: Rosenberg & Sellier, 1999) 9 ff.

29 On which, see, among others, M. Mazzamuto, *La riduzione della sfera pubblica* (Turin: Giappichelli, 2000). Following the crisis, see, among others, G. Napolitano (ed.), 'La crisi del debito sovrano e le misure di "riduzione dello Stato"' (2012) *Giornale di diritto amministrativo* 1303 ff.; F. Di Mascio and A. Natalini, 'Il contenimento della spesa pubblica e la riforma amministrativa', in G. Napolitano (ed.), *Uscire dalla crisi. Politiche pubbliche e trasformazioni istituzionali* (Bologna: il Mulino, 2012) 345 ff.

30 The risk was evidenced by G. Napolitano in 'La crisi di legittimazione e di capacità amministrativa dell'Europa', op. cit., 736.

scarce among the workforce of the national public administration: in some cases, technical skills were replaced by those of a more general nature, which were clearly unsuitable; in others, functions were outsourced to private individuals, while in yet others, business management techniques hinder the formation of specialized technical skills; lastly, where they still exist, they are directly answerable to European institutions rather than to their national governments. In particular, in the 1990s, technical knowledge was largely taken out of public administration, resulting in the technical inability to draw up projects in-house, making it institutionally difficult to assess the suitability of private project proposals. The result is ever-weaker politics, lacking both real decision-making ability in fundamental areas and internal technical elites able to make informed decisions and take action.

On the other hand, the opposite occurred in Europe, where – it is widely known – due to the particular institutional framework (two-headed interstate and community 'executive' traction, through the Council and Commission, diluted and composite regulatory power, reduced representative dynamics),[31] politics has always been weak, while the technical bodies of the main institutions are particularly effective and well prepared, so that the vulgate is that of a bureaucratic technocracy which also decides for the peoples of Europe, causing a democratic deficit.[32] On the one hand, the concept of democracy is less easily embodied than in the past; on the other, though it is increasingly difficult to make it overlap with traditional electoral and political representation, it still constitutes one of its fundamental, though not sufficient, elements.

In essence, a process of 'technification'[33] has taken place. In many sectors of the economic-financial area, the rules are now largely European, and the bureaucratic apparatuses, which are also European or national, reporting to the European institutions, are highly technical and selected on the basis of economic/financial training and methods of scrutiny. In the absence of a 'strong' political lead at the European level, and often through the construction of mechanisms that give some sectors increasing independence from the European Commission, decisions are mostly taken by the technocratic leaderships of the European institutions. They define the framework rules and adopt specific acts primarily on the basis of their technical expertise (and thus in the substantial

31 On the oscillation between intergovernmental and supranational components peculiar to the European system, see among many, C. Pinelli, 'Ipotesi sulla forma di governo dell'Unione europea' (1989) *Rivista trimestrale di diritto pubblico* 315 ff.

32 The idea of democratic deficit was famously expounded in D. Grimm, 'Does Europe Need a Constitution?' (1995) *European Law Journal* 282 ff., using a primordialist notion of *demos*, whereby the people politically precede the modern state.

33 On this, see the most recent *La tecnificazione*, S. Civitarese Matteucci and L. Torchia (eds) vol. IV of L. Ferrara and D. Sorace (eds), *Studies for the 150th anniversary of Italian Administrative Unification* (Florence: FUP, 2016), and, in particular, in addition to the introduction written by the volume's editors, the second part dedicated to *Studi sulla tecnificazione dell'economia*, 201 ff.

absence of a political filter). Over the last two decades, crucial decisions have been taken not only regarding the European continent but also the world economy and finance (on the introduction of the euro, on how to address the economic and financial crisis, how to manage certain member states' debts) on the basis of purely technical decisions by technicians, even though they have obvious political content and implications. The rules are adopted by these independent structures (insofar as they do not depend on a political and representative executive), the ECB for example.[34] The regulators and the supervisory and control apparatuses are technical. If one extends the analysis to the financial market sector or other 'networked' sectors, it becomes clear that these independent structures are deeply interconnected at the European and national levels by language, standardized conduct, and a shared, strictly technical professional culture, which, in the case of the financial markets, is grounded in economics and finance. The technical nature of regulation acts as a unifying element integrating the national and European systems, but it also isolates technical apparatuses and the sector of reference from the other orders they belong to, since such decisions are the result of high-level professional expertise, which obviously only a few possess.[35]

As has been observed,

> In this technocratic spiral, the European Union risks conforming to the ambiguous ideal of a democracy which – 'shaped by the market' (*markt-konform*) and detached from a politically mobilizable society – would fall hopelessly under the mercy of market imperatives. After that, the national selfishness that the Commission seeks to tame would create an explosive mixture with the technocratic authority exercised by the market 'experts'.[36]

In this interplay of opposites of a nation-state (as we mentioned before, this applies to Italy in particular) where there is politics without the technocracy, and a Europe in which the technocratic prevails due to the absence of politics, the forces, but also the ambiguities, of the construction of Europe have become stratified. It is no surprise that the identity problems arising from the asymmetry and imbalances described above are among the main causes of today's

34 For a definitive treatment of the ambiguity surrounding the independence and transparency of the ECB, see F. Morata, 'La Banca Centrale Europea', in S. Fabbrini (ed.), *Le istituzioni dell'Unione europea in prospettiva comparata*, in *L'Unione europea. Le istituzioni e gli attori di un sistema sovranazionale* (Rome-Bari: Laterza, 2002) 200 ff.

35 In some of these areas, judicial relief has also been introduced through sector-specific Boards of Appeals in order to reduce the number of court cases. These boards are made up of independent experts with specific and select sectoral knowledge and are therefore different from the Courts of Justice, which have general jurisdiction.

36 J. Habermas, *Nella spirale tecnocratica. Un'arringa per la solidarietà europea* (Rome: Laterza, 2014) 22.

dysfunctional order and the disconnection of citizens from the European institutions that underlies the populist movements that have gained ground throughout Europe in recent decades.[37]

2. The dilemmas of democratic legitimacy

The European institutional model essentially centres on Eurocrats, i.e., a few thousand (and rising) highly trained bureaucrats. There are just under 27,000 at the Commission, slightly over 6,000 at the Parliament, and almost 4,000 at the European Council Secretariat, with other tens of thousands of national bureaucrats making up the European 'network'. It has been argued for some decades now that this model poses problems of overall hold due to of the lack of political and democratic legitimacy and the lack of adequate counterweights capable of balancing this ontological weakness. The term 'post-national democracy' has been used to define the declining importance of national legislative powers in determining supranational policies.[38] But it has also been noted that when the sovereign debt crisis broke out, Europe "became a prisoner of its opposite: a true democratic 'trap'", as national governments took (and still take) fundamental decisions with polls and electoral deadlines in mind.[39]

2.1. Much has been written[40] on the controversial and dynamic concept of democracy,[41] the democratic deficit, the lack of transparency, and the accountability of European officials: some of these contributions are affected by ideological prejudices, but others have developed significant arguments.

37 On these aspects, particularly interesting and insightful are the proceedings of the Reconnect Project, funded by the European Commission under the Horizon 2020 programme, Principal Investigator Prof. Jan Wouters (KU Leuven): see the research project deliverables and publications at www.reconnect-europe.eu.

38 D. Curtin, *Postnational Democracy: The European Union in Search of a Political Philosophy* (The Hague: Kluwer Law International, 1997).

39 G. Napolitano, 'La crisi del debito sovrano e il rafforzamento della *governance* economica europea', in G. Napolitano (ed.), *Uscire dalla crisi*, op. cit., 419. It should be noted, on the other hand, that if the main issues of the democratic deficit in Europe had been addressed in the previous fifteen years, we would have perhaps been institutionally and politically ready to face the crisis.

40 B. Rittberger, *Building Europe's Parliament. Democratic Representation Beyond the Nation-State* (Oxford: OUP, 2005).

41 It is notoriously difficult to define the concept of democracy and establish its limits. See, in this regard, the fundamental work of L. Morlino, *Democrazie tra consolidamento e crisi* (Bologna: il Mulino, 2008); idem, *Democrazia e mutamenti. Attori, strutture, processi* (Rome: Luiss University Press, 2014). On the history of the notion of democracy, among others, see the recent M.L. Salvadori, *Democrazia. Storia di un'idea tra mito e realtà* (Rome: Donzelli, 2015). On the contents and difficulties of contemporary democracy, see S. Cassese, *La democrazia e i suoi limiti* (Milan: Mondadori, 2017). On the structure of contemporary democracies see, among others, S. Fabbrini, *Politica comparata* (Rome: Laterza, 2008).

This is not the place to reconstruct the decades-long debate in detail;[42] instead, the complex issue can be filtered through the analysis of two doctrinal contributions which, approaching the subject from opposite angles, make it possible to highlight the main institutional and administrative problems of the system, albeit within the specificity of European construction.

Mention has already been made above of an essay by Peter Lindseth from 1999,[43] to which the author has recently returned, reworking and updating his reflections first in a volume published in 2010[44] and then in a number of important recent essays. The second contribution is Deirdre Curtin's rich 2009[45] volume, which represents a quarter of a century of study in this area.

2.2. Lindseth, who looks at the topic more from a legal and formal angle, argues for the eminently administrative nature of European governance, with the consequence that the European institutions, composed of bodies of technically trained bureaucrats, are delegated by the member states, the only entities with democratic legitimation politically answerable to the electorate (input democracy), to exercise regulatory power and perform social and economic regulatory tasks. The European integration process has benefited from the crucial role of the European Court of Justice, but also from the deferential attitude long shown by national constitutional courts. The spaces of democratic legitimacy must necessarily be recovered if the system is to hold:

> Efficiency, measured in terms of realizing the gains from international coordination, cannot be divorced from other, less-quantifiable values like democratic legitimacy, without the threat of political backlash. (...) Supranational delegation is never simply a question of choosing the best or most efficient institutional design; rather, it inevitably raises concerns of democratic legitimacy that are central to the study of administrative law.[46]

From these premises, Lindseth arrives at two conclusions: on the one hand, the jurisprudential principle of the primacy of European law needs to be jettisoned, favouring normative interpretations able to maximize the member states' control over the work of the European institutions ("European Courts should regard subsidiarity, at a minimum, as an interpretive principle akin to the

42 For a recent concise reconstruction of the topic, J. Mendes, *La legittimazione dell'amministrazione dell'UE tra istanze istituzionali e democratiche*, in L. De Lucia and B. Marchetti (eds), *L'amministrazione europea e le sue regole* (Bologna: il Mulino, 2015) 89 ff.

43 P. Lindseth, 'Democratic Legitimacy and the Administrative Character of Supranationalism' (1999) 99(3) *Columbia Law Review* 628 ff.

44 P. Lindseth, *Power and Legitimacy: Reconciling Europe and the Nation-State* (Oxford: OUP, 2010).

45 D. Curtin, *Executive Power of the European Union: Law, Practices, and the Living Constitution* (Oxford: OUP, 2009).

46 P. Lindseth, *Democratic Legitimacy and the Administrative Character of Supranationalism*, op. cit., fn. 43, 737–738.

nondelegation doctrine in the United States"). On the other, it must be ruled out that the Court of Justice can have jurisdiction over *Kompetenz-Kompetenz*, i.e., over the assessment of the boundaries of the legislative competence conferred on the European institutions, so that any possible conflict between the two orders of national and supranational jurisdictions should be resolved by establishing a sort of European Conflicts Tribunal along the lines of the French Tribunal des Conflits (with the right of appeal to a political body acting as representative of the governments of the member states, as well as an op-out right). This interpretation takes its cue from some acute observations (the perception of a model with administrative origins and geared towards administration, with ensuing problems in developing the constitutional aspects of the system) and highlights some weaknesses in the model in terms of the constitutional framework, but which, with its radical consequences, jeopardizes the resilience of the entire European construction. Starting from these premises, Lindseth has developed, in recent years, the thesis of the "metabolic Constitution", in the sense of the ability to build from below the constitutional network through financial and administrative mechanisms.[47]

2.3. Deirdre Curtin tackles the problem of the democratic deficit from a realist perspective (using the legal-political method), namely the composite nature of the European order and the gradual construction of a European living constitution by means of a 'geological' process of sedimentation, which tends to build the successive encroachment of the integration process on the previous stratifications. We therefore take note of the presence of anomalies in the European order from the point of view of the democratic deficit, since executive power is fragmented into "bits and pieces"[48] (involving fourth and fifth and further (sub) branches of government and, therefore, the complex of non-majoritarian unelected agencies: administrative bodies, expert bodies, mixed public-private subjects), but the reforms aiming to gradually reduce the dimensions of the problems to make the invisible material Constitution visible are also described. Institutional fragmentation and pluralism, on the other hand, are part of the genetic patrimony of the European legal system and are dictated by the accentuated degree of conflict that arises from the multiplicity and diversity of institutional actors. In this respect, Curtin emphasizes how the renewed set-up introduced by the Lisbon Treaty, but also the tendencies of the European judiciary in recent years, have produced waves of reform aimed at smoothing out certain corners of the democratic deficit. The Lisbon reforms are examined in relation to political executive power (the European Council is described as the queen bee which directs and controls; the Council of Ministers

47 P. Lindseth, 'The Metabolic Constitution and the Limits of EU Legal Pluralism', in G. Davies and M. Avbelj (eds), *Research Handbook on Legal Pluralism and EU Law* (Northampton, MA: Elgar, 2018) 223 ff.

48 D. Curtin, 'The Constitutional Structure of the Union: A Europe of Bits and Pieces' (1993) 30 *Common Market Law Review* 17 ff.

as an institutional chameleon, and the European Commission, the 'normalized' executive), and from the administrative point of view (here Curtin carries out an interesting mapping of European civil servants European professional staff – national experts, and members of the 250 or so management committees – analyzing in depth how acts are drafted and the degree of autonomy of the bodies that make up the executive; lastly, she highlights how classic integration by stealth has been flanked by more pronounced forms of delegated legislation, which could lead to the gradual demise of comitology), and especially the 'satellites' gravitating into orbit ("the unseen hands", as Curtin defines them: ECB, Europol, Eurojust, committees, executive and auxiliary agencies, mixed European-national bodies, private delegated entities; independent or semi-independent bodies, which are also set up eminently on the basis of technical expertise). In the 1990s, some bodies were the subject of judicial investigations for maladministration and corruption. Most of these bodies, in particular some categories of 'satellites' gravitating into the orbit of the Commission, still pose considerable problems for a number of reasons: overstepping their powers (also as a result of the jurisprudential erosion of the principle of institutional balance, deriving from the so-called Meroni doctrine[49]); a high level of technical discretion; lack of transparency; participatory shortfall, and procedural[50] guarantees, in addition to access to justicial mechanisms. In the wake of the economic-financial crisis, whose effects have been asymmetrical,[51] some of these bodies have assumed a crucial position in the European institutional set-up: in particular, the ECB is now "the actor with most *de facto* political power"[52] and, although it is, of course, an independent and technical body, it is the one that, by managing the EU's monetary and financial policies, currently wields the greatest and most intrusive executive[53] power and is the one that can tip the scales of the ongoing European conflict. In Deirdre Curtin's view, possible

49 This is the well-known *ESMA* case, CJEU, Grand Chamber, 22 January 2014, Case C-270/12. On this topic see, among others, M. Simoncini, 'The Erosion of the Meroni Doctrine: The Case of the European Aviation Safety Agency' (2015) *European Public Law* 309 ff.

50 On these aspects see, in particular, G. della Cananea, *Due Process of Law Beyond the State. Requirements of Administrative Procedure* (Oxford: OUP, 2016). See also J. Mendes, *Participation in EU Rule-making. A Rights-Based Approach* (Oxford: OUP, 2011).

51 C.J. Bickerton, D. Hodson, U. Puetter, 'The New Intergovernmentalism: European Integration in the Post-Maastricht Era' (2015) 53(4) *Journal of Common Market Studies* 703.

52 D. Wilsher, 'Law and the Financial Crisis: Searching for Europe's New Gold Standard' (2014) *European Law Journal* 273. Concerning the need for some form of accountability of the ECB see, among others, C. Pinelli, 'Cittadini, responsabilità politica, mercati globali' (1997) *Rivista di Diritto Costituzionale* 60 ff.

53 D. Curtin, 'Democratic Accountability of the EU Executive Power: A Reform Agenda for Parliament', in F. Fabbrini, E. Hirsch Ballin, H. Somsen (eds), *What Form of Government for the European Union and the Eurozone?* (Oxford, UK; Portland, Oregon: Hart, 2016) 180 ff.

routes for gradually overcoming these shortcomings include allowing the Court of Justice a proactive role oriented towards bringing reuniting the organizational and functional fragmentation of the executive (it is in this sense that the jurisprudence aimed at moving beyond the pillars through the courts should be read, for example) and "constitutional geology" (constructing internal "constitutional tunnels" – *Hauptala, Pupino* and others – and the defence of internal constitutionalism against external challenges – cases *Kadi/Yusuf* and others), to protect the internal and external autonomy of the European institutions, greater transparency, removing the veneer of opacity that shrouds the activities of European bodies (especially in the more sensitive areas, such as the monetary and financial[54] market supervision sectors), greater involvement of national parliaments, particularly in the form of information and participation in debate; the affirmation of an organizational principle of accountability, through ex-post controls on results, audit procedures, and sanctioning mechanisms. For Curtin, in short, a "living, evolving, sedimentary (small 'c') constitution" is gradually taking shape in Europe and, although there is still a long way to go, we can look forward to what lies ahead with confidence: "we are at the end of the beginning and not at the beginning of the end".[55]

3. Constitutionalizing and democratizing the European order

These two different visions lead the way to some considerations which we will outline here. The process of European integration has certainly drawn nourishment from administrative law in implementing the founding treaties and constructing organizational and functional relations between European institutions and the member states. It began with top-down governance, with the institutional structures and the administrative acts, but at the same time from below with regard to the nature of structures and work.

European integration has advanced by stages since them, gradually occupying the space already belonging to the constitutional law of states, not least because the boundaries between the two areas of law are becoming increasingly blurred and there has been a process of exchange whereby constitutional law has been administrativized and administrative law has been constitutionalized.

This gradual backwards shift (from administrative law to constitutional law) has highlighted – especially in periods of stagnation and difficulty – problems with the 'democratic hold' of the system, both in terms of political and

54 On the new structure of financial market supervision and the new European authorities, see, among others, V. Cerulli Irelli, 'Dalle agenzie europee alle autorità europee di vigilanza', in M.P. Chiti and A. Natalini (eds), *Lo spazio amministrativo europeo. Le pubbliche amministrazioni dopo il Trattato di Lisbona* (Bologna: il Mulino, 2012) 137 ff.; E. Chiti, 'Le architetture istituzionali della vigilanza finanziaria', in G. Napolitano (ed.), *Uscire dalla crisi*, op. cit., 157 ff.

55 D. Curtin, *Executive Power of the European Union*, op. cit., 300–303.

institutional accountability and from the perspective of the informative and participatory visibility of procedures.

If, however, one looks at the European legal system from a dynamic perspective, its historical development allows us to appreciate the progress made over the decades, leading to greater constitutionalization of the European legal system, and the important work that the Court of Justice, in particular, has done to keep the system united, while at the same time guaranteeing a broad degree of differentiation. It is therefore a process that has to proceed with caution and follow the rhythm of the waves, so to speak, but it shows no sign of coming to a halt. It has been noted that "the Eurozone crisis has led to perhaps the most difficult period of deepening of integration since the European Communities were founded",[56] with considerable leaps forward in the area of fiscal, financial, and banking union and the competences of the European Parliament, also with greater involvement of the national parliaments. What emerged from the Lisbon Treaty was in any case considered, despite the lack of a European constitution, a significant step towards a European constitutional project,[57] but it was also remarked, less optimistically, that "it is as if all the recipes for attempting political integration were at least stretched out in the Treaties: their incompleteness and pluralism leave every possibility open from an experimentalist standpoint".[58] With the pandemic crisis, as we have seen in the previous chapter, the process of European integration has accelerated even more, with a consistent revival of the Community model and recovery of the central role of the European Commission (with the European Council retaining prominence). But, as is often the case with undulating processes, there has also been some reflux, for example in the direction of less space for the European Parliament and the parliaments of the member states, also as a result of the strict time limits required by the emergency discipline.

On the other hand, there is also the issue of the meaning of democracy that one adopts to evaluate the evolutionary processes underway.

First of all, the continental order, accused of being weak in terms of democracy, is the very one that intervenes internally (but not very effectively at this time) to counter the serious democratic shortcomings of member states (such as Hungary, Poland, Romania, and Bulgaria) and acts externally to defend the democratic values and principles of the European order (with regard to international bodies: the UN with the *Kadi* case, but also with regard to states, such as Turkey). We have already reflected on rule-of-law backsliding, but we must now at least restate that the protection of rule-of-law principles has returned, at

56 D. Kelemen, 'Towards a New Consititutional Architecture in the EU?', in F. Fabbrini, E. Hirsch Ballin, H. Somsen (eds), *What Form of Government for the European Union and the Eurozone?*, op. cit., 197 ff.

57 See, for example, I. Pernice, 'The Treaty of Lisbon: Multilevel Constitutionalism in Action' (2009) *Columbia Journal of European Law* 349 ff.

58 A. Guazzarotti, *Crisi dell'Euro e conflitto sociale. L'illusione della giustizia attraverso il mercato* (Milan: Franco Angeli, 2016) 62.

least formally, to the centre of the political agenda of the European institutions, even if, due to the war in Ukraine and the energy crisis, the severity towards Poland and Hungary of just a few months ago has slackened fairly rapidly. Moreover, and especially with regard to Poland, this is a sign of a growing political or geopolitical decision-making by the European institutions, which have applied European discipline in an asymmetric way. The question arises as to whether this increase in political decision-making is positive: in any case, at times, the political decision will also produce distortion.

Again, it should be borne in mind that the noted democratic shortcomings are often accentuated by a kind of statist presbyopia, the lack of connection between national politics and European policy, and the idea of democracy typical of nation-states. Much thought has been given, in this regard, to the new conformation of post-national democracy; in this sense, the experience of the European Union has been criticized as a form of experimentation with cosmopolitan democracy, moving in the direction of a federation beyond the nation-state: "the European Union can be understood as a decisive pact on the way to a world society governed by a constitution".[59] In recent years, however, Kantian constitutional cosmopolitanism has once again begun to fray. On the one hand, thirty years after the fall of the Berlin Wall, the crisis brought about by the Ukrainian war has accelerated the return to a geopolitical division into blocs and spheres of influence; on the other, the financial crisis has favoured the rise of populist currents, which oppose supranational integration and favour fragmentation and isolation at the European level. One thing is certain, however: in addition to taking into account the peculiarities of the European order, it must also be considered that, as part of a supranational order, one opts for a shared democracy,[60] i.e., one that is accountable not only to one's own citizens and parliaments but also to the national communities of the other member states. This phenomenon has also been called *deliberative supranationalism.*[61] Looking, for instance, at monetary and financial policies from this angle, we find consequences regarding distinct forms of legitimization of the European

59 J. Habermas, *The Crisis of the European Union: A Response* (Cambridge, UK; Medford, MA: Polity Press, 2012) 34.

From different perspectives, but with reference to the global extension of the democratic project, see J.-C. Piris, *Does the European Union Have a Constitution? Does it Need One?*, Harvard Jean Monnet Working Paper, 5/00 (Cambridge, MA: Harvard Law School, 2000); see also Y. Meny, 'Conclusioni. Una Costituzione per l'Europa?', in S. Fabbrini, *Le istituzioni dell'Unione europea in prospettiva comparata*, in *L'Unione europea. Le istituzioni e gli attori di un sistema sovranazionale*, op. cit., esp. 310.

60 S. Piattoni, 'Is the EU a Representative Democracy? The Normative Debate and the Impact of the Euro-crisisi', in F. Fabbrini, E. Hirsch Ballin, H. Somsen (eds), *What Form of Government for the European Union and the Eurozone?*, op. cit., 133 ff.

61 C. Joerges, J. Neyer, 'From Intergovernmental Bargaining to Deliberative Political Processes' (1997) 3 *European Law Journal* 273 ff.; idem, '"Deliberative Supranationalism" Revisited' (2006) 20 *EUI Law* 6.

bodies in charge of regulating and supervising them which may point towards a different outcome from what might be achieved through the traditional, national notion of democracy.

Lastly, forms of legitimation (output legitimation) that derive from a neo-functionalist reading of the integration process and are mostly linked to administrative law have been envisaged; for instance, legitimation by results has been proposed as a variant of legitimation through law, achieving high levels of economic and social development.[62]

Nevertheless, as we have seen, there are certainly areas with unresolved issues. The technically unbalanced *policy without politics*[63] typical of the European legal system leads to a lack of social legitimacy, given the substantial lack of a collective identity. This form of legitimation comes about, of course, through the sharing of a series of elements (cultural, values, social) and the passage of time, although it can be stimulated by developing mechanisms of deliberative community involvement. In this sense, action can also be taken from the procedural point of view by adopting legislation to promote transparency and the participation principle in the European legal system and the member states. For example, there has long been talk of a European law on administrative procedure, although for the time being it is still a mere proposal. But would this be sufficient to redress the lack of accountability? Or would it be necessary to take the twofold path of political representation through electoral mechanisms and by increasing the legislative power of the European Parliament? And, in so doing, provide an adequate voice for minorities and oppositions? It is clear that this solution would allow politics to enter the European order through the front door. But is such an option viable in the short term[64]? And which institutional framework and form of government should be preferred? Should the state model be transplanted to the European level? Above all, is such a sudden change desirable, or would it risk upsetting already precarious balances?

As has been remarked,

> The European recipe is complicated. If you add too much supranationalism, you risk losing the independence of the Commission and blocking the

62 M.P. Chiti, 'La legittimazione per risultati dell'Unione europea quale "comunità di diritto amministrativo"', in F. Wollenschläger and L. De Lucia (eds), *Staat und Demokratie* (Tübingen: Mohr Siebeck, 2016) 79 ff.

63 V. Schmidt, *Democracy in Europe: The EU and National Polities* (Oxford: OUP, 2006) 157 ff.

64 The science of constitutional law has long focused in great deal on this point, highlighting the possible drawbacks of a sudden shift of governance structure in favour of the European Parliament: see, among others, J.H.H. Weiler, 'Parlement européen, intégration européenne, démocratie et légitimité', in J.V. Louis and D. Waelbroek (eds), *Le Parlement européen dans l'évolution institutionnelle* (Bruxelles: Editions de l'Université de Bruxelles, 1988) 340; D. Grimm, 'Does Europe Need a Constitution?' (1995) *European Law Journal* 296.

> path to integration. But if you add too little, you risk blocking the decision-making process, or allowing some States to prevail over others. If you put too many European constraints on national political processes, you risk weakening the 'internal' accountability of national governments and parliaments. But if you put in too few, you risk weakening the 'external' accountability of domestic institutions *vis-à-vis* the citizens of other member States. If you proceed too fast in the political integration of the Union, you risk fragmenting its membership. But if you proceed too slowly, you risk undermining the ability of public institutions to govern economic and social phenomena now taking place on a territorial scale larger than the State. If you move too close to the state model, you risk having a super-State. But if you get too close, you risk entrusting highly political choices to an international organization whose democratic legitimacy appears too indirect to be sufficient.[65]

If, as we believe, it is more important to consider the issue from a perspective of becoming, we must reason, step by step and with prudence, on measures for improving the legal system, taking into account the fact that the path being travelled is new to constitutional democracies and that we are dealing with fragile mechanisms which must be handled with care and circumspection, in search of the right balance, advancing with greater or lesser speed depending on the times we are living through and the conditions created by the context.

It is no coincidence that the 2017 white paper on the Future of Europe[66] opens with a sentence uttered by Robert Schuman on 9 May 1950: "Europe will not be made all at once, or according to a single plan. It will be built through concrete achievements which first create a *de facto* solidari."

Scenario No. 5 in the white paper is "Doing much more together". But the premises laid by the European Commission document itself are not the best. On the one hand, the social dimension – solidarity, the democracy of the decision-making processes – is marginal compared to the sections devoted to the market, budget and finance, and the ability to achieve results.[67] On the other hand, as we shall see below, the context seems to point more towards scenario No. 3,

65 S. Battini, 'Review of "F. Fabbrini, E. Hirsch Ballin, H. Somsen (eds), *What Form of Government for European Union and the Eurozone?*"' (2016) *Rivista trimestrale di diritto pubblico* 252.

66 European Commission COM(2017) 2025 of 1 March 2017, *Libro Bianco sul Futuro dell'Europa. Riflessioni e scenari per l'UE a 27 verso il 2025* (Brussels: Ufficio delle pubblicazioni dell'Unione europea, 2017). The five scenarios the white paper addresses are: "Carrying on", "Nothing but the single market", "Those who want more do more", "Doing less more efficiently", "Doing much more together".

67 It is more reasonable, however, for them to be included in the so-called Five Presidents' Report, *Completing Europe's Economy and Monetary Union*, Brussels, 2015, considering that the document focused primarily on monetary and economic aspects. Yet, the 2015 document also mentioned interventions to ensure "democratic accountability, legitimacy and institutional strengthening" (p. 16 ff.).

"Those who want more do more". Compared to 2017, however, the situation has changed radically, with the pandemic crisis, the NGEU and the Conference for the Future of Europe, but also with the geopolitical crisis caused by the war in Ukraine.

That said, we may conclude by confirming that advances in procedural legitimacy and legitimation by results are certainly to be welcomed, as are other indirect forms of legitimation. But a democratic system is naturally linked to the participation of the people in political decision-making processes, which can occur through methods of representative democracy or forms of direct democracy: in short, it is clearly necessary to aim for democratic legitimization of a political[68] nature in Europe as well. It is true that state democratic systems, even those with the longest tradition, are experiencing difficulties in terms of the resilience of their democratic structures. Suffice it to think of the United States and the heated debate on the exercise of presidential prerogatives, which is putting the relationship between the federal executive and Congress under strain.[69] And there is no guarantee that representative democracy can offer protection against forms of political hijacking by economic-financial lobbies (as has also occurred in the major Western democracies in recent decades). But the difficulties encountered by national democracies do not allow us to infer that the pursuit of such democratic objectives should not be on the agenda of more developed systems, even if they are specific and of a supranational nature. It is, in short, a necessary, though not sufficient, condition, which we must strive to achieve as soon as the contextual conditions allow.

In finding the right balance, the first step is to find and maintain the correct equilibrium between economic, political, and social forces. As we shall see, this task falls primarily on the legal system and, albeit overlapping, takes priority over the object of reflection in this chapter, as it is extremely difficult to maintain a high level of democracy in an order with clearly social forces: economic, political, corporate, etc. The thesis on which we have reflected so far is that the balance between the different thrusts of the social sciences has for some time been broken, favouring economics, and that work must be done to find a new balance. Basically, as Matthias Goldmann suggested in the light

68 See, in this regard, G. Falcon, 'People, Peoples, Democratic Deficit and "Output Legitimation" in the European Union', in F. Wollenschläger and L. De Lucia (eds), *Staat und Demokratie*, op. cit., 103 ff.

69 See, most recently, J. Mashaw, D. Berke, 'Presidential Administration in a Regime of Separated Powers: An Analysis of Recent American Experience' (2018) 35 *Yale Journal of Regulation* 549. Peter Strauss was the first US scholar to examine the issue. See, among his numerous contributions, P.L. Strauss, 'The Trump Administration and Administrative Law' (2019) 94 *Chicago-Kent Law Review* 229–239; idem, 'The President and the Constitution' (2015) 65 *Case Western Reserve Law Review* 1151 ff.; idem, 'Overseer or "the Decider"? The President in Administrative Law' (2007) 75 *George Washington Law Review* 696 ff.

of Polanyi's seminal study of 1944, the mission is to "to re-embed the economy in society".[70]

Thus, after analyzing the two main weaknesses in European law, which can be effectively summarized as the 'juridification' of economic and financial rules and the 'technification' of European institutions in terms of both organization and function, it is necessary to veer decisively in the direction of European administrative law in order to examine the reasons for its success (in the face of the difficulties of European constitutional law), as well as which legal traditions have most influenced its development.

This is also necessary in order to highlight how the advances of administrative law in the European Union would come to nothing if they were not interconnected with the need to ensure a constitutional basis for the supranational system.[71]

In recent years, important steps have certainly been taken towards the constitutionalization of European Union law. This is mainly due to the repeated crises, which forced the European institutions and member states to find common solutions. The NGEU, as we have seen, is an economic-financial planning solution that combines administrative law and constitutional law. In particular, the emphasis placed by the NGEU on the rule of law has led to a considerable acceleration in constitutional terms, thanks mainly to the judgments of the European Court of Justice. In this sense, we are witnessing a gradual constitutionalization through crises and by the EU courts. Constitutionalization that also passes through mechanisms of administrative law. However, in many areas of European policies, such as migration policies and the related guarantees of human rights, not much progress has been made. It follows that there is still much to be done.

If we draw a line under what has been argued in this chapter, we can conclude that the European institutions have put in place policies that represent a balanced mix between the two theses, by Peter Lindseth and Deirdre Curtin, mentioned above. There is still a long way to go in terms of the growth of political processes, of transparency in technical mechanisms, of wider social and democratic legitimacy, but a first stretch of the path has been completed.

70 M. Goldmann, 'The Great Recurrence: Karl Polanyi and the Crises of the European Union' (2017) 23 *European Law Journal* 16.

71 This benefits both administrative law and constitutional law, but also the European Union and member states, as highlighted by P. Ridola in *Diritto comparato e diritto costituzionale europeo* (Turin: Giappichelli, 2010) 25 ff., which emphasizes the challenge facing constitutionalism today: opening up to the supranational dimension while also safeguarding the lasting spaces of statehood.

Chapter IV

The Ability of Administrative Law to Adapt and Expand as the European Legal Order Takes Shape

1 The enfranchisement of administrative law and difficulties relating to European constitutional law
2 Endogenous and exogenous legal traditions in the evolution of European administrative law: France and Germany; the United States
3 Lightweight Italian influence

1. The enfranchisement of administrative law and difficulties relating to European constitutional law

The functional evolution of the European legal system, which has taken place in successive waves, has often proved an obstacle to developing European constitutional law.[1] European administrative law,[2] on the other hand, has been able to go its own way, encountering fewer hurdles along its path.

This has led to a gradual enfranchisement of administrative law, especially over the last thirty years, accompanied by a substantial involution of the constitutional aspects of European law. This is not the place to analyze the evolutionary process in detail: we shall simply outline the main stages that have led to these different outcomes. As we have already hinted, the point of arrival is that administrative law alone, having extended beyond all expectations, is not enough to bring about integration. It requires a constitutional dimension, which, in turn, must be rooted – and grow – on terrain already laid by administrative law, in a return to a general public law perspective.

The difficulties surrounding constitutional law have arisen mainly from the circumstances we shall illustrate in this chapter. Through five successive phases of expansion in just over half a century, the population of the countries making

1 For a comparative and historical overview of European constitutional law, see P. Ridola, *Diritto comparato e diritto costituzionale europeo* (Turin: Giappichelli, 2010).
2 There is a vast literature on the foundation and development of European administrative law, but we may single out P. Craig, *UK, EU and Global Administrative Law: Foundations and Challenges*, The Hamlin Lectures (Cambridge: CUP, 2015) 313 ff.

DOI: 10.4324/9781003302094-5

up the European order has tripled, now exceeding half a billion inhabitants. Over the last twenty years, this population has grown by a third after the number of member states almost doubled during the first years of the new millennium. All this has led to a sort of aphasia of identity, which has severely weakened the ties born from a shared culture and values among the peoples of Europe (which had been stable up to the eighteenth century[3] before gradually diminishing with the introduction of borders set by the nation states[4] and weakened still further by the latest wave of new ones). The economic and financial crisis soon accentuated nationalist and populist movements.

Despite the considerable progress made over the last sixty years, the problem of which form of government to adopt has remained substantially unresolved. The historical ambiguities regarding relations between the Council and the Commission – and the ways decisions are reached – have led to an uneven

3 On this point, see the historical and cultural trajectory indicated by C. Pinelli, *Alla ricerca dell'autenticità perduta. Identità e differenze nei discorsi e nei progetti di Europa* (Naples: Editoriale Scientifica, 2017).

4 Numerous contributions have emphasized the question of identity in a variety of ways, sometimes stressing its presence but more often highlighting its absence (others, however, consider the question of identity superfluous to the construction of a legal system). It would be impossible to list such a vast bibliography here. We might simply recall an incidental, but strikingly frank, contribution to the debate: a paper by Henry G. Schermers, a leading Dutch scholar of European law, published in the Yale Law Journal for the 1991 symposium on Weiler's *The Transformation of Europe*. 'Hein' Schermers claimed that Weiler had underestimated the issue of cultural differences between the peoples of Europe, which were more pronounced than those between the inhabitants of the various states of the USA and North America as a whole: "For example, when a Dutchman speaks of Italians he often feels ill at ease. Italians are shorter and darker; they speak a language completely incomprehensible to the Dutchman. In addition, they take siestas, drink wine, and often practice a different religion. Culturally, most Dutchmen – and probably most Danes, Germans, and Englishmen – feel closer to Americans and Canadians than to Spaniards, Italians, and Greeks. This feeling of being different, this looking upon fellow Europeans as complete foreigners, affects the Common Market. For example, in the future it will be necessary to harmonize the public welfare systems of the Member States. Consequently, rich workers in Germany and the Netherlands will have to subsidize employment benefits for the poor in Greece and Portugal. At present, I doubt whether the German and Dutch labor unions (let alone the workers themselves) would be willing to make such a sacrifice. A sufficient level of solidarity does not yet exist" (H.G. Schermers, 'Comment on Weiler's "The Transformation of Europe"' (1991) 100 *Yale Law Journal* 2525 ff.). However, the situation has changed considerably since 1991. Life together in the EU by the European peoples has produced some positive results. And Art. 2 TEU has made progress in the medium term. However, identity distance remains and differences are accentuated especially in times of crisis, such as the current one, particularly in relation to sensitive issues such as financial, fiscal, and migration policies. These are the obstacles that most impede the full transition to European democratic society. On such issues, however, we refer to the optimistic reconstruction of A. von Bogdandy, *Strukturwandel des öffentlichen Rechts. Entstehung und Demokratisierung der europäischen Gesellschaft* (Berlin: Suhrkamp, 2022).

balance between the inter-state and Community approaches. Despite its increased representative and supervisory role compared with the purely consultative function of the early days, the intrinsic weakness of the European Parliament has led to a democratic deficit in terms of the traditional understanding of political representation. The complex mechanisms typical of international relations between states, which have produced variable geometries, have made it possible to identify several, but only partly overlapping, platforms. Thus, the often hybrid nature of the acts adopted by the European institutions, together with their implementation methods, the opacity and lack of accountability of the decision-making processes, the combination of hard and soft law activities, and the nature of the rulings of the Court of Justice as a true source of law (beyond the fact that the European Court has essentially played a fundamental role in the protection and affirmation of rights, despite its natural and genetic imbalance in favour of economic freedoms), have made the complex of European sources somewhat heterogeneous and elastic. The approach they adopt is more substantial than formal (suffice it to recall the theory of implicit powers and the flexibility clause), which has obvious consequences on the traditional hierarchy of sources.

All this has brought confusion regarding the attribution and exercise of powers within the European legal order, mainly because, as we have seen in previous chapters, it is an original order in which the typical features of the modern state are difficult to reproduce by merely transplanting them. In this regard, it has even been suggested that the constitutional paradigms usually evoked in relation to the European Communities are inadequate to describe these supranational structures. In fact, they are wholly administrative institutions operating as a multi-functional agency, "with executive, legislative, and adjudicative jurisdiction stretching across vast areas of economic and social regulation, unique in that it takes its mandate from multiple political principals, i.e., the Member States and their electorates". This reality is based on the assumption that

> an administrative perspective better explains the recent evolution of the EC's institutional law by viewing those changes as part of a political and legal strategy through which the Member States (the democratically-legitimate principals in the system) have sought to limit the normative autonomy of the Community as their agent, while not unduly impeding the progress of legislative and regulatory harmonisation.[5]

Admittedly, the distribution of competences was the subject of substantial interventions in the Lisbon Treaty since the measures envisaged to achieve a

5 P. Lindseth, 'Democratic Legitimacy and the Administrative Character of Supranationalism: The Example of the European Community' (1999) *Columbia Law Review* 628 ff., in particular 637 and 639. See, in this respect, the reconstruction in the previous chapter.

more adequate and more transparent distribution and definition of competencies between the Union and the member states in the draft European Constitution were substantially transposed into the treaties. The distribution of exclusive and shared competencies was better specified (as were the parallel ones and supporting actions), and the principle of attribution, aimed at delimiting the area of exclusive competencies, was reinforced. Mechanisms designed to make the distribution of powers less rigid, such as the flexibility clause and the principles of subsidiarity and proportionality, were also retained. However, there are still many grey areas. The main issue concerns the EU's external operations. Although there is a plan for a High Representative for Foreign Affairs, and foreign and security plans are fully incorporated in the Union's 'ordinary' policies, there is still a marked intergovernmental imprint on both since, in this case, it is a question of ceding areas of sovereignty in sectors that form the hard core of the states. It follows that each state is free to reach its own foreign and defence policy decisions, which means that shared external representation and a European defence system are still far off. Provision has also been made for the greater involvement of national parliaments,[6] but it remains to be seen how their roles will best be engaged.

There have been some interesting developments in the area of enhanced cooperation (Art. 20 TEU and arts. 326–334 TFEU), which may be considered to have a dual purpose: on the one hand, it can serve as a tool for overcoming deadlocks, especially in the light of the substantial enlargement of the number of member states. On the other, it may also be a way of introducing a multi-speed integration process, which may, of course, be a dynamic influence but also risks weakening the Union.[7] It has been observed, for example, that moving at different paces could strengthen the German policy of hegemony.[8] However, it should be borne in mind that, at this sensitive juncture, enhanced cooperation would be the rational choice in building an institutional architecture, especially considering the sovereignist bloc in Eastern Europe. The countries of the bloc have less democratic stability and are severely testing the principles of legal culture at the constitutional heart of the European Union. They are eroding the system's ideals and constitutional foundations from within. From this perspective, greater cooperation between the member states (some of the founding countries especially) could help boost an integration strategy based on the individual and the rights of the individual, one focused on the

6 In this regard, see the so-called Five Presidents' Report, *Completing Europe's Economy and Monetary Union*, 2015, which envisaged the assumption of critical roles for the European and the national parliaments (p. 17).

7 On this point, see one of the five scenarios in the European Commission's 2017 *White Paper on the Future of Europe* (cited above, fn. 65 chapter III), which states that only a few countries should move towards greater integration. On the advantages and disadvantages of a multi-track Europe, see, among many, J.-C. Piris, *The Future of Europe: Towards a Two-Speeds UE?* (Cambridge: CUP, 2011); P. De Pasquale, 'L'Unione europea e le nuove forme di integrazione' (2017) *Diritto pubblico comparato ed europeo* 671 ff.

8 U. Beck, *Europa tedesca* (Rome: Laterza, 2012) 45.

rule of law, the hallmark of the centuries-old Western European tradition. Integration of this kind has been contemplated several times before,[9] with renewal at the constitutional level – which, here too, can be realized by fostering integration in the administrative sphere.

The coexistence of the constitutions of the member states and the European 'Living Constitution', which has not always been an easy one, especially with regard to deep-rooted changes to the economic constitution, has led to fraught relations, especially with regard to the principles of law and how they are applied, the protection of fundamental rights, and the relationships between sources – in terms of both the theory of constitutional law and among practitioners.

In particular, the last few decades have witnessed ups and downs from the human rights perspective.[10] These have, on occasion, been marked by conflicting relations between the Court of Justice and the European Court of Human Rights. Nevertheless, it must be acknowledged that the work of the Court of Justice has led to the recognition and gradual codification of a number of values and principles, as well as the construction of a catalogue of rights that form the constitutional humus of the European Union.[11] It should, however, be emphasized that there is a wide gap between the rulings of the Court of Justice on the subject of rights, on the one hand, and the rules of the institutions responsible for the political and administrative structure of the European order, on the other. With its rulings, the European Court outlines the features of a panoply of constitutional safeguards that are sometimes not found in the measures imposed by other European institutions. There is thus a gap between institutions with political and technical powers and those with judicial functions at the European level.[12]

Nevertheless, the difficulties facing European constitutional law are reflected above all in the impasse encountered in any attempt to draft a European constitution.[13] While making no attempt to summarize the tortuous debate on a possible text, we can safely say that the process of rapprochement has been long and complex and reveals a number of positions that can only serve to demonstrate

9 See J. Delors, *Mémoires* (Paris: Plon, 2004) 577.

10 For an overall review, see, among others, G. de Búrca, 'The Evolution of EU Human Rights Law', in P. Craig and G. de Búrca (eds), *The Evolution of EU Law* (Oxford: OUP, 2011) 465 ff.; U. Bernitz, S. Weatherill (eds), *The Protection of Fundamental Rights in the EU After Lisbon* (Oxford, UK; Portland, Oregon: Hart, 2013); V. Kosta, *Fundamental Rights in EU Internal Market Legislation* (Oxford, UK; Portland, Oregon: Hart, 2015).

11 The protection of rights by the Court of Justice has been identified as one of the most positive outlooks for the European constitutional area in M. D'Alberti, *L'Unione europea e i diritti* (2016) Rivista trimestrale di diritto pubblico 761 ff.

12 Perhaps the most emblematic sector in this sense is immigration. For a recent contribution, see M. Savino, 'La crisi dei confini' (2016) *Rivista trimestrale di diritto pubblico* 739 ff.; idem, 'Creating a European Market for Refugees?' (2017) 2 *Diritto pubblico comparato ed europeo* 309.

13 The reference is to C. Pinelli, *Il momento della scrittura. Contributo al dibattito sulla Costituzione europea* (Bologna: il Mulino, 2002).

the need for political and constitutional unification.[14] There is a need for a European state with a federal structure,[15] the necessity to safeguard the specific nature of the Union[16] as a legal system; it is impossible to achieve political and constitutional union without creating a solid identity,[17] a catalogue of rights,[18] or remedying the democratic deficit.[19] There is a real need for a written European constitution[20] or, on the other hand, a non-absolute need for one, assuming the existence of a constitution (in formal as well as material terms)[21] or, in any case, a Living Constitution,[22] at least able to take the integration process forward. The implosion of the European

14 In these terms, see, for example, Y. Meny, 'La democrazia in tempi difficili', in C. Altini (ed.), *Democrazia. Storia e teoria di un'esperienza filosofica e politica* (Bologna: il Mulino, 2011) 233, critiquing Giandomenico Majone's thesis whereby the European Union, as a 'regulatory association', requires no democratic adjustment, nor does it suffer from a deficit in this regard (the reference is, of course, to G. Majone, 'The Rise of the Regulatory State in Europe' (1994) *West European Politics* 77 ff.; idem, *Regulating Europe* (London: Routledge, 1996); idem, 'Europe's "Democratic Deficit": the Question of Standards' (1998) 4 *European Law Journal* 18 ff.).

15 Among the scholars who have worked the most in this direction, we recall Deirdre Curtin and G. Federico Mancini. For the former, among the numerous contributions, see D. Curtin, 'Making a Political Constitution for the European Union' (2007) *European Journal of Law Reform* 65 ff. For the latter, see, among various other contributions, G.F. Mancini, 'Europe: The Case for Statehood' (1998) *European Law Journal* 29 ff.; idem, 'Argomenti per uno Stato unitario' (1998) *Sociologia del diritto* 7 ff.

16 Among the main supporters of this thesis, see J.H.H. Weiler, *La Costituzione dell'Europa* (Bologna: il Mulino, 2003). But for an older reflection on the nature of the European Order see, idem, *Il sistema comunitario europeo. Struttura giuridica e processi politici* (Bologna: il Mulino, 1986).

17 See, authoritatively, F. Cerutti and E. Rudolph (eds), *A Soul for Europe*, 2 vols (Leuven: Peeters, 2002).

18 Among many, L.M. Diez-Picazo, 'Una Constitucion sin declaracion de derechos? 'Reflexiones constitucionales sobre los derechos fundamentales en la Comunidad Europea' (1991) *Revista Española de Derecho Constitucional* 135 ff.

19 The debate is too vast to allow a summary of the bibliography on the subject. A brief outline is offered in S. Fabbrini, 'Le istituzioni dell'Unione europea in prospettiva comparata', in *L'Unione europea. Le istituzioni e gli attori di un sistema sovranazionale* (Rome-Bari: Laterza, 2002) 14 ff.

20 For a reconstruction of the attempt to adopt a written European Constitution and an analysis of its contents, see esp. J.-C. Piris, *The Constitution for Europe: A Legal Analysis* (Cambridge: CUP, 2006).

21 See, among others, S. Cassese, 'La Costituzione europea' (1991) *Quaderni costituzionali* 487 ff., for whom, even before the Maastricht Treaty, "There is no doubt that a European Constitution exists. It can be said that the national legal systems of the twelve countries adhering to the European Communities are part of a unitary system and that this system has a constitution, both in the sense of a constitutional order of a substantial or material kind, as understood by Dicey and Mortati, and in its formal meaning." Cassese then goes on to examine the institutional shape of the European Communities in terms of functions, organization, and competencies.

22 On the 'Living Constitution' see, for example, D. Curtin, Executive Power of the European Union: Law, Practices, and the Living Constitution (Oxford: Oxford University Press, 2009) esp. 10 ff.

constituent process in 2005, followed by the economic-financial crisis of 2007/8, meant abandoning the conventional method followed in 2003/4, which entailed a return to the intergovernmental approach (and the need to start afresh). Significant traces of the work done up to then (particularly regarding the institutional framework and the constitutional foundations of the European administration[23]) found their way into the Lisbon Treaty.[24] Still, we witnessed the remarkable downsizing of a process that had been evolving in the direction of a written pact among the peoples of Europe during the latter part of the twentieth century. Were the conditions not ripe for such a pact to hold? It is hard to say: it is certainly significant that the referendum was rejected by two 'old guard' countries (France and the Netherlands), as if to emphasize that, despite their initial presence, the principles and values underlying the constitutive act may have been lost over time (not least because of hasty and ill-considered enlargement to embrace countries in Eastern Europe). The events of Brexit and the pandemic crisis, however, showed weaknesses, but also the constitutional strength of the European legal order and the factual need for the European states to address together both economic and financial affairs and emergency issues.

In this regard, it has been observed that just as too much emphasis was laid on a European constitution during the Lisbon Treaty's gestation period, its failure, too, was overplayed in so far as the 'constitutional material'– the Living Constitution referred to above – filtered down in any case to some extent into the later treaties and continues to live on in concrete evolutionary stratifications: the process of integration has therefore never stopped. But European constitutional law has undoubtedly suffered a setback after losing its game at the turn of the millennium.

The journey of European administrative law has taken quite the opposite direction, however. European constitutional law studies, above all those regarding sources and institutional relations within the system, have been proliferating since the early decades of the millennium. From this perspective, scholarship on constitutional law got off to a head start compared with administrative law in studies on the European system. For a long time, in fact, the mere mention of European administrative law would have been considered an act of apostasy, for administrative law could only be linked to the state and could not exist beyond it. The last few decades have revealed a very different scenario, and – especially after the Single European Act – European administrative law has expanded remarkably in terms of the breadth of its functions

23 Article 298 TFEU is important in this respect. It contains the principles of independence, openness, and effectiveness of the European administration. On this Treaty provision see, among others, D. Sorace, 'Una nuova base costituzionale europea per la pubblica amministrazione', in M.P. Chiti and A. Natalini (eds), *Lo spazio amministrativo europeo. Le pubbliche amministrazioni dopo il Trattato di Lisbona* (Bologna: il Mulino, 2012) 45 ff.

24 See, esp., J.C. Piris, *The Lisbon Treaty: A Legal and Political Analysis* (Cambridge: CUP, 2010).

and competencies, as well as the development of principles and institutions and the complexity of its organization.

Thus, administrative law has freed itself of the state and has set out to explore virgin territory, experiencing a new period of flourishing and acting as a barycentre, a point of equilibrium for the legal space beyond the state.

As we shall see at the end of the volume, this is no longer sufficient since we are witnessing a two-way process of constitutionalization of administrative law and the administrativization of constitutional law,[25] which originated and developed in exactly the European context. From this point of view, administrative law can, and must, become (by identifying suitable institutional arrangements) the outrider for a renewed impetus in European constitutional law or, better – and jointly – European public law. It would not be reasonable to attempt to construct a new institutional and political structure for the Union without the decisive contribution of constitutional law.

2. Endogenous and exogenous legal traditions in the evolution of European administrative law: France and Germany; the United States

Having established this premise, namely that the European habitat has proved ideal for the development of administrative law but less so for constitutional law, it may be helpful to pause and consider the legal traditions that have most influenced the evolution of the European institutions, their bureaucracies, and administration, i.e., what these traditions have been and when they made their contribution. Doing so will highlight above all that among these traditions there is an influential law external to those of the member states: that of the United States.

The construction of the European institutions has been influenced by the major legal traditions of the most heavily industrialized countries, and administrative law is no exception.

The question of which legal systems and national legal traditions have most influenced the evolution of European administration (and, through gradual stratification, the disciplinary aspect of European administrative law) is very difficult to answer because the legal solutions adopted by the European institutions and courts have often been 'hybrid', representing a political and legal compromise between different options.

2.1. In the first decades of exploration on the subject of European administrative law, the two legal traditions that most influenced its development were undoubtedly those of France and Germany. There were several reasons for this.

25 See F. Wollenschläger's recent, 'Constitutionalisation and Deconstitutionalisation of Administrative Law in View of Europeanisation and Emancipation' (2017) *Review of European Administrative Law* 7 ff. For an older text, see S. Cassese, 'La costituzionalizzazione del diritto amministrativo' in *Studi in onore di Gaetano Silvestri*, vol. I (Turin: Giappichelli, 2016) 501 ff.

First of all, they were the two politically and economically strongest countries among the members of the European Communities. And since the United Kingdom joined much later, it is understandable that the most significant contributions to the original European legal platform came from France and Germany. As Yves Meny put it, why

> did the original community often have a Franco-Germanic flavour? (...) For the simple reason that, at that time, the German and French bureaucracies were fairly dominant and 'sold' their solutions or had them bought since it is best for a bureaucracy if it can sell to others the solutions it has already adopted. (...) In some fields, for example, the Germans were particularly adept because, especially in the economic and industrial fields, there is a much stronger tradition of standards than in other countries.[26]

Second, the French legal system has the longest tradition in the field of administrative law, so, naturally, the main structural and procedural solutions were initially inspired by this model. At the same time, Germany has a long tradition in the general principles of the rule of law, which has strongly inspired the European institutions and, in particular, the European Court of Justice.

Third, Germany and France both perceived the fundamental importance of the new EU administration from the outset. This is particularly true of Germany: its institutions immediately realized the need to send their best officials to the European institutions and studied in depth the legal regime regulating employment relations in Europe and those with the national administrations of origin.[27] Italy, for example, came to this realization very late.

2.2. Lastly, there were also reasons directly linked to institutional leadership: it must not be underestimated to what extent the history of institutions and legal principles is human-made. The institutional and legal foundations of the European Communities were mainly laid, of course, by Frenchmen Jean Monnet,[28] Robert

26 Y. Meny, 'Amministrazioni pubbliche e ordinamento europeo: esperienze comparate', in L. Vandelli, C. Bottari, D. Donati, Rimini, Maggioli (eds), *Diritto amministrativo comunitario* (Rimini: Maggioli, 1994) 264. This reasoning also applies, in the opposite sense, to other countries, such as Italy, which, due to their inability to grasp, or their underestimation of, the phenomenon, have clearly not been able to operate so incisively.

27 A. Grilli, *Le origini del diritto dell'Unione europea* (Bologna: il Mulino, 2009) 185 ff.

28 On Monnet, see, first of all, his memoirs: J. Monnet, *Mémoires* (Paris: Fayard, 1976).

Monnet's life was, of course, an adventurous one spent in pursuit of the ideal of European unity. As early as 1940, he was the mind behind Churchill's proposal for Anglo-French union before the German invasion of France: see, among others, E.R. Papa, *Storia dell'unificazione europea. Le origini e la crisi di un progetto rivoluzionario*, new edition (Florence-Milan: Giunti-Bompiani, 2017 (1st ed., Milan: Bompiani, 2006)) 64 ff.

Much has been written about the principal founder of the European order: among others, E. Roussel, *Jean Monnet 1888–1979* (Paris: Fayard, 1996); more recently M.

Schuman,[29] Paul Reuter,[30] Pierre Uri,[31] Germans Konrad Adenauer[32] and Walter Hallstein[33] (as well as, alongside them, at least Belgians Paul Van Zeeland[34] and Paul-Henri Spaak,[35] Dutchman Wim Beijen,[36] and Italian Alcide De Gasperi[37]).[38] The first two advocates general of the European Court of Justice were a Frenchman, Maurice Lagrange[39] (from 1952 to 1964), and a German, Karl Roemer (from 1953 to 1973): the extent of their influence on the development of European law has been well documented in studies on the history of the Court.[40] And in this

Adam, *Jean Monnet. Citoyen du monde. Une pensée pour aujourd'hui* (Paris: L'Harmattan, 2016); K. Schwabe, *Jean Monnet. Frankreich, Die Deutschen Und Die Einigung Europas* (Baden-Baden: Nomos, 2016).

29 See, among others, R. Poidevin, *Robert Schuman, homme d'État, 1886–1963* (Paris: Imprimerie nationale, 1986); R. Lejeune, *Robert Schuman: père de l'Europe 1886–1963: La politique, chemin de sainteté* (Paris, Fayard, 2000); H.J. Benning, *Robert Schuman: Leben und Vermächtis* (Oberpframmern, Verlag Neue Stadt, 2013); G. Knepper, *Robert Schuman: La politique pour vocation* (Paris, Éditions Salvator, 2023); M. Kontz, *Robert Schuman: Eine Biografie in Zeitzeugenberichten* (Amsterdam, Brill/Schöning, 2023).

30 Among others, J. Combacau, '*Paul Reuter, le juriste*' '*(1989)*' *Annuaire français de droit international* 7 ff.; A. Cohen, '*Le Plan Schuman de Paul Reuter entre communauté nationale et fédération européenne*' (1998) *Revue française de science politique* 645 ff.

31 The latter, an economist and Monnet's right-hand man, was the architect of the European Commission and the common market, as well as the drafter of the 1956 Spaak report, approved at the Venice conference: see, among others, M.J. Dedman, *The Origins and Development of European Union 1945–95* (London; New York: Routledge) 95–100.

32 See, among others, H.-P. Schwarz, *Adenauer. Der Aufstieg 1876–1952* (Stuttgart: DVA, 1986); idem, *Adenauer. Der Staasmann 1952–1967* (Stuttgart: DVA, 1991).

33 On the important role of Walter Hallstein, first President of the European Commission, see, recently, A. von Bogdandy, 'Von der technokratischen Rechtsgemeinschaft zum politisierten Rechtsraum – Probleme und Entwicklungslinien in der Grundbegrifflichkeit des Europarechts ('From a Technocratic Legal Community to a Politicized Legal Space: Problems and Developments in the Basic Conception of European Law')', Max Planck Institute for Comparative Public Law & International Law (MPIL) Research Paper no. 2017–12, https://ssrn.com/abstract=2971097. See also W. Loth, W. Wallace, W. Wessels, *Walter Hallstein: The Forgotten European* (New York: St. Martin's Press, 1998); M. Schönwald, *Walter Hallstein, Ein Wegbereiter Europas* (Stuttgart, Kohlhammer Verlag, 2017).

34 V. Dujardin, M. Dumoulin, *Paul Van Zeeland 1893–1973* (Bruxelles: Racine, 1997).

35 P.-H. Laurent, 'Paul-Henri Spaak and the Diplomatic Origins of the Common Market, 1955–1956' (1970) 85 *Political Science Quarterly* 373 ff.

36 A.E. Kersten, 'Beijen, Johan Willem (1897–1976)', in *Biografisch Woordenboek van Nederland*, 2013, http://resources.huygens.knaw.nl/bwn1880-2000/lemmata/bwn2/beijen.

37 See in particular, among others, P. Craveri, *De Gasperi* (Bologna, il Mulino, 2015).

38 At a later stage, as is well known, the leading role of the French at the European Commission was fundamental; suffice it to recall Robert Marjolin, François-Xavier Ortoli, Jacques Delors.

39 See R. Greaves, 'The First Advocate General, Maurice Lagrange', in N. Burrows, R. Greaves, *The Advocate General and EC Law* (Oxford: OUP, 2007).

40 See, among others, A. Grilli, *Le origini del diritto dell'Unione europea* (Bologna: il Mulino, 2009) esp. 52 ff.

regard too, the choices of some countries, including Italy, have long shown that they underestimate the phenomenon.[41]

A significant fact emerges from this list of Founding Fathers. With the exception of Monnet, who was essentially self-taught and had a cultural background in economics and several years' experience in international organizations, the other protagonists were all law graduates. This common element demonstrates, first and foremost, the importance of legal culture throughout Europe in forming the ruling class in the first half of the twentieth century. But it is also fundamental for understanding why the law was so deeply involved in the construction of the European order from the outset, quite apart from the fact that this should be taken for granted because the rules of coexistence in the new common order were being defined. Above all, it is emblematic of the prevalence of law in such a context, in order to construct a European order that would bring countries with common cultural roots together but which had become more divergent and distant in the course of a century and a half of closure and barriers between nations, a shared language had to be found. And the paradox was that, despite the close link to the experience of the modern state, legal language constituted the only common means of communication capable of keeping the Founding Fathers together in that delicate historical moment after World War II.

The role of German Walter Hallstein,[42] the first president of the European Commission from 1958 to 1967, was crucial in this respect. He was an academic, a professor of international law at the University of Frankfurt, where he also became rector. Adenauer good-naturedly reproached him for his scientific-academic approach to problems and his lack of political flair, which led to the clash with de Gaulle and the 'empty chair' crisis of 1965–66.[43] In a book of 1965, he wrote that what he was helping

41 The decisions taken often followed tortuous paths as there was no idea of sending the country's best resources either to the courts or the bureaucratic offices. An exemplary case was that of Giuseppe Federico Mancini, Italian advocate general at the Court of Justice from 1982 to 1988 (and judge of the Court of Justice from 1988 to 1999), diverted by Craxi to the Advocate General's Office after a failed attempt to have parliament elect him to the Italian Constitutional Court. Mancini, who was very successful at the Court of Justice, got there almost by chance as a second-best solution.

42 Hallstein published numerous volumes on European unity: see, among others, W. Hallstein, *United Europe. Challenge and Opportunity* (Cambridge, MA: Harvard University Press, 1962); idem, *L'unité de l'action européenne* (Losanna: CRE, 1965); idem, *La unificación de Europa: antecedentes y problema* (Buenos Aires: Instituto para la Integración de America Latina, 1966); idem, *L'Europe inachevée* (Paris: Laffont, 1970); idem, *Europa federazione incompiuta* (Milan: Rizzoli, 1971).

43 Among others, C. Malandrino, *Oltre il compromesso di Lussemburgo verso l'Europa federale: Walter Hallstein e la crisi della 'sedia vuota' (1965–66)* (Alessandria: Università del Piemonte Orientale, 2002); F. Di Nunno, *L'Italia e il compromesso di Lussemburgo, 1965–1966* (Rome: Edizioni Nuova Cultura, 2012).

to build was a Europe of diversities and their cultural synthesis, a Europe in which the Communities "are a creation of law" and "have given birth to a new legal order" in a "complete system of rules of law that autonomously and definitively governs the area entrusted to it". From his perspective as a legal theorist, he saw – from his strongly functionalist perspective – "European integration" as a "dynamic concept" in which "so-called economic integration is the core of the complete political federation".[44] He saw this original system as being built on the foundations of administrative law and the construction of a cohesive administrative-bureaucratic apparatus capable of handling European functions and policies.

And here, another key figure comes into play. The principal Founding Fathers of the European order have been mentioned above. But in addition to these political figures, there was also a *grand commis* who, working quietly in the shadows, undoubtedly constituted the nerve centre at the root of European administrative bureaucracy, driving its development, and therefore responsible for the birth of European administrative law from within. This was Frenchman Émile Noël,[45] executive secretary of the Common Market Commission from 1958 to 1967 and secretary general of the European Economic Community (later European Community) from 1967 to 1987. Born in Istanbul and ardently pro-Europe, he was a close collaborator of Jean Monnet. For three decades, Noël was at the head of the Community's administrative structure: with his impressive background and exceptional abilities, he was considered the true guide of the European Commission on a day-to-day basis throughout his extensive mandate. He introduced mechanisms typical of a ritual liturgy of sharing; he sought, through administrative structure, to give the Secretariat General and, consequently, the bureaucratic apparatus, a core position at the Thursday morning Directors-General meeting, the directors' assistants' meetings on Fridays, and the Commissioners' Heads of Cabinet on Mondays. He wielded considerable influence over recruiting new staff and informally established the criterion for respecting a national balance between officials. However, and above all, he was painstaking in assembling and cultivating "a genuinely supranational bureaucracy where a strong esprit de corps would quickly develop, but it was not immune to a technocratic mindset that the political world would soon resent".[46] This mentality, which consciously aimed to prioritize bureaucracy to the detriment of politics,

44 See E.R. Papa, *Storia dell'unificazione europea*, op. cit., 162.

45 On Noël, see esp., G. Bossuat, *Émile Noël, premier secrétaire général de la Commission européenne* (Bruxelles: Bruylant, 2011).

46 E. Calandri, M.E. Guasconi, R. Ranieri, *Storia politica e economica dell'integrazione europea. Dal 1945 ad oggi* (Naples: EdiSES, 2015) 109–110.

emerged clearly in Noël's way of considering the European order as an original system, in which "the decision does not result from a *compromis du hasard*, but rather from the independent proposal of a European institution".

We may deduce that the Franco-German axis played a fundamental role from the outset, placing its mark on the evolution of the European legal system from the point of view of administrative organization.

2.3. The primary coordinates of European administrative law were therefore inspired by French and German legal culture.[47] Their influence, as we have seen, was not represented in scholarship; on the contrary, it was initially exerted almost exclusively by practitioners and operators (or by academics on loan to the institutions). This is especially true of Germany, where the legal system's political apparatus operates independently of academia (from this point of view not entirely unlike the Italian context). This is quite the opposite of the French scenario, where scholars (and state bodies with legal competences – first and foremost the Council of State) often work alongside the political decision-making bodies, which systematically look to them for help and advice.

The French legal tradition has contributed to the development of European administrative law above all in the system of judicial review, and 'transplanting' national administrative law institutions at the European level. The organizational structure of the Court of Justice is based on the model of the French[48-] *Conseil d'Etat,* and the powers of the judges, especially their right to strike down, was inspired by Gallic administrative process: the archetypal theory of the administrative act comes from systems of administrative law and, in particular, that of France.[49] But transalpine influence over the Community's organizational apparatus is also palpable as, for example, the employment of civil servants was regulated along the lines of the French model. For historical

47 On this point, T. Tridimas, *The General Principles of EU Law*, 2nd ed. (Oxford; New York: Oxford University Press / Oxford EC law library, 2006) 23 ff. offers a very clear analysis, and his arguments are summarized here.

48 As M. Rasmussen recalls in 'The Origins of a Legal Revolution: The Early History of the European Court of Justice' (2008) *Journal of European Integration History* 83. Walter Hallstein pushed hard for the establishment of the Court of Justice, aiming to make it a judicial body not dissimilar, in its aims, from the *Bundesverfassungsgericht*. Jean Monnet, on the other hand, was not at all enthusiastic about such a solution.

Precisely for this reason, he enlisted the help of Councillor of State Maurice Lagrange (who later became the Court's first advocate general) in negotiations to build the European justice system along the lines of the *Conseil d'Etat*. After three weeks of talks, the result was a hybrid: "more than an international Court, but not quite a constitutional Court either, it was mainly an administrative Court, empowered to ensure that the HA would act within the powers granted by the Treaty" (A. Boerger-de Smedt, 'Negotiating the Foundations of European Law, 1950–57: The Legal History of the Treaties of Paris and Rome' (2012) 21 *Contemporary European History* 346).

49 The scholarship is vast, so we mention only one of the earliest studies on the subject: P. Becker, *Der Einfluß des französischen Verwaltungsrechts auf den Rechtasschutz in den Europäischen Gemeinschaften* (Hamburg: Heitmann, 1963).

reasons, then, the foundations of the European institutions and their law started with a French model but gradually moved away from this matrix over time.

The German legal tradition played a vehicular role above all in constructing the European general principles of law. This is particularly evident with regard to the principles of proportionality and legitimate expectations. The best-known example is that of proportionality, for which the Court of Justice has drawn inspiration from 'better law' or 'comparative assessment' (*wertende Rechtsvergleichung*), as it is known, which, in this case, honoured the three-step German theory of the principle of proportionality and judicial review based on the criteria of suitability, necessity, adequacy, or proportionality in the strict sense). More broadly, most of the areas relating to administrative procedure, administrative acts, and the scope of the discretionary power of European administrative activities take their inspiration from Germany.

Of interest in this regard is the thesis of Georg Nolte,[50] for whom the major German influence in the construction of European law may be attributed to the similarity, during the European Court of Justice's early days, between the theoretical position adopted by the German courts after the Second World War (which led – in the absence of an executive power, destroyed by the war – to a return to natural law) on the one hand and the search for constitutional principles capable of setting limits to the arbitrariness of the administration on the other. These principles, constructed by the German courts, formed the basis of a more extensive conceptualization of the new *Rechtsstaat* and a new constitutional order.

Shortly afterwards, the Court of Justice also sought constitutional legitimacy in order to demonstrate the supranational system's supremacy over national legal traditions. It had to solve the problem by recourse to general principles of law within a system and working with written sources inspired by the pursuit of economic objectives.

2.4. The common law made little impact in the early days of European law, due, of course, to Britain's late membership of the European Communities. But it is by no means foreign to the edifice of European institutions. Suffice it to recall, for example, the inspiration behind the structure of the EEC Commission – German and French influences aside – derived from the model of the secretariats belonging to international organizations, known to be of English origin. It should also be borne in mind that the importance of this legal tradition increased exponentially after the UK joined the European Communities. It has been noted, for example, that the work of the Court of Justice was influenced first by the French (and, to a lesser extent, the Italian) style, then by the German, and lastly, the UK style, adopting specific characteristics of the English judicial system.[51]

50 G. Nolte, 'General Principles of German and European Administrative Law: A Comparison in Historical Perspective' (1994) 57 *The Modern Law Review* 191 ff.

51 On this matter, see M.P. Chiti, 'I signori del diritto comunitario: la Corte di giustizia e lo sviluppo del diritto amministrativo europeo' (1991) 3 *Rivista trimestrale di diritto pubblico* 823.

Another influence originated in northern Europe. The Netherlands set the pattern for effectiveness and the dynamics of good administration (in this, Andreas Mathias Donner, president of the Court of Justice from 1958 to 1965, played an essential role; indeed, the judgments in the Van Gend en Loos and Costa/Enel cases were adopted under his presidency). And perhaps the greatest influence came from the Scandinavian countries (Sweden especially), with regard to implementing the principles of the rule of law, participatory democracy, and welfare. The Scandinavian influence became prominent not only with the introduction of the European Ombudsman but also in the wake of the scandal of the resignation of the Santer Commission in 1999 due to maladministration and corruption. Their model inspired an open government policy taking the cue from long-standing Scandinavian culture on such issues, with a general regime of hard law followed by soft law mechanisms, such as codes of conduct.

This was essentially an innovative hybridization phenomenon, a sort of European administrative *koine* drawing on numerous models (with a marked preference for the German and French ones):

> It is well known that the Coal and Steel Community was organized according to the French model of the *Commissariat du Plan*; the structures and functions of Euratom were borrowed from the French *Commissariat de l'energie atomique,* and the European Court of Auditors follows the lines of the German *Bundersrechtsnungshof.* The Commission is a *mélange* of still more national institutions. Its organization and rules of operation are halfway between a French ministry and the German *Bundeswirtschaftsministerium.* Some offices bear the distinct imprint of one or the other. For instance, the Secretariat General of the Commission is closely related to the General Secretariat of the French government (with the same tasks as 'memory' and general adviser to the apparatus). As for the personnel, staff regulations and careers seem to derive from the discipline of the French *fonction publique.* On the other hand, the codification of internal procedures, with the 'manual of procedures', inspection system, and ad hoc or permanent interdepartmental groups, reflect English influence.[52]

2.5. An interesting phenomenon described on several occasions in scholarship[53] is what might be called the 'feedback effect'. Principles, rules, and legal institutions are selected according to the experiences of the various member states; they are then applied and adapted to the European legal system (upstream phase). From

52 S. Cassese, 'Poteri divisi: amministrazione europea e amministrazioni nazionali', in *Studi in ricordo di Enzo Capaccioli* (Milan: Giuffrè, 1988) 26.

53 Cf. D. de Pretis, 'I principi del diritto amministrativo europeo', in M. Renna, F. Saitta (eds), *Studi sui principi di diritto amministrativo* (Milan: Giuffrè, 2012) 53 ff. Among many others, see M. Ruffert (ed.), *The Transformation of Administrative Law in Europe. La mutation du droit administratif en Europe* (Munich: Sellier, 2007).

there they radiate out again to the legal systems of the various member states (downward phase). It often happens that a principle or institution is inspired by the legal order of a particular member state, but it comes back to it when the provision is proposed at the European level. The best-known case is undoubtedly the principle of legitimate expectations, which came to Europe via the German legal system. Having passed through the filter of the European legal system, this principle then returned in various guises to the German legal order and has had a significant 'reflected' influence there.

From the political science perspective, a variant on this theme is the so-called adaptation pressure criterion, which aims to assess the extent to which national administrative traditions influence the implementation of European legislation. In this respect, of interest is a study by Christoph Knill in the late 1990s.[54] For Knill, a number of European directives were more dynamically implemented in systems in which the administrative tradition was best suited to the orientation of the European directives as a habitat for top-down legislation. In particular, with regard to the directives with the greatest impact on the need for administrative and structural reform in the member states, the United Kingdom showed the greatest ability to adapt. It had recently adopted the New Public Management reform policy (and was thus better equipped to transpose its model at the European level). On the other hand, the French administrative tradition proved less flexible, and that of Germany less so again.

2.6 It is no real surprise that the greatest influence on the evolutionary process comes from the legal traditions of the major EU member states.

Conversely, an interesting phenomenon emerging over the last few decades is the influence of the legal tradition of a nation outside the European legal system: the United States. This too comes as no surprise because US law has impacted not only on Europe but also on international bodies in a process that has impinged on the entire planet. At the same time, the United States, the most significant union of nation-states in a federal model, has always been considered a possible reference model for Europe.

American influence can be found in classic themes relating to the sphere of administrative justice, such as the intensity of judicial review. Let us consider, for example, the extent to which the 'hard look' doctrine has been absorbed by the case law of the Court of Justice, particularly between the 1990s and the early years of the new millennium.

Nevertheless, US influence (sometimes through the vector of international organizations) has been felt the strongest in the economic field thanks to the spread of the main principles regarding the organization and functioning of European institutions in European administrative law over recent decades. The most significant is the extensive network of agencies, clearly inspired by

54 C. Knill, 'European Policies: The Impact of National Administrative Traditions' (1998) 18 *Journal of Public Policy* 1 ff.

overseas practice.[55] Obvious examples are competition and antitrust law, whose development strongly reflects Anglo-American procedural mechanisms, on which the Commission and the Court of Justice have both relied to substantivize these areas. The gargantuan processes of the privatization, contractualization, outsourcing, and liberalization of the entire public sector (mainly affecting the financial markets and areas of economic interest), as well as those associated with the New Public Management business logic, also originate from Anglo-American practice. The new entrepreneurial bureaucracy, underpinned by performance and devoted to audit culture, also takes its inspiration from the United States. Even prioritizing financial objectives above the pursuit of other public goals is based on the logic of economic and financial effectiveness, which, driven by the United States and the large overseas corporations, has gained currency worldwide.[56]

There has also been an indirect influence that may, at least in part, be traced back to the United States. The idea of the artificiality of the market and the need to ensure compliance with the law, also politically influential in determining choices, was ultimately undermined.[57] Globalization led to the *lex mercatoria* (and, in particular, the financial *lex mercatoria*, which then gave rise, anomalously, to the world financial crisis of 2008) and other forms of transnational private law, implying the existence of a 'non-state objective law'. Indeed, "the 'naturalist' ideology, which appreciates the spontaneous roots of a law arising in society or business communities, has won out, so to speak, against the 'artificialist' idea on which the modern state was based".[58]

3. Lightweight Italian influence

3.1. Although Italy was one of the founding states of the European Community, it seems safe to say that its legal tradition has had minimal bearing on the evolution of European law, even though the first president of the European Court of Justice was an Italian, Massimo Pilotti.[59] In the first forty years of the Court's activity, only Alberto Trabucchi[60] and Giuseppe Federico Mancini

55 Important research could be carried out on the extent to which the American legal tradition has crossed the ocean and influenced the development of the European legal system.

56 On all these phenomena, among others, see the recent M.R. Ferrarese, *Promesse mancate. Dove ci ha portato il capitalismo finanziario* (Bologna: il Mulino, 2017), also containing further bibliographical references.

57 This role is market-conforming, not neutral; see. N. Irti, *L'ordine giuridico del mercato* (Rome-Bari: Laterza, 2004).

58 M.R. Ferrarese, *Promesse mancate*, op. cit., 172.

59 The position of the third most important 'Latin' country, Spain, was very different because Italy and France were founder members of the EEC, whereas Spain only joined in 1986, so it goes without saying that it was irrelevant until then.

60 Trabucchi's contribution was, of course, fundamental, especially for *Van Gend en Loos* and *Costa/Enel*: see E. Perillo, 'Alberto Trabucchi europeista: un tratto ancora

(who, as we have mentioned, arrived at the Luxembourg Court almost by chance as a fallback after failing to be appointed to the Italian Constitutional Court) left their mark on the orientation of its case law (in the last quarter of the century the choices were certainly more felicitous: for example, the contribution of prestigious jurists such as Antonio La Pergola and others has been fundamental; but by then most of the 'damage' had been done). This was mostly due to a provincial outlook and an underestimation of the impact (especially in the following decades) of the positions to be filled in the European sphere: politically appointed European posts were seen as a sort of 'elephant's graveyard' for declining political and professional staff: a 'golden retirement' for those who no longer had a significant contribution to make at home. If these were the usual reasons behind the choices, the nominees often lacked the motivation and vocation required to produce significant results.

3.2. If appointments from political quarters were not always felicitous, the introduction of national officials into European bodies has often proved extemporaneous, being dictated neither by thoughtful choice nor by reasoned planning. As clearly explained in an article some twenty years ago,[61] two main issues arose from bringing in national officials. The first was linked to their training (predominantly, if not exclusively, legal, making them ill-equipped to formulate proposals and discuss documents of a primarily technical or economic nature) and their behavioural characteristics (tending to shy away from responsibility, seeking refuge in political cover), as well as a structural issue (committees of experts having a less important role compared with other countries). Second, since major administrative decisions are taken by communities of technocrats in comitology committees, council working groups, and other committees of government experts,[62] the coordination procedures of the various member states are geared to ensuring the presence of their own officials in the various committees and, above all, to coordinating their positions in these committees in order to prevent contradictory and irreconcilable positions being held in different fora, have proved to be fundamental in the integration process.[63] As Balducci pointed out in 1994 (i.e., after Maastricht), apart from Luxembourg, which, being a small country, could rely on spontaneous coordination, the only nation without coordination procedures and protocols was Italy.

poco conosciuto del grande civilista patavino', in *La formazione del diritto europeo: giornata di studio per Alberto Trabucchi nel centenario della nascita, Quaderni della Rivista di diritto civile*, n. 14 (Padua: Cedam, 2007).

61 M. Balducci, 'Burocrazia comunitaria e amministrazioni nazionali nel processo decisionale dell'Unione europea' (1994) *Rivista trimestrale di scienza dell'amministrazione* 101 ff.

62 See, among others, M. Savino, *I comitati dell'Unione europea. La collegialità amministrativa negli ordinamenti compositi* (Milan: Giuffrè, 2005).

63 On why the Italian administration has been so absent in Europe, see M. Savino, 'L'amministrazione nazionale e l'Europa: l'eterna rincorsa', in L. Fiorentino (ed.), *Le amministrazioni pubbliche tra conservazione e riforme. Omaggio degli allievi a Sabino Cassese* (Milan: Giuffrè, 2008) 123 ff.

> As far as our country is concerned, not only is there no coordination between our officials working on relations with the Community institutions but our officials often do not attend committee meetings and, when they do, they have insufficient knowledge of the working languages. On several occasions, I have sat in on committee meetings as an observer, where the Italian representative, with laughable pronunciation, merely read out simple declarations of principle and kept out of the entire discussion, which he did not understand because of evident language problems.[64]

It is no wonder that our contribution has been lightweight. Of course, the situation today is quite different from a few decades ago, but how much was lost through Italy's inability to export our traditions and best practices, not to mention the failure to achieve results to its benefit? One thinks, for example, of how much the 'inaction of Italian bureaucracy' has been felt in Europe due to the country's lack of modernization in the area of structural funds.

3.3. The area where the Italian tradition was most decisive, as mentioned above, was the system of judicial protection, albeit in conjunction with those of other countries (first and foremost, France). The Italian system is often mentioned in foreign manuals of European administrative law, but only in relation to the notion of legitimate interest, and very little else.

3.4. Turning now to the role played by Italian legal scholarship, we encounter contrasting positions: it is generally considered marginal; but when it comes to European administrative law, the last three decades have seen it take centre stage.

Generally speaking – although here too the situation has changed for the better over the last 25 years – we might say that there are two main reasons why the Italian contribution to the construction of European law has been slight.

First, there is the two-way language gap: until few decades ago, Italian lawyers published almost exclusively in Italian, so practically no one can read this scholarship outside of Italy. Italian lawyers were on the margins of the continental academic circuit, which now has an extremely rich literature and operates through the lingua franca of English. The result was provincialism and isolation, and even when our jurists published innovative and academically stimulating writings, they remained outside European academic circles.

The other problem, even now, is the rigid distinction between areas of specialization, so law scholars are regimented into distinct academic fields, and interdisciplinarity is severely penalized in selection processes for academic positions. The result is a fragmented framework devoid of all-round scholars within which, as far as European law is concerned, scholars of international law and EU law considered themselves, until a few years ago, to be the repositories of sacred truth. Thus, if a constitutionalist, a commercial law specialist, an expert in employment law, or an authority on administrative law carried out studies in European law (even today, in the twenty-first century), he or she was

64 M. Balducci, op. cit., 111.

accused of encroaching on another's field and was often punished in selection procedures by purists in the micro-discipline for having addressed disciplines unrelated to the traditional scope of their professed subject area.

The extent to which Italian scholars of European law are outside the international and continental academic circuit can be illustrated by a brief example. Let us examine the fourth edition of Craig and de Búrca's (2008) texts of cases and materials pertaining to European law[65] and scan through the long lists of bibliographical references at the end of each of the 28 chapters. We find the merest trace of Italian scholarship: in over 1,200 pages, four scholars of European law, one of labour law, and one of administrative law, are cited.

Conversely, the picture that emerges from a similar experiment focusing only on European administrative law is very different. If we glance through the second edition of Paul Craig's volume on European administrative law (2012),[66] we can see (right from the first footnote) that Italian administrative law research has played a prominent role, especially in the last quarter century, thanks to Sabino Cassese and his school, the scholars linked to the *Rivista italiana di diritto pubblico comunitario*, founded in 1991 by Mario P. Chiti and Guido Greco, the *Trattato di diritto amministrativo europeo*, edited by Chiti and Greco,[67] and the Trent school led by Giandomenico Falcon.

This simple bibliographical comparison would seem to confirm that Italian administrative law scholarship has distinguished itself in what may generally be considered a somewhat limited area.

3.5. In order to appreciate the reason for the delay in understanding the emergence of a specifically European administrative law, but also to confirm that Italian legal scholarship has contributed to this process, chapter V will attempt to present a reconstruction of the historical development of European administrative law studies.

On the one hand, having focused on the traditions that have impacted on European administrative law, we must examine why scholars were slow to grasp the phenomena emerging in Europe and how, over the last few decades, administrative law has managed to carve out a significant role for itself in relation to legal developments associated with the new economic constitution and the expansion of the reforms taking place through privatization and liberalization, moving on to interpret the impact of the economic and financial crisis, as well as the pressures on the structure of European governance deriving from populism.

All this invites reflection on the role of the legal scholar (and, in particular, the scholar of administrative law), which needs to be rethought in today's scenario, as we shall see in the closing chapter.

65 P. Craig, G. de Búrca, *EU Law: Text, Cases and Materials*, 4th ed. (Oxford: OUP, 2008).

66 P. Craig, *EU Administrative Law*, 2nd ed. (Oxford: OUP, 2012).

67 M.P. Chiti and G. Greco (eds), *Trattato di diritto amministrativo europeo*, 1st ed. (Milan: Giuffrè, 1997), with one general volume and two specialist tomes; 2nd ed., 2007, with two general volumes and four specialist tomes.

Chapter V

The Science of Administrative Law and the Role of the Jurist in the Construction of the European Legal System

1 Why a diachronic analysis of the science of European administrative law?
2 The 1950s: the beginnings of European administrative law and the creation of an 'administrative atmosphere'
3 The 1960s and 1970s: the development of administration and the European Court of Justice's 'constitutionalization' of the Treaties
4 The 1980s and 1990s: the foundation of European administrative law and its science
5 The new millennium: the proactive role of administrative law studies between crisis and opportunity

1. Why a diachronic analysis of the science of European administrative law?

In order to fulfil the burdensome task of ultimate rebalancing described in the previous chapters, it is not enough to intervene only at the institutional and governance level, nor can the European Court of Justice, which, as we have seen, has been a major building-block in the construction of a Europe erected on the rule of law, take upon itself the enormous task of restructuring that is required.

It has emerged in the previous chapters that the European Commission has played, and continues to have, a fundamental role in identifying objectives suited to fostering European integration. From this point of view, the technical contribution of the Commission's officials and the members of the bodies associated with it creates an entirely new connotation, giving scientific substance to the governance choices of the European institutions. Alongside this technical aspect we also note the political contribution of the Council, the Commission's senior management, and the European Parliament, whose role has amplified over time. In a more oblique, but no less important, position in this delicate governance mechanism are the European agencies, which have made a significant mark on the acceleration of the integration process in recent decades. However, the greater prominence of the European institutions is not

DOI: 10.4324/9781003302094-6

sufficient, in isolation, to bring in a later, more cogent phase regarding the matter in question, one which is meant to lead to European political union.

Nor can this role as builder of the European 'cathedral' (a European democratic society, with its own identity, as theorized by Armin von Bogdandy[1]) be assumed exclusively by the European Court of Justice, which has played a fundamental role but already done far too much in terms of European institutional equilibria. It is well known, and has been the subject of much study,[2] that the Court of Justice has brought unprecedented subject matter and substance to European law, "drawing on the rich heritage of national legal traditions, shaped and adapted, however, into a kind of unique European *ius commune*: a common denominator of principles, ideas, and shared legal concepts. The daily work of Lagrange and Roemer is all too eloquent in this regard!".[3]

Admittedly, the European Court of Justice daily continues to make a fundamental contribution, but it is necessary, first of all, to try to create a system, a methodical analysis with a new institutional weft, implementing a technical-legal approach, at the same time presupposing an interdisciplinary knowledge base; second, the Court cannot be asked to dictate the new balances of the system in isolation since this would presuppose a legal and formal framework, even going further.[4] In recent years, the current president of the European Court of Justice, Koen Lenaerts, has strongly committed to emphasizing the Court's role as 'constitutional guide' of the European legal system, among other things, by stipulating agreements and protocols with the highest bodies of ordinary and administrative justice of the member states: an attempt to build a European judicial 'network' with the very purpose of revitalizing the integration process through the Court's 'constitutional' role (an operation that has been successful in the past).

Hence, it would appear that legal science must also share the burden of this fundamental task of reconstructing the legal platform and paradigms, precisely in view of the aspiration to elevate practical factors to the level of theoretical construction. In short, besides legislative procedure and judge-made-law, what is required is *Juristenrecht*.[5] This is an unmissable chance for legal science: it is the opportunity to return to a central position, or at least to assume a significant role once more, unlike in recent decades.

1 A. von Bogdandy, *Strukturwandel des öffentlichen Rechts. Entstehung und Demokratisierung der europäischen Gesellschaft* (Berlin: Suhrkamp, 2022).
2 See, among the most recent studies, chapter III of the book by A. von Bogdandy, *Strukturwandel des öffentlichen Rechts*, op. cit., 285 ff.
3 A. Grilli, *Le origini del diritto dell'Unione europea* (Bologna: il Mulino, 2009) 223.
4 On both points, however, of particular importance are the reflections of G. Itzcovich in *Teorie e ideologie del diritto comunitario* ("*Theories and Ideologies of Community Law*") (Turin: Giappichelli, 2006) in particular 268 ff., on the role of jurisprudence in the construction of legal orders, in the wake of the decline of the insularity of legal discourse.
5 B. Leoni, *Il diritto come pretesa* (Macerata: Liberilibri, 2004) 70–71.

Finding the keys to restoring the lost equilibria depends, first and foremost, on the science of administrative law, as it is necessary to start from an in-depth analysis – both from the historical point of view and with regard to the current organization and functioning of the European Union.

In a famous essay published immediately after World War II, Carl Schmitt argued that the scientific core of the continental jurist must be sought in the principles of law, because "It is in our preserving this indestructible core of every right against any disruptive enactment that the dignity placed in our hands lies, today in Europe more than at any other time and in any other part of the earth." Certainly, the exaltation of the principles of law by a scholar who had embraced Nazism and Fascism just a few decades earlier is striking. But if we can set aside the author's biography and the history of his ideas, focusing on the contents of the thesis he proposes, we can attempt to embrace the Plettenberg jurist's conviction, reinforced by post-war constitutionalism, that "Legal science is itself an authentic source of law." This contrasts with the French Revolutionary conception of the primacy of law, after which, in the course of the nineteenth century, scholarship doctrine ceased to be seen and valued as a science: "Positive law makes the jurist a worm in rotten wood," as Julius von Kirchmann asserted at the famous Berlin Conference of 1847. The situation worsened even more at the turn of the short century, with the so-called motorized legislation, which enabled legal science to stay abreast of sudden normative changes, so that technicians and legal practitioners, with their 'fast food' commentaries, ten-a-penny exegesis, the rudiment of the Court's latest pronouncement in textbooks, superseded academia. Motorized legislation is still being adopted to the detriment of the constructive power of the scholar-jurist. The subordination of legal science to regulatory technique "would decay into a no longer even particularly useful instrument, a prosthetic technical activity". The only possible antidote to 'légalité qui tue', against the risk of 'termitization', the point of reference of European legal science, "the first-born daughter of the modern European spirit, of modern 'western rationalism'", is the principles of law.[6]

Schmitt discerned and anticipated the important role of scholarship in the construction of European legal science, but, as has been observed,[7] he was thinking of continental scholarship in the absence of European institutions.

6 The quotations are taken from C. Schmitt, 'The Situation of European Jurisprudence, 1950', in A. von Bogdandy, R. Mehring, A. Hussain (eds), *Carl Schmitt's European Jurisprudence* (Baden-Baden: Nomos, 2022). The recent book is important because it also contains the English translation of Schmitt's 1936 essay, *The Historical Situation of German Jurisprudence*. Walter Lewald's review of the 1950 essay, and writings on Schmitt's work by Christian Tomuschat and Michael Stolleis, in addition to the editors of the volume.

7 A. von Bogdandy, *Strukturwandel des öffentlichen Rechts*, op. cit., 423 ff.

After Schmitt, there have been many theories, sometimes very different from each other, that have attempted to develop the common point of putting the right again at the centre of the system of social sciences.[8]

Today, on the other hand, as the European legal system matures we find ourselves reflecting on a single continental scientific edifice with an organic framework of European institutions that operate, in a totally new way, in the exercise of the three powers.

For these reasons, after dwelling on institutional equilibria, it is important to devote some space to the constructive capacity of European public law studies, in order to ascertain what its role has been in the past and what it is now.

This is an exploratory perspective given that, as seen above, entire libraries could be filled with tomes on the historical and institutional evolution of the European legal system and governance models. And much has also been written on the development of the European Court of Justice and its jurisprudence. These areas of study always offer new vistas to be examined, but they certainly cannot be described as virginal and unexplored.

There are very few studies, on the other hand, that aspire to carry out a systematic and organic analysis of the development of the science of European public law; of these, almost none focus in particular on European administrative law, which, as we have seen, has acquired central importance in the development of European law.

These are the reasons for this chapter's focus on the development of the science of European public law and especially administrative law. We must close the first part of the chapter here (also because of the amount of energy that a more extensive examination would require) and then, funnel-like, try to broaden the horizon of analysis again in the second part of the chapter.

Starting from the historical origins of European administrative law up to the present day might allow us to ascertain how and when (promptly or belatedly) legal science has aligned with developments and contributed to the advancement of European administrative law, to see when it has played this role most significantly, and what prospects for transformation may be discerned. It may also enable us to understand to what extent the emergence of administrative law has contributed to the transformation of legal science in various countries and whether this change is leading to the emergence of a shared and proactive European legal culture, aware of a more meaningful and less subservient and instrumental role than in the past.

As we stated earlier, ours is an attempt to understand a little-explored terrain in the history of the science of administrative law. A number of studies have been helpful in this endeavour: a fine volume by Anna Katharina Mangold[9] that

8 See, for instance, Frank Michelman's theories and, in particular, these two masterpieces: F.I. Michelman, 'Traces of Self-Government', The Supreme Court 1985 Term (1986) 100 *Harvard Law Review* 4–77; idem, 'Law's Republic', Symposium: The Republican Civic Tradition (1988) 97 *Yale Law Journal* 1493–1537.

9 A.K. Mangold, *Gemeinschaftsrecht und deutsches Recht* (Tübingen: Mohr Siebeck, 2011).

focuses, however, on German legal science in the context of a study of European law as a whole. We have also consulted works by Sabino Cassese,[10] Eberhard Schmidt-Assmann,[11] Edoardo Chiti and Joana Mendes,[12] and Filipe Brito Bastos[13] for an overview. Some of Armin von Bogdandy's essays[14] provide a theoretical framework and an outline of the conceptual foundations of underlying the edifice. An essay by Mario P. Chiti,[15] one by this author[16] (both from the early 2000s), and a couple of essays by Edoardo Chiti[17] attempt an analysis of the Italian contribution. It is, in short, a largely unexplored field of study.

Perhaps the most systemic study, revealing an exceptional cultural depth, is Armin von Bogdandy's recent book.[18] It is dedicated to the structural transformation of public law and the emergence of a European democratic society as a result of the joint contribution of the institutions of government, the courts, and continental scholarship. In particular, chapter IV of his volume focuses on the role of the jurist in the European social integration project. Von Bogdandy's work on the constructive role of legal science (not only in this work but in

10 We refer here to the list of writings cited by the author in the bibliographical note in the margins of S. Cassese, 'Diritto amministrativo europeo e diritto amministrativo nazionale: signoria o integrazione?' (2003), in idem, *Il diritto amministrativo: storia e prospettive* (Milan: Giuffrè, 2010) 399–401.

11 E. Schmidt-Assmann, *Zur Europäisierung des allgemeinen Verwaltungsrechts*, in *Festschrift für Peter Lerche* (München: C.H. Beck, 1993) 513 ff.; idem, 'Deutsches und Europäisches Verwaltungsrecht' (1993) *Deutsches Verwaltungsblatt* 924 ff.; idem, 'Das Allgemeine Verwaltungsrecht vor den Herausforderungen neuer europäischer Verwaltungsstrukturen', in *Festschrift für Günther Winkler* (Wien; New York: Springer, 1997) 995 ff.; idem, 'Die Europäisierung des Verwaltungsverfahrensrecht', in *Festgabe 50 Jahre Bundesverwaltungsgericht*, (Köln, Berlin, Bonn, München: Carl Heymanns, 2003) 487 ff.

12 E. Chiti, *La costruzione del diritto amministrativo europeo*, in M.P. Chiti (ed.), *Diritto amministrativo europeo* (Milan: Giuffrè, 2013) 45 ff.; E. Chiti and J. Mendes, 'The Evolution of EU Administrative Law', in P. Craig and G. de Búrca (eds), *The Evolution of EU Law*, 3rd edition (Oxford: OUP, 2021) 340 ff.

13 F. Brito Bastos, 'Doctrinal Methodology in EU Administrative Law: Confronting the "Touch of Stateness"' (2021) 22(4) *German Law Journal* 593 ff.

14 A. von Bogdandy, 'A Bird's Eye View on the Science of European Law: Structures, Debates and Development Prospects of Basic Research on the Law of the European Union in a German Perspective' (2000) *European Law Journal* 208 ff.; idem, 'Verwaltungsrecht im Europäischen Rechtsraum - Perspektive einer Disziplin', in A. von Bogdandy, S. Cassese, P. Huber (eds), *Handbuch Ius Publicum Europaeum*, vol. IV (Heidelberg: C.F. Müller, 2007) 3 ff.

15 M.P. Chiti, 'Le forme di azione dell'amministrazione europea', in F. Bignami and S. Cassese (eds), *Il procedimento amministrativo nel diritto europeo* (Milan: Giuffrè, 2004) 53 ff.

16 A. Sandulli, 'La scienza italiana del diritto pubblico e l'integrazione europea' (2005) *Rivista italiana di Diritto Pubblico Comunitario* 859 ff.

17 E. Chiti, 'La scienza del diritto amministrativo e il diritto pubblico ultrastatale', in L. Torchia, E. Chiti, R. Perez, A. Sandulli (eds), *La scienza del diritto amministrativo nella seconda metà del XX secolo* (Naples: Editoriale Scientifica, 2008) 129 ff.

18 A. von Bogdandy, *Strukturwandel des öffentlichen Rechts*, op. cit., 421 ff.

many others from the previous quarter century) numbers among those closest to the positions expressed in this book and is a constant source of inspiration.

This chapter is divided into two main parts. The first sections examine in depth the role played by the science of administrative law in the evolution of the European legal system, the related integration process, and the development of European administrative law. A diachronic approach is well suited here, breaking the phenomenon down into decades. Given the impossibility of an exhaustive coverage of the legal science of the various member states, which would require another book, we have decided to look in particular at the German and Italian experiences. We then offer some summary considerations, albeit in lesser detail, on the English and French scenarios, limiting ourselves to only very brief remarks regarding other countries.

The closing sections address the role of the jurist in the European integration process in more general and forward-looking terms. In this part too, the difficulty and breadth of the topic force us to limit ourselves to a somewhat impressionistic vision.

2. The 1950s: the beginnings of European administrative law and the creation of an 'administrative atmosphere'

In the 1950s, the European integration process came into being under the 'supervision', of course, of international law as the surface perception was that relations between European nations should be framed according to the normal relations between states, governed by international treaties. But even then, going deeper, the perception was growing that the nature of the institutions was such as to favour the typical dynamics of a kind of law typical of the nation-state: administrative law.[19] The ECSC (European Coal and Steel Community) was, in fact, an essentially administrative organization, possessing classic elements of international administrative organizations. It was based on the administrative agency model, with international, but above all supranational, features: as Advocate General Maurice Lagrange pointed out, the initial perception was largely one of a federal organization of six states rather than an international organization.[20] It was an *administration de mission*, following the French model, i.e., an administration that has things done rather than doing them directly.[21] Given the administrative legal systems of the six ECSC founding countries, its operations were also essentially based on the model of the administrative act. The decisions by the Court of Justice confirmed this

19 See, in this regard, M.P. Chiti, 'Le forme di azione dell'amministrazione europea', op. cit., 55 ff.

20 M. Lagrange, 'L'ordre juridique de la CECA vu à travers la jurisprudence de sa Cour de Justice' (1958) *Revue de droit public* 841 ff.

21 S. Cassese and G. della Cananea, 'The Commission of European Economic Community: The Administrative Ramifications of its Political Development (1957–1967)' (1992) *Jahrbuch für europäische Verwaltungsgeschichte* 77.

direction as judges made extensive use of principles and rules typical of administrative law and especially administrative action. Community acts were classified as administrative acts, with all that this entailed from the point of view of the nature of the act: the typical defects of legitimacy and nullity of the act, typical ways of exercising the power of decisional self-regulation, and so on.

The administrative model of the early integration process attracted the interest of the shrewdest legal scientists in France, Germany and Italy, mostly concerning the legal nature of the new supranational bodies and the acts they put in place.

Of particular note in this regard is Jean Rivero's 1958 paper on the influence of domestic laws on the Court of Justice of the ECSC.[22] The French jurist pointed out, among other things, that the Court's judicial review of the legitimacy of Community acts as envisaged by the Community judges was formed along the lines of the national legal construct of excess of administrative power. This aspect had already been understood by Pietro Gasparri in a 1957 essay published in the *Rivista trimestrale di diritto pubblico*,[23] concerning the abuse of power of Community acts; in this contribution, the Tuscan scholar demonstrated how the judicial review of *excès de pouvoir* fitted these acts perfectly. Numerous German, French, and Italian scholars also dwelt on these aspects, studying the characteristics and grounds for invalidity of Community acts, as well as measures against invalid acts, in the following decade. In particular, mention must be made of the essays by Werner Lorenz[24] and Uwe Goßmann[25] for Germany, André De Laubadère,[26] Michel Fromont,[27] and Jean-Marie Auby and Michel Fromont[28] for France; Gianguido Sacchi Morsiani,[29] Paolo De Caterini,[30] and Ugo M. Iaccarino[31] (and, later, by Umberto Fragola[32]) for Italy. These studies relating to the administrative

22 J. Rivero, 'Le problème de l'influence des droits internes sur la Cour de Justice de la CECA' (1958) 4 *Annuaire français de droit international* 295 ff.

23 P. Gasparri, 'L'eccesso di potere nel diritto della "CECA"' (1957) *Rivista trimestrale di diritto pubblico* 804 ff.

24 W. Lorenz, 'General Principles of Law: their Elaboration in the Court of Justice of the EC' (1964) *American Society of Comparative Law* 1 ff.

25 U. Goßmann, *Der Widerruf begünstingender Verwaltungsakte im Recht der Europäischen Gemeinschaften* (Köln: Gouder & Hansen, 1964).

26 A. de Laubadère, 'Les actes administratifs', in *Dix ans de jurisprudence de la Cour de justice des Communautés européennes* (Köln: Carl Heymanns, 1965) 472.

27 M. Fromont, *Rechtsschutz gegenüber der Verwaltung in Deutschland Frankreich und den Europäischen Gemeinschaften* (Köln: Carl Heymanns, 1967).

28 J.-M. Auby, M. Fromont, *Les recours contre les actes administratifs dans les Pays de la Communauté economique européenne* (Paris: Dalloz, 1971).

29 G. Sacchi Morsiani, *Il potere amministrativo delle Comunità europee e le posizioni giuridiche dei privati*, vol. I (Milan: Giuffrè, 1965).

30 P. De Caterini, *L'atto amministrativo delle Comunità europee* (Milan: Giuffrè, 1967).

31 U.M. Iaccarino, *Introduzione ad un profilo sistematico degli 'Atti' delle comunità europee. Contributo allo studio delle organizzazioni internazionali* (Naples: Jovene, 1970).

32 U. Fragola, 'Diritto amministrativo e diritto comunitario. L'atto amministrativo europeo' (1980) *Consiglio di Stato* 753 ff.

act, however, did no more than transplant parameters and institutions from domestic law into a new environment and context and did not allow a full perception of the innovative elements of Community administration.

For the rest, the doctrinal contribution of those years was mainly intended to further examine (in addition to the interventions of constitutionalists on the relations between European and national[33] sources) aspects concerning the nature and administrative organization of the ECSC and, later, the EEC.

Leading Italian public law scholars, however, expressed a marked scepticism about the new European institutions.

The last parliamentary speech of Vittorio Emanuele Orlando,[34] the founder of the Italian school of public law and president of the Council of Victory in the First World War, on 18 July 1952, was a criticism of the prospect of establishing a European Community:

> Which means giving a new constitution to a new state. This is what they have said; and so I say no, and I believe I have the right to an answer, a clarification, an explanation that reassures me that this is not possible (...). But, gentlemen, the European Constituent Assembly may imply a new form of international organisation that would then be governed by a future constitution. It will, of course, be a form of union of states: but, I repeat, of what kind? We have, as it were, a rainbow of shades (...) as to the nature of this possible union of states. For example, I have heard tell of the establishment of a European Community. What discovery would this be, in that case? There is and always has been a European Community, because a community (...) is nothing more than a collection of entities that coexist in a purely *de facto* state, so much so that jurists still call it the international community (...) So what will it be? An alliance? Fine, but that would be nothing new: history is a series of alliances (...). But what if it were a union instead? The difference would consist in permanence, in the existence of a mandatory term. International law is familiar with permanent unions, so this would not be a novelty either (...). It means that today's would be a union for the steel and coal trade. But after that, stop!"[35]

33 For example, P. Barile, 'Rapporti tra norme primarie comunitarie e norme costituzionali e primarie italiane' (1966) *La Comunità internazionale* 14 ff.

34 A. Sandulli, 'La scienza italiana del diritto pubblico e l'integrazione europea' (2005) *Rivista italiana di diritto pubblico comunitario* 863–864. Subsequently, E. Chiti, 'La costruzione del sistema amministrativo europeo', in M.P. Chiti (ed.), *Diritto amministrativo europeo* (Milan: Giuffrè, 2013) 53–54.

35 V.E. Orlando, *Sulla votazione per la nomina: a) di un membro effettivo dell'Assemblea consultiva del Consiglio d'Europa; b) di nove membri dell'assemblea della comunità europea del carbone e dell'acciaio* (Senate of the Republic, sitting of 18 July 1952), in V.E. Orlando, *Discorsi parlamentari*, Senato della Repubblica, Archivio storico (Bologna: Il Mulino, 2002) 994–996.

In 1954, Massimo Severo Giannini wrote a short critical essay on the treaty establishing the European Defence Community, whereby the union of states resulting from the treaty "takes the form of an administrative union, and the substance of a federal dictatorship", with the consequence of a serious democratic deficit in the EDC at odds "with all the principles of Europe's legal tradition".[36] And, on the other hand, it must be acknowledged that the experience of the EDC was quite different from that of the ECSC and the EEC and probably failed also because of its alleged constitutional dimension, at a time that was far from ripe.

Feliciano Benvenuti, the leader of the Veneto-Lombard school of Italian science of administrative law, had a more forward-looking idea of the new European institutions.

His 1961 essay on the legal nature of the ECSC was certainly significant. In this paper he indicated with much foresight the path that would be taken a few decades later. This was above all thanks to the construction of the objectivized legal system, which, together with the notion of function, constituted the architrave of Benvenuti's system:

> The truth is that underlying the European Coal and Steel Community is an idea that is both new and ancient, which cannot be grasped either through the usual notions of international law or with those of current domestic public law: not, therefore, by using the various formulas concerning union and cooperation between states, nor the modern concept of the sovereign state of the continental European type, so it is correct to say that the ECSC is not an international organisation, nor a national body and that, if we are to grasp its nature and value, it is necessary to refer to a different conceptual model.[37]

The ECSC, says Benvenuti, is "an autonomous sovereign body whose constitutive element is not territory but an economic activity to which political importance is given": "a corporate, non-territorial State", aiming for a substantial renewal of European public law, because

> it opens up to the possibility of a new type of supranational state, much broader than one locked within our territorial borders, a State of States that is not the federal state of territorial states, but one that, with its ancient newness, will be able to provide a new solution to the problems of the European people, who, in the diversity of its nations, is today on its way to achieving full unity of culture and civilisation,[38]

36 M.S. Giannini, 'Brevi osservazioni sul Trattato per la Comunità europea di difesa' (1954) 3 *Società* 523 ff., also in idem, *Scritti*, vol. III (Milan: Giuffrè, 2003) 867–868.
37 F. Benvenuti, *La C.E.C.A., ordinamento sovrano*, introduction to *Ordinamento della Comunità europea del carbone e dell'acciaio*, vol. I (Padua: Cedam, 1961) 1 ff., also in idem, *Scritti giuridici*, vol. III (Milano: Vita e pensiero, 2006) 2066.
38 F. Benvenuti, *La C.E.C.A., ordinamento sovrano, Scritti giuridici*, op. cit., 2059.

taking up "the formula of sovereignty of, and in, an economic sector".[39] These were insights that pointed to a fruitful way ahead, one that remained unexplored for several decades, and which rested, fundamentally, on the temporality and contingency of legal solutions and social arrangements on the one hand, and, on the other, on the unstoppable drive for the universality of social formations (in a connective tissue that leads from the freedom of the individual to the universality of society through the legal system).

Benvenuti's vision brought the notion of state back into space-time:

> The territorial state, in fact, constitutes a merely contingent solution, responding to the needs of a time and a historically determined society; therefore an essentially relative solution. We struggle to realise it, because we have been brought up in the cult of the nation-state; our entire conception of history is always a function of the territorial state, its borders, its spheres of influence, its good, or bad, neighbourly relations, namely the state identified with its territory and personified in a nation-state. All we need to do, however, is to look beyond the time of the nation states, or look beyond that short stretch of sea that separates the British Isles from the European continent, to find ourselves faced with an entirely different kind of state: the city states of pre-signorial Italy were not really nation-states or territorial states; and now England is not really a territorial state and is not even a legal entity but a collection of 'corporations'. In English society, sovereignty is subdivided into elements that are only apparently territorial but are, in reality, corporations, as is the Crown or Parliament.[40]

There would, however, be no follow-up to these insights.

Similarly, the repercussions of the indirect execution outlined in the 1957 Treaty of Rome were not grasped. While retaining the typical dualist approach of international law, it lightly outlined the organizational and functional mechanisms of what would be defined as executive federalism: according to the model studied by Jean Monnet, the supranational order was based on the national administrative structures of the member states, so the project of European integration could rest on solid foundations without removing competences or reducing the size of national administrations.[41] However, direct

39 F. Benvenuti, *La C.E.C.A., ordinamento sovrano, Scritti giuridici*, op. cit., 2076.

40 F. Benvenuti, *La C.E.C.A., ordinamento sovrano, Scritti giuridici*, op. cit., 2075.

41 As early as 1943, Jean Monnet, stationed in Algiers, set himself two objectives for European unity, the democracy of the system and its political and economic organization: "We need to attain the following goals: the re-establishment or establishment of a democratic regime in Europe, and the economic and political organisation of a 'European entity'. Achieving these two goals is essential to creating the conditions that will make peace in Europe a normal state of affairs. There will not be peace in Europe if it remains possible for regimes to be set up in which the right of opposition is not respected and in which free elections are not held.

implementation was envisaged in the areas of competition, state aid, and management of the Union's budget, with the necessary consequence that a European administration would emerge within the Commission to perform these functions.

3. The 1960s and 1970s: the development of administration and the European Court of Justice's 'constitutionalization' of the Treaties

In the 1960s, the development of the European Economic Community was marked by a pendulum-like movement, in which law and politics followed opposite directions. On the one hand, from 1963 the Court of Justice drew up the key principles of European law, carrying out a sort of 'constitutionalization' of the Treaties[42], principles that would mark the relationship between the EEC and the member states for decades to follow (direct effect, supremacy, implied powers, etc.) and that would, for a long time, allow the Community judges to play the role of 'lords' of European law. On the other hand, in 1965 the executives of the member states (in particular, Gaullist France) reacted by opposing the shift to majority decision-making in the European Council of Ministers (an event that led to the Luxembourg Compromise), increasingly concentrating decision-making power in the Council to the detriment of the Commission. This caused a sudden halt and a long stalemate in the 'political' process of European[43] integration, to which the Court of Justice further

Fulfilling these two conditions is central to restoring and maintaining all the essential forms of freedom — speech, assembly, association and so on — that are the foundations on which Western civilisation has developed." And, further on, "The countries of Europe are too small to guarantee their peoples the prosperity that modern conditions make possible and consequently necessary. They need larger markets. It is also important that they do not devote a substantial share of their resources to maintaining supposedly 'key' industries to meet the requirements of national defence, industries which are rendered obligatory by the form that States take, with their 'national sovereignty' and protectionist reflexes, such as we saw before 1939." See, in this regard, *www.cvce.eu/obj/jean_monnet_s_thoughts_on_the_future_algiers_5_august_1943-en-b61a8924–57bf-4890–9e4b-73bf4d882549.html.*

42 See, among many, K. Lenaerts, 'Some Reflections on the Separation of Powers in the European Community' (1991) *Common Market Law Review* 11 ff.

43 However, even in the period of slowdown, with its strong intergovernmental character, it achieved significant results as noted in F.W. Scharpf, 'La trappola della decisione congiunta: federalismo tedesco e integrazione europea' (1986) *Stato e mercato* 178: "In short, the history of the European Community has not lived up to the hopes of 'pro-European' politicians and 'neo-functionalist' theorists, of dynamic processes of deepening and extending the integration of functions, culminating in a European federal state. On the other hand, despite all the disappointments and frustrations, the European initiative has shown much more elasticity and resilience than the 'realist' school of international relations and the promoters, politicians and scholars, of an *Europe des patries* would have supposed. Paradoxically, the European Community appears to have become precisely that 'stable intermediate level

responded by accentuating the 'legal' process of integration. According to a well-known hypothesis, it was precisely as a result of the member states taking control of the decision-making process that it was possible to proceed along the jurisprudential route of constitutionalization[44]: this was no zero-sum game, since the states also had something to gain from the continuation of the integration process.[45]

3.1. As far as Community administration is concerned, three main lines of transformation were observed during this decade: the strengthening of the Community administration within the Commission, particularly in areas of direct execution (but not only these), giving rise to a complex architecture, with offices of external relevance; the establishment of committees, in the area of agricultural policies. This gave rise to the complex phenomenon of 'comitology', which allows the Council to exercise indirect control over the Commission in the exercise of delegated regulatory powers and to structure relations between the administrations of the member states and the Community, and the integration of the Community and national systems through the affirmation of the principles of direct effect and supremacy, through the Court of Justice's *Van Gend en Loos* and *Costa v Enel* rulings, with the result that national administrations became actual decentralized Community law implementation offices.[46]

Essentially, European administrative law can be said to have come into being in the 1960s. As Sabino Cassese recalls, in the von Lachmüller case of 1960,[47] the Court referred to "general rules of administrative law", to establish that translators working for the Commission should be subject to public law contracts.[48] But even before then, the groundwork had been laid in ECSC case law through the work of lawyers General Karl Roemer and Maurice Lagrange. In particular, in defining the status of employees of the Community institutions from case law, it helped to crystallize certain general principles of organization

between existing cooperation between nations and the emergence of a new nation' that Stanley Hoffmann (1966, p. 910) thought impossible."

44 E. Stein, 'Lawyers, Judges and the Making of a Transnational Constitution' (1981) 75 *American Journal of International Law* 1 ff.

45 On this point, see the authoritative and unsurpassed the essay by J.H.H. Weiler, 'The Transformation of Europe' (1991) 100 *Yale Law Journal* 2403 ff., translated into Italian in idem, *La Costituzione dell'Europa* (Bologna: il Mulino, 2003) 34 ff.

46 On all these aspects, see E. Chiti, 'La costruzione del sistema amministrativo europeo', op. cit., 56–65.

47 Court of Justice, judgment of 15 July 1960, C-43, 45, 48/59, *Eva von Lachmüller*, in *Racc.*, I, 907 ff. On the legal nature of the translators' employment contracts, the Court of Justice ruled that "therefore the contracts at issue come under public law and are subject to the general rules of administrative law", as a result of both the public nature of the contracting party (the Commission of the E.C.E.) and the activity performed (the service of language translation into one of the four official languages of the Community), which makes them "of the same public nature as the Commission itself".

48 S. Cassese, 'Il sistema amministrativo europeo e la sua evoluzione' (1991) *Rivista trimestrale di diritto pubblico* 771.

and functioning for the years to come. One example is the *Kergall* ruling in 1955, concerning a fixed-term official of the Common Assembly of the ECSC, which likened contracted agents employed on a fixed-term basis, but occupying posts budgeted as permanent, to civil servants. But we might also mention the *Bourgaux* judgment of 1956,[49] which classified the employment status of ECSC officials as that of a civil servant. Or else the fundamental *Algera* judgment of 1957,[50] according to which an act of employment cannot be withdrawn at will, which constitutes the first pronouncement on the subject of the revocation of European administrative acts.

And it was precisely in the 1960s that the Community courts began to develop a series of principles and rules, particularly in the field of competition, concerning the relationship between the Community administration and citizens.

3.2. Legal science in Europe remained almost totally blind to these fundamental changes, however, and the most interesting and innovative drafts were left to a very small body of personnel, mostly in the institutions operating in Brussels and Luxembourg (e.g., Émile Noël, Maurice Lagrange, etc.). This difficulty in perceiving the relevance of Community administrative law was also affected by transition to the so-called 'constitutional atmosphere', whereby scholars mainly sought to identify the characteristic features of the European constitutional order.[51]

3.3. There was one exception: German legal science, which has taken Community administrative law seriously since the 1960s and undertaken exploratory studies in this field.[52]

These studies followed the scientific direction outlined by Hans Peter Ipsen in his programmatic and methodological work of 1964, in which he argued that scientific research activity by a young German jurist in the legal field could be very productive and inspired thanks to the new horizons opened up by Community law.[53]

In short, we can say that the science of European public law effectively came into being in Germany, with the writings of Manfred Zuleeg (1969)[54] and

49 17 December 1956, *Bourgaux c. Assemblea*, in *Racc.* 1956, 449.

50 12 July 1957, *Algera c. Assemblea*, in *Racc.* 1957, 133.

51 On this, see M.P. Chiti, *Le forme di azione dell'amministrazione europea*, op. cit., 58–59.

52 Of great importance in this regard are the statistics provided by A.K. Mangold, *Gemeinschaftsrecht und deutsches Recht*, op. cit., 169 ff., concerning European law studies contained in German legal journals since the Second World War, which grew significantly from 1962 onwards, i.e., from the *Van Gend & Loos* case, and a consistent increase in studies around 1986 coinciding with the Single European Act. This demonstrates the marked interest of German legal science in European affairs.

53 H.P. Ipsen, 'Europäisches Gemeinschaftsrecht im Hochschulstudium' (1964) *Neue Juristische Wochenschrift* 961 ff., in particular 962.

54 M. Zuleeg, *Das Recht der Europäischen Gemeinschaften im Innerstaatlichen Bereich*, Kölner Schriften zum Europarecht, Band 9 (Köln: Carl Heymanns, 1969) in particular 209 ff.

Hans-Werner Rengeling (1977) among others,[55] paving the way for the more strictly administrative law-related research by Jürgen Schwarze in the 1980s, and especially for the 1988 textboook (as well as the writings of Ulrich Everling, Ingolf Pernice and Eberhard Gräbitz).

It must first of all be pointed out that these works, still at an exploratory stage, were not isolated and episodic – like, as will be seen later on in this volume, those of Gasparri and Sacchi Morsiani on the Italian scene. Rather, they formed part of an already rich and solid strand of legal and extra-judical studies on European law, unlike what was happening in other countries: in Italy, for example, for several decades the study of the Community legal system was considered the exclusive prerogative of scholars of international law. In Germany, on the other hand, the study of European institutions and their legal foundations was not the domain of international law scholars, but nor was it the exclusive province of public lawyers, so much so that scholars of private and commercial law have made important contributions to the understanding of the public aspects of the European legal system.[56] On the one hand this demonstrates the need for an ontologically interdisciplinary approach to European studies but also for such topics to be addressed by jurists with a comprehensive, all-round education. In this regard, for Germany, the academic model, which aims to educate a scientist not closed within his or her disciplinary monad, is particularly useful. For example, scholars of public international or European law need in-depth knowledge and to be able to teach both constitutional and administrative law on university courses. On the other hand, in other systems, such as the Italian one, there has been a tendency for disciplinary closure, creating artificial barriers (usually related to career advancement) between one branch of law and another; each discipline is construed as a watertight compartment, and only a researcher can productively carry out scientific research for the purposes of career advancement within its confines.

Returning to Germany, important public studies on the European legal system were carried out in the late 1960s, but especially during the 1970s, particularly in the field of constitutional law (we recall scholars such as Ipsen, Zuleeg, Gräbitz, Müller-Graff, Everling, etc.).[57]

We have already mentioned the important interdisciplinary contribution made by the *Arbeitskreis Europäische Integration* (AEI)[58] since the late 1960s. However, since the early 1960s, journals devoted to European law and integration were already in circulation; there were also series of volumes expressly dedicated to European law. Among these, of particular note were the Kölner

55 H.-W. Rengeling, *Rechtsgrundsätze beim Verwaltungsvollzug des Europäischen Gemeinschaftsrechts*, Kölner Schriften zum Europarecht, Band 27 (Köln: Carl Heymanns, 1977).

56 See, in this regard, A. von Bogdandy, 'A Bird's Eye View', op. cit., 235.

57 A painstaking reconstruction regarding the area of constitutional law can be found in A.K. Mangold, *Gemeinschaftsrecht und deutsches Recht*, op. cit., 169 ff.

58 See footnote 7 above.

Schriften zum Europarecht, a series in which the two volumes (by Zuleeg and Rengeling) conventionally considered the forerunners of European public law (containing with very promising material, in particular for European administrative law) were published.

The volume by Zuleeg, a (recently deceased) scholar of European public law and later also a judge at the Court of Justice, is devoted to the impact of EU law on national law. He develops the subject from the perspective (typical of that time), of the relationship between sources and, in particular, the conflict between Community and domestic law. In this context, in chapter 9 of the volume, Zuleeg analyses the problem of authority in the adoption of administrative measures concerning Community competence, reaching the conclusion that the substantial administrative implementation required by Community law can and, indeed, must be entrusted to the administrative apparatus of the member states and that the division of competences varies according to what European law establishes. Thus, a systematization of the subject of direct and indirect administration and the characteristics of administrative action originating in Community competences was undertaken.

However, in Hans Peter Ipsen's impressive textbook of 1972, which provides a comprehensive analysis of Community law, its administrative aspects remain wholly marginal. In his opinion, only a few provisions of the EEC Treaty referred to aspects relating to the administrative traditions of the states.[59] However, the same author noted the diffusion of the principles of administrative law proper to the member states also within the Community system, in part thanks to the creative activity in the case law of the European Court of Justice.[60] At the same time, Otto Bachof considered the path taken towards the construction of shared European legal dogmatics to be one of no return.[61]

59 H.P. Ipsen, *Europäisches Gemeinschaftsrecht* (Tübingen: Mohr Siebeck, 1972) 91–92, according to which "Die Gemeinschftsvertäge enthalten Vorschriften, die die deutsche Rechtsordnung dem (z. T. noch ungeschriebenen) allgemeinen materiellen Verwaltungrecht der Verwaltungshandlungen und dem Verwaltungsverfahrensrecht zuweist. So behandeln Art. 190, 191 EWGV, Art. 162, 163 EAGV, Art. 15 EGKSV Form und Wirksamkeit von Rechtshandlungen 164 EAGV, Art. 92 EGKSV die Vollstreckung von Akten der Gemeinschaftsorgane. Andere wichtige Materien, so die Widerruflichkeit ind Fehlerhaftigkeit solcher Akte, sind in Gemeinschaftsrecht nicht geregel, so daß Fragen der Rechtslueckenfuellung auftreten."

60 H.P. Ipsen, *Europäisches Gemeinschaftsrecht*, op. cit., 733–734. On these profiles see also, above, E.W. Fuß, *Die Europäischen Gemeinschaften und der Rechtsstaatsgedanke* (Heule: UGA, 1967) 38 ff.; G. Zieger, *Das Grundrechtsproblem in den Europäischen Gemeinschaften* (Tübingen: Mohr, 1970).

61 O. Bachof, 'Die Dogmatik des Verwaltungsrechts vor den Gegenwartsaufgaben der Verwaltung', in *Veröffentlichungen der Vereinung der Deutschen Staatslehrer*, Heft 30, von W. Martens und P. Häberle, *Grundrecht im Leistungsstaat*, von O. Bachof und W. Brohm, *Die Dogmatik des Verwaltungsrechts vor den Gegenwartsaufgaben der Verwaltung* (Berlin, New York: Walter de Gruyter, 1972) 193 ff., and in particular 236, according to which "Davon können die nationalen Dogmatiken nicht unberuehrt bleiben. Man kann sich wohl kaum vorstellen, daß auf lange Sicht eine

Barely five years later, Hans-Werner Rengeling, approaching the topic from the very angle of the general principles of European law and using a comparative method, began to fill European administrative law with subject matter. Rengeling's volume may perhaps be regarded as the first text to attempt a systematic approach to European administrative law.

Rengeling's volume also examines the distribution of competences between the Community system and those of the member states, demarcating the direct and indirect application of European law. From here he notes (stressing the lack of interest and underestimation of the importance of this aspect up to then) the close connection between the supranational system and the national systems in terms of the instruments of general administrative law employed to implement European law, a connection particularly close in the fields of administrative procedure and organization. He then moves on to a concrete analysis of various sectors allowing both direct application (e.g., competition law) and indirect application (e.g., agricultural law; right of establishment) in order to demonstrate that there are different and diverse 'layers' of application of administrative law models within the European system. Having completed this broad exploration, he tackles the main theme of his work, the general principles of administrative law, in order to show their particular importance for the indirect application of Community law.

Rengeling's work was still at an exploratory stage and, looking at it from a contemporary standpoint, was in some ways immature, but it has the following strengths: it grasped at a very early stage the relevance of the principles and the overall toolbox of administrative law within the European legal system and relations with national legal systems. It also carried out an initial and detailed fine-tuning of the usefulness and tempering of institutes and instruments of administrative law within the direct and indirect implementation procedures of Community law, at both the general level and that of the individual sectors of application; it uses both a vertical (supranational-national) and a horizontal-comparative approach (analyzing the characteristics of the different systems of administrative law). It focuses on the principles of administrative law, sensing that this angle could lead to further fruitful developments.

If the two volumes by Gianguido Sacchi Morsiani (in particular, the second, published in 1970) are the first monographic studies of European administrative law, Rengeling's monograph may be considered the first monograph on the subject of European administrative law to not only spawn a strand of studies within its own national system but also to gain a certain recognition on the international scientific scene (on the contrary, Sacchi Morsiani's books remained isolated in Italy and practically unknown outside its borders).

deutsche, eine franzoesische, eine italienischeusw. und überdies noch eine gemeineuropäische Dogmatik des Verwaltungsgeschehens unvermittelt nebeneinander bestehen können."

It should be noted, for the sake of completeness, that in Germany (as in other northern European countries and even in France) studies on European administration had become significantly more numerous from the 1970s in the wake of political science. Throughout Europe, in fact, substantial political studies research on European integration and institutions had been underway since the 1970s (see, among others, the work of Scheinman, Feld, Wiltgen, Strasser in Germany).

3.4. Italian administrative law studies, on the other hand, set the pace, while the mainstream has often expressed scepticism. This can be well illustrated by the assertive tone used by Massimo Severo Giannini in a lecture of 1967:

> we cannot speak of an administrative law of the European Communities nor of a constitutional law of the European Communities; the transposition of these notions, which are proper to the general systems in which we live, i.e., of states with systems other than Ststes, is always a gratuitous one: since it is not even of cognitive value, it is of no use.[62]

Despite the best-known twentieth-century Italian scholar of administrative law's outright rejection of the "possibility of injecting the doctrine and science of administrative law into a new phenomenon such as that of the European Communities", his words are nonetheless both interesting and indicative as they show how, towards the end of the 1960s, the opinion began to spread among scholars that an administrative law of the European Communities actually exists.

We have already mentioned studies regarding Community administrative acts from the 1950s and 1960s, but the most interesting scholarly contributions, in Italy, were those of Gianguido Sacchi Morsiani and Pietro Gasparri.

After his piece on the invalidity of Community acts (the implicit object of Giannini's criticism), in 1967 Gasparri published an essay on the relationship between politics and administration in Community law, in which he noted that the process of European integration was, on the legal level, much more advanced than was perceived on the political[63] level.

Sacchi Morsiani, the first Italian scholar to support the existence of Community administrative law, published two volumes (1965 and 1970) in which he attempted to demonstrate (with interesting results, especially in the second volume, dedicated to proceedings in the competition sector – the first dealt with the theory of acts) that the paradigms of administrative action in force in state systems could be profitably applied to the methods of exercising the power of Community institutions, analysing their characteristics and their effects on

62 M.S. Giannini, 'Profili di un diritto amministrativo delle Comunità europee', 1967, with a presentation by S. Battini, (2003) *Rivista trimestrale di diritto pubblico* 982.

63 P. Gasparri, 'Politica ed amministrazione nell'ordinamento delle Comunità europee', in *Studi in onore di Antonio Segni*, vol. II (Milan: Giuffrè, 1967) 295 ff.

private subjective legal situations. From this, the possibility of developing Community administrative law as a new and autonomous branch of administrative law arose and, above all, it followed that administrative law did not constitute a legal phenomenon exclusive to the state.[64]

In particular, Sacchi Morsiani clearly distinguished between Community administrative law (an autonomous branch of administrative law) and international administrative law, which had already been the subject of substantial studies in Germany and Italy in the first decades of the twentieth century. For him, Community administrative law constitutes the "internal administrative law of an international subject, whose system is similar, due to the complexity of its organizational and multi-subjective elements, to the state system, whose techniques it partly reproduces without, however, sharing its nature and aims".[65] The author claims "that the Community legal system is a system of administrative law in its own right", even though, as Edoardo Chiti[66] points out, a concluding chapter is needed to confirm that the initial hypothesis is fully confirmed by the analysis carried out.

3.5 German influence soon came to be felt in the northern European countries, especially in Scandinavia.

In France, on the other hand, studies on the subject paradoxically lagged far behind, given the degree of French influence over the early development of the European institutions. The separation of disciplines and the idea that administrative law should be the province of the nation-state alone meant that Rivero's warning (recalled above) was not fully grasped by French legal scholars: indeed, we might say that (with the exception of André de Laubadère and those of Jean-Marie Auby and Michel Fromont cited above) that only Rivero himself showed an awareness of the situation in his well-known contribution of 1978, in which he hoped that the process of convergence between legal systems brought about by Community law could lead to the "développement d'un droit administratif européen commun, attaché à dégager les principes essentiels d'un équilibre entre les impératifs de l'action du pouvoir et les libertés des citoyens".[67] The fact is that, in the 1960s and 1970s, the only academic studies on European administrative law concerned administrative action and the mechanisms of judicial protection. This was in contrast to the in-depth French research into the European phenomenon in other areas of the social sciences (in particular, political science).

64 G. Sacchi Morsiani, *Il potere amministrativo delle Comunità europee e le posizioni giuridiche dei privati*, vol. I, op. cit.; idem, vol. II (Milan: Giuffrè, 1970).

65 G. Sacchi Morsiani, *Il potere amministrativo delle Comunità europee e le posizioni giuridiche dei privati*, vol. I, op. cit., 4.

66 E. Chiti, 'La scienza del diritto amministrativo e il diritto pubblico ultrastatale', in L. Torchia, E. Chiti, R. Perez, A. Sandulli (eds), *La scienza del diritto amministrativo nella seconda metà del XX secolo* (Naples: Editoriale Scientifica, 2008) 148.

67 J. Rivero, 'Vers un droit commun européen: nouvelles perspectives en droit administratif', in M. Cappelletti (ed.), *New perspectives for a Common Law of Europe*, vol. I, (Firenze: EUI, 1978) 389 ff., in particular 406.

The difficulties besetting the European integration process over the decade to follow certainly contributed to this delay, most likely also as the result of the serious economic and financial crisis of the 1970s, which drew a veil of oblivion over Community administration. It continued to develop, mainly thanks to the contribution of Court of Justice case law and the administrative contribution of Commission bureaucracy, both indifferent to scholarly output (with the partial exception of German scholarship, as mentioned above).

4. The 1980s and 1990s: The foundation of European administrative law and its science

The early 1980s bore testimony to a considerable acceleration of the European integration process on the political level, which passed through the testing ground of the effectiveness of European law and its concrete implementation. The shift in this direction of the European institutional debate resulted in the 'administrative take-off' of the European legal system, on the one hand thanks to the perception of the composite and plural character of the European organization and, on the other, the complexity of European administrative law.[68] The adoption of the Single European Act (and the period leading up to it) constituted the fundamental caesura and transformation of the institutional framework in a truly supranational sense. And, in all likelihood, the full-bodied development of European environmental law also provided the 'critical mass' for the subject area to become definitively established.

European administrative law, once submerged beneath the waters, now rose decisively to the surface: administrative law studies could no longer ignore it.

4.1. The role of forerunner, but also that of systematic organizer of such confused and fragmentary material, undoubtedly belongs to Germany, home to numerous exploratory studies of the so-called general part of European administrative law by Albert Bleckmann,[69] Hans-Werner Rengeling,[70] Ulrich Everling,[71] and Hans-Hermann Kasten.[72]

68 E. Chiti, 'La costruzione del sistema amministrativo europeo', op. cit., 68–69.

69 A. Bleckmann, 'Der Verwaltungsvertrag als Handlungsmittel der Europäischen Gemeinschaften' (1981) *Deutsches Verwaltungsblatt* 889 ff., the first study dedicated to public contracts in European law.

70 H.-W. Rengeling, 'Verwaltungsverfahrens- und Verwaltungsprozeßrecht im Verhältnis zum Europäischen Gemeinschaftsrecht. Neuere Entwicklungen in der gemeinschaftsrechtlichen Rechtsprechung und Rechtsetzung' (1981) *Die Öffentliche Verwaltung* 366 ff. Subsequently, idem, 'Deutsches und europäisches Verwaltungsrecht - Wechselseitige Einwirkungen', in *VVDStRL – Veröffentlichungen der Vereinigung der Deutschen Staatsrechtslehrer* (Berlin; New York: De Gruyter, 1994) 202 ff.

71 U. Everling, 'Elemente eines europäischen Verwaltungsrechts' (1983) *Deutsches Verwaltungsblatt*, 649 ff.; idem, 'Auf dem Wege zu einem europäischen Verwaltungsrecht' (1987) in *NVwZ – Neue Zeitschrift für Verwaltungsrecht* 1 ff.

72 H.-H. Kasten, 'Entwicklung eines Europäischen Allgemeinen Verwaltungsrechts' (1985) *Die Öffentliche Verwaltung* 570 ff.

German studies of European administrative law were strongly driven by so-called special law and the adoption of European regulations and, above all, in 1985, the introduction of environmental impact assessment, upon which German public law scholars lavished particular attention. We should also consider, in this regard, the German studies on the subject of immigration and the freedom of movement of workers.[73]

Among the most important studies of the 1980s were those of Jürgen Schwarze, which proved fundamental in terms of both collation and dissemination.

In 1982, he edited a small volume as part of the often-cited Arbeitskreises Europäische Integration series,[74] in which he published the results of a study meeting held in Hamburg the previous year. In his brief introduction, Schwarze took stock of the state of the art of European administrative law, emphasizing the founding role of the Court of Justice through the development and dissemination of general principles, as well as the application and problem areas in which the foundations of a shared European administrative law were developing, in part due to the convergence of legal[75] traditions. This initial paper was then followed by other essays, including one on the principles of European administrative law.[76]

In 1988, the two volumes of *Europäisches Verwaltungsrecht*[77] were published. These, later translated into English[78] and French,[79] are conventionally considered to mark the definitive recognition and development of European administrative law. In the two volumes, subdivided, German style (a general part and a part dedicated to individual principles), Schwarze follows Rivero's direction concerning the construction (through comparison) of a common European law and continues with the approach centred on general principles, already adopted by Rengeling. This common law, however, unlike the mediaeval one, stems from case law and emanates by incorporation from a supranational system by identifying shared minimum standards.[80]

73 On these areas of study, please refer to the numerous citations in A.K. Mangold, *Gemeinschaftsrecht und deutsches Recht*, op. cit., 267 ff.

74 J. Schwarze (ed.), *Europäisches Verwaltungsrecht im Werden* (Baden-Baden: Nomos, 1982).

75 J. Schwarze, 'Europäisches Verwaltungsrecht im Werden – Einführung und Problemaufriß', in J. Schwarze (ed.), *Europäisches Verwaltungsrecht im Werden*, op. cit., 11 ff.

76 J. Schwarze, 'Der Schutz des Gemeinschaftsbürgers durch allgemeine Verwaltungsrechtsgrundsätze im EG-Recht' (1986) in *NJW - Neue Juristische Wochenschrift* 1067 ff.

77 J. Schwarze, *Europäisches Verwaltngsrecht*, voll. I and II (Baden-Baden: Nomos, 1988).

78 J. Schwarze, *European Administrative Law* (London: Sweet & Maxwell, 1992).

79 J. Schwarze, *Droit administratif européen* (Bruxelles: Bruylant, 1994).

80 In this regard, Luis María Diez Picazo in his review of the English edition of the work: L.M. Diez Picazo, 'La formación de un derecho administrativo europeo' (1993) *Revista Española de Derecho Constitucional* 300.

What is striking in Schwarze's work is the almost total concentration on sources, principles of action and techniques of regulation, while only a few opening pages are devoted to the structural aspects of administrative organization. The key, and practically sole, topic is the principle of legality and the consequences of breaching it, as well as other general principles in the European legal system (equality, proportionality, legal certainty, legitimate expectations, procedural principles). In short, the approach is that of administrative law linked to the tradition of the legal method, centred on a systematic approach and the legality of acts rather than the innovations of the European system, consisting of effectiveness, consensuality, and the informality of its structural and functional aspects.

The technique used, as we mentioned, is asymmetrical comparison, i.e., the experience of the main member states is compared with that of the Community as a whole. Another of the work's characteristics is its extremely detailed description; the collection of case law and scholarly literature is thorough and complete: it contains practically all the scholarship produced at that time. If there is one aspect that deserves a special mention in Schwarze's volume, it is the emergence of a careful mapping of Community 'territory'. What is lacking, however, flanking the in-depth study of organizational aspects (in many cases together with an analysis of operation), is a strong idea of system and a reflection on the original features of European administrative law. In the final part, he highlights, on the one hand, the interdependence between European legal systems through the vehicular function of the Community legal system and the dramatic emergence of a common European law, emphasizing, on the other, the integration and disappearance of the boundaries between constitutional and administrative law.

Another undoubted merit of Schwarze's work is that, following his cue, a solid line of research developed in order to complete the analysis and underpin the new discipline from the theoretical point of view. Of particular importance in the early 1990s were some *Habilitationsschrifts*, especially those of Michael Brenner[81], Claus Dieter Classen,[82] Thomas von Danwitz,[83] Stefan Kadelbach,[84] and Hermann-Josef Blanke,[85] all published by Mohr in the well-known Ius

81 M. Brenner, *Der Gestaltungsauftrag der Verwaltung in der Europäischen Union* (Tübingen: Mohr, 1996).

82 C.D. Classen, *Die Europäisierung der Verwaltungsgerichtsbarkeit. eine vergleichende Untersuchung zum deutschen, französischen und europäischen Verwaltungsprozeßrecht* (Tübingen: Mohr, 1996).

83 T. von Danwitz, *Verwaltungsrechtliches System und europäische Integration* (Tübingen: Mohr, 1996). By von Danwitz see also the interesting exposition in idem: *Europäisches Verwaltungsrecht* (Berlin, Heidelberg: Springer, 2008).

84 S. Kadelbach, *Allgemeines Verwaltungsrecht unter europäischem Einfluß* (Tübingen: Mohr Siebeck, 1999).

85 H.-J. Blanke, *Vertrauensschutz im deutschen und europäischen Verwaltungsrecht* (Tübingen: Mohr, Siebeck, 2000).

Publicum series (later Mohr Siebeck). The work of Armin Hatje was also important in this regard.[86]

Nevertheless, in the 1990s, the most significant contribution, both in methodological and substantive terms, was that of the creators of the *Neue Verwaltungsrechtswissenschaft* and, above all, Eberhard Schmidt-Assmann, Wolfgang Hoffmann-Riehm, and Andreas Voßkuhle.

The driving force behind the reform of German administrative law, under the impetus of European administrative law, was most certainly Eberhard Schmidt-Assmann. He had already highlighted the profound and revolutionary influence of European law on national administrative law indicated in two essays published in 1993 (and in subsequent writings in the 1990s).[87] But the emergence of new trends was above all the result of his exceptional ability to promote legal culture. The 'capacity for focus', mobilization, and concentration on long-term projects spawned by the *Neue Verwaltungsrechtswissenschaft*, with the ten position volumes, published between 1993 and 2004, *Schriften zur Reform des Verwaltungsrechts*, including the one dated 1999 (Band 6), dedicated to the *Strukturen des Europäischen Verwaltungsrechts*, were particularly emblematic of the 1990s.

Here, the main transformations in administrative law were examined, one of which, the Europeanization of German administrative law, was undoubtedly at the forefront, which meant that not only the methodological coordinates but also the very subject matter of the discipline had to be rewritten from scratch.

What lay at the heart of the proposals of the *Neue Verwaltungsrechtswissenschaft* was no longer the legal principle of legality but that of *politische Steuerung* ('governance'), a principle derived from other social sciences, sociology in particular. Through this 'governance', the model of horizontal networks replaces the hierarchical one and the mechanisms of parliamentary control, and the state is no longer at centre stage: the role of the state, in this fluid and dynamic reality, becomes that of promoter of interactions within and between networks, and the centre of gravity shifts to the supranational and transnational levels. The shift in focus of the scientific analysis of administrative law led to enormous growth in the spectrum of analysis, which, at this point, can no longer be limited to the narrow confines of the legal method but must extend to the territories of the other social sciences. This, in particular, implies the analysis of reality and, therefore, a realistic attitude; concentration on effects and consequences; an intra-, multi-, and interdisciplinary approach, the tendency to use *Schlüsselbegriffe* (key terms: e.g. *Kooperation, Privatisierung, Steuerung*) and *Leitbilder* (guiding visions: e.g. the *schlanker Staat* or lean state; *lernende Verwaltung*, the learning administration), the tendency to focus in detail on areas of the so-called special law. In essence, this involves the emergence of

86 A. Hatje, *Die gemeinschaftsrechtliche Steuerung der Wirtschaftsverwaltung* (Baden-Baden: Nomos, 1998).

87 See footnote 17 above.

principles from the analysis of reality and subsequent subsumption into guiding ideas.[88]

Schmidt-Aßmann transposed this thorough analysis of the new tendencies into a dense 1998 volume of a methodological stamp, *Das allgemeine Verwaltungsrecht als Ordnungsidee*,[89] which can be considered the reference text for the construction of the new school. A little like the way Orlando's *Technical Criteria* served as the reference essay for the Italian school of public law in the late nineteenth century.

What is striking about Schmidt-Aßmann's undertaking is the overall shift of the problematic focus onto the themes and models of organization (especially *Steuerung* and *Kooperation*) following the profound *Europäisierung des Verwaltungsrechts* (Schmidt-Aßmann speaks of *Europäisierung des Recht durch Recht* in this regard) and the equally felt *Europäisierung der Verwaltungsstrukturen*, through the growing influence of economics and the concepts of 'network' and 'coordination' (as well as the innovative elements already highlighted in Voßkuhle's already mentioned paper); but, at the same time, renewed confidence in the concept of the legal system and in the possibility of tracing changes back to the legal tradition and the normativity of the system. While the profound transformation of models would seem to be unable to allow a hypothesis merely of reconciliation with the past.

All the work of analysis and reflection was brought together in the three volumes of the *Grundlagen des Verwaltungsrechts*[90] together with a new methodological reflection through which he came

> to see the study of administrative law as a 'science of direction' (*Steuerungswissenschaft*), i.e., a decision-oriented and advisory science (with regard to the legislator, for example), called to analyse the elements (actors, procedures, goals, instruments, and effects) of the relations between

88 On the *Neue Verwaltungsrechtswissenschaft*, see esp. A. Voßkuhle, 'The Reform Approach in the German Science of Administrative Law: The "Neue Verwaltungsrechtswissenschaft"', in *The Transformation of Administrative Law in Europe* (München: Sellier, European Law Publishers, 2007) 89 ff.

89 E. Schmidt-Aßmann, *Das Allgemeine Verwaltungsrecht als Ordnungsidee. Grundlagen und Aufgaben der verwaltungsrechtlichen Systembildung* (Berlin: Springer, 1998, 2nd ed., revised and expanded, 2004).

90 W. Hoffmann-Riem, E. Schmidt-Aßmann, A. Voßkuhle (eds), *Grundlagen des Verwaltungsrechts*, vol. I, *Methoden, Maßstäbe, Aufgaben, Organisation*, 2nd ed. (München: C.H. Beck, 2012); W. Hoffmann-Riem, E. Schmidt-Aßmann, A. Voßkuhle (eds), *Grundlagen des Verwaltungsrechts*, vol. II, *Informationsordnung, Verwaltungsverfahren, Handlungsformen* 2nd ed. (München: C.H. Beck, 2012; 1st ed., 2008); W. Hoffmann-Riem, E. Schmidt-Aßmann, A. Voßkuhle (eds), *Grundlagen des Verwaltungsrechts*, vol. III, *Personal, Finanzen, Kontrolle, Sanktionen, Staatliche Einstandspflichten*, 2nd ed. (München: C.H. Beck, 2013). On the first two volumes, see L. De Lucia's review in (2013) *Rivista trimestrale di diritto pubblico* 1076 ff.

administration and society and systematically investigate their reciprocal influences.[91]

And, in spite of this radical transformation, he is keen to reaffirm that he remains within the horizon of traditional dogma, not preaching the *Neue Verwaltungsrechtswissenschaft*, methodological pluralism or a trans- and interdisciplinary discourse (but, in the opposite sense, the cited Voßkuhle essay).

This conclusion (at the state of the art) would seem, however, to represent a step backwards with respect to the radical and fundamental path of innovation that he outlined.

4.2. The role of Italian administrative law studies, however, was not a secondary one. On the contrary, we may even say it has been of considerable importance.

In Italy, European administrative law made its entrance thanks to the scientific intuition and exploratory curiosity of Sabino Cassese. First, with two papers at conferences in 1982 and 1983, on European[92] bureaucracy and on the relations between international organizations and national[93] administrations (both published in 1985) and then, above all, with a 1985 IEAP study on European[94] administration (published in 1987).

The study constitutes a milestone in European administrative law studies, since it outlines the underlying European model of the public arena, an area which the author would work on in the decades to follow, also outlining the particular characteristics of management committees, torn between the centrifugal force of the national administrations (with the Council acting as a check on the Commission) and the centripetal force of the Commission, aiming to realize a European administrative style (breaking, therefore, with the national model of the 'state-as-a-unit'). One of the central original features of European administrative law is, in Cassese's opinion, the neo-corporative model represented by the US interest representation model, which, however, presents itself differently from its American guise,

91 In this regard, L. De Lucia, 'Il diritto amministrativo tedesco e il rinnovamento della dogmatica giuridica' (2015) *Rivista trimestrale di diritto pubblico* 1.

92 S. Cassese, 'Theoretical Sketch of the Cooperative and Mutidimensional Nature of Community Bureaucracy', in J. Jamar e W. Wessels (eds), *Community Bureaucracy at the Crossroads – L'administration communautaire à l'heure du choix* (Bruges: De Tempel, 1985) 39 ff.

93 S. Cassese, *Relations between International Organizations and National Administrations: General Report*, in IISA, XIX International Congress of Administrative Sciences, *Proceeding* (Bruxelles: Kluwer, 1985) 161 ff.

94 S. Cassese, 'Divided Powers: European Administration and National Bureaucracies', in S. Cassese (ed.), *The European Administration. L'Administration Européenne* (Bruxelles: IISA, 1987) 5 ff.; also in Italian under the title of *Poteri divisi: amministrazione europea e amministrazioni nazionali*, in *Studi in onore di Enzo Capaccioli* (Milan: Giuffrè, 1988) 159 ff.

> as here the interests to be represented and representing are also those of the state and government. Hence the phenomenon referred to elsewhere as the 'public arena', because governments and private individuals compete with equal rights (but not on an equal footing, as we have seen) in exploiting regulatory differences and presenting and asserting their interests, consequently placing states and private individuals on the same plane. This represents the greatest contribution of European integration to the diminishing role of nation-states.[95]

Another significant characteristic is that of cooperation, which manifests itself through mixed bodies and composite procedures. On the other hand, the European Union is a composite public organization by its very nature: as such, it makes no sense to speak of a multilevel structure, because

> the Union is not (only) a higher plane of legal construction, overlapping with the states. It conditions them, interfering at all levels and thus profoundly transforming the traditional legal orders. But this happens – and herein lies the characteristic feature – without the Union taking the place of the states as in the British Empire's 'indirect rule' model, already tried and tested in the 1500s by the Ottoman Empire in its relations with subject countries such as Egypt, Moldavia, Armenia, Kurdistan, and Transylvania[96]

(and, in the author's opinion, it is thanks to this very nature and history that transformation into a European federal state and convergence into a single and simplified form is impossible). Furthermore, the Europeanization of national administrative laws and the consequent 'pooling' of entire sectors of administrative law is leading towards the convergence of administrative systems and osmosis between the various legal models.

Turning, lastly, to the method of study. For Cassese, the reform process induced by European administrative law is the ultimate proof of the need for a plurality of methodologies, to the effect that every subject area calls for the application of the method or methods best suited to analysing it.[97] He therefore rejected the idea that the legal method was the only approach a jurist could adopt along with the systematic conception of law and legal dogmatics that developed during the late nineteenth century and most of the twentieth century.

95 S. Cassese, 'Il diritto amministrativo europeo presenta caratteri originali?' (2003) *Rivista trimestrale di diritto pubblico* 50.

96 S. Cassese, 'L'Unione europea come organizzazione pubblica composita' (2000) 5 *Rivista Italiana di Diritto Pubblico Comunitario* 987, now in idem, *La crisi dello Stato* (Roma-Bari: Laterza, 2002) 71.

97 see S. Cassese, 'Il sorriso del gatto, ovvero dei metodi nello studio del diritto pubblico' (2006) *Rivista trimestrale di diritto pubblico* 597 ff.

It is also worth mentioning a study by Gaetano D'Auria towards the late 1980s.[98] It was part of an ambitious French research project directed by Charles Debbasch,[99] which constituted the actual birth of European administrative law studies beyond the Alps. But it was only in the early 1990s that studies and scholars of European administrative law began to proliferate in Italy, in an unstoppable process of expansion: Mario P. Chiti,[100] Guido Greco,[101] Claudio Franchini,[102] Giacinto della Cananea,[103] Alberto Massera,[104] Giandomenico Falcon,[105] Luisa Torchia,[106] Roberto Caranta,[107] Eugenio Picozza,[108]

98 G. D'Auria, 'L'administration italienne et l'intégration européenne', in C. Debbasch (ed.), *Administrations nationales et intégration européenne*, Annales européennes d'administration publique, Centre de Recherches Administratives d'Aix-Marseille (Paris: CNRS, 1987) 76 ff.

99 Ch. Debbasch (ed.), *Administrations nationales et intégration européenne*, op. cit., with contributions by, among others L. Dubouis (Rapport français), A. François-D. Vandercammen (Rapport belge), G. D'Auria (Rapport italienne), S. Beissel-Merten (Rapport luxembourgeoise), and J. Dutheil de la Rochère (Rapport britannique).

100 M.P. Chiti, 'Il coordinamento delle politiche comunitarie e la riforma degli apparati di governo', in Associazione per gli Studi e le Ricerche Parlamentari, *Quaderno n. 1, Seminari 1989–1990* (Milan: Giuffrè, 1991) 235 ff.; idem, 'I signori del diritto comunitario: la Corte di giustizia e lo sviluppo del diritto amministrativo europeo' (1991) 3 *Rivista trimestrale di diritto pubblico* 823.

101 G. Greco, 'Profili di diritto pubblico italo-comunitario', in G. Greco (ed.), *Argomenti di diritto pubblico italo-comunitario* (Milan: Giuffrè, 1989) 3 ff.

102 C. Franchini, 'L'integrazione europea e il governo delle politiche comunitarie in Italia: organizzazione amministrativa e rapporti con le Comunità europee' (1990) 30 *Rivista di diritto europeo* 37 ff.; idem, 'L'impatto dell'integrazione comunitaria sulle relazioni al vertice dell'amministrazione: poteri governativi e poteri amministrativi' (1991) *Rivista trimestrale di diritto pubblico* 775 ff.; idem, *Amministrazione italiana e amministrazione comunitaria* (Padua: Cedam, 1st ed. 1992, 2nd ed. 1993).

103 G. della Cananea, 'Cooperazione e integrazione nel sistema amministrativo delle Comunità europee: la questione della "comitologia"' (1990) *Rivista trimestrale di diritto pubblico* 655 ff.

104 A. Massera, 'Il ruolo dell'amministrazione alla luce dell'Atto Unico Europeo' (1991) *Rivista trimestrale di diritto pubblico* 783 ff.; idem, 'Una nozione comunitaria di pubblica amministrazione', in Aa.Vv., *El desenvolupament del dret administratiu europeu*, Generalitat de Catalunya, Escola d'Administración Pública de Catalunya (Barcelona: Generalitat de Catalunya, 1993) 55 ff.; idem, 'L'amministrazione e i cittadini nel diritto comunitario' (1993) *Rivista trimestrale di diritto pubblico* 19 ff.

105 G. Falcon, 'Dal diritto amministrativo nazionale al diritto amministrativo comunitario' (1991) *Rivista italiana di diritto pubblico comunitario* 351 ff.; idem, 'Alcune osservazioni sullo sviluppo del diritto amministrativo comunitario' (1993) *Rivista trimestrale di diritto pubblico* 74 ff.

106 L. Torchia, *Il controllo pubblico della finanza privata* (Padua: Cedam, 1992).

107 R. Caranta, *Giustizia amministrativa e diritto comunitario* (Naples: Jovene, 1992).

108 E. Picozza, 'Alcune riflessioni circa la rilevanza del diritto comunitario sui principi del diritto amministrativo italiano' (1992) *Rivista italiana di diritto pubblico comunitario* 1209 ff.

Of these, Claudio Franchini's book on co-administration can be considered (in addition to those of Sacchi Morsiani) the first Italian monographic study on European administrative law and the first volume in Europe to emphasize the importance of the organization of European administration in terms of relations with national administrations.

These works made it possible to enter unexplored territories, particularly in the area of administrative organization: in addition to the aforementioned volume by Franchini, the studies by Alberto Massera on the functional notion of public administration, those of Giacinto della Cananea on comitology, and Luisa Torchia on independent authorities were veritable milestones in the construction of European administrative law and its repercussions on the transformations of national laws.

The first Italian textbook on European administrative law was published in 1990.[109] Towards the end of the year, an international conference on National Administrative Rights and European Administrative Law was held in Rome, the findings of which were collected in the 1991 *Rivista trimestrale di diritto pubblico*.[110]

1991 saw the first issue of the *Rivista italiana di diritto pubblico comunitario*, edited by Mario P. Chiti and Guido Greco, and it is still one of the most important journals in the field of public law. In 1997, the same authors directed an exceptional work of analysis of European administrative law, which gave rise to the three volumes of the *Trattato di diritto amministrativo europeo* (with one general part and two special parts).[111] In 1999, Mario P. Chiti published the first edition of the handbook *Diritto amministrativo europeo*,[112] a teaching aid with a coherent and capillary structure and, above all, an in-depth analysis of principles and institutes. By the second half of the 1990s, the discipline was fully established, and courses in Italian universities multiplied.

Lastly, it should be noted that, after his prophetic exploratory essay of 1961, Benvenuti variously reflected once again on the European legal system between 1985 and 1994. The first of these reflections was in a lecture at a conference in Lugano,[113] then in a well-known essay in 1989, *Europe without Borders*, the Venetian jurist, working on overcoming the notion of borders and, consequently, territory and state sovereignty, expounded on the idea of Europe as a "functional structure, and no longer a national and territorial one, [in which]

109 M. Airoldi, *Lineamenti di diritto amministrativo comunitario* (Milan: Giuffrè, 1990).

110 In (1991) *Rivista trimestrale di diritto pubblico* 769 ff.

111 M.P. Chiti and G. Greco (eds), *Trattato di diritto amministrativo europeo* (Milan: Giuffrè, 1997).

112 M.P. Chiti, *Diritto amministrativo europeo* (Milano: Giuffrè, 1999).

113 F. Benvenuti, 'Le Alpi per l'Europa. Prolusione', in *Le Alpi per l'Europa: una proposta politica. Economia, territorio e società. Istituzioni politica e società*, Atti del II Convegno (Lugano, 14–16 March 1985) (Milan: Giuffrè, 1988), also in idem, *Scritti giuridici*, vol. V (Milano: Vita e pensiero, 2006) 4039 ff.

borders are disappearing, and the sphere within which nation States realise their sovereignty is increasingly shrinking".

> If we succeed in believing that nation-states can at least coexist alongside what can be called 'functional states', if we succeed in perceiving this reality as a prelude to tomorrow's reality, then we can also be aware that today's efforts will end up imposing consciousness of that social reality, inevitably led in the end to transitioning from an economic reality to a political reality, which we call Europe. A non-state reality, certainly, but one endowed with the non-territorial but transnational character that will be the hallmark of the states of the future: a Community that will not be so much territorial as centred on identical interests and needs: interests and needs that, in other words, are not purely economic but enlightened by the ideality that comes from shared traditions of history and thought, in a word, from a common civilisation.[114]

And also in a paper published three years later, he reiterated that "the European system is not one of a federal state but, if you will, of a Community".[115]

Lastly, in a report delivered in 1994, he found many concrete signs of the objectification of the European order, noting that

> this breaking down of the rigid nineteenth-century figure of a pyramidal state was hastened thanks to the privatisation movements now common to all the member states of the European Union, while giving form to precisely those independent authorities that tend, in broad areas such as economics or mass communications, to strike a balance that does not correspond to a subjectivised interest but to an ordinal and therefore objective interest.[116]

In the space of little more than five years, between 1990 and 1997, European administrative law, having flowed quietly under the surface, now became a disruptive torrent; once a neglected area of study, it was now a cutting-edge discipline of administrative law. And an organized, composite, and nationwide movement of scholars had finally come into being.

4.3. Something not dissimilar took place in the United Kingdom, where research by Trevor Hartley, Francis Snyder, Carol Harlow, Vincent Wright, Alec Stone Sweet, Paul Craig, Richard Rawlings, and Takis Tridimas soon contributed to the growing number of studies on the subject. Paul Craig can

114 F. Benvenuti, 'Europa senza confini' (1989) *Nuova antologia* 249 ff., also in idem, *Scritti giuridici*, vol. V, op. cit., 4101–4102.

115 F. Benvenuti, 'Verso il '93 e oltre', in *Studi in memoria di Franco Piga*, vol. II (Milan: Giuffrè, 1992) 1077 ff., also in idem, *Scritti giuridici*, vol. V, op. cit., 4303.

116 F. Benvenuti, 'Dalla sovranità dello Stato persona alla sovranità dell'ordinamento' (1995) *Jus* 193 ff., also in idem, *Scritti giuridici*, vol. V, op. cit., 4378.

currently be regarded as the leading scholar on European administrative law, having published the world's best-known textbook on the subject.

The contribution of the study of English administrative law to European administrative law has been fundamental in many ways: giving importance to historical and evolutionary aspects, attention to organizational structure and structural models in the search for an institutional balance; the centrality of general principles, which constitute the skeleton around which European administrative law is fleshed out, the decisive role of the courts and their case law in constructing this law, and the openness to alternative forms of protection.

As we have already observed, European administrative law has made enormous progress over the last three decades, and a not inconsiderable part of the merit can be ascribed to scholars from across the Channel and the dedication and organization of their work.

4.4. Important progress has also been made in France, thanks to Pierre Delvolvé, Jean-Bernard Auby, Jacqueline Dutheil de la Rochère, Jacques Ziller, and others, albeit about a decade behind Italy and England.

Spain entered the Community late (at the time of the Single European Act), but in the last thirty years its legal scholars (Ricardo Alonso García, Francisco Balaguer Callejón, Luis Ortega Álvarez, Elisenda Malaret i García, Luis María Díez-Picazo Gimenez, as well as new generations of scholars, including Daniel Sarmiento, and many others) have fully made up for lost time and brought a significant contribution to European administrative law studies.

Irish scholars have produced growing numbers of important studies in recent decades, not least thanks to Deirdre Curtin's contribution to European law.

Portuguese and Greek scholars on the one hand and Belgian and Dutch academics on the other have also made growing numbers of contributions over the last quarter century.

Lastly, it should be noted that European public law studies are not cultivated and enlarged solely on the Continent. There are important scholars and research centres on the American continent, where leading public law scholars in North America number among the foremost scholars of European public law (e.g., Daniel Halberstam and Mathias Reimann at Michigan Law School) and also, more specifically, of European administrative law (among others, Peter Lindseth, Peter Strauss, Susan Rose Ackerman, Francesca Bignami).

4.5. In short, between the 1990s and the early years of the new millennium, the main themes of European administrative law were subject to much in-depth examination: the new organizational models, the principles and procedural modalities of administrative action, provisions on responsibility, forms of justice, not to mention the numerous sectorial disciplines, including the fundamental one of the new law of economics, stemming from the European integration process, constituting a thorough and broad-ranging study in which the Italian science of administrative law has made an important and leading contribution.

It may be argued, as a conclusion to this brief parenthesis, that a handful of scholars scattered across the Continent and in close contact (Jürgen Schwarze, Eberhard Schmidt-Aßmann and a few others in Germany; Sabino Cassese, Mario P. Chiti and a few others in Italy; Paul Craig, Carol Harlow and some others in the United Kingdom; Jean-Bernard Auby and some others in France) laid the mature foundations of European administrative law, just as Joseph Weiler built the foundations of European[117] constitutional law in the 1970s.

5. The new millennium: the proactive role of administrative law studies between crisis and opportunity

The first two decades of the new millennium are characterized by contradictory phenomena in the development of European administrative law.

First of all, there was a move in the direction of stabilizing the disciplinary framework, strengthened by the steps taken by the constitutional platform of the European legal system. However, the partial failure of the attempt to draw up a European Constitution led to the step forward represented by the Lisbon Treaty, which produced a redefinition of the Union's constitutional principles and values, including with regard to the administrative side.

The severe global economic and financial crisis has brought about a change in the relationship between the European institutions and the member states, resulting in significant changes, including at the administrative level. If these have once again led to developments in intergovernmental terms, they are also pointing towards a new phase in the evolution of European administrative law (at least, this is what seems to be evident from the new regulations of the banking union and fiscal unions), moving in the direction of networks of independent administrations, composite administrations, and cooperative mechanisms and procedures.

The European Union, which, up to now, had only expanded, is seeing, thanks to Brexit, the first worrying signs of disintegration, and public law scholars are focusing not only on the study of procedural mechanisms but also on the consequences on the overall structure of the Union resulting from the departure of the United Kingdom.

The recent pandemic and war crises, as observed above, have been a major stress test for the European legal system, to which the European institutions have responded with extremely long-term actions, but producing content that, through the NGEU and REPowerEU, have significantly revitalized the process of European integration and strengthened the role of European administrative law.

117 It should be noted, on the other hand, that original studies were taking place at around the same time: the first textbook on European administrative law, by Schwarze, dates back to 1988, and already in 1989 Sabino Cassese published the first edition of his textbook, *Le basi del diritto amministrativo*, which contained a chapter dedicated to European administrative law (S. Cassese, *Le basi del diritto amministrativo* (Turin: Einaudi, 1989) 297 ff.).

These changes have led to further rapprochement between administrative and European constitutional law as a solution to the complex situation can be found, on the legal plane, in these two cores of public law.

Essentially, based on what has gone before, it may be assumed that, in the midst of the crisis besetting the common project, the European legal system will be able to produce its own antibodies and ensure the next step forward in the European integration process.

5.1. In the twenty years in question, European administrative law studies have made great strides, constituting an embryonic science at the continental level, wholly transcending national barriers. There has therefore been talk of the gradual development of a common European administrative culture as a condition for the success of the European integration process.[118]

Here, however, the question becomes somewhat awkward and the subject of rather heated debate, not only in Europe, and is closely connected to the related topic of the Europeanization of domestic administrative law.

Some maintain the real possibility of the emergence (even the current existence) of a European legal culture, arguing that there is already an extensive common substratum, thanks to the vertical and horizontal convergence produced by European administrative law. Others oppose this optimistic view (deeming it utopian) because, in concrete terms, the differences and divergences between legal systems, traditions, and cultures are still so strong and solid that the possible emergence of a common European legal culture is not credible.

Another factor to take into consideration is the 'model' of legal culture. Will it be of a kind close to the *Neue Verwaltungsrechtswissenschaft* or to the continental liberal European legal tradition? The former would appear preferable, but there is still much uncertainty and divergence of opinion on this point.

And, in any case, even leaving aside methodology, one cannot fail to recognize that if one speaks of general principles of action, independent authorities, models of transparency, and forms of judicial review on the unlawful actions of the administration, one can easily weave together a scientific dialogue to demonstrate the now common matrix of legal training.

With regard to the progress made in the 2000s, it would be too complex here to describe the multiple ramifications of administrative law studies, which can now boast several Continent-wide legal journals, numerous treatises and reference texts, series of studies, and hundreds of monographs. We must not fail to mention – in addition to the three volumes of the *Grundlagen* edited by Schmidt-Aßmann, Hoffmann-Riem and Voßkuhle – the five volumes published so far of the treatise on *Ius Publicum Europaeum*, edited by Armin von Bogdandy, Sabino Cassese, and Peter Huber, which have enabled further in-depth exploration of the points of commonality and convergence among the various European legal systems in the light of the influence of European law.

118 K.-P. Sommermann, 'Gemeineuropäische Verwaltungskultur als Gelingensbedingung europäischer Integration?' (2015) *Die öffentliche Verwaltung* 449 ff.

To gain an idea of the complexity and degree of disciplinary maturity achieved by European administrative law, suffice it to look over and compare the indices of the four reference works on the subject in France, Germany, the United Kingdom, and Italy: the third edition of the *Traité* by Jean-Bernard Auby and Jacqueline Dutheil de la Rochère (2022), the volume edited by Oswald Jansen and Bettina Schöndorf-Haubold on European composite administration (2011), the third edition of Paul Craig's textbook (2018), and the second edition of the volume edited by Mario P. Chiti (2018).

Consequently, there is now a mature and largely shared and coherent picture of the 'system' configurations in the European legal system and administrative law, both in terms of general principles and functions and the aspects pertaining to organization, finance, procedure, and judicial review.

But it also reveals the plurality of approaches and the asymmetrical capabilities to go into greater depth of the various continental legal cultures, which thus allow the *summa* of European administrative law to be translated into a sort of melting pot: the irrepressible German tendency for taxonomic 'heaviness' and solidity of subject matter and, in particular, the propensity to start from a general concept and then go into extreme depth in examining the normative and applicative discipline of a single sector; the more 'ethereal', but original and creative, Italic tendency to grasp the trends and theoretical coordinates that emerge from concrete analysis of the terrain covered; the great French architectural ability to build sets and sub-sets, matryoshka-like, but preserving lightness and verticality; and the enviable solidity and essentiality of the English edifice, with its immovable divisions and ability to move easily between normative and jurisprudential analysis.

Ultimately, it is clear that to speak of Italian, French, German, or English administrative law or even to speak of European administrative law makes less and less sense, because, by now, on the continental level there is only 'administrative law', with its various facets and expressions. European law is so interwoven with national laws that it has become one with them, and it increasingly makes little sense to limit legal analysis within the territorial borders of states. But there is more: there can be various expressions of legal evolution, depending on the different contexts in which it operates and the centuries-old traditions to be taken into account. Its trends and development are, however, becoming recognizable and shared, regardless of specific national applications.

Brexit will certainly be a loss for the development of continental legal culture, considering the fundamental contribution brough by Anglo-Saxon scholars to the development of a common European law.

5.2. European administrative law is now not only studied on the Continent, but it also attracts the attention of universities and research institutes around the world and is considered an important laboratory for the study of relations between administrations belonging to different systems and different levels of government.

Albeit with a much broader scope (European law as a whole), an essay by Piet Eeckhout published a few years ago in a US legal journal explained very well to non-European scholars the four reasons why EU law has become so influential across the globe.[119] The first is the constant and adaptable questioning of the aims and boundaries of the European legal system. The second is the autonomy of the European legal system and its importance for relations with international bodies. The third is the relationship between economic freedoms and the protection of individual rights, and, lastly, the primacy of European law over national ones.

As Sabino Cassese points out, "The most important phenomenon in the two hundred years of administrative law is the development, in the last quarter of a century, of an administrative law that only belongs in part to a state, while the other part pertains to a supranational non-state body".[120] At the administrative level, the European legal system has engendered very particular forms of emersion, representation, and balancing of interests, which, as noted above, have produced the phenomenon of the so-called public arena.[121]

All this has attracted the growing attention of scholars in North and South America, Asia, and Oceania to the vicissitudes of European public law as an example of a non-federal 'regional' order, whose model dates back to the mediaeval tradition but is endowed with a strong heritage both in terms of a robust democratic fabric and a centuries-old legal culture. On the other hand, the proliferation of study centres dedicated to European law (focusing in particular on public law) in American universities also constitutes a strong pole of attraction for the more authoritative European scholars. Thus, the centre of gravity of European law studies is increasingly shifting outside the Continent, and one wonders whether a community of scholars of European public law[122] and, within it, of European administrative law, is thus coming into being, consolidating a European administrative law that can operate recognizing a common substratum, while maintaining the irrepressible differences stemming from the different legal traditions.

A particularly interesting example is the European Legal Studies Program of the University of Michigan Law School, directed by Daniel Halberstam. Halberstam, currently Eric Stein Collegiate Professor of Law at the University of Michigan, has been both a clerk at the US Supreme Court and a judicial fellow at the European Court of Justice. Under Eric Stein's influence, Ann Arbor has established itself as an important overseas crosspoint for European law studies.

European public law is also an important subject at the Columbia University Law School, with its European Legal Studies Center. There is a Global Faculty

119 P. Eeckhout, 'The Growing Influence of European Union Law' (2011) 33 *Fordham International Law Journal* 1490 ff.

120 S. Cassese, 'Il diritto amministrativo europeo presenta caratteri originali?', 2003, in idem, *Il diritto amministrativo: storia e prospettive* (Milan: Giuffrè, 2010) 388.

121 S. Cassese, *Il diritto amministrativo europeo presenta caratteri originali?*, op. cit., 389.

122 On this trend of European legal studies taking root overseas, see A. von Bogdandy, 'A Bird's Eye View on the Science of European Law', op. cit., 208, analyzing certain critical aspects.

Program at New York University's Law School, the Law School at the University of Notre Dame, and so on.

In view of Mercosur, albeit in much looser terms, the topic of European administrative law is also of growing interest in South American states. Courses on European law (including from the public law perspective) are also becoming more common in Asian universities.

As we might deduce from the description presented here, the vicissitudes of European administrative law are unique, and this is also true of its evolutionary timeline. It has gone, in the space of barely a quarter of a century, from being misunderstood to become a science of worldwide importance.

It is a timeline that runs parallel to the substance of European law mentioned at the beginning of this volume: the process of European integration has taken place thanks to a melting pot of knowledge and a mixture of disciplines. This entails the need to adopt a different methodological paradigm for the study of European law: it must bear the hallmarks of an interdisciplinary[123] approach, a characteristic that gradually spilled over into national contexts.

In conclusion, in just a handful of decades, European public law and its science have not only taken shape in original ways, but they have also profoundly and irreversibly altered the context of reference.

Now, in the wake of the waves of continuous upheaval produced by the global economic and financial crisis, the discipline, together with the entire legal system, will have to prove to be not only young, but resilient and tough.

But it will also have to prove that it can make a proactive contribution to the construction of the new European order. As we have attempted to show above, law (and also the science of law) has so far played an ancillary and mostly instrumental role in the process of European integration, being secondary to the economic-financial objectives of the order.

It is certainly true that steps forward have also been made on the legal plane, but, in the last quarter century especially, they have been made precisely in order to obtain, first and foremost, results in the domain of economics.

On the contrary, the science of public law, no longer a servant but in prime position, is called upon to make a constructive and proactive contribution of its own for redressing the balance of the push from the various social sciences. We might consider, for example, financial and monetary issues, social rights, the complex phenomenon of immigration, and the closely related question of the free movement of persons.

How law can be an instrument of redressing balance, and what legal science contribute in this direction will be addressed in the next section.

123 J.H.H. Weiler, 'The Reformation of European Constitutionalism' (1997) 35 *Journal of Common Market Studies* 97. In this regard, in addition to the studies of Armin von Bogdandy and Sabino Cassese cited above, also see A.K. Mangold, *Gemeinschaftsrecht und deutsches Recht*, op. cit., in particular, 7 ff.

Chapter VI

The Law in the New European Legal Order

1 The resilience of a Europe built on the rule of law: the end of the line or quick stop?
2 Interdisciplinarity with the law in first place?
3 Public law driving towards 'utopian realism'

1. The resilience of a Europe built on the rule of law: the end of the line or quick stop?

We have seen that Europe has undergone various evolutionary phases, some of them marked by strong imbalances between the subject and methods of the social sciences in order to 'manage' the legal system.

Leaving aside the centuries-long age of religion (or spirituality, as it is sometimes called), the most significant social influence on our continent for roughly a millennium[1], the legal method led by Germany, prevailed from the nineteenth century and the early part of the twentieth century, bringing about a wave of dogmatism, formalism, positivism, statism, and the predominance of the state over the individual: this era, the age of the birth of the administrative state, brought us to World War I. The 1920s and 1930s were characterized – also due to severe economic crisis – by the supremacy of politics over the other social sciences, which pathologically translated into authoritarianism, totalitarianism, nationalism, imperialism, the erosion of individual rights, and the occupation of the state by a part of civil society. This, the age of the authoritarian state, led to World War II. From the mid-1980s to the present day, as we have seen, 'economic cretinism', to use the Gramscian[2] expression, prevailed over the other social sciences, leading to neo-liberalism, mercantilism, monetarism, the emergence of global private powers, market deregulation, the

1 This imbalance also produced ills of its own, such as the holy wars, the Inquisition, and religious fundamentalism, to name but a few examples.
2 A. Gramsci, *Quaderni del carcere*, vol. II, quad. no. 7, para. 13 (Turin: Einaudi, 2007) 863–864. The paragraph is dedicated to 'Einaudi e il materialismo storico', and Gramsci speaks of economic cretinism referring to economic propagandists.

DOI: 10.4324/9781003302094-7

compression of social rights, populism, leaderism, and neo-nationalism: the severe economic and financial crisis has brought out the worst of this way of conceiving social arrangements, and we do not yet know where all this may lead, but certainly the prospects are not rosy.

What can be gleaned from cycles in history is that law, politics, economics, and the other social sciences should proceed in a mutual equilibrium, in a relationship of mutual exchange and support. When the rapport between these sciences becomes asymmetrical, and one of them prevails over the others, which become merely instrumental, the system's defences and counterweights are weakened, and the systems collapse, bringing the dire consequences that history has shown us.

As far as the European order is concerned, we have seen the extent to which the global economic crisis has highlighted its weaknesses. In the light of the dominance of a certain economic-financial interest over others, and the failed attempt to adopt a European constitution, the system's shortcomings in the spheres of politics, identity, value, and constitution now came to the fore (also as a result of a too hasty expansion).

Crises can be useful for legal systems if they are understood as opportunities for their growth and maturation. It is no mere chance that all the previous 'crises' that have hit Europe in recent decades have turned out to be growth fevers, symptoms to identify ills, and have helped to find antibodies and take important steps towards integration. The serious difficulties of the day, concerning politics and identity, as well as the economy and finance, may also be an opportunity to integrate and harmonize the systems of the member states, moving in the direction of a truly united Europe.

These crisis years have seen steps forward in the direction of unity, such as the attempt to achieve a European banking union,[3] an objective which is still a long way off, principally due to the absence of the so-called third pillar, the deposit insurance system.[4] Similar steps could also be taken in the areas of fiscal union, defence, and foreign policy.

But what the governments of the member states will have to reflect on is the goal: whether they intend to exclusively build a Europe of economic interests and, therefore, extend the territory of the supranational entity exclusively to compete more strongly with the other world economic blocs, or whether they also intend to build a Europe of the peoples, grounded in its Graeco-Roman cultural roots and eighteenth-century Enlightenment thinking. If the idea is the

3 On this *ex multis*, see S. Cassese, 'La nuova architettura finanziaria europea' (2014) *Giornale di diritto amministrativo* 79 ff.; L. Torchia, 'L'Unione bancaria europea: un approccio continentale?' (2015) *Giornale di diritto amministrativo* 11 ff.; E. Chiti and G. Vesperini, *The Administrative Architecture of Financial Integration. Institutional Design, Legal Issues, Perspectives* (Bologna: il Mulino, 2015).

4 On the legal repercussions of the European Banking Union, an in-depth analysis is provided in G. Lo Schiavo (ed.), *The European Banking Union and the Role of Law* (Cheltenham, UK; Northampton, MA: Elgar, 2019).

former, it is obvious that the order will be rather precarious: as long as it is worthwhile, all will be well, but once the economic benefit disappears, cracks will appear, and the social model will collapse.

If, on the other hand, the intention is to create a European order as the home of the European peoples, then the route must be reset to different coordinates, relying strongly on education and culture to foster a common European consciousness. But first of all, the balance of the social model must be restored, so that the contributions of the 'partial systems' of the social sciences and the distinct methods become symmetrical and exchangeable once again, which will ensure impartiality and the reconstitution of interdisciplinary union.

The institutional path to follow could be one of enhanced cooperation. In this regard, the hypothesis of splitting, i.e., the creation – alongside the market union that currently encompasses almost the whole of Europe – of a nucleus of just a few founding countries, which would move in the direction of closer political integration, adopting "a new institutional paradigm, the union of states operating according to one version or another of the logic of the multiple separation of powers",[5] has been put forward. Nevertheless, the institutional confusion – both horizontal and vertical – that largely followed the severe economic and financial crisis, which showed the limits of a purely economic perspective of integration,[6] was remarked, along with the risk that differentiated forms of integration could lead to a neoliberal dead end, creating "a post-political and post-democratic environment".[7]

In this regard, the recent developments in the migration crisis are symptomatic. Suffice it to recall, in particular, the failure to redistribute the burden of receiving a million refugees who arrived in Europe via the Balkans in 2015 (so-called relocation) and the related problem of burden-sharing, which is paralyzing the reform of the common asylum system now under discussion. It is common knowledge that the countries of the Visegrád bloc are resisting the introduction of a European quota system for the reception of applicants for international protection, and this veto leads one to suppose that, in the not-too-distant future, it may be necessary to proceed through intensified cooperation.[8]

Integration should therefore also progress on other levels: through a small and cohesive group of forerunner countries, which, having historically shared the founding principles of the democratic state, are capable of also building unity in diversity on the constitutional, political, and social planes.

In recent years, the question has often been asked whether the story of a united Europe has already come to an end (a success, but also a very short

5 S. Fabbrini, *Sdoppiamento. Una prospettiva nuova per l'Europa* (Rome: Laterza, 2017) 117.
6 S. Fabbrini, *Sdoppiamento*, op. cit., 121.
7 A. Somma, *Europa a due velocità. Postpolitica dell'Unione europea* (Reggio Emilia: Imprimatur, 2017) 206.
8 See, in this regard, *www.europarl.europa.eu/legislative-train/theme-towards-a-new-policy-on-migration/file-revision-of-the-dublin-regulation*.

story, with a sudden fall). However, it could well be that the best years are yet to come. For this to happen, however, we need to understand how to restore balance and, before that, what the role of the various social sciences should be. Due to the legal slant that inevitably underpins this research, we must ask, first and foremost, what the role of law in the contemporary age should be, in an attempt to piece together an order oriented towards the political union of Europe and its peoples.[9]

In short, behind every crisis lurks an opportunity: the important thing is to know how to grasp it. On the other hand, the very course of the birth of the European order (which took shape thanks to a series of international contingencies and, in particular, the East-West conflict on the Continent and the Cold War in general) shows that "political ideas and projects geared to a qualitative leap presuppose a constellation of particular impulses for action and decision if they are to be taken into consideration and become realistically possible".[10] Could it be that we have now reached the moment to bring about a change to the structure, in terms of political equilibria and the supranational order, to take the step that has so often failed (with the EDC, the EPC, and the European Constitution)?

2. Interdisciplinarity with the law in first place?

What is the role of the jurist today? Social scientists have been asking themselves these questions over the last years, even coming to radical conclusions, such as, among others, the end of law[11] and jurists,[12] the evaporation of law,[13] the inability of law to interpret the contemporary age, the uselessness of law, or even worse, the ill effects of law.

9 On the topic of political union, on which public law scholars have been working for almost three decades, see, among others, C. Pinelli, 'Ipotesi sulla forma di governo dell'Unione europea (1989) *Rivista trimestrale di diritto pubblico*', 315 ff.; J.P. Jacqué, J.H.H. Weiler, 'On the Road to European Union: A New Judicial Architecture: An Agenda for the Intergovernmental Conference' (1990) *Common Market Law Review* 185 ff.

10 E. Böckenförde, *Diritto e secolarizzazione. Dallo Stato moderno all'Europa unita*, (Rome-Bari: Laterza, 2007), 173.

11 See, among others, P. Rossi (ed.), *Fine del diritto?* (Bologna: il Mulino, 2011); A. Zaradny, N. Wolff, T. Fleury Graff (eds), *La fin du droit* (Paris: Mare Martin, 2016).

12 See, for example, R. Susskind, *The End of Lawyers? Rethinking the Nature of Legal Services* (Oxford: Oxford University Press, 2008), where legal services are understood as a shrinking market, and a future for lawyers is seen only if they are willing to reposition themselves in close connection with the IT and business sectors.

13 Or rather, the dumbing down of legal discourse through the economy and the mechanistic logic of the market society, on which, among others, see A. Supiot, *Lo spirito di Filadelfia. Giustizia sociale e mercato totale* (Milan: Et Al., 2011).

These are catastrophic and reductionist readings, devoid of substance. What, then, should the role of law be? Is it really reduced to a mere infrastructure, to be used at will to create a system? Is law currently a mere "mouthpiece of economic laws" or merely the "source of a conceptual order derived from economics"[14]? Or is it also subject matter (specific and technical, different from other scientific substance) and, if so, does it contribute to adding content to the fabric of the legal order? Is the legal sphere still autonomous, and can the jurist's technical knowledge still be put to use independently of the substantive primacy of economics?

These are recurrent questions in the contemporary debate, demonstrating the malaise surrounding legal studies in search of a new identity.

À quoi nous sert le droit? This, for example, is the question posed, from the sociological standpoint, by Jacques Commaille in a recent essay[15] aiming at encouraging dialogue between the social sciences, based on the assumption that law does still serve a purpose. He emphasizes the dual nature of law, arguing that it serves, in a generally 'closed' and dogmatic sense, to point to and identify 'transcendent Reason' and thus impose itself on society, while also aiming, from a more 'open' and realistic viewpoint, to interpret social processes and become the key to understanding society's needs, aspirations, and claims. Commaille describes the profound transformation that has also taken place in the legal field, both in its connection to the territory – no longer exclusively linked to the state, but as the jurist is called to a two-way glocal approach, globalized and localized at the same time – and in its relationship with time, which is now inexorably accelerating, so that the need for justice is also closely linked to the time factor. Lastly, he shows how these institutional and social transformations have undermined the closed understanding of law as 'transcendent Reason', so that, as the construction of a social model of the democratic type is still indispensable, it can only be achieved through the hybridization of the two legal meanings and also, therefore, through a dialogue between law and the other social sciences.

À quoi sert le droit? also prompts François Ost, adopting an interdisciplinary approach, to return to the primordial meaning of the concept of law, reconstructing its uses, functions, and purposes in a book that can be numbered among the most significant in the early years of the millennium thanks to its influence on the legal sphere.[16] Ost takes his cue from a scenario that was unthinkable until a few years ago, namely, that of a post-legal society, a society without law or, better, "une société dans laquelle le droit se serait dissous dans un océan de normativité indistincte". The proliferation of technical and managerial standards and indicators, stemming from the culture of performance and management, the normalization of objects, and the standardization of practices,

14 A. Somma, *Europa a due velocità*, op. cit., 209.
15 J. Commaille, *À quoi nous sert le droit?* (Paris: Gallimard, 2015).
16 F. Ost, *À quoi sert le droit? Usages, functions, finalité* (Bruxelles: Bruylant, 2016).

ethical norms, the diffusion of technological instruments of social control, the "l'empire des normes chiffrées", the "gouvernance sans véritables normes, en se pechant sur l'empire des statistiques et la nébuleuse des *nudges*"[17] have produced chaos and reduced the empire of law to a mere archipelago. Thus, we encounter formally non-legal norms that are endowed with real normative capacity and, conversely, formally legal norms that have dubious material normativity, as they lack the 'statut de règle de droit'. Thus, Ost wonders what is lost when a social model decides to do without law and what the real contribution of law to social[18] relations is. Even more fundamentally, the author reflects (in the course of a philosophical and anthropological interlude) about man and the new humanism, about the Greek and Roman cultural matrix that is required today in order to answer the question: "quel homme pour quel droit? (…) c'est notre image de l'homme, en effet, qui détermine le type de société et de droit que nous voulons defendre".[19] For Ost, law has its own extrinsic and intrinsic purposes: the most eminent extrinsic purposes are democracy, justice, what constitutes the human; but there are also others, such as the preservation of the established order.

> Dans ces conditions, la recherche la plus importante porte sur les finalités 'intrinsèques': celle que l'on attribue au droit, si et seulement si, on en subordonne les fonctionnalités à la promotion de la démocratie, la recherche de la justice et le souci de conforter la constitution de l'humain.[20]

It follows that the intrinsic functions of law concern the intensity and extent to which the technical functions of law are imparted in order to pursue democracy and justice. Ost identifies three intrinsic purposes of law: "1) définir un équilibre social général, (2) susceptible d'être imposé par la contrainte, et cependant (3) de nature à être remis en cause dans le cadre de procédures déterminées".[21] Thus, for Ost, balance, shared obligation, and certain procedural renewal are intrinsic aims of democratic and just legal systems; these are requirements that must operate in tandem, because working in isolation would lead to negative outcomes: law is the effort to civilize force.

Interpreted in these terms, the concept of law is imbued with substance and is not reduced to the role of mere infrastructure. The notion of endogenous legal content, on the other hand, dates back to the eighteenth century and is not only associated with the common law tradition across the Channel (for William Blackstone, the sovereign is merely the repository of law, serving to secure justice for the individual), but above all to the *Staatslehre* of the Germanic

17 F. Ost, 'De l'internomativité à la concurrence des normativités: quels sont le role et la place du droit?' (2018) *Les Cahiers de droit*, 10.
18 F. Ost, *À quoi sert le droit? Usages, functions, finalité*, op. cit., 1–5.
19 F. Ost, op. cit., 12.
20 F. Ost, op. cit., 8.
21 F. Ost, op. cit., 337.

tradition of the eighteenth and nineteenth centuries. From this flowed some important offshoots at the turn of the twentieth century: Santi Romano,[22] for example, supported the conceptual autonomy of law, unlike Giovanni Gentile, who reduced the law to ethics, and Benedetto Croce, who reduced it to economics. Carl Schmitt, on the other hand, reduced it to politics.

And if law is a second-level concept, not as primaeval as morality, spirituality, politics, and economics (and thus, in certain historical periods, called upon by religion, politics, and economics in a marginal function, adapting it to their own ends[23]), it is nonetheless essential and autonomous, with its own 'politically militant' intrinsic aims, one might say. In pursuing them, the law is naturally oriented towards engineering and constitutionalizing society, in search of proportion and, therefore, the right balance between the multiple interests found in life in society and between the impulses of the various social sciences. These are to be pursued through reasonable and shared principles, which can adapt in line with changes in society.

The legal platform thus derives its ontological inspiration from the harmonization of impulses coming from the various social sciences: law puts a brake on the primordial instincts that lead to the abuse of one social science over the others. And it is thus called upon to play a fundamental role in creating a synthesis of the goals of the other sciences at any specific time in history, in transforming the impulses, needs, and claims they present into rules (with the requirements mentioned above) and reconstructing the lost balance between the various social sciences. The law, in this context, is at the same time the

22 See, in particular, Santo Romano's two masterpieces: S. Romano, *The Legal Order*, edited and translated by M. Croce (London: Routledge, 2018; first Italian edition: *L'ordinamento giuridico*, Pisa: Spoerri, 1918); idem, *Frammenti di un dizionario giuridico* (Milan: Giuffrè, 1947). On Santi Romano's theories see, among others, A. Sandulli, 'Santi Romano and the Perception of the Public Law Complexity' (2009) 1 *Italian Journal of Public Law* 1–38.

23 On this point, N. Irti, *Il diritto nell'età della tecnica* (Naples: Editoriale Scientifica, 2016) 13 is clear: "Il volere, da cui nasce e si svolge il diritto, mira a raggiungere uno *scopo*. Volontà di scopo – potrebbe dirsi –, che sceglie mezzi e strumenti adatti. Già questo è un primo incontro con la tecnica, se per tecnica intendiamo l'*adeguazione dei mezzi al fine*, il non restare al di qua né andare al di là del risultato atteso. L'energia normativa non va sciupata e neppure risparmiata, ma messa a razionale servizio dello scopo. La tecnica del diritto è appunto in questa *commisurazione*, nel chiedere alla volontà altrui non meno e non più del sacrificio necessario. L'analisi economica del diritto, venuta in moda ai nostri giorni, solleva un vecchio e secolare problema. È appena da soggiungere che la *razionale scelta dei mezzi* nulla ha a vedere con la *razionale scelta dei fini*: il fine offre il criterio per calcolare la razionalità dei mezzi, ma non c'è alcun criterio per calcolare la razionalità dei fini. Qui, nel preferire l'uno all'altro fine, o nell'ordinarli secondo un prima e un dopo, si agita la storia dell'uomo: fedi religiose, visioni del mondo, ideologie politiche, interessi economici. Conflitti si accendono e si spengono, alleanze si concludono e si sciolgono: e alleanze e conflitti lasciano traccia nella storia delle legislazioni."

instrument to attain this new balance and the end to achieve by finding the right proportion.[24]

3. Public law driving towards 'utopian realism'

What kind of jurist and, in particular, what kind of public lawyer can realize such an ambitious objective, capable of revitalizing European integration process in the right direction?

There are some who believe that the path by which the jurist can once again become part of the elites seeking to build the social order is that of dogmatics, previously traced by Gerber and Laband, following in the footsteps of Savigny and Puchta.[25] This originates from neo-constructivism,[26] neo-dogmatism, and conceptual[27] abstractionism, all of which have evolved in the German-speaking environment especially, in both private and public law in recent decades. They seek to re-position the jurist at centre stage, using a legal method, very close, *mutatis mutandis*, to the traditional Savignian historical school method, interpreted from a Gerberian perspective. It is an axiomatic method, based on a closed order, the establishment of a system, the deductive process, and univocal interpretation.

History has already shown what this way of conceiving law can lead to, and this type of jurist seems the least suited to achieving the objective outlined in the previous paragraph.

To understand a development process as complex as the European one, built, as we have seen, on the foundation of a plurality of social sciences, jurists cannot operate in isolation.[28] Instead, they must be open to a plurality of methodologies pluralism and the study of the other social sciences, grasping the variables of the topical method and ready to adopt a differentiated approach to

24 See, again, N. Irti, *Il diritto nell'età della tecnica*, op. cit., 33: "C'è un'alternativa ineludibile: o il diritto, fedele alle antiche radici, si ritira nell'ombra, spaurito e inerme dinanzi all'immane potenza della tecno-economia, la quale sceglierà, essa stessa, la sede giuridica dei singoli affari; o il diritto, nelle forme del dominio imperiale o degli accordi inter-statuali, sarà capace di raggiungere quella potenza e di piegarla alla propria disciplina."

25 Entire libraries have been written on Savigny and the theoretical output of the historical school. *Ex multis*, see the important 1964 lecture, recently published in Italian, by E. Böckenförde, *Diritto e secolarizzazione. Dallo Stato moderno all'Europa unita*, op. cit., 3 ff.

26 A. von Bogdandy, 'The Past and Promise of Doctrinal Constructivism: A Strategy for Responding to the Challenges Facing Constitutional scholarship in Europe' (2009) 7 *International Journal Constitutional Law* 364–400.

27 Santi Romano spoke of "logomachie concettualistiche" (conceptualist logomachy) in 'Giurisprudenza scolastica', in idem, *Frammenti di un dizionario giuridico* (Giuffrè: Milan, 1953, reprinted from the original) 112.

28 M. Brutti, 'La solitudine del presente', in I. Birocchi and M. Brutti (eds), *Storia del diritto e identità disciplinari: tradizioni e prospettive* (Turin: Giappichelli, 2016) 295 ff.

a problem according to the different conditions that present themselves, while safeguarding their technical and genetic heritage.

The role of the scholar of public law could perhaps be something akin to Benvenuti's 'utopian realism',[29] that is, having an ability to read prismatic reality by assuming a proactive and constructive attitude: being a builder of cathedrals who does not go down the road of legal dogmatics or remain isolated in an ivory tower but is in full contact with the other social sciences and their findings. And this too in function of piecing together the new order (and, as it were, controlling its hold) to ensure a balance between the different thrusts of the social sciences and to direct the content of the resulting melting pot towards aims of democracy and justice.

The public law scholar should be equipped for the in-depth field studies required by administrative law but should also aspire to return to the militant reconstruction of a constitutional order – the construction, through a return to the 'constitutional phase', of a European public law policy.

Jurists should be 'open' but neither naive nor superficial: they should be able to engage with different methodologies through the filter of legal technique, but must be careful not to get caught up in the languages and methods of other sciences, as sometimes happens overseas. Being fully conversant with legal technique, which is at the heart of legality and its goals, and jealously defending their genetic heritage, the European jurist may thus aim for the construction of a democratic and institutionally balanced order.

A move in this direction will lead on the one hand to the demise of the insularity of legal discourse and on the other to the inadequacy of the theory that the legal order is the keystone of constitutional and institutional construction, given the current complexity of institutional arrangements.[30]

It follows that this is not so much an epistemological matter, other than for the purpose of recording changes in methodological variety and plurality. The basic issue lies in the purpose of juridicity: in practice, jurists note and avail themselves of the different methods, according to their usefulness, to construct, applying juridical technique, the best balance to maintain the system.

The jurist and the law must therefore not seek supremacy (indeed, there are no longer the premises for this to happen) or even hegemony over the other sciences; rather, they are called upon to play a dual role. In their relations with the other sciences, they must use their specific technique alongside, and on a par with, other social scientists; in pursuing intrinsic goals, the law must act as a

29 On the oxymoron of 'utopian realism' and its subject matter see, more specifically, U. Allegretti, 'Benvenuti e le potenzialità del realismo utopico' (2017) *Rivista trimestrale di diritto pubblico* 2017, 65 ff. without necessarily embracing the non-law hypothesis assumed in J. Carbonnier, *Flessibile diritto. Per una sociologia del diritto senza rigore* (Milan: Giuffrè, 1997) 25 ff.

30 On these issues, see the in-depth examination in G. Itzcovich, *Teorie e ideologie del diritto comunitario* (*Theories and Ideologies of Community Law*) (Turin: Giappichelli, 2006) 268 ff.

sextant, guiding the whole scientific edifice towards balance, calculability, and orderly solutions to problems, always keeping the guarantee of fundamental rights in sight.

This may, perhaps, be the path the scholar of law should take so that they – and public law – may once again participate actively as part of the scientific elite that guides social orders. The role of the scholar of law must no longer be one of supremacy, but rather of primacy, marked, in a wide-ranging Europeanist vision, by a platonic fair balance[31] of economics, politics, and law,[32] in pursuit of Monnet's dream of the political and economic union of the peoples of Europe, governed by a democratic legal regime: "Nous ne coalisons pas des États, nous unissons des hommes."[33]

31 The reference is to Plato's *Philebus*, which closes with a hierarchy of values, the first of which is precisely the right balance and what is directly derived from it, endowed with proportion and beauty.

32 Moreover, in G. Pasquino, *L'Europa in trenta lezioni* (Turin: Utet, 2017) 65, we read that at present there seems to be a lack of vision, a far-reaching strategic aspiration: "Attualmente, non esistono personalità politiche – ma neppure fuori della politica – che abbiano mostrato una visione europeistica di respiro, che si siano affermate con la promessa non semplicemente di governare meglio l'Europa che c'è, ma di costruire un'Europa migliore, l'Europa che vorremmo. Mancano i politici, mancano i predicatori, mancano i profeti. Mancano quelli che Schumpeter definirebbe gli imprenditori politici, uomini o donne che sappiano cogliere la richiesta di maggiore unificazione oppure che sappiano trasformare le delusioni dell'Unione europea in promesse di cambiamenti realizzabili."

33 J. Monnet, *Mémoires* (Paris: Fayard, 1976). The sentence was uttered on 30 April 1952, in a speech to the National Press Club in Washington. And, in a subsequent speech in Strasbourg on 11 September 1952, Monnet recalled that "Cette union européenne ne peut pas se fonder seulement sur les bonnes volontés. Des règles sont nécessaires. Les événements tragiques que nous avons vécus, ceux auxquels nous assistons, nous ont peut-être rendus plus sages. Mais les hommes passent, d'autres viendront qui nous remplaceront. Ce que nous pourrons leur laisser, ce ne sera pas notre expérience personnelle, qui disparaîtra avec nous; ce que nous pouvons leur laisser, ce sont les institutions. La vie des institutions est plus longue que celle des hommes et les institutions peuvent ainsi, si elle se sont bien construites, accumuler et transmettre la sagesse des générations successives."

Epilogue

We have attempted in this volume to develop the following line of reasoning.

1. We started from the observation that the European order, which has managed to ensure the peoples of Western Europe experience peace and prosperity and masterfully overcome the numerous crises that have befallen it, is now experiencing the most complex challenges in its short history. To formulate a diagnosis, we had to examine the very origins of the European integration process.

By looking at the past in this manner, we have understood that the supranational European order has a very different genetic heritage from those of the modern nation-states. These possessed a well-defined legal (and philosophical) lineage, as law (and philosophy) constituted recognized social sciences during the seventeenth and eighteenth centuries. Thus, it fell primarily to legal systems to guide the European continent's economic, political, and social development from the seventeenth to the nineteenth century. Economics was scarcely more than an embryonic science, and the foundations of sociology would be laid over the course of the nineteenth century. Not that, even then, rulers made decisions without considering political and economic factors, but these were matters of fact and, as such, were not grounded in a robust scientific and methodological framework.

During the eighteenth and nineteenth centuries, the state and the law were closely interconnected: the law was considered functional to the state, and the state existed in function of the law. This interdependence was accomplished through a process of the juridicization of politics and/or the politicization of law. The law organized and regulated the exercise of political power, both in terms of constraining the exercise of sovereign command and from the point of view of the individual guarantees recognized by the rule of law. Indeed, almost every aspect of the modern state 'speaks the language of law'.

The genome of the supranational European order contains a wealth of chromosomes. By the mid-twentieth century, several other social sciences had matured alongside law; these include economics, sociology, political science, and statistics. The European Union is therefore a unique system, not only because of its inherently composite nature but also because it was built on a

DOI: 10.4324/9781003302094-8

fusion of methodologies from the social sciences. Among these, economic concerns alongside the legal method gained significant prominence as matters of policy were intentionally left to the national states, and the priority at the European level was principally economics and technocratic-bureaucratic matters. Through the functionalist model, the objective of integration was pursued via the market, particularly in seeking to implement the ordoliberal theories of the social market economy. As has been observed, "European integration has always been driven by political factors (...). Yet, while the ends were always political, the means were always economic."[1]

In this context, the role of law has primarily been to contain and channel the unrelenting forces of the economy (at the supranational level) and politics (emanating from national states), providing a concrete constitutional foundation for the process of economic integration (referred to as 'Integration through Law'). However, this dual genome has meant that practitioners have come to perceive the creation of rules as a set of incentives and a system of cost-benefit analyses that guide their behaviours in terms of economic advantages and disadvantages, as well as establishing the relationship between ends and means. Such a perspective can be interpreted through the lens of utility-effectiveness/efficiency-economic viability on one hand, and proportionality/benefit on the other, in an approach that gravitates towards an empirical methodology, prioritizing the study of public and private behaviours over the formulation of rules and emphasizing not only legality, equality, and solidarity but also objectives, results, and social well-being.

2. In the early decades of the integration process, practitioners largely embraced the principles of the Freiburg Ordoliberal School. Originating in Germany, these principles emerged in response to both state totalitarianism, advocating for the transformation of the state into a regulator, and unfettered market liberalism, emphasizing the need to establish rules for the market in the form of an 'ordo'. Instead, an alternative concept known as the 'third way' emerged, positioned between economic planning and economic-financial deregulation. Proponents of ordoliberalism maintained that society is structured into multiple closely interconnected, distinct, and equal spheres (law, politics, economics) brought together through subsidiarity. Within this *schema*, law assumes a fundamental role in shaping and giving substance to the economy, which can only exist as a combined social and legal construct. The balanced coexistence of economics, politics, and law determines the proper functioning of markets, particularly the principle of free competition that drives economic growth and, consequently, social progress. This perspective presents an institutional view of the economic system, wherein the legal framework centres around the fundamental goal of safeguarding competition in the market, which becomes the primary public interest to be preserved. In this context, public

1 R. Baldwin and C. Wyplosz, *The Economics of European Integration*, 5th ed. (Maidenhead: MacGraw-Hill Education, 2015) 31.

institutions proactively safeguard the economic order and embrace a holistic conception of the economy and the market. There is thus a constant interaction between economics and law, both in terms of procedure and the construction of operating rules for the system.

The socio-economic landscape underwent a profound metamorphosis during the 1980s and, above all, the 1990s, under a dual impulse to deregulate, on the one hand, and to bring about the corporatization of public entities on the other. This paradigm shift was inspired by reforms introduced in the English-speaking world, particularly in the United States and Britain. Additionally, within the European framework, a third force emerged: constraints imposed on public finances. Social benefits were drastically reduced through the strict application of algorithms in a highly technical process. While the administration of these benefits rested with individual member states, the European order exerted substantial influence through its financial mechanisms.

Departing from the foundations of the social market economy, there was now a shift towards neoliberal approaches, propelled by privatization and liberalization policies alongside the adoption of private-sector strategies in the public sector. This transition was accomplished thanks to a decisive turn towards analytical approaches and econometrics involving the development of mathematically valid algorithms. This transition marked a move away from earlier realistic perspectives and a divergence from other social sciences. There was also a desire to align economics with the precision found in the exact sciences, given the assumption of the systematic completeness of economics and its classification as a science.

At the same time, the principles of Thatcherian New Public Management facilitated transplanting organizational and management methods from the commercial onto the public sector, giving rise to a 'corporatization' process termed 'results-oriented administration'. This favoured an instrumental and teleocratic view of the legal order, emphasizing productivity and contractual arrangements in a transition that relegated the nomocratic perspective, inherent to political philosophy and cultivated over centuries within European legal and political culture, to a marginal position.

As a consequence, the trajectory of European law has taken a strikingly different route from that of state law, with the consequence that the function of law is now very different from that of the last three hundred years.

The new European legality, as has been observed, "is already born hybrid: its legitimacy comes not only from *auctoritas* (formally valid 'legislative' law) but also and above all from *ratio* (the substantive and procedural rights and principles of justice)".[2] Essentially, the shift that has occurred is a movement away from a state-level rule of law to a community of law, defined as such by the Court of Justice to describe the blend derived from European treaties and the general principles of the legal order as discerned by the courts.

2 M. Vogliotti, *Legalità*, in *Enciclopedia del diritto*, Annali VI, 2013, 410 ff.

Still, this legality was born hybrid primarily thanks to its dual genetic makeup, as we mentioned earlier: the model was forged on a European functionalist foundation that evolved within and for the market, employing predominantly economic methods (and, to a lesser extent, sociological and political methods), and after an initial period of equilibrium, in the last quarter of a century, economics has come to dominate the scene.

3. The unique characteristic of the evolution of the European order is that the economic method has 'penetrated' the legal sphere through a process of 'juridification', and the law has been employed as an 'infrastructure' to strategically disseminate the economic method within the order.

Management rules have been translated into legal principles, and, by focusing on economic rationality, this 'juridification' has transformed the content and notion of legality itself: if "legal action is no longer synonymous with efficient action, then it is inevitable that efficiency will inspire the legal reconstruction of administrative action".[3] Juridified efficiency has led to the deviant transformation of the inherently dynamic nature of an economic process, that of achieving results, into a prescriptive and formalized given, rigidifying and morphing it into legalism. The consequence has been a logical and systemic[4] short-circuit.

The neoliberal-style economic constitution that emerged from all this has ultimately shaped the integration process across its various phases, as clearly emerges from recent developments. The sovereign debt crisis led to the formulation of an original regulatory framework in which financial interests (and their related technical aspects) crafted a new economic governance structure. This regulatory arrangement is characterized by exceptions and exceptionalism, where European institutions possessing specific technical expertise and a minimal degree of democratic legitimacy end up wielding substantially unlimited powers.[5]

This regulatory system, operating interchangeably with forms of hard and soft law, generates a series of paradoxes. Norms produce deregulation, which allows entities with primarily technical competencies to enjoy a reasonable degree of discretion. The discretionary power of national administrations is thus considerably diminished, although it is 'reclaimed' by European-level institutions equipped with technical expertise:

3 A. Romano Tassone, 'Sulla formula "amministrazione per risultati"', in *Scritti in onore di Elio Casetta*, vol. II (Naples: Jovene, 2001) 823.

4 In this regard, M. Everson has pointed out the need to recuperate the role of law with its distinct characteristics, in order to address and overcome "its current malaise of totalizing economic rationalization". This re-emphasis on the role of law aims to offset the overwhelming dominance of economic considerations and their totalizing impact: 'Ordoliberal Escape from Societas Economica: Re-establishing the Normative' in J. Hien and C. Joerges (eds), *Ordoliberalism, Polanyi, and the Theodicy of Markets* (Oxford: Hart, 2017) 210.

5 See the recent C. Joerges, 'The Overburdening of Law by Ordoliberalism and the Integration Project', in J. Hien and C. Joerges (eds), *Ordoliberalism, Law and the Rule of Economics* (Oxford, UK; Portland, OR: Hart, 2017) 179 ff.

> While legal regulation of a public nature essentially operates based on the compliance/non-compliance binomial (of behaviours and acts) with respect to legal norms – built on the judgments of legitimacy/illegitimacy that enable judicial review – the new governance largely revolves around evaluations. Especially, it centres on the distinct success/failure conceptual pair in the economic performance of States and their planned or implemented policies.[6]

4. The European institutional model revolves around a few thousand (approximately 40,000 and growing) bureaucrats with excellent technical skills supplemented by national bureaucrats in the European 'network'. This model of post-national democracy – as we may call a system where national legislative powers in shaping supranational policies –, while ensuring high technical quality, poses challenges concerning political and democratic legitimacy and the absence of adequate checks and balances to offset this inherent weakness.

In response to the extreme dominance of politics during the second quarter of the twentieth century, which led to the horrors of World War II, the European 'spillover' was functionally rooted in the supremacy of technical expertise in the absence of politics. This form of 'output legitimacy' has been termed 'technocratic legitimacy'. The supranational order deliberately evolved in an 'apolitical' direction, although it exercised, in reality, a strong influence on politics and the structure of society. With almost no central political authority, reliance on the virtues of technical expertise from epistemic communities became essential. This naturally facilitated the emergence of administrative law, which was able to evolve and adapt within such a favourable environment.

In Europe, decisions are largely made by the technical leadership of the European institutions, in the absence of a 'strong' central political authority. These leaders define the framework rules and adopt specific acts principally based on their technical expertise. The rules enacted by these independent structures (which do not rely on a political and representative executive) – for example, the European Central Bank – are technical. The regulators, supervisory, and control apparatuses are also technical. If we extend our examination to the so-called networked sectors, we may observe that these independent structures, at both European and national level, are deeply interconnected through shared language, standardized practices, and a common professional culture, all of which are strictly technical. This culture is economically and financially oriented in the context of the financial markets. The technical nature of regulation serves as a unifying and integrating element between national and European apparatuses; however, it also isolates them and their respective sectors from the other areas of the legal systems to which they belong.

6 L. De Lucia, '"Pastorato" e "disciplinamento" nella *governance* economica europea' (2015) *Diritto pubbico* 890.

In some member states (such as Italy), the opposite phenomenon has occurred: there is politics but no technical expertise, as the internal technical competencies within public entities have been significantly reduced, creating a paradox where some states have politics but lack technical experts to support decision-making, while the European Union is dominated by technical aspects in the absence of politics.

Such a paradox arises because, as democratic safeguards are extended, decision-making processes become less efficient, and vice versa. Typically, what is gained in democracy is lost in efficiency, and vice versa. Moreover, it is crucial to strike an appropriate balance to ensure that the European public perceives the decisions adopted as the ideal means of pursuing the common interest.

In the discourse surrounding 'democratic deficit', two predominant stances emerge.

The first perspective, advocated in particular by Peter Lindseth, argues that European governance is primarily administrative. Consequently, European institutions, comprising bodies of technically skilled bureaucrats, are delegated by the member states – the only entities with politically democratic legitimacy answerable to the electorate (input democracy) – to exercise normative power and perform tasks of social and economic regulation. Alongside the lingering political primacy of nation-states, this perspective indirectly suggests the emergence of the constitutional drive of the European order, through the workings of technical and administrative mechanisms. This could potentially lead to a new constitutional framework within a kind of 'metabolic constitution'. Thus, the connection between administrative law and European constitutional law would arise from the bottom up, facilitated by bolstering the administrative processes.

The second thesis, as outlined by Deirdre Curtin and others, revolves around the composite nature of the European order and the gradual construction of a living European constitution. This perspective views interventions aimed at European integration as sedimentary layers that accumulate over time, much like different geological strata. This approach acknowledges the current democratic deficit but also takes into account the progress made over past decades and what will be achieved in the years to come. In any case, fragmentation and institutional pluralism are an intrinsic part of the European order and stem from the significant conflict arising from the multitude and diversity of institutional actors and interests at play. As such, the solutions for gradually overcoming the current deficit are, in the short-to-medium term, facilitated by the proactive role of the Court of Justice, the dissemination of transparency mechanisms, the greater involvement of national parliaments, and the reinforcement of the organizational principle of accountability.

In reality, from both perspectives, the development follows the path of a gradual evolution. Consequently, contrary to the firmly established originalist approach of the United States, the viewpoint leans more towards the perspective of ongoing development, involving cautious and gradual reasoning vis-à-vis measures for improving the legal framework. It takes into account that the path ahead is uncharted for constitutional democracies and that these mechanisms are fragile and need to be handled carefully and prudently, seeking the right balance and advancing at varying speeds, depending on the times and the context.

In recent years, various forms of procedural legitimacy have been suggested, involving enhanced procedural guarantees, an emphasis on outcomes, and other indirect forms of legitimacy. The introduction of such mechanisms is both important and desirable; however, if the focus is on a material constitution, it is clear that the destiny of a constitutional democratic order is linked to the participation of the people in political decision-making processes using appropriate means. In short, it appears necessary to aim for a democratic legitimacy of a political nature.

5. The functional evolution and progressive development of the European legal framework, on the one hand, and the delegation of political matters primarily to the member states while focusing on technical-economic competencies, have posed challenges to the advancement of European constitutional law. Conversely, European administrative law has been able to operate within its sphere with relative ease, encountering few obstacles along its course, and this has led to the gradual emancipation of administrative law, especially over the last three decades, along with a substantial weakening of the constitutional aspects of the European order.

The difficulties surrounding constitutional law have been felt in several respects: first, a weakness emerges in terms of identity; second, in relation to government, especially with regard to democratic deficit and the lack of transparency and participation in the decision-making process, and, last, in relation to flexibility in the way laws are made. Despite the achievements of the Treaty of Lisbon, a number of unresolved issues persist concerning the allocation of competences. Regarding the protection of rights, although the Court of Justice has made significant progress, a certain asymmetry with respect to the European Convention on Human Rights and a substantial gap between the pronouncements of the European court and practical application by other European institutions remain.

These ambiguities took their toll on the failed attempt to adopt the European Constitution. While it is true that many of its contents made their way into the Treaty of Lisbon, its failure represented a significant setback for European constitutional law.

In stark contrast, the fate of European administrative law has been very different. Until only a few decades ago, administrative law could be associated with the nation-state alone and extended no further. Nevertheless, the last few decades have witnessed a change in direction. Particularly in the wake of the Single European Act, European administrative law has grown exponentially in terms of the scope of its functions and competencies, the depth of its development regarding principles and institutes, and the complexity and capillarity of its organizational structures. Administrative law has transcended the confines of the nation-state, venturing into unexplored realms both at the continental and global levels. It has undergone a renaissance, serving as a centre of gravity and equilibrium within the legal space beyond the nation-state.

However, today, this is no longer sufficient. The bidirectional process of the constitutionalization of administrative law and the infusion of administrative elements into constitutional law, which originated and developed within the European context, demands that administrative and constitutional law studies proceed hand in hand. From this standpoint, administrative law can act as a trailblazer, stimulating a renewed impetus in European constitutional law or, more precisely, European public law. Erecting a new institutional and political framework for the Union is not a reasonable possibility without the decisive contribution of constitutional law. In this regard, there has been discussion of a 'Strukturwandel' (structural transformation) of European public law and a constitutionally grounded architectural design for the legal system and European democratic society, as enshrined in Article 2 of the Treaty on European Union (TUE).[7]

In the evolutionary trajectory of European administrative law, the Italian legal tradition has held minimal sway, while those of France and Germany have assumed pivotal roles, particularly in the early phases. Furthermore, the contributions of the United Kingdom, the Scandinavian countries, and the Netherlands have also been significant. However, over the past three decades, the American legal tradition has played an increasingly prominent role, possibly due to the North American origin of the principles and institutions of economic regulation.

6. The aim is to restore the lost balance between law, economics, and politics. As Europe's history shows, some phases in its evolution have been marked by significant imbalances between social forces and the direction of legal development.

After a millennium of dominance by religion and the spiritual sphere, between the nineteenth century and the beginning of the twentieth the Savignian and Hegelian law-oriented framework came to dominate, bringing with it a surge of dogmatism, formalism, positivism, statism, and state primacy over individuals. This era, marking the birth of the administrative state, culminated in the First World War. In the aftermath of the global conflict and the severe economic crisis it spawned, politics took precedence over other social sciences, leading to authoritarianism, totalitarianism, nationalism, imperialism, the curtailment of individual rights, and a segment of civil society taking over the state. This era of authoritarian states ultimately culminated in the Second World War. Over the past three decades, the economic method has overwhelmingly overshadowed other social sciences in a shift that became especially

7 See A. von Bogdandy, *Strukturwandel des öffentlichen Rechts. Entstehung und Demokratisierung der europäischen Gesellschaft* (Berlin: Suhrkamp, 2022).

pronounced during the economic and financial crisis, marking an era of neoliberalism characterized by the narrowing of social rights and the erosion of democratic constitutional safeguards.

Additionally, economic and financial leverage has become a decisive factor in geopolitics and international relations. These historical cycles illustrate the importance of maintaining a balanced interaction between law, politics, economics, and other social sciences in a mutually beneficial exchange. When one of these disciplines takes undue prominence over the others, relegating them to subservient or instrumental roles, the defence mechanisms and checks within the system weaken, potentially leading legal and political orders to the point of collapse.

To establish a well-balanced European system, one must first determine whether the emphasis should be solely on a common market, shaping Europe as an economic powerhouse on a global scale, or if the aspiration is to forge a 'Europe of its peoples'. The former approach can only result in a temporary and weak instrumental partnership on the political, social, and identity levels. Such an arrangement would hold as long as it is economically advantageous, but as soon as this is not the case, each member might well go its own way. If the intention is to establish a European order that serves as a home for the European peoples, then the trajectory must be charted anew, guided by different coordinates: "If Europe does not wish to run aground, it must no longer come across as a technical-pragmatic construct of economic rationality; it must manifest itself as an idea of order and reflect the political will of not only European individuals but also the collective will of the European peoples."[8]

The foremost imperative is to restore balance within the social model, reinstating symmetry and reciprocity among the contributions from various 'partial systems' while fostering the collaborative use of distinct methodologies. This would ensure that no single perspective dominates and would re-establish interdisciplinary partnerships.

In this direction, could the path to follow involve greater cooperation among a small and cohesive group of countries, aiming for a union that goes beyond merely economic aspects and extends to the constitutional and political levels? These countries might roughly be the original founding members of the European project. Given their historical alignment with the foundational principles of democratic States, they may be in a position to construct a new European order centred on unity in diversity. This approach would have ramifications on the constitutional, political, and social planes while upholding fundamental rights. However, alongside the potential advantages of this solution, there are also possible drawbacks, particularly in the domains of foreign policy and geopolitical dynamics. The complexities of international relations and the evolving global landscape could make this course more arduous to navigate today than it would have been a few years ago.

8 E. Böckenförde, *Diritto e secolarizzazione. Dallo Stato moderno all'Europa unita* (Rome–Bari: Laterza, 2007) 200–201.

7. Indeed, confronting the challenge of re-establishing a balanced sense of purpose cannot be accomplished solely through institutional changes or governance reforms. Even though the European Court of Justice has played and continues to play an essential role, it cannot, in isolation, define a new order through its jurisprudential guidelines, as it has done in the past. It is imperative that, alongside other stakeholders, the legal community assume the responsibility of constructing and proposing solutions effectively capable of reconciling means and ends, even when these may conflict. In doing so, it must take into account the profound transformative phenomena that have characterized recent decades, primarily driven by technological revolution and economic globalization.

Indeed, the importance of European public law has become particularly evident in the contexts of the pandemic and the Ukrainian crisis. European institutions have been profoundly transformed, reinforcing the political dimension through the Next Generation EU (NGEU) and REPowerEU initiatives. These measures have greatly fortified the community method and the roles of the European Council, notably the European Commission, by means of budgetary instruments and an economic programme aligned with the pursuit of specific public interests.

In this monograph we have traced the journey of European public law, revealing a trajectory rich in accomplishments. Cultivation of this field through a fruitful synergy between jurisprudence and academia has woven a dense tapestry of principles and institutions that underpin the organization and operation of European institutions, as well as the relationships between these entities and national institutions. This field has seen remarkable growth and an expanding influence, attracting scholarly attention across Europe and beyond its borders, fostering the development of a common European legal culture.

However, the task assigned to the scholar of European public law is broader, primarily entailing the reassertion of distinct substantive legal content. We are currently navigating, as previously mentioned, a profound resurgence of the rule of law on the continental level. Yet, this resurgence is enacted through protection mechanisms, employing financial instruments and implementing sanctioning or nudging mechanisms. Despite the chaos within the normative framework, bringing order to the vast array of sources is becoming increasingly challenging in a scenario where formally non-legal norms possess actual normative significance while, conversely, the material normativity of the rule may be questionable.

It is therefore necessary to retrace the authentic roots of European juridicity, once again emphasizing the intrinsic and extrinsic purposes of law, one rich in substance, that resists being confined to the role of mere infrastructure. While it remains true that law is a second-order concept, not a primal one like morality, spirituality, politics, and economics, and has historically been tugged in various directions when religion, politics, and economics have – adapting it to their purposes – at times utilized it albeit marginally and instrumentally for their own ends,[9] it is also true

9 On this point, a passage from N. Irti's work *Il diritto nell'età della tecnica*, (Naples: Editoriale Scientifica, 2016) 13, is clear: "The will, from which law is born and

that juridicity has some characteristics that set it apart. In its intrinsic and 'advocatory' purposes, one could say, law serves to guide society via its normative value, in the pursuit of proportionality and, therefore, the right balance among the multiple interests inherent in collective life and the diverse influences of the various social sciences. This can be achieved by adopting reasonable and shared norms capable of constantly adapting to the ever-evolving social landscape.

Consequently, the legal platform is naturally inspired by the configuration and restraint of impulses from the various social sciences. Law acts as a constraint upon the primal instincts that might otherwise lead to the dominance of one social science over others. In this sense, it assumes a fundamental role in synthesizing the objectives pursued by other sciences at a specific historical juncture. Its primary function is to transform the impulses, demands, and assertions of other social sciences into rules that will align with the criteria mentioned earlier.

Thus, the imperative lies in restoring the lost equilibrium among the various social sciences. In this context, law is both the means to attain a new balance and the objective to be pursued by discovering the ideal proportion.[10]

The substantial commitment expected of the academic community necessitates a redefinition of the role of legal scholars in the direction of what could be termed 'utopian realism', implying the ability to perceive the numerous facets of reality while adopting a proactive and constructive approach capable of restoring primacy. Jurists should no longer live in isolation within their secluded domain but must fully engage with other social sciences and their findings to weave the very fabric of the emerging order, with the overarching goal of preserving equilibrium amid the diverse forces arising from the 'partial systems'

unfolds, is to achieve a purpose. A will of purpose, one might say, which chooses suitable means and instruments. This is already a first encounter with technique, if by technique we mean *adapting means to ends*, not staying on this side or going further than the expected result. Normative energy should be neither wasted nor hoarded but put to rational service for the purpose. The technique of law lies precisely in this proportionality, in demanding from the will of others no less and no more than the necessary sacrifice. The economic analysis of law, which is currently in vogue, raises an age-old and eternal problem. It is just worth adding that the *rational choice of means* has nothing to do with the *rational choice of ends*: the end provides the criterion for calculating the rationality of the means, but there is no criterion for calculating the rationality of the ends. Here, in favouring one purpose over another, or in arranging them in a sequence, the tapestry of human history unfurls: religious faiths, worldviews, political ideologies, and economic interests come to life. Conflicts kindle and fade; alliances are forged and severed; and both alliances and conflicts etch their imprints upon the pages of legislative history."

10 Again, as N. Irti contends in *Il diritto nell'età della tecnica*, "There is an inescapable alternative: either law, true to its ancient roots, retreats into the shadows, fearful and defenceless in the face of the immense power of techno-economics, which will itself choose the legal framework for individual affairs; or law, in the forms of imperial dominance or inter-state agreements, will be capable of attaining that power, bending it to its own discipline."

within the social sciences. The ultimate aim is to steer the resulting product towards constitutional ideals of democracy and justice.[11]

In conclusion, the law can and should serve as an infrastructure, but it must not depart from its fundamental purposes, which are deeply embedded in the genetic heritage of the major Western industrialized cultures – namely, democracy and justice. What is required is a return to the moment of writing, to the 'constitutional moment', and the deeper meaning of 'integration through law', a return to the original post-war era when law, politics, and economics fused into an effective partnership, a return to the Philadelphia Declaration of 1944, which expressed the aspiration to build a new international order based on law and justice, and the guarantee of fundamental rights, in the aftermath of the horrors of the Second World War.

8. These are the areas where the future of Europe will be decided in the coming years. It will become clear whether, as hoped, a true union of European peoples within a democratic framework that rectifies imbalances through legal means can be achieved. In such a vision, concepts like community, solidarity, and dignity must not remain mere rhetorical flourishes but manifest as tangible realities.

In 1945, in the shadow of the horrors of World War II, an influential Florentine legal scholar, Giovanni Miele, urged jurists to adopt a radical change of focus:

> The social sciences, especially law, need to distance themselves from their abstract and formal nature which has abetted various forms of tyranny so effectively. Rather, they must adopt procedures to elevate all that is noble and enduring in the human spirit: freedom, justice, solidarity, neighbourly love, and the spirit of fraternity. In this light, a profound re-examination of concepts that hold particular sway in this domain becomes compelling and should be undertaken without delay. For jurists, this will involve re-examining the complex reality of the State, the nature of its responsibilities, the distribution of its organs and functions, its relationships with individuals, the relationships of individuals with their peers, and the autonomy of individuals and groups.[12]

11 This could enable the law to endure even in the current critical phase, albeit resting on new foundations. As G. Teubner remarks in *Diritto policontesturale. Prospettive giuridiche della pluralizzazione dei mondi sociali* (Naples: La Città del Sole, 1999) 78, the law has survived all the challenges it has had to face over the past two centuries: "Marx, Weber, and Ehrlich, along with, among contemporary legal theories: legal pluralism, institutionalism, critical legal studies, private government theories, autopoiesis, and the economic analysis of law – have all vigorously contested the hierarchy of law in which '[t]he King's Two Bodies' resided. However, none have achieved unequivocal success."

12 G. Miele, 'Umanesimo giuridico' (1945) *Rivista di diritto commerciale*, now in idem, *Scritti giuridici*, vol. II (Milan: Giuffrè, 1987) 445.

But as early as ten years before, Thomas Mann, foreseeing a sombre future, had expressed his desire for the rise of

> a militant humanism, a humanism that would discover its own strength and become imbued with the conviction that the principles of freedom, tolerance, and doubt must not allow themselves to be exploited and overshadowed by shameless and undoubting fanaticism. If European humanism has become incapable of a vigorous rebirth of ideas, and if it is no longer capable of invigorating its soul with a determined zest for life, it will perish, and the name of Europe will be nothing more than a historical expression from which it would be better to seek refuge in timelessness neutrality.[13]

The legal order and personal freedom converge in the Europe of constitutional structural transformation, seeking to offset the asymmetries brought about by financial dominance and the new geopolitical landscape. This places an obligation on legal scholars, especially public law researchers, to chart the parameters for achieving a proportionate balance between economics and politics in the pursuit of constructing a European democratic society.

Once again, it is necessary to fight for the law. In a Europe witnessing a worrying resurgence of populism and nationalism, it is once again crucial to uphold the idea that law is not the unconscious outcome of a people's spirit but the privileged tool through which societal progress and the legal order can be realized. The goal is to consistently use the law to attain collective functional outcomes through the recognition of individual rights and freedoms.

From this point of view, as a synthesis of centuries-old European intellectual thought in the field of legal sciences, Article 2 TEU – which has long been considered a purely programmatic legislative provision, as has happened in the past also fundamental articles of the Italian Constitution – could really constitute, in coordination with other articles of the European treaties and thanks to the interpretation of the courts, the constitutional basis through which the law can be put back at the centre, on the basis of the theorization of several layered movements of thought over several centuries. A not non-instrumental concept of law, working for dialogue and collaboration between social sciences: a *primus inter pares* rather than an authoritarian leader. This will only come about if the tyrant of our times, economic-financial power, will give way to the force of the law.

13 T. Mann, Acthung, *Europa! Essays* 1933–1938 (Berlin: Fischer Verlag, 1995) 95–96.

Bibliography

Airoldi M., *Lineamenti di diritto amministrativo comunitario* (Milan: Giuffrè, 1990).

Allegretti U., 'Benvenuti e le potenzialità del realismo utopico' (2017) *Rivista trimestrale di diritto pubblico* 65–72.

Amato G., 'Il mercato nella Costituzione' (1992) *Quaderni costituzionali* 7–19.

Amato G., Conclusioni, in G. Montedoro and E. Reviglio (eds), *La legge di bilancio e di stabilità: le politiche economiche possibili fra diritto costituzionale e diritto europeo. Dibattito fra economisti e giuristi* (Rome: Dike, 2017) 127–130.

Armstrong J.A., *The European Administrative Elite*, 1973 (Princeton: Princeton Legacy Library, 2015).

Armstrong J.A., *Nations before Nationalism*, 1982 (Chapel Hill, NC: UNC Press Enduring Editions, 2009).

Asor Rosa A., *Il grande silenzio. Intervista sugli intellettuali* (Roma-Bari: Laterza, 2009).

Auby J.-M. and Fromont M., *Les recours contre les actes administratifs dans les Pays de la Communauté economique européenne* (Paris: Dalloz, 1971).

Bachof O., 'Die Dogmatik des Verwaltungsrechts vor den Gegenwartsaufgaben der Verwaltung', in *Veröffentlichungen der Vereinung der Deutschen Staatslehrer*, Heft 30, von W. Martens und P. Häberle, *Grundrecht im Leistungsstaat*, von O. Bachof und W. Brohm, *Die Dogmatik des Verwaltungsrechts vor den Gegenwartsaufgaben der Verwaltung* (Berlin; New York: Walter de Gruyter, 1972) 193–364.

Badie B. and Birnbaum, P., *Sociologie de l'Etat* (Paris: Grasset, 1979).

Baldassarre A., 'Diritti sociali', in *Enciclopedia giuridica*, vol. XI (Roma: Istituto della Enciclopedia italiana, 1989) 1–34.

Balducci M., 'Burocrazia comunitaria e amministrazioni nazionali nel processo decisionale dell'Unione europea' (1994) *Rivista trimestrale di scienza dell'amministrazione* 101–156.

Baldwin R., Cave M., and Lodge M. (eds), *Understanding Regulation: Theory, Strategy, and Practice* (Oxford; New York: Oxford University Press, 2012).

Baldwin R. and Wymplosz C., *The Economics of European Integration*, 5th ed. (Maidenhead, UK: MacGraw-Hill Education, 2015).

Baraggia A. and Bonelli M, 'Linking Money to Values: The New Rule of Law Conditionality Regulation and its Constitutional Challenges' (2022) 23 *German Law Journal* 131–156.

Barberis M., *Europa del diritto. Sull'identità giuridica europea* (Bologna: il Mulino, 2008).

Barile P., *Rapporti tra norme primarie comunitarie e norme costituzionali e primarie italiane* (Padova: Cedam, 1966).

Basedow J., Dietze J., Griller S., Kellerbauer M., Klamert M., Malferrari L., Scharf T., Schnichels D., Thym D., Tomkin J., 'European Integration: Quo vadis? A critical commentary on the PSPP judgment of the German Federal Constitutional Court of May 5, 2020' (2021) 19 *I-CON* 188–207.

Bataveljic D., *European Federalism* (Saarbrücken: Lambert Academic Publishing, 2018).

Battini S., 'Review of "F. Fabbrini, E. Hirsch Ballin, H. Somsen (eds), What Form of Government for European Union and the Eurozone?"' (2016) *Rivista trimestrale di diritto pubblico* 246–252.

Beck U., *Europa tedesca. La nuova geografia del potere* (Rome: Laterza, 2012).

Becker P., *Der Einfluß des französischen Verwaltungsrechts auf den Rechtasschutz in den Europäischen Gemeinschaften* (Hamburg: Heitmann, 1963).

Benvenuti F., 'Dalla sovranità dello Stato persona alla sovranità dell'ordinamento' (1995) *Jus* 14–19.

Benvenuti F., 'Dalla sovranità dello Stato persona alla sovranità dell'ordinamento', in F. Benvenuti *Scritti giuridici*, vol. V (Milano: Vita e pensiero, 2006) 4367–4380.

Benvenuti F., 'Europa senza confini' (1989) *Nuova antologia* 249–260.

Benvenuti F., 'Europa senza confini', in F. Benvenuti, *Scritti giuridici*, vol. V (Milano: Vita e pensiero, 2006) 4093–4106.

Benvenuti F., 'Le Alpi per l'Europa. Prolusione', in F. Benvenuti, *Le Alpi per l'Europa: una proposta politica. Economia, territorio e società. Istituzioni politica e società*, Atti del II Convegno (Lugano, 14–16 March 1985) (Milan: Giuffrè, 1988) 15–24.

Benvenuti F., 'Le Alpi per l'Europa. Prolusione', in F. Benvenuti, *Scritti giuridici*, vol. V (Milano: Vita e pensiero, 2006) 4039–4050.

Benvenuti F., 'Verso il '93 e oltre', in *Scritti giuridici*, vol. V (Milano: Vita e pensiero, 2006) 4291–4304.

Benvenuti F., 'Verso il '93 e oltre', in *Studi in memoria di Franco Piga*, vol. II (Milan: Giuffrè, 1992) 1077–1093.

Benvenuti F., 'La C.E.C.A., ordinamento sovrano', introduction to *Ordinamento della Comunità europea del carbone e dell'acciaio*, vol. I (Padua: Cedam, 1961) 1–41.

Benvenuti, F., *Scritti giuridici*, vol. V (Milano: Vita e pensiero, 2006).

Benvenuti M., *Libertà senza liberazione. Per una critica della ragione costituzionale dell'Unione europea* (Naples: Editoriale Scientifica, 2016).

Beqiraj J. and Moxham L., 'Reconciling the Theory and the Practice of the Rule of Law in the European Union Measuring the Rule of Law' (2022) 14 *Hague Journal on the Rule of Law* 1–26.

Bergonzini C., 'The Italian Constitutional Court and Balancing the Budget: Judgment of 9 February 2015, no. 10; Judgment of 10 March 2015, no. 70' (2016) 12(1) *European Constitutional Law Review* 177–191.

Berman H.J., *Law and Revolution*, vol. I, *The Origin of the Western Legal Tradition* (Cambridge, MA: Belknap Press, 1998).

Berman H.J., *Law and Revolution*, vol. II, *The Impact of the Protestant Reformation on the Western Legal Tradition* (London; Cambridge, MA: Belknap Press, 2003).

Berman P.S., *Global Legal Pluralism: A Jurisprudence of Law beyond the Borders* (New York:Cambridge University Press, 2012).

Bernitz U. and Weatherill S. (eds), *The Protection of Fundamental Rights in the EU After Lisbon* (Oxford; Portland: Hart, 2013).

Bickerton C.J., Hodson D. and Puetter U., 'The New Intergovernmentalism: European Integration in the Post-Maastricht Era' (2015) 53(4) *Journal of Common Market Studies* 703–722.

Bifulco R. and Nato A. (eds), *The Concept of Sovereignty in the EU: Past, Present and the Future*, in https://reconnect–europe.eu/wp–content/uploads/2020/05/D4.3.pdf, 2020.

Bifulco R., *Diritto e generazioni future. Problemi giuridici della responsabilità intergenerazionale* (Milan: Franco Angeli, 2008).

Bilancia F., 'Spending review e pareggio di bilancio. Cosa rimane dell'autonomia locale?' (2014) *Diritto pubblico* 45–86.

Bilancia F., *La crisi dell'ordinamento giuridico dello Stato rappresentativo* (Padua: Cedam, 2000).

Bin R., Caretti, P., and Pitruzzella G., *Profili costituzionali dell'Unione europea. Processo costituente e governance economica*, 2nd ed. (Bologna: Il Mulino, 2015).

Black, D., *The Theory of Committees and Elections* (Cambridge: Cambridge University Press, 1958).

Black D., 'On the Rationale of Group Decision-making' (1948) 56 *Journal of Political Economy* 23–34.

Blanke H.-J., *Vertrauensschutz im deutschen und europäischen Verwaltungsrecht* (Tübingen: Mohr Siebeck, 2000).

Blauberger M. and van Hüllen V., 'Conditionality of EU Funds: An Instrument to Enforce EU Fundamental Values?' (2021) 43(1) *Journal of European Integration* 1–16.

Bleckmann, A., 'Der Verwaltungsvertrag als Handlungsmittel der Europäischen Gemeinschaften' (1981) *Deutsches Verwaltungsblatt* 889–898.

Böckenförde E., 'The Rise of the State as a Process of Secularization', 1967, in *Religion, Law and Democracy: Selected Writings*, section II, 'Law and Secularity' (Oxford: Oxford University Press, 2020) 152–167.

Böckenförde E.-W., 'Carrying Weimar Constitutional Theory into the Bonn Republic' (2018) *Constellations* 225–241.

Böckenförde E., 'The Constituent Power of the People: A Liminal Concept of Constitutional Law', 1982, in *Constitutional and Political Theory: Selected Writings*, section II, 'Constitutional Theory' (Oxford: Oxford University Press, 2017).

Böckenförde E., *Diritto e secolarizzazione. Dallo Stato moderno all'Europa unita* (Roma-Bari: Laterza, 2007).

Böckenförde E.-W., *Staat–Nation–Europa: Studien zur Staatslehre, Verfassungstheorie und Rechtsphilosophie* (Frankfurt am Main: Suhrkamp Verlag, 1999).

Böckenforde E.-W., *Staat, Verfassung, Demokratie. Studien zur Verfassungstheorie und zum Verfassungsrecht* (Berlin: Suhrkamp, 1991).

Böckenförde E.-W., *Staat, Gesellschaft, Freiheit. Studien zur Staatstheorie und zum Verfassungsrecht* (Berlin: Suhrkamp, 1976).

Boerger-de SmedtA., 'Negotiating the Foundations of European Law, 1950–57: The Legal History of the Treaties of Paris and Rome' (2012) 21 *Contemporary European History* 339–356.

Böhme, M., *Why We Need to Renew Democracy in Europe: A Brief Excursus on the Democratic Deficit of the European Union* (Munich: GRIN, 2013).

Bonetti P., *Introduzione a Croce* (Roma-Bari: Laterza, 2005).

Bossuat G., *Émile Noël, premier secrétaire général de la Commission européenne* (Bruxelles: Bruylant, 2011).

Brack N. and Gürkan S. (eds), *Theorizing the Crises of the European Union* (London: Routledge, 2020).

Brenner M., *Der Gestaltungsauftrag der Verwaltung in der Europäischen Union* (Tübingen: Mohr Siebeck1996).

Bressanelli E. and Chelotti N., 'The shadow of the European Council: Understanding Legislation on Economic Governance' (2016) 38(3) *Journal of European Integration* 511–525.

Brito Bastos F., 'Doctrinal Methodology in EU Administrative Law: Confronting the "Touch of Stateness"' (2021) 22(4) *German Law Journal* 593–624.

Brutti M., 'La solitudine del presente', in I. Birocchi and M. Brutti (eds), *Storia del diritto e identità disciplinari: tradizioni e prospettive* (Turin: Giappichelli, 2016) 295–318.

Brutti, M., 'Per la scienza giuridica europea (riflessioni su un dibattito in corso)' (2012) *Rivista trimestrale di diritto pubblico* 905–932.

Buchanan, J.M., 'Constitutional Economics', in J. Eatwell, M. Milgate, and P. Newman (eds), *The Invisible Hand* (London: Macmillan, 1989) 79–87.

Buchanan J.M. and Tullock G., *The Calculus of Consent: Logical Foundations of Constitutional Democracies* (Ann Arbor: University of Michigan Press, 1962).

Burgess M., *Federalism and the European Union: The Building of Europe, 1950–2000* (London; New York: Routledge, 2000).

Burgess, M., *Federalism and European Union: Political Ideas, Influences, and Strategies in the European Community 1972–1986* (London; New York: Routledge, 1989).

Calabresi, G., 'Some Thoughts on Risk Distribution and the Law of Torts' (1961) 70 *Yale Law Journal* 499–553.

Calandri, E., Guasconi, M.E., and Ranieri R., *Storia politica e economica dell'integrazione europea. Dal 1945 ad oggi* (Naples: EdiSES, 2015).

Campagnolo U., *Repubblica Federale Europea. Unificazione giuridica dell'Europa*, 1945 (Soveria Mannelli: Rubbettino, 2004).

Campagnolo U., *Verso una Costituzione federale per l'Europa. Una proposta inedita del 1943* (Milan: Giuffrè, 2003).

Cantaro A., *Costituzione e ordine economico* (Acireale: Bonanno, 1994).

Capogrosso F., *Shared sovereignty and denationalisation of statehood in the European Union: Has Governance eclipsed Government?* (Munich: GRIN, 2009).

Caraffini P., 'De Gaulle, the 'Empty Chair Crisis' and the European Movement' (2015) 7 *Perspectives on Federalism* 163–189.

Caranta R., *Giustizia amministrativa e diritto comunitario* (Naples: Jovene, 1992).

Carbonnier J., *Flessibile diritto. Per una sociologia del diritto senza rigore* (Milan: Giuffrè, 1997).

Caroni P., *La solitudine dello storico del diritto. Appunti sull'inerenza di una disciplina altra* (Milan: Giuffrè, 2009).

Cassese S., *Advanced Introduction to Global Administrative Law* (London: Elgar, 2021).

Cassese S., *A World Government?* (Sevilla: Global Law Press/Editorial Derecho Global, 2018).

Cassese S., *La democrazia e i suoi limiti* (Milan: Mondadori, 2017).

Cassese S., 'La costituzionalizzazione del diritto amministrativo', in *Studi in onore di Gaetano Silvestri*, vol. I (Turin: Giappichelli, 2016) 501–518.

Cassese S., 'La nuova architettura finanziaria europea' (2014) *Giornale di diritto amministrativo* 79–82.

Cassese S., 'Diritto amministrativo europeo e diritto amministrativo nazionale: signoria o integrazione?' (2003), in *Il diritto amministrativo: storia e prospettive* (Milan: Giuffrè, 2010) 393–402.

Cassese S., 'Il diritto amministrativo europeo presenta caratteri originali?' (2003) *Rivista trimestrale di diritto pubblico* 35–52.

Cassese S., 'Il diritto alla buona amministrazione' (2009) *European Review of Public Law 1037–1047.*

Cassese S., 'Il sorriso del gatto, ovvero dei metodi nello studio del diritto pubblico' (2006) *Rivista trimestrale di diritto pubblico* 597–611.

Cassese S., *Lo spazio giuridico globale* (Roma-Bari: Laterza, 2003).

Cassese S., 'Giuristi ed economisti: metodo e metodi nello studio del diritto' (2002) 3 *Giornale di Diritto Amministrativo* 341–342.

Cassese S., *La crisi dello Stato* (Roma-Bari: Laterza, 2001).

Cassese S., 'L'Unione europea come organizzazione pubblica composita' (2000) 5 *Rivista Italiana di Diritto Pubblico Comunitario* 987–992, also in *La crisi dello Stato* (Roma-Bari: Laterza, 2002) 67–73.

Cassese S., 'Il sistema amministrativo europeo e la sua evoluzione' (1991) *Rivista trimestrale di diritto pubblico* 769–774.

Cassese S. and della Cananea G., 'The Commission of European Economic Community: The Administrative Ramifications of its Political Development (1957–1967)' (1992) *Jahrbuch für europäische Verwaltungsgeschichte* 75–94.

Cassese S., 'La Costituzione europea' (1991) *Quaderni costituzionali* 487–508.

Cassese S., *Le basi del diritto amministrativo* (Turin: Einaudi, 1989).

Cassese S., 'Le rivoluzioni politiche del ventesimo secolo e la secolarizzazione della scienza giuridica', in Aa.Vv., *Nuovi moti per la formazione del diritto, Atti del Convegno Internazionale, Rome, C.N.R., 2–3 June 1987* (Padua: Cedam, 1988) 379–386.

Cassese, S., 'Poteri divisi: amministrazione europea e amministrazioni nazionali', in *Studi in onore di Enzo Capaccioli* (Milan: Giuffrè, 1988) 159–168.

Cassese S., 'Divided Powers: European Administration and National Bureaucracies', in S. Cassese (ed.), *The European Administration – L'administration Européenne* (Bruxelles: IISA, 1987) 5–19.

Cassese S., 'Theoretical Sketch of the Cooperative and Mutidimensional Nature of Community Bureaucracy', in J. Jamar and W. Wessels (eds), *Community Bureaucracy at the Crossroads – L'administration communautaire à l'heure du choix* (Bruges: De Tempel, 1985) 39–46.

Cassese S., 'Relations between International Organizations and National Administrations: General Report', in *IISA, XIX International Congress of Administrative Sciences, Proceedings* (Bruxelles: Kluwer, 1985) 159–204.

Cerulli Irelli V., 'Dalle agenzie europee alle autorità europee di vigilanza', in M.P. Chiti and A. Natalini (eds), *Lo spazio amministrativo europeo. Le pubbliche amministrazioni dopo il Trattato di Lisbona* (Bologna: il Mulino, 2012) 137–163.

Cerulli Irelli V., *Amministrazione pubblica e diritto privato* (Turin: Giappichelli, 2011).

Cerutti F. and Rudolph E. (eds), *A Soul for Europe*, 2 vols (Leuven: Peeters, 2002).

Cesarano F., *Monetary Theory and Bretton Woods. The Construction of an International Monetary Order* (New York: Cambridge University Press, 2006).

Chabod F., *Storia dell'idea di Europa* (Bari: Laterza, 1961).

Chessa O., *La Costituzione della moneta. Concorrenza, indipendenza della banca centrale, pareggio di bilancio* (Naples: Jovene, 2016).

Chevallier J., 'Management public and droit' (2008) *Politiques et management public* 93–100.

Chiti E., 'Managing the Ecological Transition of the EU: The European Green Deal as a Regulatory Process' (2022) 59(1) *Common Market Law Review* 19–48.

Chiti E. and Mendes J., 'The Evolution of EU Administrative Law', in P. Craig and G. de Búrca (eds), *The Evolution of EU Law*, 3rd ed. (Oxford: Oxford University Press, 2021) 339–372.

Chiti E., 'La costruzione del diritto amministrativo europeo', in M.P. Chiti (ed.), *Diritto amministrativo europeo* (Milan: Giuffrè, 2013) 45–88.

Chiti E. and Teixeira P.G., 'The constitutional implications of the European responses to the financial and public debt crisis' (2013) 50 *Common Market Law Review* 683–708.

Chiti E., 'Le architetture istituzionali della vigilanza finanziaria', in G. Napolitano (ed.), *Uscire dalla crisi. Politiche pubbliche e trasformazioni istituzionali* (Bologna: il Mulino, 2012) 157–196.

Chiti E. and Mattarella B.G. (eds), *Global Administrative Law and EU Administrative Law: Relationships, Legal Issues and Comparison* (Berlin-Heidelberg: Springer, 2011).

Chiti E., 'La scienza del diritto amministrativo e il diritto pubblico ultrastatale', in L. Torchia, E. Chiti, R. Perez, A. Sandulli (eds), *La scienza del diritto amministrativo nella seconda metà del XX secolo* (Naples: Editoriale Scientifica, 2008) 145–169.

Chiti E. and Franchini C., *L'integrazione amministrativa europea* (Bologna: il Mulino, 2003).

Chiti M.P., 'La legittimazione per risultati dell'Unione europea quale "comunità di diritto amministrativo"', in F. Wollenschläger and L. De Lucia (eds), *Staat und Demokratie* (Tübingen: Mohr Siebeck, 2016) 79–102.

Chiti M.P., 'Le forme di azione dell'amministrazione europea', in F. Bignami and S. Cassese (eds), *Il procedimento amministrativo nel diritto europeo* (Milan: Giuffrè, 2004) 53–86.

Chiti M.P., *Diritto amministrativo europeo* (Milan: Giuffrè, 1999).

Chiti M.P. and Greco, G. (eds), *Trattato di diritto amministrativo europeo*, 1st ed. (Milan: Giuffrè, 1997).

Chiti M.P., 'I signori del diritto comunitario: la Corte di giustizia e lo sviluppo del diritto amministrativo europeo' (1991) 3 *Rivista trimestrale di diritto pubblico* 796–831.

Chiti M.P., 'Il coordinamento delle politiche comunitarie e la riforma degli apparati di governo', in *Associazione per gli Studi e le Ricerche Parlamentari, Quaderno n. 1, Seminari 1989–1990* (Milan: Giuffrè, 1991) 235–254.

Ciocca P., 'Machiavelli e l'economia' (2013) *Rivista di storia economica* 249–260.

Civitarese Matteucci S. and Halliday S. (eds), *Social Rights in Europe in an Age of Austerity* (London: Routledge, 2017).

Civitarese Matteucci S. and Torchia L. (eds), *La tecnificazione*, vol. IV of the studies for the 150th anniversary of Italian administrative unification, L. Ferrara and D. Sorace (eds), (Florence: FUP, 2016).

Civitarese Matteucci S. and Torchia L., 'La tecnificazione dell'amministrazione', in S. Civitarese Matteucci and L. Torchia (eds), *La tecnificazione*, vol. IV of the studies for the 150th anniversary of Italian administrative unification, L. Ferrara and D. Sorace (eds), (Florence: FUP, 2016) 7–48.

Civitarese Matteucci S., 'L'identità delle scienze giuridiche nel mondo giuridico "plurale" – "Questa è l'acqua"', in V. Barsotti (ed.), *L'identità delle scienze giuridiche in ordinamenti multilivello* (Rimini: Maggioli, 2014) 29–49.

Classen C.D., *Die Europäisierung der Verwaltungsgerichtsbarkeit. eine vergleichende Untersuchung zum deutschen, französischen und europäischen Verwaltungsprozeßrecht* (Tübingen: Mohr Siebeck, 1996).

Cloots E., De Baere G., and Sottiaux S. (eds), *Federalism in the European Union* (Oxford, UK; Portland, OR: Hart, 2012).
Close, C.W., *State Formation and Shared Sovereignty: The Holy Roman Empire and the Dutch Republic, 1488–1696* (Cambridge: Cambridge University Press, 2021).
Coase R.H., 'The Nature of the Firm' (1937) 4 *Economica* 386–405.
Coase R.H., 'The Problem of Social Cost' (1960) 3 *Journal of Law & Economics* 1–44.
Cohen A., 'Le Plan Schuman de Paul Reuter entre communauté nationale et fédération européenne' (1998) *Revue française de science politique* 645–663.
Combacau J., 'Paul Reuter, le juriste' (1989) *Annuaire français de droit international* 7–19.
Commaille J., *À quoi nous sert le droit?* (Paris: Gallimard, 2015).
Copelovitch M., 'No, this isn't Europe's "Hamiltonian moment"', on *washingtonpost.com*, 27 May2020.
Corso G., 'I diritti sociali nella Costituzione italiana' (1981) *Rivista trimestrale di diritto pubblico* 755–784.
Costa P., *Civitas. Storia della cittadinanza in Europa*, vol. IV, *L'età dei totalitarismi e della democrazia* (Roma-Bari: Laterza, 2001).
Costa P. and Zolo D. (eds), *The Rule of Law: History, Theory and Criticism* (Dordrecht: Springer, 2007).
Courty G. and Devin G., *La construction européenne*, 3rd ed. (Paris: La Découverte, 2010, 1st ed., 2001).
Craig P. (ed.), *ReNEUAL Model Rules on EU Administrative Procedure* (Oxford: Oxford University Press, 2017).
Craig P., *UK, EU and Global Administrative Law: Foundations and Challenges*, The Hamlin Lectures (Cambridge: Cambridge University Press, 2015).
Craig P., 'Economic Governance and the Euro Crisis: Constitutional Architecture and Constitutional Implications', in M. Adams, F. Fabbrini, and P. Larouche (eds), *The Constitutionalization of European Budgetary Constraints* (Oxford, UK; Portland, OR: Hart, 2014) 19–40.
Craig P., *EU Administrative Law*, 2nd ed. (Oxford: Oxford University Press, 2012).
Craig P., 'The Nature of the Community: Integration, Democracy, and Legitimacy', in P. Craig and G. de Búrca (eds), *The Evolution of EU Law*, 2nd ed. (Oxford: Oxford University Press, 2011) 12–45.
Craig P., 'Formal and Substantive Conceptions of the Rule of Law: An Analytical Framework' (1997) *Public Law* 467–487.
Craig P. and de Búrca G., *EU Law: Text, Cases and Materials*, 4th ed. (Oxford: Oxford University Press, 2008).
Crane D.A., 'Ordoliberalism and the Freiburg School', in D.A. Crane and H. Hovenkamp (eds), *The Making of Competition Policy: Legal and Economic Sources* (New York: Oxford University Press, 2013) 252–281.
Croce B., *Riduzione della filosofia del diritto alla filosofia dell'economia*, 1907 (Milan: Giuffrè, 2016).
Croce B., *Storia d'Europa nel secolo decimonono* (Bari: Laterza, 1932).
Curtin D., 'Democratic Accountability of the EU Executive Power: A Reform Agenda for Parliament', in F. Fabbrini, E. Hirsch Ballin, and H. Somsen (eds), *What Form of Government for the European Union and the Eurozone?* (Oxford, UK; Portland, OR: Hart, 2016) 171–194.
Curtin D., *Executive Power of the European Union: Law, Practices, and the Living Constitution* (Oxford: Oxford University Press, 2009).

Curtin D., 'Making a Political Constitution for the European Union' (2007) *European Journal of Law Reform* 65–76.

Curtin D., *Postnational Democracy: The European Union in Search of a Political Philosophy* (The Hague: Kluwer Law International, 1997).

Curtin D., 'The Constitutional Structure of the Union: A Europe of Bits and Pieces' (1993) 30 *Common Market Law Review* 17–69.

D'Alberti M., 'Comparazione giuridica, diritto europeo e diritto globale', in G. della Cananea and C. Franchini (eds), *Il diritto che cambia, Liber amicorum Mario Pilade Chiti* (Naples: Editoriale Scientifica, 2016) 179–188.

D'Alberti M., 'L'Unione europea e i diritti' (2016) *Rivista trimestrale di diritto pubblico* 761–777.

D'Alberti M., 'Diritto amministrativo e diritto privato: nuove emersioni di una questione antica' (2012) *Rivista trimestrale di diritto pubblico* 1019–1028.

D'Auria G., 'L'administration italienne et l'intégration européenne', in C. Debbasch (ed.), *Administrations nationales et intégration européenne*, Annales européennes d'administration publique, Centre de Recherches Administratives d'Aix-Marseille (Paris: CNRS, 1987) 71–84.

D'Ottavio G., *L'Europa dei tedeschi. La Repubblica Federale di Germania e l'integrazione europea, 1949–1966* (Bologna: il Mulino, 2012).

Dani M., *Il diritto pubblico europeo nella prospettiva dei conflitti* (Padua: Cedam, 2013).

Dani M., Chiti E., Mendes J., Menéndez A.J., Schepel H., and Wilkinson M., '"It's the political economy…!" A Moment of Truth for the Eurozone and the EU' (2021) 19 *International Journal of Constitutional Law* 309–327.

Dani M., Mendes J., Menendez A.J., Wilkinson M., Schepel H., and Chiti E., 'At the End of the Law: A Moment of Truth for the Eurozone and the EU', *VerfBlog*, 15 May2020.

Davidoff Solomon S. and Zaring D., 'The Dealmaking State: Executive Power in the Trump Administration' (2018) 106 *Georgetown Law Journal* 1097–1138.

Dawson M. and de Witte F., 'Constitutional Balance in the EU after the Euro-crisis' (2013) 73(4) *Modern Law Review* 817–844.

De Bellis M., 'European Financial Supervision after the Crisis: Multi-Speed Models within a Two-Track Framework', in E. Chiti and G. Vesperini (eds), *The Administrative Architecture of Financial Integration: Institutional Design, Legal Issues, Perspectives* (Bologna: il Mulino, 2015) 61–92.

De Bellis M., *La regolazione dei mercati finanziari* (Milan: Giuffrè, 2012).

De Bellis M., 'EU and Global Private Regulatory Regimes: The Accounting and Auditing Sectors', in E. Chiti and B.G. Mattarella (eds), *Global Administrative Law and EU Administrative Law: Relationships, Legal Issues and Comparison* (Berlin: Springer, 2011) 269–292.

De Bellis M., 'Public Law and Private Regulators in the Global Legal Space' (2011) *International Journal of Constitutional Law* 425–448.

De Bellis M., 'Unificazione, differenziazione e tecnificazione nella regolazione europea dei mercati finanziari' (2015) *Rivista italiana di diritto pubblico comunitario* 1553–1579.

de Búrca G. (ed.), *EU Law and the Welfare State: In Search of Solidarity* (Oxford: Oxford University Press, 2005).

de Búrca G., 'Poland and Hungary's EU Membership: On Not Confronting Authoritarian Governments' (2022) 20 *International Journal of Constitutional Law* 13–34.

de Búrca G., 'The Evolution of EU Human Rights Law', in P. Craig and G. de Búrca (eds), *The Evolution of EU Law* (Oxford: Oxford University Press, 2011) 480–505.

de Búrca G. and de Witte, B. (eds), *Social Rights in Europe* (Oxford: Oxford University Press, 2005).

De Carolis M., *Il rovescio della libertà. Tramonto del neoliberalismo e disagio della civiltà* (Macerata: Quodlibet, 2017).

De Caterini P., *L'atto amministrativo delle Comunità europee* (Milan: Giuffrè, 1967).

de Laubadère A., 'Les actes administratifs', in *Dix ans de jurisprudence de la Cour de justice des Communautés européennes* (Köln: Carl Heymanns, 1965) 472–487.

De Lucia L., 'Il diritto amministrativo tedesco e il rinnovamento della dogmatica giuridica' (2015) *Rivista trimestrale di diritto pubblico* 1–27.

De Lucia L., '"Pastorato" e "disciplinamento" nella governance economica europea' (2015) *Diritto pubbico* 867–908.

De Lucia L., 'Recensione a: *Grundlagen des Verwaltungsrechts*, vol. I, *Methoden, Maßstäbe, Aufgaben, Organisation*, a cura di W. Hoffmann-Riem, E. Schmidt-Aßmann, A. Voßkuhle, München, 2012, 2° edizione, XLVIII, 1446; Grundlagen des Verwaltungsrechts, vol. II, Informationsordnung, Verwaltungsverfahren, Handlungsformen, a cura di W. Hoffmann-Riem, E. Schmidt-Aßmann, A. Voßkuhle, München, 2012, 2° edizione, LII, 1859' (2013) *Rivista trimestrale di diritto pubblico* 1076–1084.

De Pasquale P., 'L'Unione europea e le nuove forme di integrazione' (2017) *Diritto pubblico comparato ed europeo* 671–686.

de Pretis D., 'I principi del diritto amministrativo europeo', in M. Renna and F. Saitta (eds), *Studi sui principi di diritto amministrativo* (Milan: Giuffrè, 2012) 41–60.

de Witte B., 'The European Union's COVID–19 Recovery Plan: The Legal Engineering of an Economic Policy Shift' (2021) 58 *Common Market Law Review* 635–682.

de Witte B., 'Euro Crisis Responses and the EU Legal Order: Increased Institutional Variation or Constitutional Mutation?' (2015) 11 *EU Constitutional Law Review* 434–457.

de Witte B., 'Treaty Games: Law as Instrument and as Constraint in the Euro Crisis Policy', in F. Allen, E. Carletti, and S. Simonelli (eds), *Governance for the Eurozone: Integration or Disintegration?* (Philadelphia, PA: FIC Press, 2012) 139–160.

Dedman M.J., *The Origins and Development of European Union 1945–95* (London; New York: Routledge).

della Cananea G. and Galetta D.U. (eds), *Codice ReNEUAL del procedimento amministrativo dell'Unione europea* (Naples: Editoriale Scientifica, 2016).

della Cananea G., 'Uniformità e varietà del diritto nello "spazio giuridico europeo"', in G. della Cananea and C. Franchini (eds), *Il diritto che cambia, Liber amicorum Mario Pilade Chiti* (Naples: Editoriale Scientifica, 2016) 233–242.

della Cananea G., *Due Process of Law beyond the State: Requirements of Administrative Procedure* (Oxford: Oxford University Press, 2016).

della Cananea G., *L'Unione europea. Un ordinamento composito* (Roma-Bari: Laterza, 2003).

della Cananea G., *Indirizzo e controllo della finanza pubblica. Un tema al centro del dibattito istituzionale: la finanza pubblica nazionale e l'Unione economica e monetaria* (Bologna: il Mulino, 1996).

della Cananea G., 'Cooperazione e integrazione nel sistema amministrativo delle Comunità europee: la questione della "comitologia"' (1990) *Rivista trimestrale di diritto pubblico* 655–702.

Delors J., *Mémoires* (Paris: Plon, 2004).

Dermine P., 'The EU's Response to the COVID–19 Crisis and the Trajectory of Fiscal Integration in Europe: Between Continuity and Rupture' (2020) 47(4) *Legal Issues of Economic Integration* 337–358.

Di Cataldo V., *A che cosa serve il diritto* (Bologna: il Mulino, 2017).

Di Mascio F. and Natalini A., 'Il contenimento della spesa pubblica e la riforma amministrativa', in G. Napolitano (ed.), *Uscire dalla crisi. Politiche pubbliche e trasformazioni istituzionali* (Bologna: il Mulino, 2012) 345–382.

Di Nunno F., *L'Italia e il compromesso di Lussemburgo, 1965–1966* (Rome: Edizioni Nuova Cultura, 2012).

Diamond L., 'Facing Up to the Democratic Recession' (2015) 26 *Journal of Democracy* 141–155.

Diamond L., *The Spirit of Democracy: The Struggle to Build Free Society Throughout the World* (New York: Times Books/Henry Holt & Co., 2008).

Diez Picazo L.M., 'La formación de un derecho administrativo europeo' (1993) *Revista Española de Derecho Constitucional* 297–301.

Diez-Picazo L.M., 'Una Constitucion sin declaracion de derechos? 'Reflexiones constitucionales sobre los derechos fundamentales en la Comunidad Europea' (1991) *Revista Española de Derecho Constitucional* 135–155.

Dorso G., 'Equilibrio ed egemonia' (1944) *Aretusa* 93–94.

Dugato M., *Le società per la gestione dei servizi pubblici locali* (Milan: Ipsoa, 2001).

Dugato M., *Atipicità e funzionalizzazione nell'attività amministrativa per contratti* (Milan: Giuffrè, 1996).

Dujardin V. and Dumoulin M., *Paul Van Zeeland 1893–1973* (Bruxelles: Racine, 1997).

Dyson K., *Conservative Liberalism, Ordo–liberalism, and the State: Disciplining Democracy and the Market* (Oxford: Oxford University Press, 2021).

Dyson K., *States, Debt and Power: "Saints" and "Sinners" in European History and Integration* (Oxford: Oxford University Press, 2014).

Echebarria Fernández J., 'A Critical Analysis on the European Union's Measures to Overcome the Economic Impact of the COVID–19 Pandemic' (2020) 5(3) *European Papers*, 1399–1423.

Editorial, 'Not Mastering the Treaties: The German Federal Constitutional Court's PSPP Judgment' (2020) 57 *Common Market Law Review* 965–978.

Eeckhout P., 'The Growing Influence of European Union Law' (2011) 33 *Fordham International Law Journal* 1490–1521.

Eliantonio M., Korkea-Aho E., and Stefan O. (eds), *EU Soft Law in the Member States: Theoretical Findings and Empirical Evidence* (London: Hart, 2021).

Esposito R., *A Philosophy for Europe: From the Outside* (Cambridge, UK; Medford, MA: Polity Press, 2018)

European Commission, COM(2017)2025 of 1 March 2017, *Libro Bianco sul Futuro dell'Europa. Riflessioni e scenari per l'UE a 27 verso il 2025* (Brussels: Ufficio delle pubblicazioni dell'Unione europea, 2017).

Everling U., 'Auf dem Wege zu einem europäischen Verwaltungsrecht' (1987) *NVwZ – Neue Zeitschrift für Verwaltungsrecht* 1–9.

Everling U., 'Elemente eines europäischen Verwaltungsrechts' (1983) *Deutsches Verwaltungsblatt*, 649–658.

Everson M., 'Ordoliberal Escape from Societas Economica: Re-establishing the Normative' in J. Hien and C. Joerges (eds), *Ordoliberalism, Polanyi, and the Theodicy of Markets* (Oxford: Hart, 2017) 201–212.

Everson M., 'The Fault of (European) Law in (Political and Social) Economic Crisis' (2013) *Law Critique* 107–129.

Fabbrini F., *Next Generation EU. Il futuro di Europa e Italia dopo la pandemia* (Bologna: il Mulino, 2022).

Fabbrini F., 'The Legal Architecture of the Economic Responses to COVID–19: EMU beyond the Pandemic' (2021) 60 *Journal of Common Market Studies* 186–203.

Fabbrini F., *Economic Governance in Europe: Comparative Paradoxes and Constitutional Challenges* (Oxford: Oxford University Press, 2016).

Fabbrini S., 'Intergovernmentalism and Its Limits: Assessing the European Union's Answer to the Euro Crisis' (2013) 46 *Comparative Political Studies* 1003–1029.

Fabbrini S., *Sdoppiamento. Una prospettiva nuova per l'Europa* (Rome: Laterza, 2017).

Fabbrini S. (ed.), *Democracy and Federalism in the European Union and the United States: Exploring Post-national Governance* (London; New York: Routledge, 2004).

Fabbrini S., 'Le istituzioni dell'Unione europea in prospettiva comparata', in S. Fabbrini (ed.), *L'Unione europea. Le istituzioni e gli attori di un sistema sovranazionale* (Roma-Bari: Laterza, 2002) 3–37.

Falcon G., 'People, Peoples, Democratic Deficit and "Output Legitimation" in the European Union', in F. Wollenschläger and L. De Lucia (eds), *Staat und Demokratie* (Tübingen: Mohr Siebeck, 2016) 103–112.

Falcon G., 'Alcune osservazioni sullo sviluppo del diritto amministrativo comunitario' (1993) *Rivista trimestrale di diritto pubblico* 74–84.

Falcon G., 'Dal diritto amministrativo nazionale al diritto amministrativo comunitario' (1991) *Rivista italiana di diritto pubblico comunitario* 351–370.

Fasone C. and Lindseth P., 'Europe's Fractured Metabolic Constitution: From the Eurozone Crisis to Coronavirus Response', Working Papers Series, SOG-WP61/2020, Luiss School of Government, October2020.

Fasone C., 'The Constitutional Role of Independent Fiscal Institutions in the Eurozone' (2019) 23 *German Law Journal* 257–279.

Fasone C. and Lupo N., 'The Union Budget and the Budgetary Procedure', in R. Schütze and T. Tridimas (eds), *Oxford Principles of European Union Law*, vol. I, *The European Union Legal Order* (Oxford: Oxford University Press, 2018) 809–843.

Fasone C., 'Towards a Strengthened Coordination between the EU and National Budgets: A Complementary Role and a Joint Control for Parliaments?' (2018) 40 *Journal of European Integration* 265–279.

Fauri F., *L'Unione europea. Una storia economica* (Bologna: il Mulino, 2017).

Ferrarese M.R., *Promesse mancate. Dove ci ha portato il capitalismo finanziario* (Bologna: il Mulino, 2017).

Ferrarese M.R., *Diritto sconfinato. Inventiva giuridica e spazi nel mondo globale* (Roma-Bari: Laterza, 2006).

Ferrera M., 'Breaking the "Caging" Mentality: Ordoliberalism, Responsibility and Solidarity in the EU', in J. Hien and C. Joerges (eds), *Ordoliberalism, Law and the Rule of Economics* (Oxford, UK; Portland, OR: Hart, 2017) 115–128.

Fikentscher W., Hacker P., and Podszun R. (eds), *FairEconomy: Crises, Culture, Competition and the Role of Law* (Berlin-Heidelberg: Springer, 2013).

Fikentscher W., *Culture, Law and Economics* (Berne; Durham: Staempfli/Carolina Academic Press, 2004).

'Findings of the international conference on National Administrative Rights and European Administrative Law ("Diritti amministrativi nazionali e diritto amministrativo europeo"), Rome, 12 December 1990' (1991) *Rivista trimestrale di diritto pubblico* 741–865.

Forsthoff E., *Der Staat der Industriegesellschaft. Dargestellt am Beispiel der Bundesrepublik Deutschland* (Berlin: Beck, 1984).

Forte P., 'Oggetti giuridici. Note e primi appunti sulla loro esistenza' (2015) *Costituzionalismo* 45–102.

Fox-Genovese E., *The Origins of Physiocracy: Economic Revolution and Social Order in Eighteenth Century France* (Ithaca, NY: Cornell University Press, 1976).

Fragola U., 'Diritto amministrativo e diritto comunitario. L'atto amministrativo europeo' (1980) *Consiglio di Stato* 753–758.

Franchini C., 'L'impatto dell'integrazione comunitaria sulle relazioni al vertice dell'amministrazione: poteri governativi e poteri amministrativi' (1991) *Rivista trimestrale di diritto pubblico* 775–782.

Franchini C., 'L'integrazione europea e il governo delle politiche comunitarie in Italia: organizzazione amministrativa e rapporti con le Comunità europee' (1990) 30 *Rivista di diritto europeo* 17–38.

Franchini C., *Amministrazione italiana e amministrazione comunitaria* (Padua: Cedam, 1st ed. 1992, 2nd ed. 1993).

Friedman M., 'The Methodology of Positive Economics', in *Essays in Positive Economics* (Chicago: University of Chicago Press, 1953) 3–46.

Fromont M., *Rechtsschutz gegenüber der Verwaltung in Deutschland Frankreich und den Europäischen Gemeinschaften* (Köln: Carl Heymanns, 1967).

Fuß E.W., *Die Europäischen Gemeinschaften und der Rechtsstaatsgedanke* (Heule: UGA, 1967).

Gal M.S., Bakhoum M., Drexl J., Fox E.M., and Gerber D.J. (eds), *The Economic Characteristics of Developing Jurisdictions: Their Implications for Competition Law* (Cheltenham, UK; Northampton, MA: Elgar, 2015).

Galetta D.U., 'Il diritto a una buona amministrazione europea come fonte di essenziali garanzie procedimentali nei confronti della pubblica amministrazione' (2005) *Rivista italiana di diritto pubblico comunitario* 819–857.

Galgano F., *Lex mercatoria. Storia del diritto commerciale* (Bologna: il Mulino, 1993).

Gallo D., *Public Services and EU Competition Law: The Social Market Economy in Action* (Abingdon, UK; New York: Routledge-Giappichelli, 2021).

Gasparri P., 'L'eccesso di potere nel diritto della "CECA"' (1957) *Rivista trimestrale di diritto pubblico* 804–826.

Gasparri P., 'Politica ed amministrazione nell'ordinamento delle Comunità europee', in *Studi in onore di Antonio Segni*, vol. II (Milan:Giuffrè, 1967) 295–308.

Gerbet P., *La construction de l'Europe*, 4th ed. (1st ed., 1983), (Paris: Armand Colin, 2007).

Giannini M.S., 'Profili di un diritto amministrativo delle Comunità europee', 1967, with an introduction by S. Battini (2003) 4 *Rivista trimestrale di diritto pubblico* 979–988.

Giannini M.S., 'In principio sono le funzioni', 1959, in M.S. Giannini, *Scritti*, vol. IV (Milan: Giuffrè, 2004) 719–724.

Giannini M.S., 'Brevi osservazioni sul Trattato per la Comunità europea di difesa' (1954) 3 *Società* 523–530.

Gilbert M., *Storia politica dell'integrazione europea* (Roma-Bari:Laterza, 2005).

Giraudi G., *Ripensare l'Europa. Storia, processi e sfide dell'integrazione europea* (Soveria Mannelli: Rubbettino, 2008).

Giubboni S., *Social Rights and Market Freedoms in the European Constitution: A Labour Law Perspective* (Cambridge: Cambridge University Press, 2009).
Glencross A. and Trechsel A.H. (eds), *EU Federalism and Constitutionalism: The Legacy of Altiero Spinelli* (Lanham, MD: Lexington, 2010).
Goldmann M., 'The Great Recurrence: Karl Polanyi and the Crises of the European Union' (2017) 23 *European Law Journal* 272–289.
Goßmann U., *Der Widerruf begünstingender Verwaltungsakte im Recht der Europäischen Gemeinschaften* (Köln: Gouder & Hansen, 1964).
Gouzy P., *Les pioniers de l'Europe communautaire* (Losanne: Centre des Recherches Européennes, 1968).
Gramsci A., *Quaderni del carcere* (Turin: Einaudi, 2007).
Greaves R., 'The First Advocate General, Maurice Lagrange', in N. Burrows and R. Greaves, *The Advocate General and EC Law* (Oxford: Oxford University Press, 2007) 59–88.
Greco G., 'Profili di diritto pubblico italo-comunitario', in G. Greco (ed.), *Argomenti di diritto pubblico italo-comunitario* (Milan: Giuffrè, 1989) 3–88.
Grilli A., *Le origini del diritto dell'Unione europea* (Bologna: il Mulino, 2009).
Grimm D., 'Does Europe Need a Constitution?' (1995) *European Law Journal* 282–302.
Grogan J. and Beqiraj J., 'The Rule of Law as the Perimeter of Legitimacy for COVID–19 Responses', in J. Grogan and A. Donald (eds), *Routledge Handbook of Law and the COVID–19 Pandemic* (Abingdon, UK; New York: Routledge2022) 349–369.
Grossi P., *A History of European Law* (Hoboken: Wiley-Blackwell, 2010); Italian ed., *L'Europa del diritto* (Roma-Bari: Laterza, 2009).
Grossi P., *L'Europa del diritto* (Roma-Bari: Laterza, 2009).
Grossi P., *L'invenzione del diritto* (Roma-Bari: Laterza, 2017)
Grossi P., *Ritorno al diritto* (Roma-Bari: Laterza, 2015).
Guazzarotti A., *Neoliberismo e difesa dello Stato di diritto in Europa. Riflessioni critiche sulla costituzione materiale dell'UE* (Milano: FrancoAngeli, 2023).
Guazzarotti A., *Crisi dell'euro e conflitto sociale. L'illusione della giustizia attraverso il mercato* (Milan: Franco Angeli, 2016).
Haas E.B., *The Uniting of Europe: Political, Social, and Economic Forces 1950–57* (Stanford: Stanford University Press, 1958).
Haas P.M., 'Epistemic Communities and International Policy Coordination' (1992) *International Organization* 1–35.
Habermas J., *Nella spirale tecnocratica. Un'arringa per la solidarietà europea* (Roma-Bari: Laterza, 2014).
Habermas J., *The Crisis of the European Union. A Response* (Cambridge, UK; Medford, MA: Polity Press, 2012).
Hallstein W., *Europa federazione incompiuta* (Milan: Rizzoli, 1971).
Hallstein W., *L'Europe inachevée* (Paris: Laffont, 1970).
Hallstein W., *La unificación de Europa: antecedentes y problema* (Buenos Aires: Instituto para la Integración de America Latina, 1966).
Hallstein W., *L'unité de l'action européenne* (Losanna: CRE, 1965).
Hallstein W., *United Europe: Challenge and Opportunity* (Cambridge, MA: Harvard University Press, 1962).
Harris P., Lock A., and Rees P. (eds), *Machiavelli, Marketing and Management* (London: Routledge, 2000).

Hatje A., *Die gemeinschaftsrechtliche Steuerung der Wirtschaftsverwaltung* (Baden-Baden: Nomos, 1998).

Heinemann-Grüder A. (ed.), *Federalism Doomed? European Federalism Between Integration and Separation* (New York: Berghahn Books, 2002).

Helleiner E., *Forgotten Foundations of Bretton Woods: International Development and the Making of the Postwar Order* (Ithaca, NY: Cornell University Press, 2014).

Hespanha A.M., La culture juridique Européenne. Synthèse d'un millenaire (Aix-en-provence: Le poisson volant, 2015); Italian ed., *La cultura giuridica europea* (Bologna: il Mulino, 2012).

Hien J. and Joerges C. (eds), *Ordoliberalism, Law and the Rule of Economics* (Oxford, UK; Portland, OR: Hart, 2017).

Hirschl R., 'The Judicialization of Politics', in G.A. Caldeira, R.D. Kelemen, K.E. Whittington (eds), *The Oxford Handbook of Law and Politics* (Oxford: Oxford University Press, 2008) 253–274.

Hoffmann-Riem W., Schmidt-Aßmann E., and Voßkuhle A. (eds), Grundlagen des Verwaltungsrechts, vol. III, *Personal, Finanzen, Kontrolle, Sanktionen, Staatliche Einstandspflichten*, 2nd ed. (München: C.H. Beck, 2013).

Hoffmann-Riem W., Schmidt-Aßmann E., and Voßkuhle A. (eds), Grundlagen des Verwaltungsrechts, vol. I, *Methoden, Maßstäbe, Aufgaben, Organisation*, 2nd ed. (München: C.H. Beck, 2012).

Hoffmann-Riem W., Schmidt-Aßmann E., and Voßkuhle A. (eds), Grundlagen des Verwaltungsrechts, vol. II, *Informationsordnung, Verwaltungsverfahren, Handlungsformen*2nd ed. (München: C.H. Beck, 2012; 1st ed., 2008).

Holman C., *Machiavelli and the Politics of Democratic Innovation* (Toronto: University of Toronto Press, 2018).

Hooghe L. and Marks G., 'European Integration and Democratic Competition' (2004) *Europäische Politik* 1–8.

Hooghe L. and Marks G., *Multi-Level Governance and European Integration* (Lanham: Rowman & Littlefield, 2001).

Hyvärinen A., 'Opening Statements', in A. Kocharov (ed.), *Another Legal Monster? An EUI Debate on the Fiscal Compact Treaty*, EUI Working Paper LAW 2012/09 (Fiesole: European University Institute, 2012) 8–9.

Iaccarino U.M., *Introduzione ad un profilo sistematico degli 'Atti' delle comunità europee. Contributo allo studio delle organizzazioni internazionali* (Naples: Jovene, 1970).

Ipsen H.P., *Europäisches Gemeinschaftsrecht* (Tübingen: Mohr Siebeck, 1972).

Ipsen H.P., 'Europäisches Gemeinschaftsrecht im Hochschulstudium' (1964) *Neue Juristische Wochenschrift* 961–967.

Irti N., *Il diritto nell'età della tecnica* (Naples: Editoriale Scientifica, 2016).

Irti N., *Un diritto incalcolabile* (Turin: Giappichelli, 2016).

Irti N., *L'ordine giuridico del mercato* (Roma-Bari: Laterza, 2004).

Irti N., *Nichilismo giuridico* (Roma-Bari: Laterza, 2004).

Irti N. and Severino E., *Dialogo su Diritto e tecnica* (Roma-Bari: Laterza, 2001).

Issing O., 'The COVID–19 Crisis: A Hamilton moment for the European Union?' (2020) *International Finance* 340–347.

Itzcovich G., *Teorie e ideologie del diritto comunitario* [Theories and ideologies of community law] (Turin: Giappichelli, 2006).

JacquéJ.P.and Weiler J.H.H., 'On the Road to European Union – A New Judicial Architecture – An Agenda for the Intergovernmental Conference' (1990) *Common Market Law Review* 185–207.

Joerges C., 'The Overburdening of Law by Ordoliberalism and the Integration Project', in J. Hien and C. Joerges (eds), *Ordoliberalism, Law and the Rule of Economics* (Oxford, UK; Portland, OR: Hart, 2017) 179–200.

Joerges C. and Giubboni S., 'Diritto, politica ed economia nella crisi europea' (2014) *Rivista critica del diritto privato* 343–368.

Joerges C. and Neyer J., '"Deliberative Supranationalism" Revisited' (2006) EUI Working Paper LAW no. 2006/20.

Joerges C. and Neyer J., 'From Intergovernmental Bargaining to Deliberative Political Processes' (1997) 3 *European Law Journal* 273–299.

Jones E., Kelemen R.D., and Meunier S., 'Failing Foward? The Euro Crisis and the Incomplete Nature of European Integration' (2016) 49(7) *Comparative Political Studies* 1010–1034.

Kadelbach S., *Allgemeines Verwaltungsrecht unter europäischem Einfluß* (Tübingen: Mohr Siebeck, 1999).

Kapoor S., 'This Isn't Europe's "Hamilton" Moment', on *politico.eu*, 22 May2020.

Kasten H.-H., 'Entwicklung eines Europäischen Allgemeinen Verwaltungsrechts' (1985) *Die Öffentliche Verwaltung* 570–574.

Kelemen D., 'Towards a New Consititutional Architecture in the EU?', in F. Fabbrini, E. Hirsch Ballin, H. Somsen (eds), *What Form of Government for the European Union and the Eurozone?* (Oxford, UK; Portland, OR: Hart, 2016) 197–216.

Kersten A.E., 'Beijen, Johan Willem (1897–1976)', in *Biografisch Woordenboek van Nederland*, 2013, http://resources.huygens.knaw.nl/bwn1880-2000/lemmata/bwn2/beijen.

Klabbers J. and Palombella G. (eds), *The Challenge of Inter-Legality* (Cambridge, UK; New York: Cambridge University Press, 2019).

Knill C., 'European Policies: The Impact of National Administrative Traditions' (1998) 18 *Journal of Public Policy* 1–28.

Koslowski P. (ed.), *The Theory of Capitalism in the German Economic Tradition: Historism, Ordo–liberalism, Critical Theory, Solidarism* (Berlin; Heidelberg: Springer, 2000).

Kosta V., *Fundamental Rights in EU Internal Market Legislation* (Oxford, UK; Portland, OR: Hart, 2015).

Kostantinides T., *The Rule of Law in the European Union. The Internal Dimension* (Oxford, UK; Portland, OR: Hart, 2017).

Kovačević B., *Europe's Hidden Federalism: Federal Experiences of European Integration* (London; New York: Routledge, 2019).

Krick E. and Holst C. (eds), *Experts and Democratic Legitimacy: Tracing the Social Ties of Expert Bodies in Europe* (Abingdon, UK; New York: Routledge, 2021).

Krisch N. (ed.), *Entangled Legalities beyond the State* (Cambridge: Cambridge University Press, 2022).

Kumm M., 'The Cosmopolitan Turn in Constitutionalism: An Integrated Conception of Public Law' (2013) *Indiana Journal of Global Legal Studies* 605–628.

Labriola G. and Romeo F. (eds), *Niccolò Machiavelli e la tradizione giuridica europea* (Naples: Editoriale Scientifica, 2016).

Labriola G.M., *La fisiocrazia come scienza nuova. Economia e diritto tra antico e moderno* (Naples: Editoriale Scientifica, 2004).

Lagrange M., 'L'ordre juridique de la CECA vu à travers la jurisprudence de sa Cour de Justice' (1958) *Revue de droit public* 841–865.

Laurent P.-H., 'Paul-Henri Spaak and the Diplomatic Origins of the Common Market, 1955–1956' (1970) 85 *Political Science Quarterly* 373–396.

Laursen F. (ed.), *The EU and Federalism: Polities and Policies Compared* (London; New York: Routledge, 2010).

Lenaerts K., 'Some Reflections on the Separation of Powers in the European Community' (1991) *Common Market Law Review* 11–35.

Leoni B., *Il diritto come pretesa* (Macerata: Liberilibri, 2004).

Liebert U., Gattig A., and Evas T. (eds), *Democratising the EU from below? Citizenship, Civil Society and the Public Sphere* (London: Routledge, 2018).

Lindberg L.N., *The Political Dynamics of European Economic Integration* (Stanford: Stanford University Press, 1963).

Lindseth P. and Fasone C., 'Rule-of-Law Conditionality and Resource Mobilization: The Foundations of a Genuinely "Constitutional" EU?', 12 *Verfassungsblog* (11 December2020), https://verfassungsblog.de/rule–of–law–conditionality–and–resource–mobilization–the–foundations–of–a–genuinely–constitutional–eu/.

Lindseth P., 'The metabolic constitution and the limits of EU legal pluralism', in G. Davies and M. Avbelj (eds), *Research Handbook on Legal Pluralism and EU Law* (Northampton, MA: Elgar, 2018) 223–242.

Lindseth P., *Power and Legitimacy: Reconciling Europe and the Nation-state* (New York; Oxford: Oxford University Press, 2010).

Lindseth P., 'Democratic Legitimacy and the Administrative Character of Supranationalism' (1999) 99(3) *Columbia Law Review* 628–738.

Lo Schiavo G. (ed.), *The European Banking Union and the Role of Law* (Cheltenham, UK; Northampton, MA: Elgar, 2019).

Lorenz W., 'General Principles of Law: Their Elaboration in the Court of Justice of the EC' (1964) *American Society of Comparative Law* 1–29.

Losurdo F., *Lo Stato sociale condizionato. Stabilità e crescita nell'ordinamento costituzionale* (Turin: Giappichelli, 2016).

Loth W., Wallace W., and Wessels W., *Walter Hallstein: The Forgotten European* (New York: St. Martin's Press, 1998).

Luciani M., 'Diritti sociali e livelli essenziali delle prestazioni pubbliche nei sessant'anni della Corte costituzionale' (2016) 3 *Rivista AIC* 1–18.

Luciani M., 'Costituzionalismo irenico e costituzionalismo polemico' (2006) *Giurisprudenza costituzionale* 1643–1668.

Luciani M., 'Sui diritti sociali', in *Studi in onore di Manlio Mazziotti di Celso*, vol. II (Padua: Cedam, 1995) 97–134.

Luciani M., 'Nuovi diritti fondamentali e nuovi rapporti fra cittadini e pubblica amministrazione' (1985) *Rivista critica del diritto privato* 61–79.

Luhmann N., 'Selbst-thematisierungen des Gesellschaftssystems', in *Soziologische Aufklärung*, vol. II (Köln: Westdeutscher, 1975) 72–102.

Macchia M. et al., 'Studi sulla tecnificazione dell'economia', in S. Civitarese Matteucci and L. Torchia (eds), *La tecnificazione*, vol. IV of L. Ferrara and D. Sorace (eds), Studies for the 150th anniversary of Italian administrative unification, Part II, Florence: FUP, 2016) 201–276.

Maduro M. and Kahn P. (eds), *Democracy in Times of Pandemic* (Cambridge, UK; New York: Cambridge University Press, 2020).

Mair P., *Governare il vuoto. La fine della democrazia dei partiti* (Soveria Mannelli: Rubbettino, 2016).
Majone G., 'Delegation of Regulatory Powers in a Mixed Polity' (2002) *European Law Journal* 319–339.
Majone G., 'Europe's "Democratic Deficit": the Question of Standards' (1998) 4 *European Law Journal* 5–28.
Majone G., *Regulating Europe* (London: Routledge, 1996).
Majone G., 'The Rise of Regulatory State in Europe' (1994) 17 *West European Politics* 77–101.
Malandrino C., *Oltre il compromesso di Lussemburgo verso l'Europa federale: Walter Hallstein e la crisi della 'sedia vuota' (1965–66)* (Alessandria: Università del Piemonte Orientale, 2002).
Mancini G.F., 'Argomenti per uno Stato unitario' (1998) *Sociologia del diritto* 7–27.
Mancini G.F., 'Europe: The Case for Statehood' (1998) *European Law Journal* 29–42.
Mangold A.K., *Gemeinschaftsrecht und deutsches Recht* (Tübingen: Mohr Siebeck, 2011).
Mann T., 'Attenzione, Europa!', 1935, in T. Mann, *Moniti all'Europa* (Milan: Mondadori, 2017) 95–96.
Mashaw J., Berke D., 'Presidential Administration in a Regime of Separated Powers: An Analysis of Recent American Experience' (2018) 35 *Yale Journal of Regulation* 549–616.
Massera A., 'L'amministrazione e i cittadini nel diritto comunitario' (1993) *Rivista trimestrale di diritto pubblico* 19–48.
Massera A., 'Una nozione comunitaria di pubblica amministrazione', in Aa.Vv., *El desenvolupament del dret administratiu europeu*, Generalitat de Catalunya, Escola d'Administración Pública de Catalunya (Barcelona: Generalitat de Catalunya, 1993) 55–78.
Massera A., 'Il ruolo dell'amministrazione alla luce dell'Atto Unico Europeo' (1991) *Rivista trimestrale di diritto pubblico* 783–795.
Mattarella B.G., *Burocrazia e riforme. L'innovazione nella pubblica amministrazione* (Bologna: il Mulino, 2017).
Matthijs M., 'Powerful Rules Governing the Euro: The Perverse Logic of German Ideas' (2015) *Journal of European Public Policy* 375–391.
Mazzamuto M., *La riduzione della sfera pubblica* (Turin: Giappichelli, 2000).
Mazziotti di Celso M., 'Diritti sociali', in *Enciclopedia del diritto*, vol. XII (Milan: Giuffrè, 1964) 802–807.
McKay D., *Federalism and European Union: A Political Economy Perspective* (Oxford: Oxford University Press, 2000).
Melis G., 'Introduzione', in A. Varni and G. Melis (eds), *Burocrazie non burocratiche. Il lavo ro dei tecnici nelle amministrazioni tra Otto e Novecento* (Turin: Rosenberg & Sellier, 1999) 9–14.
Mendes J. and Venzke I. (eds), *Allocating Authority: Who Should Do What in European and International Law?* (Oxford, UK; Portland, OR: Hart/Bloomsbury, 2020).
Mendes J., 'La legittimazione dell'amministrazione dell'UE tra istanze istituzionali e democratiche', in L. De Lucia and B. Marchetti (eds), *L'amministrazione europea e le sue regole* (Bologna: il Mulino, 2015) 89–116.
Mendes J., *Participation in EU Rule-making: A Rights-Based Approach* (Oxford: Oxford University Press, 2011).
Meny Y., 'Amministrazioni pubbliche e ordinamento europeo: esperienze comparate', in L. Vandelli, C. Bottari, D. Donati (eds), *Diritto amministrativo comunitario* (Rimini: Maggioli, 1994) 245–270.

Meny Y., 'La democrazia in tempi difficili', in C. Altini (ed.), *Democrazia. Storia e teoria di un'esperienza filosofica e politica* (Bologna: il Mulino, 2011) 309–324.

Meny Y., 'Conclusioni. Una Costituzione per l'Europa?', in S. Fabbrini, Le istituzioni dell'Unione europea in prospettiva comparata, in *L'Unione europea. Le istituzioni e gli attori di un sistema sovranazionale* (Roma-Bari: Laterza, 2002) 298–310.

Merusi F., *La legalità amministrativa fra passato e futuro. Vicende italiane* (Naples: Editoriale Scientifica, 2016).

Merusi F., *La legalità amministrativa. Altri sentieri interrotti* (Bologna: il Mulino, 2012).

Merusi F., 'Per un divieto di cartolarizzazione del rischio di credito' (2009) *Banca borsa e titoli di credito* 253–263.

Merusi F., *Sentieri interrotti della legalità. La decostruzione del diritto amministrativo* (Bologna: il Mulino, 2007).

Merusi F., *Diritto contro economia. Resistenze istituzionali all'innovazione economica* (Turin: Giappichelli, 2006).

Merusi F., *Democrazia e autorità indipendenti. Un romanzo "quasi" giallo* (Bologna: il Mulino, 2000).

Messori M., 'Processo all'economia. Demografia, democrazia, mercati, felicità' (2018) *Astrid–online.it*.

Miele G., 'Umanesimo giuridico', 1945, in G. Miele, *Scritti giuridici* (Milan: Giuffrè, 1987) vol. II, 445–456.

Mihaeschu Evans B.C., *The Right to Good Administration at the Crossroads of the Various Sources of Fundamental Rights in the EU Integrated Administrative System* (Baden-Baden: Nomos, 2015).

Mitrany D., *A Working Peace System: An Argument for the Functional Development of International Organization*, 1943 (Chicago: Quadranglite Books, 1966).

Moliterni A., *Amministrazione consensuale e diritto privato* (Milan: Giuffrè, 2016).

Monnet J., *Mémoires* (Paris: Fayard, 1976).

Morata F., 'La Banca Centrale Europea', in S. Fabbrini (ed.), Le istituzioni dell'Unione europea in prospettiva comparata, in *L'Unione europea. Le istituzioni e gli attori di un sistema sovranazionale* (Roma-Bari: Laterza, 2002) 200–226.

Moravcsik A., *The Choice for Europe: Social Purpose and State Power (from Messina to Maastricht)* (Ithaca: Cornell University Press, 1998).

Morelli U., *Storia dell'integrazione europea* (Milan: Guerini, 2011).

Morlino L., *Democrazia e mutamenti. Attori, strutture, processi* (Rome: Luiss University Press, 2014).

Morlino L. and Palombella G. (eds), *Rule of Law and Democracy: Inquiries into Internal and External Issues* (Leiden; Boston: Brill Academic Publishing, 2010).

Morlino L., *Democrazie tra consolidamento e crisi* (Bologna: il Mulino, 2008).

Napolitano G. (ed.), *Foreign Direct Investment Screening – Il controllo degli investimenti esteri diretti* (Bologna: il Mulino, 2020).

Napolitano G., 'La crisi di legittimazione e di capacità amministrativa dell'Europa' (2016) *Rivista trimestrale di diritto pubblico* 717–738.

Napolitano G. (ed.), 'La crisi del debito sovrano e le misure di "riduzione dello Stato"' (2012) *Giornale di diritto amministrativo* 1303–1318.

Napolitano G., *Pubblico e privato nel diritto amministrativo* (Milan: Giuffrè, 2003).

Napolitano G. and Abrescia M., *Analisi economica del diritto pubblico* (Bologna: il Mulino, 2009).

Nato A., *La cittadinanza sociale al tempo della crisi economica* (Rome: Cacucci, 2020).

Nolte G., 'General Principles of German and European Administrative Law: A Comparison in Historical Perspective' (1994) 57 *The Modern Law Review* 191–212.

Núñez Ferrer J., 'Reading between the Lines of Council Agreement on the MFF and Next Generation EU', CEPS Policy Insights no. 2020–18, July2020.

Oakeshott M., *Rationalism in Politics and Other Essays*, New expanded ed. (Indianapolis: Liberty Fund, 1991) (1st ed., 1962).

Olivi B., Santaniello R., *Storia dell'integrazione europea. Dalla guerra fredda ai giorni nostri*, 3rd ed. (Bologna: il Mulino, 2015 (1st ed., 2005)).

Olivi B., *L'Europa difficile. Storia politica dell'integrazione europea 1948–2000*, 2nd ed. (Bologna: il Mulino, 2000 (1st ed., 1993)).

Orlando V.E., 'Sulla votazione per la nomina: a) di un membro effettivo dell'Assemblea consultiva del Consiglio d'Europa; b) di nove membri dell'assemblea della comunità europea del carbone e dell'acciaio' (Senate of the Republic, sitting of 18 July 1952), in V.E. Orlando, *Discorsi parlamentari*, Senato della Repubblica, Archivio storico (Bologna: Il Mulino, 2002) 993–996.

Ost F., *À quoi sert le droit? Usages, functions, finalité* (Bruxelles: Bruylant, 2016).

Palermo F., *La forma di Stato dell'Unione europea. Per una teoria costituzionale dell'integrazione sovranazionale* (Padua: Cedam, 2005).

Palombella G., *È possibile una legalità globale? Il rule of law e la governance del mondo* (Bologna: il Mulino, 2012).

Palombella G. and Walker N. (eds), *Relocating the Rule of Law* (Oxford, UK; Portland, OR: Hart, 2008).

Papa E.R., *Storia dell'unificazione europea. Le origini e la crisi di un progetto rivoluzionario* (Florence-Milan: Giunti-Bompiani, 2017, 1st ed., Milan: Bompiani, 2006).

Pasquino G., *L'Europa in trenta lezioni* (Turin: Utet, 2017).

Pech L., 'The Rule of Law in the EU: The Evolution of the Treaty Framework and the Rule of Law Toolbox', RECONNECT, Working Paper 7, March2020, 2–35.

Pech L. and Scheppele K., 'Illiberalism Within: Rule of Law Backsliding in the EU' (2017) 19 *Cambridge Yearbook of European Legal Studies* 3–47.

Perillo E., 'Alberto Trabucchi europeista: un tratto ancora poco conosciuto del grande civilista patavino', in *La formazione del diritto europeo: giornata di studio per Alberto Trabucchi nel centenario della nascita*, Quaderni della Rivista di diritto civile, no. 14 (Padua: Cedam, 2007) 189–202.

Pernice I., 'The Treaty of Lisbon: Multilevel Constitutionalism in Action' (2009) *Columbia Journal of European Law* 349–407.

Piattoni S., 'Is the EU a Representative Democracy? The Normative Debate and the Impact of the Euro-crisis', in F. Fabbrini, E. Hirsch Ballin, H. Somsen (eds), *What Form of Government for the European Union and the Eurozone?* (Oxford, UK; Portland, OR: Hart, 2016) 133–150.

Picozza E., 'Alcune riflessioni circa la rilevanza del diritto comunitario sui principi del diritto amministrativo italiano' (1992) *Rivista italiana di diritto pubblico comunitario* 1209–1241.

Piers Ludlow N., 'Challenging French Leadership in Europe: Germany, Italy, the Netherlands and the Outbreak of the Empty Chair Crisis of 1965–1966' (1999) 8 *Contemporary European History* 231–248.

Pierson P., 'The Path to European Integration: A Historical Institutionalist Analysis' (1996) 29(2) *Comparative Political Studies* 123–163.

Pinder J., *Altiero Spinelli and the British Federalists: Writings by Beveridge, Robins and Spinelli* (London: Federal Trust for Education, 2005)

Pinelli C., 'Conditionality and Economic Constitutionalism in the Eurozone' (2019) 11 *Italian Journal of Public Law* 22–42.

Pinelli C., *Alla ricerca dell'autenticità perduta. Identità e differenze nei discorsi e nei progetti di Europa* (Naples: Editoriale Scientifica, 2017).

Pinelli C., 'Il doppio cappello dei governi tra Stati e Unione europea' (2016) *Rivista trimestrale di diritto pubblico* 639–649.

Pinelli C., *Il momento della scrittura. Contributo al dibattito sulla Costituzione europea* (Bologna: il Mulino, 2002).

Pinelli C., 'Cittadini, responsabilità politica, mercati globali' (1997) *Rivista di Diritto Costituzionale* 43–90.

Pinelli C., 'Ipotesi sulla forma di governo dell'Unione europea' (1989) *Rivista trimestrale di diritto pubblico* 315–338.

Pino G. and Villa V. (eds), *Rule of Law. L'ideale della legalità* (Bologna: il Mulino, 2016).

Piris J.-C., *The Lisbon Treaty: A Legal and Political Analysis* (Cambridge: Cambridge University Press, 2010).

Piris J.-C., *The Constitution for Europe: A Legal Analysis* (Cambridge: Cambridge University Press, 2006).

Piris J.-C., *Does the European Union Have a Constitution? Does it Need One?*, Harvard Jean Monnet Working Paper, 5/00 (Cambridge, MA: Harvard Law School, 2000).

Pistor K., *The Code of Capital: How to Creates Wealth and Inequality* (Princeton, New Jersey: Princeton University Press, 2019).

Poggi G., *Forms of Power* (Milton, Australia: Polity, 2013).

Poggi G., *The State: Its Nature, Development and Prospects* (Milton, Australia: Polity, 2013); Italian ed., *Lo Stato* (Bologna: Il Mulino, 1992)

Poidevin R., *Robert Schuman, homme d'État, 1886–1963* (Paris: Imprimerie nationale, 1986).

Polanyi K., *The Great Transformation: The Political and Economic Origins of Our Time*, 1944 (Boston: Beacon Press, 2001).

Ponce J., 'Good Administrations and Administrative Procedures' (2005) *Indiana Journal of Global Legal Studies* 551–588.

Posner R.A., 'The Decline of Law as an Autonomous Discipline' (1987) 100 *Harvard Law Review* 761–780.

Posner R.A., *Economic Analysis of Law* (Boston: Little Brown & Co., 1973).

Preterossi G., *Ciò che resta della democrazia* (Roma-Bari: Laterza, 2015).

Psygkas A., *From the "Democratic deficit" to a "Democratic surplus" in Europe* (New York: Oxford University Press, 2017).

Raffini L., *La democrazia in mutamento. Dallo Stato-Nazione all'Europa* (Florence: FUP, 2010)

Rapone L., *Storia dell'integrazione europea*, 2nd ed. (Rome: Carocci, 2015, 1st ed., 2002).

Rasmussen M., 'The Origins of a Legal Revolution: The Early History of the European Court of Justice' (2008) *Journal of European Integration History* 77–98.

Rasmussen H., *On Law and Policy in the European Court of Justice: A Comparative Study in Judicial Policy-Making* (Dordrecht: Nijohoff, 1986).

Rengeling H.-W., 'Deutsches und europäisches Verwaltungsrecht – Wechselseitige Einwirkungen', in *VVDStRL – Veröffentlichungen der Vereinigung der Deutschen Staatsrechtslehrer* (Berlin; New York: De Gruyter, 1994) 202–239.

Rengeling H.-W., 'Verwaltungsverfahrens- und Verwaltungsprozeßrecht im Verhältnis zum Europäischen Gemeinschaftsrecht. Neuere Entwicklungen in der gemeinschaftsrechtlichen Rechtsprechung und Rechtsetzung' (1981) *Die Öffentliche Verwaltung* 366–370.

Rengeling H.-W., *Rechtsgrundsätze beim Verwaltungsvollzug des Europäischen Gemeinschaftsrechts*, Kölner Schriften zum Europarecht, Band 27 (Köln: Carl Heymanns, 1977).

Requejo F. and Nagel K.-J. (eds), *Federalism beyond Federations: Asymmetry and Processes of Resymmetrisation in Europe* (London; New York: Routledge, 2016).

Ridola P., *Diritto comparato e diritto costituzionale europeo* (Turin: Giappichelli, 2010).

Rifkin J., *The Green New Deal: Why the Fossil Fuel Civilization Will Collapse by 2028, and the Bold Economic Plan to Save Life on Earth* (New York: St. Martin's Press, 2019).

Rittberger B., *Building Europe's Parliament. Democratic Representation Beyond the Nation-State* (Oxford: Oxford University Press, 2005).

Rivero J., 'Vers un droit commun européen: nouvelles perspectives en droit administratif', in M. Cappelletti (ed.), *New Perspectives for a Common Law of Europe*, vol. I, (Firenze: EUI, 1978) 389–406.

Rivero J., 'Le problème de l'influence des droits internes sur la Cour de Justice de la CECA' (1958) 4 *Annuaire français de droit international* 295–308.

Romano Tassone A., 'Sulla formula "amministrazione per risultati"', in *Scritti in onore di Elio Casetta*, vol. II (Naples: Jovene, 2001) 813–825.

Romano S., *Frammenti di un dizionario giuridico* (Milan: Giuffrè, 1953).

Rossi P. (ed.), *The Boundaries of Europe: From the Fall of the Ancient World to the Age of Decolonisation* (Berlin: Di Gruyter Akademie Forschung, 2015).

Rossi P. (ed.), *Fine del diritto?* (Bologna: il Mulino, 2011).

Rossi P., *L'identità dell'Europa* (Bologna: il Mulino, 2007).

Roussel E., *Jean Monnet 1888–1979* (Paris: Fayard, 1996).

Ruffert M. (ed.), *The Transformation of Administrative Law in Europe. La mutation du droit administratif en Europe* (Munich: Sellier, 2007).

Ruggie J.G., 'International Regimes, Transactions, and Change: Embedded Liberalism in the Postwar Economic Order' (1982) *International Organization* 379–415.

Sacchi Morsiani G., *Il potere amministrativo delle Comunità europee e le posizioni giuridiche dei privati*, vol. I (Milan: Giuffrè, 1965).

Sacchi Morsiani G., *Il potere amministrativo delle Comunità europee e le posizioni giuridiche dei privati*, vol. I (Milan: Giuffrè, 1970).

Sacco R., 'Legal Formants: A Dynamic Approach to Comparative Law (Installment I of II)' (1991) 39(1) *American Journal of Comparative Law* 1–34.

Sacco R., 'Legal Formants: A Dynamic Approach to Comparative Law (Installment II of II)' (1991) 39(2) *American Journal of Comparative Law* 343–401.

Saitto F., *Economia e Stato costituzionale. Contributo allo studio della "Costituzione economica" in Germania* (Milan: Giuffrè, 2016).

Salerno G.M., *L'efficienza dei poteri pubblici nei principi dell'ordinamento costituzionale* (Turin: Giappichelli, 1999).

Sales I. and Melorio S., 'Le mafie nel PIL', in E. Ciconte, F. Forgione, I. Sales (eds), *Atlante delle mafie. Storia, economia, società, cultura*, vol. IV (Soveria Mannelli: Rubbettino, 2016) 15–35.

Saliba I.C., *The Influence of Federalism on the process of European Integration: The aim of the study is to shed light on the influence of federalism throughout the process of European Integration* (Saarbrücken: Lambert Academic Publishing, 2014).

Salvadori M.L., *Democrazia. Storia di un'idea tra mito e realtà* (Rome: Donzelli, 2015).

Sandulli A., 'Il bazooka giurisdizionale tedesco e la politica monetaria della Banca Centrale Europea' (2020) *Rivista italiana di diritto pubblico comunitario* 363–374.

Sandulli A., 'Il diritto quale infrastruttura per i poteri privati? A proposito di un libro di Katharina Pistor' (2021) 27 *Diritto pubblico* 999–1013.

Sandulli A., 'La scienza italiana del diritto pubblico e l'integrazione europea' (2005) *Rivista italiana di Diritto Pubblico Comunitario* 859–898.

Saurugger S., *Theoretical Approaches to European Integration* (New York: Palgrave MacMillan, 2014).

Sauter W., 'The Economic Constitution of the European Union' (1998) *Columbia Journal of European Law* 27–68.

Savino M., 'Creating a European Market for Refugees?' (2017) 2 *Diritto pubblico comparato ed europeo* 309–316.

Savino M., 'La crisi dei confini' (2016) *Rivista trimestrale di diritto pubblico* 739–759.

Savino M., 'L'amministrazione nazionale e l'Europa: l'eterna rincorsa', in L. Fiorentino (ed.), *Le amministrazioni pubbliche tra conservazione e riforme. Omaggio degli allievi a Sabino Cassese* (Milan: Giuffrè, 2008) 123–167.

Savino M., *I comitati dell'Unione europea. La collegialità amministrativa negli ordinamenti compositi* (Milan: Giuffrè, 2005).

Scharpf F.W., 'La trappola della decisione congiunta: federalismo tedesco e integrazione europea' (1986) *Stato e mercato* 175–216.

Scheingold S.A., *The Law in Political Integration: The Evolution and Integrative Implications of Regional Legal Processes in the European Community* (Harvard: Harvard University Center for International Affairs, 1971).

Schermers H.G., 'Comment on Weiler's "The Transformation of Europe"' (1991) 100 *Yale Law Journal* 2525–2536.

Schiavone A., *Ius. L'invention de droit en Occident* (Paris: Belin Editeur, 2011); Italian ed., *Ius. L'invenzione del diritto in Occidente* (Turin: Einaudi, 2010).

Schmidt Jr. R.J., *Reading Politics with Machiavelli* (Oxford: Oxford University Press, 2018).

Schmidt V.A., 'Theorizing Institutional Change and Governance in European Responses to the COVID-19 Pandemic' (2020) *42(8) Journal of European Integration* 1177–1193.

Schmidt V.A., 'Democracy and Legitimacy in the European Union Revisited: Input, Output and "Throughput"' (2013) 61(1) *Political Studies* 2–22.

Schmidt V.A., *Democracy in Europe: The EU and National Polities* (Oxford: Oxford University Press, 2006).

Schmidt V.A., *The Futures of European Capitalism* (Oxford: Oxford University Press, 2002).

Schmidt-Aßmann E., 'Introduction: European Composite Administration and the Role of European Administrative Law', in O. Jansen and B. Schöndorf-Haubold (eds), *The European Composite Administration* (Mortsel: Intersentia, 2011).

Schmidt-Aßmann E., *Das Allgemeine Verwaltungsrecht als Ordnungsidee. Grundlagen und Aufgaben der verwaltungsrechtlichen Systembildung* (Berlin: Springer, 1998, 2nd ed., revised and expanded, 2004).

Schmidt-Assmann E., 'Die Europäisierung des Verwaltungsverfahrensrecht', in *Festgabe 50 Jahre Bundesverwaltungsgericht* (Köln; Berlin; Bonn; München: Carl Heymanns, 2003) 487–506.

Schmidt-Assmann E., 'Das Allgemeine Verwaltungsrecht vor den Herausforderungen neuer europäischer Verwaltungsstrukturen', in *Festschrift für Günther Winkler* (Wien; New York: Springer, 1997) 995–1011.

Schmidt-Assmann E., 'Deutsches und Europäisches Verwaltungsrecht' (1993) *Deutsches Verwaltungsblatt* 924–936.

Schmidt-Assmann E., 'Zur Europäisierung des allgemeinen Verwaltungsrechts', in *Festschrift für Peter Lerche* (München: C.H. Beck, 1993) 513–527.

Schmitt C., 'The Situation of European Jurisprudence, 1950', in A. von Bogdandy, R. Mehring, A. Hussain (eds), *Carl Schmitt's European Jurisprudence* (Baden-Baden: Nomos, 2022) 9–47.

Schütze R., *From Dual to Cooperative Federalism. The Changing Structure of European Law* (Oxford: Oxford University Press, 2009).

Schwabe K., *Jean Monnet. Frankreich, Die Deutschen Und Die Einigung Europas* (Baden-Baden: Nomos, 2016).

Schwarz H.-P., *Adenauer. Der Aufstieg 1876–1952* (Stuttgart: DVA, 1986).

Schwarz H.-P., *Adenauer. Der Staasmann 1952–1967* (Stuttgart: DVA, 1991).

Schwarze J., *Droit administratif européen* (Bruxelles: Bruylant, 1994).

Schwarze J., *European Administrative Law* (London: Sweet & Maxwell, 1992).

Schwarze J., 'Der Schutz des Gemeinschaftsbürgers durch allgemeine Verwaltungsrechtsgrundsätze im EG-Recht' (1986) *NJW – Neue Juristische Wochenschrift* 1067–1073.

Schwarze J. (ed.), *Europäisches Verwaltngsrecht im Werden* (Baden-Baden: Nomos, 1982).

Schwarze J., 'Europäisches Verwaltngsrecht im Werden – Einführung und Problemaufriß', in J. Schwarze (ed.), *Europäisches Verwaltngsrecht im Werden* (Baden-Baden: Nomos, 1982) 11–22.

Schwarze J., *Europäisches Verwaltngsrecht*, vols I and II (Baden-Baden: Nomos, 1988).

Senden L., *Soft Law in European Community Law* (Oxford, UK; Portland, OR: Hart, 2004).

Shapiro M., 'The Problems of Independent Agencies in the United States and the European Union' (1997) *Journal of European Public Policy* 276–277.

Simoncini M., 'The Erosion of the Meroni Doctrine: The Case of the European Aviation Safety Agency' (2015) *European Public Law* 309–342.

Somma A., *Europa a due velocità. Postpolitica dell'Unione europea* (Reggio Emilia: Imprimatur, 2017).

Sommermann K.-P., 'Gemeineuropäische Verwaltungskultur als Gelingensbedingung europäischer Integration?' (2015) *Die öffentliche Verwaltung* 449–455.

Sorace, D., 'Una nuova base costituzionale europea per la pubblica amministrazione', in M.P. Chiti and A. Natalini (eds), *Lo spazio amministrativo europeo. Le pubbliche amministrazioni dopo il Trattato di Lisbona* (Bologna: il Mulino, 2012) 45–85.

Spinelli A., 'Europeismo', in *Enciclopedia del Novecento* (Rome: Istituto della enciclopedia italiana, 1977) 855–864.

Spinelli A., Il piano economico della democrazia italiana, 1944, in A. Spinelli, *La rivoluzione federalista. Scritti 1944–1947*, edited by P. Graglia (Bologna: Il Mulino, 1996).

Steil B., *The Marshall Plan: Dawn of the Cold War* (New York: Simon & Schuster, 2018).

Stein E., 'Lawyers, Judges and the Making of a Transnational Constitution' (1981) 75 *American Journal of International Law* 1–27.

Stelkens U. and Andrijauskaitė A., *Good Administration and the Council of Europe: Law, Principles and Effectiveness* (Oxford: Oxford University Press, 2020).

Stone Sweet A., La Corte di Giustizia europea, in S. Fabbrini (ed.), *L'Unione europea. Le istituzioni e gli attori di un sistema sovranazionale* (Roma-Bari: Laterza, 2002) 73–102.

Stone Sweet A., *The Juridical Construction of Europe* (Oxford: Oxford University Press, 2000).

Strauss L., Thoughts on Machiavelli (Glencoe, IL: The Free Press, 1958).

Strauss P.L. (ed.), 'The Trump Administration and Administrative Law', Symposium (2019) 94 *Chicago-Kent Law Review* 229.

Strauss P.L., 'The President and the Constitution' (2015) 65 *Case Western Reserve Law Review* 1151–1173.

Strauss P.L., 'Overseer or "the Decider"? The President in Administrative Law' (2007) *George Washington Law Review* 696–760.

Sunstein C., 'Paradoxes of the Regulatory State' (1990) 57 *University of Chicago Law Review* 407–441.

Supiot A., *Homo juridicus: On the Antropoligical Function of the Law* (London; New York: Verso, 2017).

Supiot A., *Lo spirito di Filadelfia. Giustizia sociale e mercato totale* (Milan: Et Al., 2011).

Susskind R., *The End of Lawyers? Rethinking the Nature of Legal Services* (Oxford: Oxford University Press, 2008).

Tamm D., 'The History of the Court of Justice of the European Union since its Origin', in A. Rosas, E. Levits, Y. Bot (eds), *The Court of Justice and the Construction of Europe: Analyses and Perspectives on Sixty Years of Case-law – La Cour de Justice et la construction de l'Europe. Analyses et perspectives de soixante ans de jurisprudence* (The Hague: Asser Press, 2013) 9–35.

Tarquini A. (ed.), *Il primato della politica nell'Italia del Novecento* (Roma-Bari: Laterza, 2016).

Teubner G., 'Juridification: Concepts, Aspects, Limits, Solutions', in G. Teubner (ed.), *Juridification of Social Spheres: A Comparative Analysis in the Areas of Labor, Corporate, Antitrust and Social Welfare Law* (Berlin; Boston: De Gruyter, 2012) 3–48.

Teubner G., *Nuovi conflitti costituzionali. Norme fondamentali dei regimi transnazionali* (Milan: Bruno Mondadori, 2012).

Teubner G., *Diritto policontesturale. Prospettive giuridiche della pluralizzazione dei mondi sociali* (Naples: La Città del Sole, 1999).

Torchia L., 'In crisi per sempre? L'Europa tra ideali e realtà' (2016) *Rivista trimestrale di diritto pubblico* 617–620.

Torchia L., 'L'Unione bancaria europea: un approccio continentale?' (2015) *Giornale di diritto amministrativo* 11–15.

Torchia L., *Il governo delle differenze. Il principio di equivalenza nell'ordinamento europeo* (Bologna: il Mulino, 2006).

Torchia L., *Il controllo pubblico della finanza privata* (Padua: Cedam, 1992).

Tridimas T., *The General Principles of EU Law*, 2nd ed. (Oxford; New York: Oxford University Press/Oxford EC Law Library, 2006).

Triepel H., *Die Hegemonie. Ein Buch von führenden Staaten* (Stuttgart; Berlin: Kolhammer, 1938).

Tuori Ka. and Tuori Kl., *The Eurozone Crisis: A Constitutional Analysis* (New York: Cambridge University Press, 2014).

Ursi R., *Le stagioni dell'efficienza. I paradigmi giuridici della buona amministrazione* (Rimini: Maggioli, 2016).

van den Brink T., Luchtman M., and Scholten M. (eds), *Sovereignty in the Shared Legal Order of the EU: Core Values of Regulation and Enforcement* (Cambridge, UK: Intersentia Uitgevers, 2015).

Varsori A., *La Cenerentola d'Europa? L'Italia e l'integrazione europea dal 1947 a oggi* (Soveria Mannelli: Rubbettino, 2010).

Vauchez A., *Democratizing Europe: The Centrality and Salience of Europe's Independent Branch* (New York: Palgrave, 2015).

Vesperini G., *Il vincolo europeo sui diritti amministrativi nazionali* (Milan: Giuffrè, 2011).

Vogliotti M., *Les nouveaux chemins de la légalité. Au-delà de la modernité juridique* (Bruxelles: Presses de l'Université Saint-Louis, 2020).

Vogliotti M., 'Legalità', in *Enciclopedia del diritto. Annali*, vol. VI (Milan: Giuffrè, 2013) 371–435.

von Bogdandy A., *Strukturwandel des öffentlichen Rechts. Entstehung und Demokratisierung der europäischen Gesellschaft* (Berlin: Suhrkamp, 2022).

von Bogdandy A., 'Von der technokratischen Rechtsgemeinschaft zum politisierten Rechtsraum – Probleme und Entwicklungslinien in der Grundbegrifflichkeit des Europarechts (From a Technocratic Legal Community to a Politicized Legal Space – Problems and Developments in the Basic Conception of European Law)', Max Planck Institute for Comparative Public Law & International Law (MPIL) Research Paper No. 2017–12, https://ssrn.com/abstract=2971097.

von Bogdandy A., 'Le sfide della scienza giuridica nello spazio giuridico europeo' (2012) *Il diritto dell'Unione europea* 225–239.

von Bogdandy A. and Bast J., *Principles of European Constitutional Law* (London: Hart/Beck/Nomos, 2011).

von Bogdandy A., 'Founding Principles', in A. von Bogdandy and J. Bast (eds), *Principles of European Constitutional Law*, 2nd rev. ed. (Oxford; Munich: Hart/Beck, 2010) 11–54.

von Bogdandy A., 'The past and promise of doctrinal constructivism: A strategy for responding to the challenges facing constitutional scholarship in Europe (2009) 7 *International Journal Constitutional Law* 364–400.

von Bogdandy A., 'Verwaltungsrecht im Europäischen Rechtsraum. Perspektive einer Disziplin', in A. von Bogdandy, S. Cassese, P. Huber (eds), *Handbuch Ius Publicum Europaeum*, vol. IV (Heidelberg: C.F. Müller, 2007) 3–36.

von Bogdandy A., 'A Bird's Eye View on the Science of European Law: Structures, Debates and Development Prospects of Basic Research on the Law of the European Union in a German Perspective' (2000) *European Law Journal* 208–238.

von Danwitz T., *Europäisches Verwaltungsrecht* (Berlin; Heidelberg: Springer, 2008).

von Danwitz T., *Verwaltungsrechtliches System und europäische Integration* (Tübingen: Mohr, 1996).

Voßkuhle A., 'The Reform Approach in the German Science of Administrative Law: The "Neue Verwaltungsrechtswissenschaft"', in *The Transformation of Administrative Law in Europe* (München: Sellier, European Law Publishers, 2007) 85–101.

Wakefield J., *The Right to Good Administration* (Alphen aan den Rijn: Kluwer, 2007).

Waldron J., 'Legislation and the Rule of Law' (2007) *Legisprudence* 91–123.

Watson A., *Il trapianto di norme giuridiche. Un "approccio" di diritto comparato*, 1974 (Naples: ESI, 1984).

Weber M., *The Protestant Ethic and the Spirit of Capitalism*, 1920 (Oxford; New York: Oxford University Press, 2010).
Weber M., R. Stammlers "Überwindung" der materialistischen Geschichtsauffassung', in J. von Winckelmann, (ed.), *Gesammelte Aufsätze zur Wissenschaftslehre* (Tübingen: Mohr, 1988) 291–383.
Weber M., *Economy and Society*, vol. I, part III, 'Forms of Power'; vol. IV, part IX, 'Sociology of Power', Section II, 1922 (Berkeley, LA; London: University of California Press, 1978).
Weeks J., 'A "Hamiltonian moment" for Europe', on *socialeurope.eu*, 14 July 2020.
Weiler J.H.H., 'Europe in Crisis: On "political messianism", "legitimacy" and the "rule of law"' (2012) *Singapore Journal of Legal Studies* 248–268.
Weiler J.H.H., 'The Geology of International Law: Governance, Democracy and Legitimacy' (2004) *Heidelberg Journal of International Law* 547–562.
Weiler J.H.H., *La Costituzione dell'Europa* (Bologna: il Mulino, 2003).
Weiler J.H.H., 'The Reformation of European Constitutionalism' (1997) 35 *Journal of Common Market Studies* 97–131.
Weiler J.H.H., 'To Be a European Citizen-Eros and Civilization' (1997) *Journal of European Public Policy* 495–519.
Weiler J.H.H., 'The Transformation of Europe' (1991) 100 *Yale Law Journal* 2403–2483.
Weiler J.H.H., 'Parlement européen, intégration européenne, démocratie et légitimité', in J.V. Louis and D. Waelbroek (eds), *Le Parlement européen dans l'évolution institutionnelle* (Bruxelles: Editions de l'Université de Bruxelles, 1988) 325–348.
Weiler J.H.H., 'The Community System: The Dual Character of Supranationalism' (1981) 1 *Yearbook of European Law* 267–306.
Weiler J.H.H., *Il sistema comunitario europeo. Struttura giuridica e processi politici* (Bologna: il Mulino, 1986).
Wilsher D., 'Law and the Financial Crisis: Searching for Europe's New Gold Standard' (2014) 20 *European Law Journal* 241–283.
Wollenschläger F., 'Constitutionalisation and Deconstitutionalisation of Administrative Law in View of Europeanisation and Emancipation' (2017) *Review of European Administrative Law* 7–79.
Woodruf D.M., 'The Moral and Normative Dimension of "the Economic" and the Ordoliberal Tradition', in J. Hien and C. Joerges (eds), *Ordoliberalism, Polanyi, and the Theodicy of Markets* (Oxford: Hart, 2017) 215–228.
Zamparini L. and Villani-Lubelli U. (eds), *Features and Challenges of the EU Budget* (Cheltenham: Edward Elgar, 2019).
Zaradny A., Wolff N., and Fleury Graff T. (eds), *La fin du droit* (Paris: Mare Martin, 2016).
Zieger G., *Das Grundrechtsproblem in den Europäischen Gemeinschaften* (Tübingen: Mohr, 1970).
Zielonka J., *Disintegration: How to Save the European Union* (Roma-Bari: Laterza, 2015).
Zimmermann R., *The Law of Obligations: Roman Foundations of the Civilian Tradition* (Oxford: Oxford University Press, 1996).
Zolo D., 'Teoria e critica dello Stato di diritto', in P. Costa and D. Zolo (eds), *Lo Stato di diritto. Storia, teoria, critica* (Milano: Feltrinelli, 2002) 17–88.
Zorgbibe C., *Histoire de la construction européenne* (Paris: Puf, 1993).
Zuckert C.H., *Machiavelli's Politics* (Chicago: University of Chicago Press, 2017).
Zuleeg M., *Das Recht der Europäischen Gemeinschaften im Innerstaatlichen Bereich*, Kölner Schriften zum Europarecht, Band 9 (Köln: Carl Heymanns, 1969).

Index

Adenauer, Konrad, 113–114
Administration de mission, 129
Administrative Law, 5–7, 12, 27, 43, 54, 56, 63, 70, 85, 90–91, 97, 100, 103, 104–157, 174–175; European, 124–157; science of, 123–157
Alonso García, Ricardo, 152
Amato, Giuliano, 70
Arbeitskreis Europäische Integration – AEI, 137, 143
Auby, Jean-Marie, 141
Auby, Jean-Bernard, 152–153, 155

Bachof, Otto, 138
Balaguer Callejón, Francisco, 152
Balducci, Massimo, 121–122
Beccaria, Cesare, 15, 18
Beijen, Wim, 113
Bentham, Jeremy, 17
Benvenuti, Feliciano, 21, 132–133, 150–151, 166
Bignami, Francesca, 152
Black, Duncan, 48
Blanke, Hermann-Josef, 144
Bleckmann, Albert, 142
Bobbio, Norberto, 21
Böckenförde, Ernst-Wolfgang, 19, 31, 47, 50, 176
Bodin, Jean, 18
von Bogdandy, Armin, 125–126, 128, 154, 175
Böhm, Franz, 49
Brenner, Michael, 144
Bretton Woods, 45
Brexit, 2, 110, 153, 155
Brito Bastos, Filipe, 128
Buchanan, James, 48
Bureaucracy, 42, 80, 88, 93, 111, 115, 120–122

Caffi, Andrea, 36
Calabresi, Guido, 48
Campagnolo, Umberto, 36
Caranta, Roberto, 149
Caroni, Pio, 25
Cassese, Sabino, 23, 26, 55, 83, 87, 118, 123, 128, 135, 147–148, 153–154, 156
Cattaneo, Carlo, 36
Chicago School, 48, 51, 69
Chiti, Edoardo, 128, 140
Chiti, Mario P., 123, 128, 149–150, 153, 155
Classen, Claus Dieter, 144
Clinton, Bill, 47
Coase, Ronald, 47
Cold War, 46, 161
Colorni, Eugenio, 36
Comitology, 121, 135, 150
Commaille, Jacques, 162
Conditionality, 61–62
Conference for the Future of Europe, 101–102
Conseil d'État, 116
Constitutional law, 5, 7, 71, 97, 103, 104–111, 125; European, 153
Costa, Paolo, 36
Cost/benefit balance, 42–43
Costums Union, 43
Court of Justice of the European Union, 7, 28, 32, 37, 42–43, 45, 59, 77, 94, 97–98, 103, 106, 108, 113, 116–120, 124–125, 127, 129–130, 134, 138, 142–143, 170, 173, 176
Craig, Paul, 26, 123, 151, 155

Crisis, 159: economic and financial, 55, 96, 176; empty chair, 31, 45, 115; pandemic, 1, 2, 29, 55, 60, 64, 80–81, 177; ukranian, 1, 2, 39, 40, 46, 57, 68, 72, 78, 83, 99, 102, 177
Croce, Benedetto, 22, 164
Cuoco, Vincenzo, 15
Curtin, Deirdre, 94, 96–97, 103, 173

Dahrendorf, Ralf, 28
von Danwitz, Thomas, 144
Daseinvorsorge, 37
D'Auria, Gaetano, 149
Debbasch, Charles, 149
de Búrca, Gráinne, 123
De Caterini, Paolo, 130
De Gasperi, Alcide, 113
de Gaulle, Charles, 31, 88, 115
de Laubadère, André, 130, 140
Deliberative supranationalism, 99
della Cananea, Giacinto, 149–150
De Lucia, Luca, 171
Delvolvé, Pierre, 152
Democracy, 85–103; illiberal, 59; liberal, 86; participatory, 118
Democratic constitutionalism, 12, 101
Democratic deficit, 36–37, 84, 93, 99, 106, 173
Deregulation, 46, 49, 69, 74
Díez-Picazo Gimenez, Luis María, 152
von Dietz, Constantin, 49
Donner, Mathias, 118
Duguit, Léon, 21
Durkheim, Émile, 21
Dutheil de la Rochère, 152, 155

Economic and Monetary Union – EMU, 43
Eeckhout, Piet, 155
Effectiveness, 43
Efficiency, 37, 66, 75, 80, 94, 173
Embedded liberalism, 50
End of law, 161
Enhanced cooperation, 107, 160
Eucken, Walter, 49
European agencies, 96, 124
European Anti-Fraud Office – OLAF, 63
European Banking Union – EBU, 34, 159
European Central Bank – ECB; 34, 56, 76–77, 83, 91, 96, 172
European Coal and Steel Community, 129–132, 136
European Commission, 39, 56, 61, 64, 79, 81, 88, 91, 98, 100–101, 117–120, 124, 134–135, 147
European Constitution, 2, 5, 20, 43, 46–47, 98, 107, 109–110, 153, 159, 161, 173–174
European Council, 61, 91, 124, 147
European Court of Human Rights, 108
European Defence Community – EDC, 132, 161
European democratic society, 3, 4, 125, 128
European Economic Community, 68, 131–132, 134
European identity, 14–15, 125
European institutions, 23
European integration, 74
European legal order, 23
European Ombudsman, 118
European Parliament, 36, 98, 100, 106, 124
European Political Community – EPC, 161
European Public Prosecutor's Office – EPPO, 63
European Recovery Program – ERP, 44
European Securities and Markets Authority – ESMA, 34, 37, 54
European Semester, 64–65
European Stability Mechanism – ESM, 76
European System of Financial Supervision – ESFS, 33–34
European Union Budget, 34, 59, 61
European Union Constitution, 108–111
European Union external relations, 107
Europe of the people, 159–160, 176
Everling, Ulrich, 137, 142
Excès de pouvoir, 130

Falcon, Giandomenico, 123, 149
Fall of Berlin Wall, 46, 99
Fiscal Compact, 76
Forsthoff, Ernst, 37, 85
Fragola, Umberto, 130
Franchini, Claudio, 149–150
Free competition, 49
Freiburg School, 49–51, 68, 169
French Revolution, 18, 126
Friedman, Milton, 51
Fromont, Michel, 130, 140
Functionalism, 20

Gasparri, Pietro, 130, 137, 140
Gentile, Giovanni, 22, 164
Gény, François, 21

Gerber, Carl Friedrich, 165
Giannini, Massimo Severo, 21, 132, 140
Glass Steagall Act, 47
Globalization, 46, 68, 83, 120
Goldmann, Matthias, 102–103
Good administration, 81
Goßmann, Uwe, 130
Gräbitz, Eberhard, 137
Gramsci, Antonio, 158
Great Depression, 2
Greco, Guido, 123, 149–150
Grossi, Paolo, 13
Grossmann- Dörth, Hans, 49
Grotius, Hugo, 16
Guicciardini, Francesco, 15, 17

Habermas, Jürgen, 28, 55, 72, 92
Halberstam, Daniel, 152, 156
Hallstein, Walter, 31, 37, 39, 113–114
Hard law, 118
"Hard look" doctrine, 120
Harlow, Carol, 151, 153
Hartley, Trevor, 151
Hatje, Armin, 145
Hauriou, Maurice, 34
Hegel, Georg Wilhelm Friedrich, 49
Hobbes, Thomas, 16, 49
Hoffmann-Riehm, Wolfgang, 145, 154
Heber, Peter, 154
Humanism, 21, 179–180
Hungary, 2, 53, 59, 62–63, 98–99

Iaccarino, Ugo M., 130
Inequality, 44
Integration through Law, 27, 45
Interest representation model, 147
International Accounting Standards Board – IASB, 75
International Monetary Fund – IMF, 76, 87
Ipsen, Hans Peter, 136, 138
Irti, Natalino, 20, 164, 177–178
Italian Constitutional Court, 86
Italian Constitution, 71, 180; art. 1, 27; art. 81, 71, 75; art. 97, 71
Italian President of the Republic, 86
Ius commune, 125
Ius Publicum Europaeum, 154

Jansen, Oswald, 155
von Jhering, Rudolf, 21
Judicial activism, 87
Judicialization, 71, 81
Judicial review, 130, 154
Juridification, 103, 171
Juristenrecht, 125

Kadelbach, Stefan, 144
Kant, Immanuel, 19, 21, 99
Kantorowincz, Hermann, 21
Kasten, Hans-Hermann, 142
Kelsen, Hans, 19
Knill, Christoph, 119
von Kirchmann, Julius, 20, 126
Kompetenz-Kompetenz, 95

Laband, Paul, 165
Lagrange, Maurice, 113, 125, 129, 135–136
Lampe, Adolf, 49
La Pergola, Antonio, 121
Law and economics, 22, 47
Legal certainty, 37
Legal culture, 114, 116, 124–157
Legal formant, 13
Legality, 37, 44, 73, 75, 170–171
Legal scholarship, 116, 122–123, 124–157
Legal science, 19, 124–157
Legitimacy, 41, 85–103, 170, 174; by results, 100; democratic, 85–103; lack of, 36; output, 85, 100, 172
Lenaerts, Koen, 125
Liberalization, 52, 74
Lindseth, Peter, 94–95, 103, 106, 152, 173
Lisbon Treaty, 39, 95, 98, 106, 110, 153
Living Constitution, 94–95, 108–110
Lorenz, Werner, 130
Luhmann, Niklas, 25

Maastricht Treaty, 46, 74
Machiavelli, Niccolò, 15, 17
Malaret i García, Elisenda, 152,
Management by objectives, 52
Mancini, Alberto Federico, 121
Mangold, Anna Katharina, 127
Mann, Thomas, 180
Marshall Plan, 44, 51, 68
Massera, Alberto, 149–150
Mendes, Joana, 128
Meny, Yves, 112
Meroni doctrine, 96
Metabolic Constitution, 6, 95, 173
Methods of European integration, 14; community, 33–34, 37, 56–57; intergovernmental method, 33–34, 52
Miele, Giovanni, 179

von Mises, Ludwig, 88
Mitrany, David, 30
Models of European integration, 29 ff.; confederalism, 35; federalism, 35; historical institutionalism, 32; intergovernmental liberalism, 26; multi-level governance, 32; neo-functionalism, 26, 30–31, 37, 42, 44; neo-institutionalism, 26, 42; rational choice institutionalism, 33; social constructionism, 33; transgovernmentalism, 26
Modern State, 4, 14–16, 18–19, 22–23, 28–29, 31, 37, 66; foundations of, 23
Monnet, Jean, 30, 112, 114–115, 133, 167
Montesquieu, 17
Mosca, Gaetano, 18
Motorized legislation, 126
Müller-Armack, Alfred, 49
Müller-Graff, Peter-Christian, 137
Multiannual Financial Framework – MFF, 59

National Recovery and Resilience Plan – NRRP, 64–65, 79
Neo-constructivism, 165
Neo-cooperative model, 147
Neo-functionalism, 26
Neo-liberalism, 51, 69, 72, 74, 158, 171, 176
Neue Verwaltungsrechtswissenschaft, 145, 154
New Green Deal, 59
New public management, 52, 74, 120, 170
Next Generation EU – NGEU, 51, 57, 59–60, 63–66, 73, 78–79, 81, 83, 102–103, 153, 177
Nöel, Émile, 115, 136
Nolte, George, 117

Open method of coordination, 37
Ordoliberalism, 49–50, 68, 72–73, 169
Organization for Economic Cooperation and Development – OECD, 44
Orlando, Vittorio Emanuele, 131, 146
Ortega Álvarez, Luis, 152,
Ost, François, 162–163

Pandemic Emergency Purchase Programme – PEPP, 81
Pareto, Vilfredo, 18
Pernice, Ingolf, 137
Philadelphia declaration, 179
Phisiocracy, 18
Picozza, Eugenio, 149
Pilotti, Massimo, 120
Pluralism, 41
Poland, 2, 59, 62–63, 98–99
Polanyi, Karl, 8, 28, 47, 67, 103
Policy without politics, 100
Political Theology, 14
Populism, 59, 99, 158, 180
Posner, Richard, 48
Primacy of law, 24, 126
Private powers, 28
Privatization, 52, 74
Progressive Conservatism, 18
Proportionality, 42, 50, 107, 117, 178
Protection of the EU financial interests, 34, 57, 60, 62–63; PIF Directive, 63
Puchta, Georg Friedrich, 165

Radbruch, Gustav, 21
Rational-legal theory, 24
Rawlings, Richard, 151
Reagan, Ronald, 46
Recovery and Resilience Facility – RRF, 57, 63–65, 79
Reimann, Mathias, 152
Rengeling, Hans-Werner, 137–139, 142–143
RePowerEU, 57, 78, 153, 177
Reuter, Paul, 113
Rivero, Jean, 130, 140, 143
Rivista trimestrale di diritto pubblico, 130
Roemer, Karl, 113, 125, 135
Role of Law, 23, 34, 158–167, 177–180; functional, 20; infrastructural, 53, 66, 70–71, 79–81, 171; instrumental, 15, 18, 34, 70, 180
Romagnosi, Gian Domenico, 15, 36
Romano, Santi, 21, 34, 164
Romano Tassone, Antonio, 171
Röpke, Wilhelm, 49
Rose Ackerman, Susan, 152
Rosselli, Carlo, 36
Rossi, Ernesto, 36
Rule of law,24, 41, 44, 54, 57, 59–60, 65, 118; backsliding, 57, 59–60, 98
Rüstow, Alexander, 49

Sacchi Morsiani, Gianguido, 130, 137, 139–141, 150
Sacco, Rodolfo, 13
Sarmiento, Daniel, 152
von Savigny, Friedrich Karl, 165
Schmidt, Vivien, 4, 89

Schmidt-Aßmann, Eberhard, 128, 145–146, 153–154
Schmitt, Carl, 14, 19–20, 126, 164
Schöndorf-Haubold, Bettina, 155
Schuman, Robert, 30, 101, 113
Schwarze, Jürgen, 137, 143–144, 153
Secularism, 14, 16
Separation of powers, 160
Service of General Economic Interest – SGEI, 89
Single European Act, 142
Single Market, 43
Six Pack, 76
Smith, Adam, 18
Snyder, Francis, 151
Social citizenship, 51
Social cohesion, 51
Social dumping, 51
Social market economy, 49
Social rights, 38, 46, 50
Soft law, 118
Solidarity, 44–45, 77
Sovereignty, 24; shared, 42, 99
Spaak, Paul-Henri, 113
Spillover effect, 87–88, 172
Spinelli, Altiero, 36, 86
Spinoza, Baruch, 16
State and market, 50
Stein, Eric, 27, 156
Stigler, George, 51–52
Stone Sweet, Alec, 27, 151
Strauss, Peter, 152
Structuralism, 19
Subsidiarity, 42, 49–50, 94, 107
Support to mitigate Unemployment Risks in an Emergency – SURE, 79
Sustainability, 55, 59, 66

Technocracy, 37, 42, 85, 89–93, 121, 172; without politics, 86, 100
Thatcher, Margareth, 46, 52, 170
Throughput, 89
Torchia, Luisa, 33, 149–150
Totalitarianism, 49
Trabucchi, Alberto, 120
Transparency, 37, 52, 89, 93, 154
Treaty of Rome, 133
Treaty on European Union – TEU; art. 2: 4, 105, 175, 180; art. 7: 59, 62; art. 20: 107
Treaty on the Functioning of the European Union – TFEU; art. 125: 46; art. 126: 46; art. 130: 46; art. 298: 110; art. 317: 60; art. 322: 60; artt. 326–334: 107
Trentin, Silvio, 36
Tridimas, Takis, 151
Tullock, Gordon, 48

Uri, Pierre, 113
Useful effect, 43
Utopian realism, 166, 178

Venice Commission, 44
Ventotene Manifesto, 35
Verri, Pietro, 15
Vico, Giambattista, 15
Visegrád bloc, 160
Voßkuhle, Andreas, 145–147, 154

Weber, Max, 14, 21, 24, 44, 88
Weiler, Joseph H.H., 27, 35, 68, 153, 157
Welfare State, 50, 118
World Bank, 45
World Trade Organization – WTO, 87
World War I, 25, 67, 131, 158, 175
World War II, 2, 8, 14, 25, 36, 45, 47, 67–68, 85, 87, 117, 126, 158, 172, 175, 179
Wright, Vincent, 151

van Zeeland, Paul, 113
Ziller, Jacques, 152
Zimmermann, Reinhard, 24
Zuleeg, Manfred, 136–138

FSC
www.fsc.org
MIX
Papier | Fördert gute Waldnutzung
FSC® C083411

Kolibri 360 GmbH
Ferdinand-Jühlke-Straße 7
99095 Erfurt, Deutschland
produktsicherheit@kolibri360.de